SEXUAL KNOWLEDGE

Austrian and Habsburg Studies

General Editor: Gary B. Cohen, Center for Austrian Studies,
University of Minnesota

Volume 1
Austrian Women in the Nineteenth and Twentieth Centuries: Cross-Disciplinary Perspectives
Edited by David F. Good, Margarete Grandner, and Mary Jo Maynes

Volume 2
From World War to Waldheim: Culture and Politics in Austria and the United States
Edited by David F. Good and Ruth Wodak

Volume 3
Rethinking Vienna 1900
Edited by Steven Beller

Volume 4
The Great Tradition and its Legacy: The Evolution of Dramatic and Musical Theater in Austria and Central Europe
Edited by Michael Cherlin, Halina Filipowicz, and RIchard L. Rudolph

Volume 5
Creating the Other: Ethnic Conflict and Nationalism in Habsburg Central Europe
Edited by Nancy M. Wingfield

Volume 6
Constructing Nationalities in East Central Europe
Edited by Pieter M. Judson and Marsha L. Rozenblit

Volume 7
The Environment and Sustainable Development in the New Central Europe
Edited by Zbigniew Bochniarz and Gary B. Cohen

Volume 8
Crime, Jews and News: Vienna 1890–1914
Edited by Daniel Mark Vyleta

Volume 9
The Limits of Loyalty: Imperial Symbolism, Popular Allegiances, and State Patriotism in the Late Habsburg Monarchy
Edited by Laurence Cole and Daniel L. Unowsky

Volume 10
Embodiments of Power: Building Baroque Cities in Europe
Edited by Gary B. Cohen and Franz A. J. Szabo

Volume 11
Diversity and Dissent: Negotiating Religious Differences in Central Europe, 1500–1800
Edited by Howard Louthan, Gary B. Cohen, and Franz A. J. Szabo

Volume 12
"Vienna is Different": Jewish Writers in Austria from the Fin de Siècle to the Present
Hillary Hope Herzog

Volume 13
Sexual Knowledge: Feeling, Fact, and Social Reform in Vienna, 1900–1934
Britta McEwen

Volume 14
Journeys Into Madness: Mapping Mental Illness in the Austro-Hungarian Empire
Edited by Gemma Blackshaw and Sabine Wieber

Volume 15
Territorial Revisionism and the Allies of Germany in the World War
Edited by Marina Cattaruzza, Stefan Dyroff and Dieter Langewiesche

Volume 16
The Viennese Café and Fin-de-Siècle Culture
Edited by Charlotte Ashby, Tag Gronberg and Simon Shaw-Miller

Volume 17
Understanding Multiculturalism: The Habsburg Central European Experience
Edited by Johannes Feichtinger and Gary B. Cohen

Volume 18
Sacrifice and Rebirth: The Legacy of the Last Habsburg War
Edited by Mark Cornwall and John Paul Newman

Volume 19
Tropics of Vienna: Colonial Utopias of the Habsburg Empire
Ulrich E. Bach

SEXUAL KNOWLEDGE

Feeling, Fact, and Social Reform in Vienna, 1900–1934

Britta McEwen

berghahn
NEW YORK • OXFORD
www.berghahnbooks.com

First edition published in 2012 by
Berghahn Books
www.berghahnbooks.com

© 2012, 2016 Britta McEwen
First paperback published in 2016

All rights reserved. Except for the quotation of short passages for the purposes of criticism and review, no part of this book may be reproduced in any form or by any means, electronic or mechanical, including photocopying, recording, or any information storage and retrieval system now known or to be invented, without written permission of the publisher.

Library of Congress Cataloging-in-Publication Data

McEwen, Britta, 1973-
  Sexual knowledge : feeling, fact, and social reform in Vienna, 1900–1934 / Britta McEwen.
    p. cm. – (Austrian and Habsburg studies ; v. 13)
  Includes bibliographical references and index.
  ISBN 978-0-85745-337-2 (hardcover) – ISBN (paperback) 978-1-78533-037-7 – ISBN 978-0-85745-338-9 (ebook)
  1. Sexology–Austria–Vienna–History. 2. Sex instruction–Austria–Vienna–History. 3. Social problems–Austria--Vienna–History. I. Title.
  HQ18.A9M35 2012
  306.709436'13–dc23   2011037634

British Library Cataloguing in Publication Data

A catalogue record for this book is available from the British Library

ISBN 978-0-85745-337-2 (hardback)
ISBN 978-1-78533-037-7 (paperback)
ISBN 978-0-85745-338-9 (ebook)

CONTENTS

Acknowledgments		vii
Introduction	Vienna as a Laboratory for Sexual Knowledge	1
Chapter 1	City Hall and Sexual Hygiene in Red Vienna	26
Chapter 2	Sexual Education Debates in Late Imperial and Republican Vienna	54
Chapter 3	Popular Sexual Knowledge for and about Women	91
Chapter 4	Clinic Culture	118
Chapter 5	Emotional Responses: Hugo Bettauer's Vienna Weeklies	144
Chapter 6	Local Reform on an International Stage: The World League for Sexual Reform in Vienna	175
Conclusion	Sexual Knowledge between Science and Social Reform	196
Bibliography		199
Index		215

Acknowledgments

I would like to thank the UCLA Graduate Division and Department of History for tremendous support in the early days of this project. Travel grants from the UCLA Center for the Study of Women, the UCLA Center for European and Russian Studies, and the Berkeley Center for European Studies enabled me to make many trips to central Europe. A Creighton University Faculty Research Fellowship and a Paul Klemperer Fellowship from the New York Academy of Medicine helped me track down several medical sources once back in the United States. I am indebted to the Fulbright Commission of Austria for accepting and supporting my academic interests while in Vienna. Finally, I am grateful to several publishers for allowing me to publish substantially revised and updated versions of research that has appeared elsewhere. Parts of chapter 1 are reprinted with permission from an article that was first published in the *Austrian History Yearbook* (Volume XVI 2010). Sections of chapter 2 first appeared in two publications: *Sharing Sexual Knowledge: A Cultural History of Sex Education in Twentieth Century Europe and North America* (London: Routledge, 2009) and *Sexualität, Unterschichtenmilieus und ArbeiterInnenbewegung* (Leipzig: Akademische Verlagsanstalt, 2003).

In Austria, I wish to thank the unflagging and suspiciously cheerful staff at the *National Bibliothek*, who never limited my requests nor blinked at their titles. I am also very grateful to the staffs at the *Archive der österreichischen Arbeiterbewegung*, the *Gesellschaft der Ärzte in Wien*, and the *Stadt- und Landesarchiv* for the city of Vienna. I also enjoyed the encouragement of Viennese scholars and feminists Sandra Eder, Maria Mesner, Sonja Niederacher, Karin Riegler, and Annemarie Steidl. Most of all, I wish to thank Gundi Herold, who led me into the *Wienerwald* every week for constitutionals, language lessons, and loving moral support during my times in Vienna.

In the United States, I am particularly grateful to the members of my dissertation committee and the regular attendees of the UCLA European History

Colloquium. I cannot overemphasize my intellectual and human debt to David Sabean; he has been a true *Doktor-Vater* and inspiration. It is to him that I owe my introduction to Ann Przyzycki DeVita at Berghahn Books, who in turn found two attentive and constructive readers for my manuscript. I am very grateful for their comments. Finally, I was lucky enough to enter UCLA with a cohort that has challenged and upheld me. Their society has shaped my scholarship more than anything else. My special thanks to Amy Woodson-Boulton, Claudia Verhoeven, Andrea Mansker, and Patricia Tilburg.

My deepest gratitude remains to the family and friends who supported me through the process of writing this book: the Slobodas, the Shoups, Amy Turbes, Christy Rentmeester, Betsy Elliot-Meisel, Julie Fox, Jean McEwen, Jamie McEwen, Nana Olivas, Kristin Justice, and Erik Lund. This book is dedicated to my long-suffering parents, Carol McEwen and Matthew Zukowski, whom I will never be able to repay.

Introduction

VIENNA AS A LABORATORY FOR SEXUAL KNOWLEDGE

Prelude

For much of the year 1900, eighteen-year-old Ida Bauer spent an hour a day with her doctor, Sigmund Freud. Freud had been hired by Bauer's father, whom he had already treated for syphilis several years earlier. Freud's task in treating Ida Bauer, however, was to discover the source of the hysteria she suffered from, which left her with a dry cough, a limp, and occasional vaginal discharge. She was also entertaining suicidal thoughts. Bauer explained to Freud her relationships with Herr and Frau K., family friends who, Bauer maintained, had acted inappropriately towards her. In the course of their conversations, Bauer spoke openly to Freud about the sexual issues that seemed to undergird her relationship to the Ks. Herr K., she claimed, had made sexual advances towards her while both families were vacationing in the *Sudtirol*. Frau K., on the other hand, had befriended her, perhaps, Ida thought now, in order to better obtain access to Ida's father, with whom Ida believed she was having an affair.

Ida Bauer's father had his own ideas about what was causing his daughter's mental distress. Frau K. had warned him that his daughter was preoccupied with sexual knowledge and had spent her vacation days reading sexologist Paolo Mantegazza's *Physiology of Love* and other "books of that sort."[1] Ida's imagination, her father postulated, had become over-excited by such reading material and had fabricated a seduction scene with Herr K. out of the thin mountain air. Using dream analysis, the concept of sexual sublimation, and his new theory of repression, Freud came to similar, if more complex, conclusions. Ida, still maintaining her version of the story, left Freud's care abruptly on New Year's Eve, 1900.

Five years later, Freud published Ida Bauer's case history (renaming her "Dora"), which became a pillar of psychoanalytic theory.

Both Freud and the Bauers have great significance for the history explored in this book. Freud's role as the leader of a psychoanalytic movement that revolutionized mental health care and the ways in which the western world thinks about sex makes him both an historical actor in the history of Vienna and a methodological model for the history of sexuality. The Bauer family also played a further role in the history of Vienna. Ida Bauer experienced depression as an adult and sought psychoanalytic treatment again in the interwar years. During that time her brother, Otto Bauer, led the Austrian Social Democratic Workers' Party (henceforth SDAP) through the tumultuous political changes of Austria's First Republic, 1918 to 1934. His party held the majority on Vienna's city council and was able to remake wide swaths of the city's geography and cultural landscape in radical and innovative ways. Aside from pockets of support in Austria's provincial capitals, however, the SDAP's power was isolated. The Austrian countryside during the First Republic voted overwhelmingly in favor for the Christian Social Party (CSP), which engaged in a *Kulturkampf* with the SDAP that eventually resulted in the brief Civil War of 1934, after which Otto Bauer and the rest of his party's leadership fled to Brno, in the new state of Czechoslovakia. Four years later, Sigmund Freud left Vienna at the insistence of the National Socialists, who controlled Austria from 1938 to 1945.

The remarkably turbulent political events that are encompassed within this story, from the demise of the Austro-Hungarian Empire, through World War I and the founding of the Austrian Republic, and finally to the violent regime changes of the 1930s, have the ability to overshadow Vienna's rich cultural history. In this book, however, these events serve as the political background to an examination of sexual knowledge in Vienna. I will argue that the production and distribution of sexual knowledge in Vienna underwent a dramatic shift during the years 1900 to 1934: from a form of scientific inquiry practiced largely by medical specialists to a social reform issue engaged by and intended for a wide audience.

Let us return for a moment to Ida Bauer in 1900. It is clear that whatever went wrong for her that summer in the Alps, it revolved around questions about sexual knowledge and behavior. In his conversations with Ida Bauer that fall, Freud repeatedly questioned the extent of sexual knowledge she possessed and the nature of the sexual behavior she believed was taking place around her. What had she been reading that summer? What did Herr K. want from her? Was the relationship between her father and Frau K. sexual? How did her father's history of venereal infection and professed impotence affect his ability to conduct a romantic affair? When Freud published these inquiries five years later, he was very aware that fellow physicians would react with "astonishment and horror" to the plain ways in which he had discussed sexual matters with an eighteen-year-old girl from a middle-class family.[2] Freud defended himself from would-be critics by making the bold assertion that it was "possible for a man to talk to girls and women upon sexual matters of every kind without doing them harm and without bringing suspicion upon himself," so long as one did so in a dry and direct manner and could "make them feel convinced that it [was] unavoidable."[3] Indeed, Freud predicated his treatment of Ida Bauer on the belief that hysteria could not be cured without discussing sexual matters. Bringing sexual matters into the open disarmed them, according to Freud. Any injury sexual topics caused on a conscious level was preferable to the far greater damage they could have as unconscious ideas or fantasies. Talking about sex was necessary for psychoanalytic treatment. Rather than tip-toe around the subject, Freud recommended a different tack: "The right attitude is: 'pour faire une omelette il faut casser des oeufs.'"[4]

The social pretense of respectable women's ignorance of sexual matters was one of the eggs that Freud cracked while constructing his theories of sexuality and the unconscious. Feminist critics of Freud have further suggested that Ida Bauer herself was "cracked" by Freud, a casualty of his assumptions about women.[5] This book will not engage in those controversies. The questions that surrounded Ida Bauer's treatment, however, invite us to think about the history of sexual knowledge in Vienna and its importance to the city's larger history. Both contemporary social critics and modern historians of *fin-de-siècle* Vienna have described it as a city suffused with sex.[6] However, this description disappears in the post-Imperial historiography of the city. Certainly sex was at the heart of the conversations in which Freud engaged Ida Bauer: what she knew, where she had received her knowledge, and why she believed certain sexual behavior to be improper. This book is at base an attempt to apply these questions to a wider range of historical actors in Vienna, including those who inherited the former Imperial capital: the citizens of the First Republic.

The Problem

The history of sexual knowledge in Vienna established in this book is the result of a series of inquiries into both urban and epistemological cultural changes. Its story is concerned with the ways knowledge about sex was made and shared in Vienna, beginning with the explosion of sexual science in the late Imperial period and ending with the incomplete cultural revolution wrought by the SDAP, which ended in 1934. First, I have focused on the shift in the purpose of sexual knowledge in Vienna, as understood by those who created and disseminated it. Whereas *fin-de-siècle* sexology sought to classify and heal individuals as a medical science, sexual knowledge in the interwar years was employed to heal the social body: the truncated, diseased, and impoverished population of the newly created Republic of Austria. This shift refocused sexual knowledge away from sexological taxonomies of aberrant sexual behaviors and towards advising heterosexual, reproductive couples, whom numerous social reform movements targeted as central to the regeneration of society. Imagining and implementing national regeneration through such citizens meant that bodies, hygiene, families, and reproduction would need to be redefined and restructured to fit the needs of the new state. Much as Freud had done in his treatment of Ida Bauer, the young Republic would have to talk about sex in radically new ways. Second, I have sought to explain how the discourse of sexual danger, especially regarding venereal infection, intensified in Vienna during the first third of the twentieth century. I argue that this intensification was the direct result of World War I and the ensuing concern that women and children would be infected with venereal disease (VD) carried by returning soldiers. Particular kinds of narratives were used to express sexual danger to both medical and popular audiences. I will also call attention to the employment of emotional testimonies and melodrama by those who wished to illustrate sexual danger in disease, reproduction, or ignorance. Throughout the story told here, I emphasize the politically and culturally specific context of sexual knowledge in Vienna. Unlike other European capitals, Vienna did not produce a body of pronatalist legislation or ideology during the years 1900 to 1934.[7] Likewise, despite Austria's overwhelmingly Roman Catholic population and the strength of political Catholicism on a national level, contraception advice, distribution, and research were both legal and widespread during the First Republic. I will argue that developments such as these were made possible by Vienna's position as the successive capital of two very unusual countries; the Austro-Hungarian Empire, a supra-national and polyglot entity, and the Republic of Austria, a nation that no native political party supported. In both cases, Vienna stood apart as a state within a state, with a politics and culture distinct from the larger political body.

Methodology

The most significant methodological choice I have made in this work is to limit the range of inquiry to a city, rather than a nation. Although my research is inspired by the growing literature that links sexuality to nationalism, I have not found this approach to be useful in thinking about either the Austro-Hungarian Empire or the First Austrian Republic.[8] Instead, I have treated Vienna as the most politically and culturally contested space within both regimes. The primary political opponents in the struggle to produce and control sexual knowledge in Vienna, from 1900 to 1934, were those of social democracy and political Catholicism. Neither political party could be described as nationalistic.[9] Both developed out of nineteenth-century, multi-national Imperial conditions; when the Empire was dismantled after World War I, both parties favored union with Germany over the creation of an independent Austria. Yet lack of native nationalism did not lead any of Austria's politicians to doubt Vienna's position as a world capital.[10]

Before the World War I, Vienna was governed by the Christian Social Party and was the jewel of the Empire's "golden triangle" of capitals. After the war, the city was recognized as a province of Austria, granted the right to self-taxation, and controlled by the SDAP. Unlike any other European capital, interwar Vienna was socialist-run through and through, a kind of exhibition piece for what could be achieved in the name of the working class. Throughout the First Republic, however, armed militias representing socialists, Catholics, communists, and monarchists clashed in street skirmishes, culminating in a civil war whose last battles were fought in Vienna's municipal housing complexes. The extraordinary position of Vienna during the years 1900 to 1934 makes a study circumscribed by nationalist concepts irrelevant.

My methodological approach to the problem of sexual knowledge in Vienna has been shaped by my sources, the bulk of which have been published. These include hundreds of sex manuals, advice columns, Catholic theological texts, medical journals, children's sexual education pamphlets, and municipal reports. Where possible, I have sought out the records of the associations that produced this body of literature, which has allowed me to look at the way that sex became a reform movement. These associational records provide me with a picture of how people performed the act of organization: what their meetings were like, where their money came from, what rules they created for themselves. Finally, I have used documents from city, state, and political party archives. These include city administration records, personnel records, clinic forms, and propaganda materials.[11]

I approach sexual knowledge from the position of cultural history. Rather than define a "sexuality" for early twentieth-century Vienna, I have sought to understand how people in Vienna thought about sex, what they did with that knowledge, and how that knowledge changed over time. To do so, I have employed three major analytical tools. The first is an analysis of contemporary discourses of sexual knowledge.[12] Discursive analysis, most famously employed by Michel Foucault, forces the historian to suspend temporarily all the points of view of a given debate, making them momentarily equal and divorcing them from any eventual "truth" or outcome. This exercise allows the historian to study the components of a past debate, the relationships between ideas, the format of information, and any attempts to control or limit discussion. Discursive analysis is especially useful for my project because it breaks down the distinctions between hard sciences, like biology, and soft or "pseudo" sciences, such as eugenics.[13] These distinctions among sexual knowledge, perhaps clear to modern historians, were extremely fluid in the early twentieth century. By taking seriously the multiplicity of beliefs about sexual behavior and the moral and hygienic consequences thereof, I am better able to recreate the cultural context of sexual knowledge in Vienna as it was understood by the historical actors who shaped it.

My approach to sexual discourse employs two further analytical tools. The first is the concept of a "horizon of possibility," originally used by Lucien Febvre to investigate the mental life of historical subjects.[14] Carlo Ginzburg has invoked a "horizon of possibility in culture," to defend historical investigations of individuals who might not be representative of the dominant culture, but nevertheless help historians to think about the limits of what was possible to think in a given era.[15] I have adapted this concept to think about the significance of some of the unusual sources I have uncovered and the often-marginalized authors or sex reform groups that produced them. Using a horizon of possibility has helped me work with many kinds of published sexual knowledge, particularly those texts without edition histories. Without such evidence, it is difficult to construct an argument about the popular reception of some of the most innovative sexual information produced in Vienna. I have approached these texts as delineators of what was possible when people wrote and reasoned about sex. The second analytical addition to discursive analysis employed in this work is the concept of "emotional regimes," which has been most fully defined by William Reddy.[16] This method of analysis identifies the systems within a society that govern the ways its citizens are asked to feel. I chose to use the methods of emotional history because my sources revolve around emotion: seduction and betrayal, romantic and familial love, fear of childbirth, and so on. Much of the sexual information available in early twentieth-century Vienna was conveyed in melodramatic language that appealed to the individual's sense of justice and responsibility. I have used the concept of emotional regimes to identify which emotions were discussed in relation to sex, as well as the social attitudes and personal attributes that combined to make possible desired (or undesired) emotions about sex and sex knowledge. My methodology is designed to illuminate the possibilities open to Viennese historical actors as they thought, felt, and communicated sexual knowledge.

Historiography

Modern Austrian history has been written to explain failure: the failure of Liberalism in the late nineteenth century and Social Democracy in the interwar years; the decline of empirical thought and the rise of irrationalism among intellectual elites; the loss of World War I and the dissolution of the Austro-Hungarian Empire; the failure of Jewish assimilation and the rise of anti-Semitism; and the inability to create a culture of nationalism that might have prevented the *Anschluß* with Germany in 1938. This approach has usefully exploited the numerous failures of Austrian history and used them as entry points of political and cultural explanation.

Carl Schorske transformed the explanatory model of failure into one of crisis and cultural innovation in *Fin-de-Siècle Vienna: Politics and Culture*, which argues that the Liberal bourgeoisie of late Imperial Vienna retreated into aesthetics and intellectual life in response to an increasingly frozen parliamentary system and the rise of the CSP in Vienna.[17] Schorske drew upon the increase of political irrationalism and the cultural legacy of Roman Catholicism to explain Viennese cultural modernism as struggle between *Sein und Schein*: "reality and illusion," or "being and appearing." This has been an enormously profitable avenue for historians, and a great deal of the recent historiography of Vienna has been written in dialogue with or as a critique of Schorske's work. Schorske's use of cultural figures to illuminate political and intellectual shifts has been appropriated by historians and extended to studies of Ludwig Wittgenstein, Karl Kraus, Richard von Krafft-Ebing, and Otto Weininger.[18] John Boyer has worked to clarify the voting patterns of the Viennese Liberal bourgeoisie, and has shown that in many cases the class base identified by Schorske actually voted against Liberalism and for CSP politicians like Karl Lueger, who won his first election in 1895 and served as Vienna's mayor from 1897 to 1910.[19] Wolfgang Maderthaner and Lutz Musner have studied the social, cultural, and economic ruptures that separated Vienna's elite inner city from the working-class *Vorstadt*.[20] Harriet Anderson questioned the paucity of women in the cultural historiography of late Imperial Vienna, and has used her study of Viennese women's movements to suggest that some contemporary political drives transcended a Liberal/Catholic split.[21] Finally, historians Ivar Oxaal and Michael Pollack have criticized Schorske for his reluctance to credit Vienna's Jewish presence (10 percent of the population in 1900) with meaning other than as the victims of antisemitism.[22] This critique is carried out most fully by Steven Beller, who has used the *Gymnasium* records of late Imperial Vienna to establish that over 50 percent of graduates from a liberal bourgeois background who qualified to enter university, and thus practice culture-shaping professions, were Jewish.[23]

Historians of anti-Semitism in Austria have led the process of extending cultural histories of Vienna into the interwar years. Austrian and American historians have explored the culture of interwar Vienna, which was dominated by a deepening political polarization, by emphasizing political theory, crisis, and violence.[24] Anton Pelinka has explained political culture in the First Republic as a *Lager System*, in which the SDAP, CSP, and Pan-German Party functioned as camps that socialized members through youth groups, educational programs, and cultural organizations, binding individuals into deep patterns of membership that, on a national level, resulted in a "centrifugal democracy" in which consensus was impossible.[25] In this sense, interwar Austria was very similar to Weimar Germany. Many historians have worked to define this political camp system and establish its effects on city life in Vienna. Josef Weidenholzer has argued that the education innovations and worker festivities sponsored by the SDAP were conscious efforts to uproot and replace Catholic patterns of culture in Vienna.[26] Conversely, Melanie A. Sully has interpreted the SDAP's focus on socio-cultural reform as a sign of the party's inability to effect political change on a national level.[27] This criticism is implicit in Helmut Gruber's work, which shows that the translation of Austromarxist ideals into social reform in interwar Austria was marked by an oftentimes clumsy, top-down approach by the SDAP to its working-class constituency.[28] The persistence of religious belief in the daily life of socialist-controlled Vienna in the interwar period has been explored by historians, as have the limits of socialist reform vis-à-vis women.[29] This literature has been central to helping me frame sexual reform within the volatile political context of interwar Austria.

As will become clear in the following chapters, a wide range of actors were drawn to the project of making public basic information about sex. Catholics, socialists, and others worked to improve the health of the people, mental and physical, by creating and disseminating sexual knowledge. But particularly in the First Republic, sex information became politicized. Catholics emphasized purity and chastity (for the glory of God) when explaining sex to their audiences; socialists largely echoed these messages while appealing to the health of the greater population and the importance of upright, clean living. So while both sides may have justified their actions differently, the end goal was very similar. Like many of their Weimar colleagues, sex reformers in Vienna were committed to creating a viable *Volk* through hygiene and education. Unlike many Berlin progressives, however, the Viennese showed a grudging appreciation for the power of the Roman Catholic Church to structure sexual forms of knowledge in terms of confession and revelation. This uneasy cohabitation between a Catholic heritage and a socialist future in interwar Vienna gave a different nuance to the discourse of sex reform than was found in Weimar Germany, particularly when it came to the issue of abortion, as we shall see. The bi-polar politics of interwar Austria left deep marks in what could be achieved in the realm of sexual knowledge.

Because the Austrian Republic was so fragile and so bitterly contested, historians have been largely unable to approach interwar history in a non-partisan way: that is, without setting up political winners and losers to be championed or reviled. The composite result has been a doomsday-narrative of the Republic for all parties involved: the fall of socialist Vienna in 1934, the betrayal of Christian Social ideals by the clerico-fascist wing that led the *Christliche Ständestaat* ("Christian Corporate State") of 1934 to 1938, the mutinous putsch attempts against the *Ständestaat* led by Austrian National Socialists, and the *Anschluß* invasion of Austria by Nazi Germany in 1938. This narrative divides interwar Austrian culture between political enemies and makes it very difficult to uncover shared concerns or discussions. This book tries to mitigate the weight of interwar Austria's doomsday narrative in two ways. First, I have approached sexual knowledge in Vienna as a process that spans the late Imperial and Republican periods, producing a heterogeneous corpus of research and reform that was still very fluid in 1934. Second, I have chosen a very political topic—sex—and attempted to show how it transcended traditional political boundaries in interwar Vienna. Sex research and reform in the period my book covers was an international undertaking, avidly followed by scientists and activists eager to apply new methods in Vienna. Within Austria, sexual knowledge production and distribution divided opinion within parties and occasionally drew erstwhile political enemies together. Clearly, this is not a book that seeks to explain the failure of Austrian liberalism in the *fin-de-siècle* or even the eventual ecstatic reception of Adolf Hitler in 1938. Rather, it underlines some of the cultural continuities between these events and suggests an alternate sphere of work and activism that expanded in this time frame.

Because the larger argument of this book posits a shift in sexual knowledge that has not been addressed in the historiography, I want to use fuller historical narratives to introduce my understanding of sex as a science and as a social reform movement. In the next two sections, I wish to set up the key issues and historiography surrounding these problems.

Sex as Science

Nineteenth-century medical authorities and specialists who theorized about sex were known as sexologists. Working from anatomical, hormonal, and inheritable models of human wellness and abnormality, sexologists attempted to map out the entire range of human sexual preference and behavior. They did so with very little recourse to individual psychic drives, resting their findings instead on the physiological information that was being produced in centers of medical learning across Europe. Many sexologists, including Havelock Ellis in England and Magnus Hirschfeld in Germany, argued for the normalization of non-procreative desires and the abolition of anti-homosexual legislation. However, sexology also drew from the ground-breaking work of Bénédict Augustin Morel (*Theory of Degeneration*, 1857) and Cesare Lombroso (*Criminal Man*, 1876) to argue that non-procreative sexual activities were not (merely) immoral choices but rather symptoms of degeneration: inherited tendencies that played out in the sexual lives of abnormal or atavistic human beings.[30] This approach to sexual behavior transformed sexual activities, such as same-sex penetration, into sexual identities, such as homosexuality. Sexology suggested that sexual activity, including perverse activity (defined as that which did not have coitus as its goal) was determined by natural laws. In doing so, sexology challenged the authority of Church and state to define sexual issues. Rather than require penance or legal penalty from individuals who engaged in abnormal sexual practices, sexology argued that they deserved scientific study and, in some cases, medical treatment.

As literary critic Rita Felski has pointed out, the world of sexual science created in the nineteenth century "brings to mind sepia-tinted images of earnest Victorian scholars laboring over lists of sexual perversions with the taxonomical zeal of an entomologist examining insects."[31] Indeed, perhaps the most famous sexological study produced in this period was a taxonomy. University of Vienna Professor of Psychiatry Richard von Krafft-Ebing's *Psychopathia sexualis*, first published in 1886, detailed a world of sexual perversion and abnormality. *Psychopathia sexualis* began as a slim, 110-page thinking-through of the relationship between legal structures and medical authorities in criminal cases involving sexual activity. Krafft-Ebing revised the text eleven times before his death in 1902, adding new definitions and case studies to each addition and expanding the tome to 437 pages, including illustrations.[32] The categories of homosexuality, masochism, pedophilia, and fetishism were either coined or given their modern definition by Krafft-Ebing. His taxonomy of sexual behavior made Vienna a capital of sexology.

At the close of the nineteenth century, the University of Vienna Medical School where Krafft-Ebing taught was one of the most prestigious in the world. Its departments of physiology, psychiatry, and dermatology and venereal disease played important roles in the development of sexual science. In the physiology department, luminaries including Ernst Fleischel, Sigmund Exner, and Josef Breuer collaborated with Ernst Mach (from the physics department) to develop new theories of cerebral localization, perception, and memory. These researches, inspired by Charles Darwin's theses, attempted to reconstruct the history of evolution via the brain layouts of organisms. Exner's work, in particular, anticipated what would today be called evolutionary psychology. His physiological explanations of psychic phenomena claimed that man's moral behaviors were outgrowths of instinct, as he argued in a famous 1891 lecture to his colleagues, "Morality as a Weapon in the Struggle for Existence."[33] In the psychiatry department, led by the internationally acclaimed neuroanatomy expert Thomas Meynert, mental behaviors were explained through physiological findings. Krafft-Ebing, when he joined the department in 1889, built direct links between asylum and university psychiatry and succeeded in making psychiatry-neuropathology an independent medical specialty in 1903.[34] Finally, the dermatology and venereal disease department helped to create the new science of bacteriology, which under the name mycology had previously been the domain of botanists. Here, Ernest Finger pioneered modern research on gonorrhea, while his colleague Edward Lang (working at the Second Department of Venereal Disease at Vienna's General Hospital) used bacteriology to argue successfully that syphilis, gonorrhea, and soft chancre were clinically and etiologically different diseases.

In Vienna, as in the rest of Europe, sexual knowledge produced by the university medical faculty was combined with insights from psychiatry, criminal anthropology, and biology. The largest schism within the resulting interdisciplinary realm of sexology was rooted in the competing biological theories of Lamarck and Darwin and the ways these theories were used to explain social processes. Understanding how traits were passed through successive generations of human beings was critical to sexology because many of its conclusions about sexual deviance were based upon ideas of inherited weaknesses. Lamarckian models of reproduction argued that the environment and acquired characteristics of each generation could have immediate effects upon the genetic make-up of its offspring. Degeneration worked as cause and symptom of the same illnesses in this school of thought; the human embryo adapted to the environment of the womb, modifying to survive the poisons and behaviors of its mother. As the practices and environments of human beings changed, Neo-Lamarckians argued, so would humans themselves. Urbanization and industrialization thus threatened to produce ever-weaker and more degenerate cohorts. Darwinian theory, on the other hand, posited that generational change happened at a glacial rate. Sexual selection in each generation favored the strongest and thus most capable of reproduction, slowly modifying each species according to the traits selected and amplified by thousands of generations. We have already seen that the Vienna Medical School's physiology department, in particular, was animated by Darwin's work. Yet Viennese sexual science in the late nineteenth century drew liberally from both Darwinian and Neo-Lamarckian thought. The latter survived at the University of Vienna well into the interwar period, most famously in the hereditary experiments of Paul Kammerer.[35] Both Darwinian and Neo-Lamarckian theories of hereditary transmission of traits were used extensively to construct social reform movements in the late nineteenth and early twentieth centuries. I will take up this discussion below, after introducing a final development in Viennese sexual science: the psychoanalytic revolution.

Psychoanalysis, as developed by Freud and modified by his students in the early twentieth century, shared important roots with sexual science.[36] Neo-Lamarckian scientists would have recognized in Freud's work a modified version of their own environmental theories, now extended into child development. However, psychoanalysis's approach to sexual functions was fundamentally different from that of sexology; rather than look for objective, physiological causes of sexual deviance, psychoanalysis explored a subjective world of motivations and drives that determined action on an individual level. Yet sexological and psychoanalytical practices developed as theories about and answers to the same kinds of medical ailments, including hysteria, impotence, and homosexuality. Furthermore, in *fin-de-siècle* Vienna these practices developed side by side. As historian William McGrath has shown, Freud was convinced that physiological and psychological processes were identical and that the disorders of his patients could be best illuminated using both psychoanalytical and biochemical explanations.[37] The methods of dream analysis and free association Freud developed in his psychoanalytic practice allowed him to expose phenomena hidden by biological medicine, but were not intended to replace it. In the case-study produced by Freud's work with Ida Bauer, for instance, Freud reframed the either psychical or somatic question of the roots of hysteria by arguing for both, claiming that hysterical physical symptoms repeated themselves only when they had psychical significance.[38]

Thus, according to Freud, Ida Bauer's recurring cough had a psychological meaning welded onto it: the belief (gleaned from reading sexological textbooks) that her otherwise impotent father and Frau K. were engaging in oral sex.[39]

Unlike sexology, psychoanalysis was not interested in insisting upon a unity of meaning for sexual behaviors and abnormalities. On the contrary, as his analysis of Ida Bauer shows, Freud argued that single symptoms could correspond to and express multiple meanings, according to the nature of the suppressed thoughts that were struggling to express themselves through physical signs.[40] The therapeutic technique Freud developed—the "talking cure"—was purely psychological, but he maintained that it also revealed the organic bases of neuroses. In this way, Freud combined and transformed the current medical and sexological traditions in Vienna to create a new way of thinking about sex as "not simply interven[ing], like a *deus ex machina*, on one single occasion" in an individual's life, but rather as "the key to the problem of psychoneuroses and of the neuroses in general."[41] In particular, Freud's 1905 *Three Essays on the Theory of Sexuality* reframed the central questions of sexology. In it, he constructed a theory of infantile sexuality and child development that explained homosexuality, masturbation, fetishism, and sadomasochism as symptoms not of degeneration, but rather as signs of an incomplete or abnormal development of an individual's natural sexual drives. Freud's ideas, like those of many sexual researchers before him, were dismissed as "Jewish science" in Vienna. The anti-Semitic reception of these ideas remains an untold story in Central European history. As the following chapters unfold, we will see that several of Vienna's most polarizing figures in the realm of public sexual knowledge production were Jewish, as well. The uncomfortable position of being a religious outsider speaking to a deeply Catholic culture about sex is explored more fully in chapter 5.

Although Freud is not a major character in the narrative this book creates, two early "defectors" from Freud's psychoanalytic circle, Alfred Adler and Wilhelm Reich, deserve special introduction.[42] On the cusp of World War I, Alfred Adler broke with Freud over the supremacy of sexual matters in individual development. Social and cultural factors, he argued, played far greater roles in the formation of individual subjectivity. Adler developed his own brand of personality analysis that stressed the ability to work with others as the most important human characteristic. His emphasis on cooperation, as well as his critique of the prevailing social hierarchy as causing "inferiority-complexes," made Adler's theories very popular with the Social Democratic ideologues that envisioned the interwar period's *neue Menschen*. In 1919, he was invited by the city of Vienna to direct an experimental teaching college.[43] Wilhelm Reich, on the other hand, produced psychoanalytic theories that were less agreeable to Vienna's city council. In 1922, when the Vienna Psychoanalytic Dispensary was opened, Reich worked with Freud to bring individualistic private practice to a larger public. His experiences in the free clinic led him to argue that, among its lower-class patients, the "release of sexual tensions through genital satisfaction immediately reduced the breaking through of pathological drives."[44] Reich's "Theory of the Orgasm," which claimed that all neuroses (as well as social problems such as rape and prostitution) could be cured through regular sexual satisfaction, was formulated between 1922 and 1926. In 1929, Reich broke with Freud and founded the Socialistic Society for Sexual Advice and Research, which operated several sex counseling clinics in Vienna beginning in 1930. In these centers, Reich taught that abstinence, the prohibition of masturbation, and the compulsion to marry were injurious attempts by parental and state authorities to suppress sexuality in young people and thus create more submissive subjects. Reich's Society used experimental psychoanalytic science to free the Viennese of what he considered to be unhealthy social-sexual constraints.

Both Alfred Adler and Wilhelm Reich modified Freudian psychoanalytic theory in ways that allowed psychoanalytic insights to be applied on a social, rather than an individual level. They refocused their diagnoses onto a social body that required healing, and participated in the massive, heterogeneous project of social renewal through medical and scientific intervention that dominated the late nineteenth and early twentieth century. This project used sexual science in its arguments for social reform.

Sex as a Social Reform Movement

The sexual knowledge produced by sexology and psychoanalysis in the *fin-de-siècle* was interpreted by a wide variety of social reform groups in the early twentieth century. In the German-speaking world, the movements involved in appropriating and spreading sexual knowledge included social purity campaigns against prostitution, Neo-Malthusian birth-control supporters, feminists, antifeminists, Monists, and proponents of eugenics.[45] In Vienna, as elsewhere, the science of sex was interpreted in highly contested ways.

Two of the most popular authors to interpret the science of sex at the turn of the century were Ernst Haeckel and Otto Weininger. Haeckel's 1899 best-seller, *The Riddle of the Universe*, popularized Darwin for German audiences and argued for a spirituality-based unity of matter in the universe. Alfred H. Kelly has demonstrated the popularity of this belief system, which Haeckel called Monism, among the German working classes before World War I.[46] Monism deified the workings of nature, redefining processes including sexual intercourse and reproduction as holy. We know that pre-war Vienna also supported a Monist League, which held meetings and led Sunday hiking expeditions through the Vienna Woods.[47] Vienna's Monist League was led by sociologist Rudolf Goldscheid, whose theories of *Menschenökonomie* ("economy of humanity") called for quality over quantity in the production of citizens. As Edward Ross Dickenson has shown, Monism offered a lighter version of the Darwinian evolutionary theory that was very attractive to feminists and socialists.[48] In Vienna, Monism in general (and Goldscheid's ideas in particular) was used by Neo-Malthusian socialists and feminists who supported family limitation through birth control. Otto Weininger's spectacular *Sex and Character*, in contrast, inspired feminist outrage when it appeared in 1903.[49] *Sex and Character* employed a Neo-Lamarckian reading of sexual characteristics on a cellular level to argue for moral and sexual purity. Weininger had attended a wide range of lectures by the medical faculty at the University of Vienna, including those of Krafft-Ebing and Exner.[50] His philosophical inquiry into male and female differences rested upon the biological boundaries of gender that Weininger established, using his scientific training at the University of Vienna, in the first part of *Sex and Character*. In the second, philosophical section of the text, Weininger identified sexuality and reproduction as inherently feminine and thus something to be overcome. Jews, too, were infected with femininity, and linked with a crassly scientific worldview in Weininger's attack on the emptiness of modernity.[51]

Weininger's anti-Semitism has been contextualized from a number of angles.[52] His descriptions of women as potentially disease-bearing and immoral, however, must be understood in the context of contemporary Viennese debates on venereal disease and prostitution. Prostitution was a visible part of life in *fin-de-siècle* Vienna's city center, from the ancient *Graben* to the edges of the newly installed *Ringstrasse*. Historian Karin Jusek has analyzed the tremendous social debate over prostitution during this period.[53] Socialists, Catholic action groups, feminists, and medical experts argued for greater purity and/or venereal disease prophylaxis in Vienna, attacking both prostitutes and their clientele as agents of racial and moral degeneration via syphilitic infection. During this time, the city sidewalks were divided into sexual commerce zones, "marked off by the police with an invisible line where [prostitutes] might carry on their trade."[54] These "line girls" formed the least expensive and most obvious legion of prostitutes, and registered with the police at the rate of roughly 2,000 a year.[55] Beginning in 1873, Vienna struggled under a system of semi-regulated prostitution that strove to sanitize (through compulsory health inspections of any woman on the street) the lowest ranks of venal sex workers and turned a blind eye to less accessible brothels and clubs. The specter of syphilis prompted civil hygiene administrators to demand municipal registration and observation of prostitutes, yet Vienna, capital of Catholicism in central Europe, never officially legalized the sale of sex. Caught between these mandates were the bourgeois city fathers, who allowed the charade to limp along as best it could. For critics of the system, the hypocrisy of prostitution was merely a synecdoche for Viennese Liberalism.

The most dangerous aspect of venal sex according to the medical experts participating in *fin-de-siècle* prostitution debates was the risk of syphilitic infection. During this period, syphilis was understood as a multi-stage disease that began with sores on the genitals or swollen lymph nodes near the groin. These primary symptoms would quickly dissipate, but the microorganisms that caused the disease, identified in 1905 by Berlin microbiologists Schaudinn and Hoffmann, remained in the bloodstream, and could invade the spinal cord and lining of the brain within a year. If the body's immune system did not conquer the T. pallidium organism, the patient could begin showing signs of neurosyphilis—speech problems, inability to raise the eyelids, mania, dementia, and paralysis—sometimes a full decade after the original infection. In 1906, German pathologist August Paul von Wassermann developed a blood test for syphilis that could identify the disease at all stages. Syphilis research, treatment development, and moral sermonizing were major discourses within the Viennese medical community. For the year 1901, the index of the prestigious *Wiener medizinische Wochenschrift*, the empire's oldest medical journal, listed syphilis as the most frequent subject for articles and book reviews. Recommended treatments ranged from simple courses of mercury massaged into the body and scalp to complex contraptions that blew hot air on the genitals of comfortably seated, still-clothed patients.[56] In 1909, Berlin physician Paul Ehrlich announced that the chemical preparation salversan blocked the development of primary and secondary syphilis, if used immediately after infection.[57] In the face of this incurable disease, hygiene became the watchword of concerned doctors, who increasingly advised the state in their roles as *Obersanitätsrath, Sanitätsberichter*, and even *Sectionschef und Sanitätsreferent* of the Imperial Ministry of Interior. The overarching message of the medical community vis-à-vis syphilis is reflected in a succinct aphorism from *Obersanitätsrath* Dr. Rudolf von Jaksch: "The future of medicine lies in prophylaxis. The best prophylaxis is purity."[58]

Purity was also the maxim favored by Catholic women's associations in late Imperial Vienna. The women's movement in Vienna demanded the abolition of prostitution but was divided in its approach to the problem. The *Christlicher Wiener Frauenbund* (Christian League of Viennese Women), an anti-Semitic and anti-emancipation political league, campaigned for abolition in combination with the promotion of chastity and religious feeling. The anticlerical *Allgemeine Österreichischen Frauenvereins* (Austrian Women's Association), a much smaller organization primarily dedicated to enlarging women's educational opportunities, favored abolition on the grounds that prostitution represented an institutionalized method of class and gender exploitation.[59] The *AöF* argued that only love could make a sexual relationship moral. Both groups formulated their opposition to hygiene regulation in ways modeled on Josephine Butler's campaign against the British Contagious Diseases Acts.[60] Wrongful detention of women suspected of prostitution was decried, as was the hypocrisy of hygienic surveillance of prostitutes but not their clients. In addition, both groups argued that feminine sexuality should be returned to its "natural" sphere of marriage and motherhood. Beginning in 1907, the *Österreichischer Bund für Mutterschutz* (Austrian League for the Protection of Mothers) offered a more radical interpretation of sexuality for women. Free union, supported by the German *BfM* president Helene Stöcker, was vigorously debated by the *BfM* in Vienna.[61] Stöcker called for a *neue Ethik* ("new morality") that recognized human sexuality as natural and life affirming. Prostitution, defined by the *BfM* as any sexual relationship (including marriage) entered into for financial gain, was described as the inevitable result of moral corruption and inequality between the sexes. The Austrian *BfM*, like its German counterpart, supported equal rights and state support for mothers regardless of their marital status. In the working-class district of Ottakring, the *BfM* opened a charitable home to care for unmarried pregnant women before and after the birth of their children in 1908. Many of the *BfM*'s members went on to participate in the Viennese sex reform movement documented by this book.

German-speaking feminists of the late Imperial period used a range of arguments in their campaigns for free union and mothers' rights, including eugenic proposals. The *Bund für Mutterschutz* demanded state care for illegitimate children on the grounds that they, as products of freely chosen sexual relations, represented an untapped resource of genetic strength available to the *Volk*.[62] To better insure the health of children, the *BfM* also petitioned state authorities to institute mandatory medical examinations for prospective marriage partners. Viennese feminist Grete Meisel-Hess, a supporter of the *Allgemeine Österreichischen Frauenvereins* and the *BfM*, criticized capitalist culture as thwarting racial improvement by presenting monetary obstacles to "true" sexual selection. Because property was inherited under capitalism, it was possible for biologically inferior offspring to prosper and reproduce simply because they had been born into rich families. Meisel-Hess argued that only socialism would provide equal rights, for women and for the poor, and thus restore the proper conditions for sexual selection and survival of the fittest.[63] In the meantime, she suggested that the mothers and children should form the primary units of society, with the state replacing the father as their protector and means of support. Historian Ellinor Melander has shown that Meisel-Hess's philosophy was deeply influenced by Ernst Haeckel's Monism and the eugenic proposals of Alfred Ploetz.[64] Recent scholarship suggests similar stimuli for the *Bund für Mutterschutz*, presenting overwhelming evidence that democratic, socialist, and eugenic principles coexisted in German and Austrian feminism.[65]

Eugenics was a pan-European approach to racial improvement whose novelty as a social movement lay in its concentrated focus on human reproduction. The neologism was created in 1883 by Francis Galton, a statistician and scientist whose work on the inheritability of talent suggested that, using selective sexual partnership, the human race could improve itself through collective breeding habits. Eugenics was based on Darwinian principals of evolutionary progress and on modifications of Darwinian theory known as "social Darwinism." The later movement, spearheaded by Herbert Spencer, drew a strong analogy between the competitive processes at work in nature within and between the species and the competitive processes at work within the social order. Eugenics and social Darwinism were popularized in Germany and Austria by Alfred Ploetz, whose 1895 book *The Efficiency of Our Race and the Protection of the Weak* coined the term *Rassenhygiene* ("racial hygiene"). Ploetz argued for a pure Germanic race that purged itself of weak members, rather than protecting them through social welfare policy. He suggested that reproduction be planned to maximize positive qualities in offspring, that sickly children be mercifully destroyed, and that the most inferior males of society be sent to the front line during wartime.[66] Ploetz described human beings as deposits of "positive" and "negative" biological materials. These poles were in turn used by a wide range of eugenic thinkers, in Germany and elsewhere, to describe eugenic policy itself. Positive eugenics, to this day, refers to state-directed programs intended to create a strong population, including maternity benefits, family health care, municipal housing, hygiene education programs, and selective access to contraception. Negative eugenics refers to attempts to eliminate racial imperfection in a given population, such as immigration quotas, sterilization of the unfit, limitation of marriage rights, and elimination of unwanted members of society.

Although both Ploetz and Haeckel's work assumed a hierarchy of racial worthiness that placed Germanic people above all others, it is important to stress that their ideas were embraced and interpreted by people of all political persuasions. Eugenics, *Rassenhygiene*, and social Darwinism were not exclusively associated with fascist politics until 1935, when biological racism was institutionalized in National Socialist Germany through the Nuremberg laws. The period under discussion in this book supported a spectrum of eugenic thought, ranging from the strictly hereditarian, to policies of interventionist social medicine, and finally to more loosely environmentalist arguments. As my research shows, many proponents of social democracy in Vienna were also supporters of eugenics. For socialists, state planners, feminists, and birth control advocates, eugenics was a means of making talk about sex scientific. In both the late Imperial and Republican years, scientific sexual discourse was a powerful tool for those who sought to undermine the authority of the Roman Catholic Church and its representatives in Viennese government, the Christian Social Party. Eugenics helped a variety of people to make arguments about sex and sexual morality that were not dependant on Christian concepts of marriage, fidelity, and chastity.

Eugenics was concerned first and foremost with the production of healthy children through careful control over heterosexual coupling. This is also true for the majority of the sources I have used in this book; be they conservative or progressive, most authors in this period concerned themselves with heterosexual, reproductive knowledge for the people of Vienna. The silence regarding homosexuality in these sources is almost total. Although there are brief mentions of same-sex desire, homosexual knowledge production in this period seems beyond the project of most sex reformers in Vienna. Certainly young men in *Gymnasium* might be familiar with same-sex love from the classical texts they studied, and there was a flourishing homosexual culture in Imperial Vienna, replete with clubs, cafés, and committees that continued into the interwar period.[67] While public knowledge and concern over homosexuality played an important part of crafting and policing heterosexuality in other European contexts, this was not the case in early twentieth-century Vienna.[68] Knowledge production in the interwar years in particular focuses almost exclusively on heterosexuality. Homosexuality, like other "deviant" or non-reproductive subjects such as masturbation and abortion, is an important adumbration on this material rather than a subject in its own right. Where possible, I comment on its presence, yet this book is about the construction of heterosexual knowledge.

The Book

Each of the six chapters of this book is intended to open up major avenues of sexual inquiry and knowledge in Vienna. They illustrate an expansion of sexual *Aufklärung* (literally, "enlightenment") in all sectors of urban society, including workers, women, and children. In each chapter, sexual discussions like those Freud had with Ida Bauer in 1900 are replayed and reworked for ever-wider audiences. Although centered around disparate events and historical characters, each chapter returns to the issues I found to be central in my research: sexual hygiene and education, sex advice and birth control information, and romantic and familial love.

Chapter 1, entitled "City Hall and Sexual Hygiene in Red Vienna," focuses on the discussion of sex throughout the creation of Vienna's socialist municipal health and hygiene system. I argue that Social Democratic sexual doctrine created a new form of *Verantwortlichkeit*, or responsibility, which served as a secular argument for the previously Catholic imperative of sexual continence. I also contextualize the eugenic arguments that Vienna's Director of Welfare, Dr. Julius Tandler, used to convey the importance of *Vorantwortlichkeit* to medical professionals, civil servants, and the citizens of Vienna. Tandler turned traditional eugenics on its head by insisting that social welfare programs, far from diluting the process of "survival of the fittest," actually accelerated constitutional improvements within the *Volk*.

The following two chapters focus on the radical redirection of sexual knowledge that took place in the First Republic: away from the realm of educated professionals and towards women and children of all classes. Chapter 2 is called "Sexual Education Debates in Late Imperial and Republican Vienna." The question of sexual knowledge for children was highly contested in the early twentieth century. All of the Austrian parties involved in this debate, from conservative

Catholics to fringe socialists, viewed sexual education as a major tool in the construction of a child's view of their gender role and thus their role in society. Shaping children's ideas about sex was an integral part of sex reform in Vienna. Chapter 3, "Popular Sexual Knowledge for and about Women," follows the explosion in the public sphere of sexual information intended for adults, and particularly women. I analyze the sexual knowledge published in advice books and newspaper columns intended for female audiences, and suggest that the popular press helped to both create and advertise the ideal of companionate marriage. This new understanding of sexual partnership, I show, was vehemently countered by the Roman Catholic Church. However, a deliberately Catholic tone of confession was cultivated even in socialist and woman-centered publications, which created an opportunity for women to testify to their sexual distress and demand new roles for themselves in the family and society.

Chapter 4 is called "Clinic Culture." It highlights the introduction of clinical sexual advice and care open to all Viennese citizens following World War I. A municipal Marriage Advice Center, an independent constellation of reproductive rights clinics, and a series of communist sexual advice offices all offered *Sprechstunden* ("office hours") consultations intended for workers but open to the general public. Clinic culture in Vienna, shaped by post-war material poverty and women's increasing demands for birth control, encouraged a new moral interpretation of sexual activity, marriage, and reproduction. I also suggest the limits of official Social Democratic policy regarding *Sexualnot* ("sexual misery" or "sexual emergency"), a popular term used to justify a variety of sexual reforms. Chapter 5, "Emotional Responses: Hugo Bettauer's Vienna Weeklies," revisits the sensational case of a Viennese journalist and publisher who was censored by the municipal government, charged for the corruption of youth, and ultimately assassinated for producing sexual information. In the pages of his Viennese weeklies, I argue, Bettauer created an emotional regime of pleasure and compassion at odds with Catholic concepts of purity and socialist calls for sexual responsibility.

My final chapter is "Local Reform on an International Stage: The World League for Sexual Reform in Vienna." This seven-day event was open to the public, as was a special hygiene exhibit on loan from the Vienna Museum of Sociological and Economic Sciences. Over 2,000 participants and guests listened to Viennese representatives interact with their international colleagues. Using the debates from the WLSR's Vienna conference, in which many of the sex reform advocates from my chapters squared off against each other, I frame the particularities of Viennese sexual knowledge within international scientific and social reform movements.

The story told in this book thus does not establish a sexuality for the city of Vienna, but rather provides a close look at the ways in which sexual knowledge was shared publicly. A break occurred following World War I that emphasized new models of heterosexual love and behavior. Of course, we may never know how precisely lives were impacted by this new discourse in the early twentieth century. However, as the chapters of this book will illustrate, it is clear that the voices that joined this fraught conversation were full of emotion. Fear, confusion, and shame are present, but so is hope. The sea change that occurred in the types of sexual knowledge produced made possible a new attitude towards the body and its attendant pleasures, even as it emphasized the dangers of desire. In many cases we are left to imagine for ourselves what individual Viennese citizens did with this knowledge; we may hope that it gave them courage to live and love.

Notes

1. Sigmund Freud, *Dora: An Analysis of a Case of Hysteria* (New York: Simon and Schuster, 1997) 19.
2. Freud, *Dora*, 41.
3. Freud, *Dora*, 41.
4. Freud, *Dora*, 42.
5. The literature of feminist responses to Freud and Freudian theory is enormous. With regards to Freud's treatment of Dora, *In Dora's Case: Freud—Hysteria—Feminism*, edited by Charles Bernheimer and Claire Kahane (New York: Columbia University Press, 1985), offers a comprehensive, chronological overview of psychoanalytic readings of the case, beginning with Jacques Lacan's 1951 essay "Intervention on Transference." The most sustained, historically contextualized feminist analysis of *Dora* is made by Hannah S. Decker in *Freud, Dora, and Vienna 1900* (New York: The Free Press, 1991).
6. Karl Kraus and Otto Weininger are two of the most famous critics of turn-of-the-century Vienna's sexual culture and hypocrisies. These and other sexual critiques emphasize regulated prostitution, venereal disease, and multiple political sexual scandals. See Franz X. Eder, "Erotisierendes Wissen. Zur Geschichte der 'Sexualisierung' im Wiener Fin de Siècle," in *Erotik, Versuch einer Annährung. Austellungskatalog des Historisches Museums der Stadt Wien* (Wien: Historisches Museum, 1990), 20–28.
7. Perhaps the most pronatalist capitals of interwar Europe were Paris and Rome. In both countries, motherhood was understood as the corresponding female sacrifice to male sacrifice in war. Pronatalist laws in these cities included the severe limitation of contraception devices and information, financial support to large families, the legislation of tax breaks, the development of a science of infant health and care (*puériculture*), social assistance for mothers, and, famously, medals for the mothers of especially large families. See Mary Louise Roberts, *Civilization Without Sexes: Reconstructing Gender in Postwar France, 1917–1927* (Chicago: University of Chicago Press, 1994); Marie-Monique Huss, "Pronatalism in the Inter-War Period in France," in *Journal of Contemporary History* 25:1 (January 1990), 39–68; Victoria de Grazia, *How Fascism Ruled Women: Italy, 1922–1945* (Berkeley: University of California Press, 1992); David G. Horn, "Constructing the Sterile City: Pronatalism and Social Sciences in Interwar Italy," in *American Ethnologist* 18:3 (August 1991), 581–601; Lauren E. Forcucci, "Battle for Births: The Fascist Pronatalist Campaign in Italy 1925 to 1938," in *Journal of the Society for the Anthropology of Europe* 10:1 (2010), 4–13.
8. See George Mosse, *Nationalism and Sexuality: Middle-Class Morality and Sexual Norms in Modern Europe* (Madison: University of Wisconsin Press, 1985); Isabel V. Hull, *Sexuality, State, and Civil Society in Germany, 1700–1815* (Ithaca: Cornell University Press, 1996); Miranda Pol-

lard, *Reign of Virtue: Mobilizing Gender in Vichy France* (Chicago: University of Chicago Press, 1998); and Eric Naiman, *Sex in Public: The Incarnation of Early Soviet Ideology* (Princeton: Princeton University Press, 1997).

9. This study does not take into account the stance of the German nationalists of interwar Austria on sex and public sexual information. I did not find enough materials in my research to support a sustained comparison between German nationalism, Catholicism, and socialism.

10. Post-World War I plans for a combined Germany and Austria called for the creation of two capitals, Berlin and Vienna, and a government that could rotate between them on a yearly basis.

11. My project has also been shaped by a lack of certain sources, particularly the treatment records of interwar Vienna's marriage and birth control advice clinics and the investigations sponsored by Vienna's Socialistic Society for Sexual Consultation and Sexual Research. Both of these bodies of information seem to have been destroyed during the 1930s, either by the clerico-fascist forces that took control of Austria in 1934 or the National Socialists who ruled after 1938.

12. This approach was pioneered by Michel Foucault, who used it to show how institutions such as asylums, prisons, and clinics created hierarchies of knowledge and thus augmented their own power. Since then, Foucault's theses on sexuality, agency, and self-hood have been challenged by historians in fruitful ways. See especially Lynn Hunt, "Foucault's Subject in *The History of Sexuality*," in Domna C. Stanton (ed.), *Discourses of Sexuality from Aristotle to Freud* (Ann Arbor: University of Michigan Press, 1992), 78–93; John E. Toews, "Foucault and the Freudian Subject: Archeology, Genealogy, and the Historicization of Psychoanalysis," in Jan Goldstein (ed.), *Foucault and the Writing of History* (Oxford: Blackwell, 1994); Jeffery Weeks, *Sex, Politics, and Society: The Regulation of Sexuality Since 1800* (London: Longman, 1989); Thomas Laqueur, *Making Sex: Body and Gender from the Greeks to Freud* (Cambridge: Harvard University Press, 1990). My own use of Foucault is very limited: rather than establish a hierarchy of knowledge or a history of bio-power and its deployment, I use discursive analysis to emphasize the plurality of sexual knowledge.

13. Jan Goldstein makes this point eloquently in her introduction to *Foucault and the Writing of History* (Oxford: Blackwell, 1994), 2–15.

14. Lucien Febvre, *The Problem of Unbelief in the Sixteenth Century*, translated by Beatrice Gottlieb (Cambridge: Harvard University Press, 1982).

15. Carlo Ginzburg, *The Cheese and the Worms: The Cosmos of a Sixteenth-Century Miller*, translated by John and Anne Tedeschi (Baltimore: Johns Hopkins Press, 1976).

16. William M. Reddy, *The Navigation of Feelings: A Framework for the History of Emotions* (Cambridge: Cambridge University Press, 2001). The concept of "emotionology" first outlined by Peter and Carol Stearns has also been useful to this project, especially as it requires that historians distinguish between an official emotional regime and records of individual emotional expression. See Peter N. Stearns and Carol Z. Stearns, "Emotionology: Clarifying the History of Emotions," *American Historical Review* 90 (October 1985), 813–836. For a review of the historiography of emotions, see Barbara H. Rosenwein, "Worrying about Emotions in History," *American Historical Review* 107 (June 2002), 821–845.

17. Carl Schorske, *Fin-de-Siècle Vienna: Politics and Culture* (New York: Vintage Books, 1981).

18. See Allen Janik and Stephen Toulmin, *Wittgenstein's Vienna* (New York: Simon and Schuster, 1973); Edward Timm, *Karl Kraus, Apocalyptic Satirist: Cultural Catastrophe in Habsburg Vienna* (New Haven: Yale University Press, 1986); Jacques Le Rider, *Modernity and Crises of Identity: Culture and Society in Fin-de-Siècle Vienna*, translated by Rosemary Morris (New York: Continuum, 1993); Harry Oosterhuis, *Stepchildren of Nature: Krafft-Ebing, Psychiatry, and the Making of Sexual Identity* (Chicago: University of Chicago Press, 2000); Chandak Sengoopta, *Otto Weininger: Sex, Science, and the Self in Imperial Vienna* (Chicago: University of Chicago Press, 2000).

19. John W. Boyer, *Political Radicalism in Late Imperial Vienna: Origins of the Christian Social Movement, 1848–1887* (Chicago: University of Chicago Press, 1981) and *Culture and Political Crisis in Vienna: Christian Socialism in Power, 1997–1918* (Chicago: University of Chicago Press, 1995).
20. Wolfgang Maderthaner and Lutz Musner, *Die Anarchie der Vorstadt: Das andere Wien um 1900* (Frankfurt am Main: Campus Verlag, 1999).
21. Harriet Anderson, *Utopian Feminism: Women's Movements in fin-de-siècle Vienna* (New Haven: Yale University Press, 1992).
22. Ivar Oxaal, "Editor's Introduction: Perspectives and Problems," in Ivar Oxaal (ed.), *Jews, Anti-Semitism, and Culture in Vienna* (New York: Routledge and Kegan Paul Ltd., 1987), 2–11; Michael Pollok, "Cultural Innovation and Social Identity in Fin-de-Siècle Vienna," in Ivar Oxaal (ed.), *Jews, Anti-Semitism, and Culture in Vienna* (New York: Routledge and Kegan Paul Ltd., 1987), 59–74.
23. Steven Beller, *Vienna and the Jews, 1867–1938: A Cultural History* (Cambridge: Cambridge University Press, 1989). See also Bruce F. Pauley, *From Prejudice to Persecution: A History of Austrian Anti-Semitism* (Chapel Hill: University of North Carolina Press, 1992) and Evan Burr Bukey, *Hitler's Austria: Popular Sentiment in the Nazi Era, 1938–1945* (Chapel Hill: University of North Carolina Press, 2000).
24. Gerhard Botz, *Gewalt in der Politik: Attentate, Zusammenstöße, Putschversuche, Unruhen in Österreich, 1918–1938* (München: Wilhelm Fink Verlag, 1983); Anson Rabinbach, *The Crisis of Austrian Socialism: From Red Vienna to Civil War, 1927–1934* (Chicago: University of Chicago Press, 1983); Rolf Steininger, "12 November 1918 bis 13 März 1938: Stationen auf dem Weg zum 'Anschluß,'" in Rolf Steininger und Michael Gehler (Hg.), *Österreich im 20. Jahrhundert: Von der Monarchie bis zum Zweiten Weltkreig* (Wien: Bòhlau, 1997), 99–152; Fritz Weber, "Hauptprobleme der wirtschaftlichen und sozialen Entwicklung Österreichs in der Zwischenkriegszeit," in Franz Kadrnoska (Hrsg.) *Aufbruch und Untergang: Österreichische Kultur Zwischen 1918 und 1938* (Wien: Europaverlag, 1981), 593–622.
25. Anton Pelinka, *Austria: Out of the Shadow of the Past* (Boulder: Westview Press, 1998), 30 and 15, respectively. See also Detlef Lehnert, "Politisch-kulturelle Integrationsmilieus und Orientierungslager in einer polarisierten Massengesellschaft," in Emmerich Tálos, Herbert Dachs et al. (Hg), *Handbuch des politischen Systems Österreich* (Wien: Manzsche Verlags- und Universitätsbuchhandlung, 1995), 431–443. The *Handbuch* also features a helpful set of essays on the six largest political parties of the First Republic.
26. Josef Weidenholzer, *Auf dem Weg zum 'Neuen Menschen': Bildungs- und Kulturarbeiter österreichischen Sozialdemokratie in der Ersten Republik* (Wien: Europaverlag, 1981).
27. Melanie A. Sully, *Continuity and Change in Austrian Socialism: The Eternal Quest for the Third Way* (Boulder: East European Monographs, 1982), and Sully, "Social Democracy and the Political Culture of the First Republic," in Anson Rabinbach (ed.), *The Austrian Socialist Experiment: Social Democracy and Austromarxism, 1918–1934* (Boulder: Westview Press, 1985).
28. Helmut Gruber, *Red Vienna: Experiment in Working-Class Culture, 1919–1934* (Oxford: Oxford University Press, 1991). See also Helmut Gruber, "Reflections on the Problematique of Socialist Party Culture and the Realities of Working-Class Life in Red Vienna," in Helmut Konrad (Hg.), *Die deutsche und die österreichische Arbeiterbewegung zur Zeit der Zweiten Internationale* (Wien: Europaverlag, 1982), 647–661.
29. On Catholicism, see Wolfgang Maderthaner, "Kirche und Sozialdemokratie. Aspekte des Verhältnisses von politischem Klerikalismus und sozialistischer Arbeiterschaft bis zum Jahre 1938" in Helmut Konrad und Wolfgang Maderthaner, *Neuere Studien zur Arbeitergeschichte*, Band III (Wien: Europaverlag, 1984), 527–558; Ernst Hainisch, "Das System und die Lebenswelt des Katholizismus," in Emmerich Tálos, Herbert Dachs et al. (Hg) *Handbuch des politischen Systems Österreich* (Wien: Manzsche Verlags- und Universitätsbuchhandlung, 1995), 444–453.

On the limits of socialist reform, see Helmut Gruber, "The 'New Woman': Realities and Illusions of Gender Equality in Red Vienna," in Helmut Gruber and Pamela Graves (eds.), *Women and Socialism, Socialism and Women: Europe between the Two World Wars* (New York: Berghahn Books, 1998), 57–94, and Karin Lehner, *Verpönte Eingriffe: sozialdemokratische Reformbestrebungen zu den Abtreibungsbestimmungen in der Zwischenkriegseit* (Wien: Picus Verlag, 1989).

30. The best historical analysis of these key texts remains Daniel Pick's *Faces of Degeneration: A European Disorder, 1948–1918* (Cambridge: Cambridge University Press, 1989).
31. Rita Felski, "Introduction," in Lucy Bland and Laura Doan (eds.), *Sexology in Culture: Labeling Bodies and Desires* (Chicago: University of Chicago Press, 1998), 1.
32. Harry Oosterhuis, *Stepchildren of Nature: Krafft-Ebing, Psychiatry, and the Making of Modern Sexual Identity* (Chicago: University of Chicago Press, 2000), 47. For a reading of Krafft-Ebing as a psychologist, rather than a sexologist, see Renate Hauser, "Krafft-Ebing's Psychological Understanding of Sexual Behavior," in Roy Porter and Mikuláš Teich (eds.), *Sexual Knowledge, Sexual Science: The History of Attitudes to Sexuality* (Cambridge: Cambridge University Press, 1994), 210–227.
33. Erna Lesky, *The Vienna Medical School of the 19th Century* (Baltimore: The Johns Hopkins University Press, 1976), 494.
34. Lesky, *Vienna Medical School*, 345.
35. As a university-trained scientist who was also a member of the Monist League, Kammerer illustrates well the fluidity between hard and soft sciences. See his attempt to combine both in *Lebensbeherrschung: Grundsteinlegung zur organischen Technik* (München: Geschäftsstelle des Deutschen Monistenbundes, 1919).
36. An excellent guide to these affinities is Sander Gilman, "Sigmund Freud and the Sexologists: A Second Reading," in Roy Porter and Mikuláš Teich (eds.), *Sexual Knowledge, Sexual Science: A History of Attitudes to Sexuality* (Cambridge: Cambridge University Press, 1994), 323–347.
37. William J. McGrath, *Freud's Discovery of Psychoanalysis: The Politics of Hysteria* (Ithaca: Cornell University Press, 1986), 18.
38. Freud, *Dora*, 33.
39. Freud maintained that the unconscious sexual fantasies that caused such suffering in hysterics like Ida Bauer were not the result of precocious sexual knowledge gleaned from sexology books. Rather, these unconscious fantasies were the same ones that perverts made real and acted out in the pages of books like *Psychopathia Sexualis*. Freud, *Dora*, 43.
40. Freud, *Dora*, 46.
41. Freud, *Dora*, 105.
42. A third early "defector" of Freud's circle, Otto Gross, was committed to sexual liberation through free love, a fascinating avant-garde cause that, although popular in some circles, did little to educate the wider public on sexual knowledge.
43. Malachi Hacohen, *Karl Popper – The Formative Years, 1902–1945* (Cambridge: Cambridge University Press, 2000), 92. Popper was a member of the league before World War I.
44. Wilhelm Reich, *The Function of the Orgasm: Sex-Economic Problems of Biological Energy*, translated by Theodore P. Wolfe (New York: Noonday Press, 1942), 58.
45. A great deal of research has been done on the sex reform movement in Germany. Some of the findings most useful to this work have been: Atina Grossman, *Reforming Sex: The German Movement for Birth Control and Abortion Reform, 1920–1950* (New York: Oxford University Press, 1995); Cornelie Usborne. *The Politics of the Body in Weimar Germany: Women's Reproductive Rights and Duties* (Ann Arbor: The University of Michigan Press, 1992); Anne Taylor Allen, *Motherhood and Feminism in Germany, 1870–1914* (New Brunswick: Rutgers University Press, 1991); Reinhard Mocek, "The Program of Proletarian *Rassenhygiene*," *Science in Context* 11:3–4 (1998), 609–617; Lutz D.H. Sauerteig, "Sex, Medicine, and Morality During the First

World War," in Roger Cooter, Mark Harrison et al. (eds.), *War, Medicine, and Modernity* (London: Sutton Publishing, 1998), 167–188.
46. Alfred H. Kelly, "Darwinism and the Working Class in Wilhelmine Germany," in Seymour Drescher, David Sabean, and Allan Sharlin (eds.), *Political Symbolism in Modern Europe* (New Brunswick: Transaction Books, 1982), 146–167. See also Paul Ziche (Hg.), *Monismus um 1900: Wissenschaftskultur und Weltanschauung* (Berlin: Verlag für Wissenschaft und Bildung, 2000) and Daniel Gasman, *The Scientific Origins of National Socialism: Social Darwinism and the German Monist League* (London: MacDonald & Co., 1971) for later applications of Monism.
47. Hacohen, *Karl Popper*, 67.
48. Edward Ross Dickinson, "Reflections on Feminism and Monism in the Kaiserreich," *Central European History* 34:2 (June 2001), 191–230.
49. Two of Vienna's most prominent first-wave feminists, Rosa Mayreder and Grete Meisel-Hess, first entered political debate while responding to *Sex and Character*.
50. Otto Weininger, "Curriculum Vitae," reprinted in Hannah Rodlauer (Hg.) *Otto Weininger: Eros und Psyche. Studien und Briefe, 1899–1902* (Wien: Österreichische Akademie der Wissenschaften, 1990), 210–211.
51. Two excellent guides to Weininger's complicated arguments are David S. Luft, *Eros and Inwardness in Vienna: Weininger, Musil, Doderer* (Chicago: University of Chicago Press, 2003) and Chandak Sengoopta, *Otto Weininger: Sex, Science, and Self in Imperial Vienna* (Chicago: University of Chicago Press, 2000).
52. These range from investigations of the Imperial educational system to psychoanalytic hypotheses of Jewish self-hatred. See Barbara Hyams and Nancy A. Harrowitz, "A Critical Introduction to the History of Weininger Reception," in Nancy A. Harrowitz and Barbara Hyams (eds.), *Jews and Gender: Responses to Otto Weininger* (Philadelphia: Temple University Press, 1995), 3–20; Jacques Le Rider, *Le cas Otto Weininger* (Paris: Presses Universitaires de France, 1982); on Weininger's education: Hannelore Rodlauer, "Fragments from Weininger's Education (1895–1902)," in Nancy A. Harrowitz and Barbara Hyams (eds.), *Jews and Gender: Responses to Otto Weininger* (Philadelphia: Temple University Press, 1995), 35–58; on the theory of Jewish self-hatred: Theodor Lessing, *Der jüdische Selbsthaß* (Berlin: Jüdischer Verlag, 1930).
53. Karin J. Jusek, *Auf der Suche nach der Verlorenen: Die Prostitutionsdebatten im Wien der Jahrhundertwende* (Wien: Löcker Verlag, 1994).
54. Stephan Zweig, *The World of Yesterday* (New York: Viking Press, 1943), 85.
55. Jusek, *Verlorenen*, 116. This number obviously does not reflect the amount of unregistered or "illegal" prostitutes practicing in Vienna. Police estimates in the 1870s judged that registered prostitutes made up only 10 percent of the population of working women on the street. Jusek, *Verlorenen*, 114.
56. Dr. Karl Ullmann, "Referate," *Wiener medizinische Wochenschrift* (Jg. 49, 11 August 1900), 1592.
57. Salversan was ineffective for cases in which neurosyphilis had already presented itself. Syphilis was not cured until 1944, when penicillin (discovered in 1929) proved successful in treating all stages of the disease. See Edward Shorter, *A History of Psychiatry from the Era of the Asylum to the Age of Prozac* (New York: John Wiley and Sons, Inc., 1997), 195.
58. "Aphorisms," *Wiener medizinische Wochenschrift* (Jg. 50, 29 December 1900), 15. This special fiftieth anniversary issue of the *WmW* featured aphorisms from its readers all over Europe and provides an excellent portrait of the state of medicine in 1900. Jaksch was stationed in Prague.
59. For 1905, the *AöF* counted just over 300 members, compared to the *CWF*'s 14,000. See Anderson, *Utopian Feminism*, 42. However, the *AöF*'s members were much more prolific speechmakers and theoreticians. Many of their members became politicians during the interwar years, once women were given the vote.

60. For analysis of Josephine Butler, see Judith R. Walkowitz, *City of Dreadful Delight: Narratives of Sexual Danger in Late-Victorian London* (Chicago: University of Chicago Press, 1992).
61. In a review article celebrating its twenty-fifth anniversary, the Austrian *BfM* obliquely referred to its inability to unanimously support free union by calling itself "the quieter sister" of the German *BfM*. Hans Paradeiser, "25 Jahre 'Bund für Mutterschutz'," *Blätter für das Wohlfahrtswesen,* (Jg. 31, Jänner/Februar 1932), 6–9.
62. See Anne Taylor Allen, "Feminism, Venereal Disease, and the State in Germany, 1890–1918," *Journal of the History of Sexuality* 4:1 (July 1993), 27–50.
63. Ideas summarized from Grete Meisel-Hess, *Der Sexuelle Krise* (Jena: 1909), 288–314.
64. Ellinor Melander, "Toward the Sexual and Economic Emancipation of Women: The Philosophy of Grete Meisel-Hess," *History of European Ideas* 14:5 (1992), 695–713.
65. See Kristin McGuire, "Helene Stöcker's 'neue Ethik' from 1905–1915," Paper presented at the German Historical Institute Conference *Sexuality in Modern German History* (October 2002); Dickinson, "Reflections on Feminism and Monism," 203; Allen, "Feminism," 34–35.
66. See Michael Burleigh and Wolfgang Wippermann, *The Racial State: Germany 1933–1945* (Cambridge: Cambridge University Press, 1991), 32.
67. On the use of classical texts to discuss same-sex desire, see Peter Singer, *Pushing Time Away: My Grandfather and the Tragedy of Jewish Vienna* (New York: Harper Collins, 2003). For a reading of Vienna's homosexual cultures, see Neda Bei, Wolfgang Förster, Hanna Hacker, and Manfred Lang (eds.), *Das Lila Wien um 1900: Zur Ästhetik der Homosexualitäten* (Wien: promedia, 1986) and Hanna Hacker, *Frauen und Freundinnen: Studien zur weiblichen Homosexualität am Beispiel Österreich 1870–1938* (Weinheim: Beltz Verlag, 1987).
68. For French and German contexts, see Carolyn J. Dean, *The Frail Social Body: Pornography, Homosexuality, and Other Fantasies in Interwar France* (Berkeley: University of California Press, 2000) and Tracie Matysik, *Reforming the Moral Subject: Ethics and Sexuality in Central Europe, 1890–1930* (Ithaca: Cornell University Press, 2008), respectively.

Chapter 1

CITY HALL AND SEXUAL HYGIENE IN RED VIENNA

In late November 1920, one of the few pre-war chaired Jewish professors of Vienna's University Medical School was appointed to head the municipality's newly created public health and welfare office. Dr. Julius Tandler was a professor of anatomy, a founding member of the Austrian Society for Population Politics, and the creator of a scientific journal dedicated to research into improving the human constitution. He had served on various health committees in the fledgling Austrian Republic before ascending to his new title as *amtsführenden Stadtrat für Wohlfahrtswesen und soziale Verwaltung der Stadt Wien*. Tandler's unofficial title was no less impressive: within a few years, he was popularly known as "the medical pope of Social Democracy."[1] As head of interwar Vienna's Welfare Office, Tandler shaped municipal health and welfare policy into a particular form of social medicine designed to strengthen and replenish the city's population. To do so, he stressed public sexual hygiene and private responsibility as crucial to the city's collective health.

World War I dramatically altered political and material conditions in Vienna. At the end of the war, Vienna stood as the capital of a truncated rump state that no native political party supported. The three years following the war brought starvation to much of the city, which also suffered from one of the most severe housing shortages in Europe. Families separated and were abandoned in the former Imperial capital of Vienna, as homecoming soldiers either failed to return at all or sought economic advantage in the former crown lands now organized into discrete countries. According to a special wartime commissioned report from the Austrian Society of Doctors, venereal disease, tuberculosis, alcoholism and infant mortality rates had risen to new levels.[2] Perhaps the greatest threat to Vienna, however, was the collapse of the fragile coalition government ruling the nation.

During Julius Tandler's fourteen-year tenure as Minister of Public Health, a *Kulturkampf* was waged between the Social Democratic Workers Party (henceforth SDAP) that held the majority on Vienna's City Council and the Christian Social Party that controlled the provinces. In a period of almost continual political and economic crisis, Julius Tandler's mandate was to heal a war-broken population and engender *neue Menschen*—literally, new people—whose healthy, orderly lives would help rebuild the nation.

Austrian historiography is rich in biographical studies of the SDAP party members who shaped interwar Vienna's political culture. The theory of political change they developed, Austromarxism, rejected any form of dictatorship (including dictatorship of the proletariat) in favor of democratic election. The Austromarxists believed that the material and cultural progress achieved by Vienna's Social Democratic city council would persuade their fellow countrymen to vote for the SDAP. Deeply committed to this "democratic revolution," Austromarxism was critical of both the communist and fascist revolutions that took place among Austria's interwar neighbors: Bavaria, Hungary, Italy, and Germany. The texts of Social Democratic ideologues Victor Adler, Karl Renner, and Otto Bauer have been anthologized, analyzed, and psychoanalyzed.[3] Historians have called attention to the critical roles played by SDAP leaders Karl Seitz, Vienna's popular interwar mayor; Otto Glöckel, who democratized Vienna's educational system; Hugo Breitner, who developed "Red" Vienna's progressive income and luxury taxes; Theodor Körner, who argued (unsuccessfully) for an armed seizure of power in the face of increasing paramilitary violence; and Robert Danneberg, who oversaw the construction of over 60,000 new apartments in Vienna. Although Vienna's welfare system was famous in interwar Europe, Julius Tandler has not received the same historical attention as his SDAP peers. The very aspects of his career that make him so central to this work have, I believe, discouraged other researchers from including him in the historiographical pantheon of Social Democratic leadership. As this chapter will illustrate, Tandler's interwar municipal welfare and hygiene innovations were plainly concerned with the regeneration, through sexual reproduction, of Austria's population. He, more than any other SDAP leader, was responsible for transforming scientific sexual knowledge into social programs designed to reshape Viennese ideas about sex.

Vienna's reputation as a city suffused with illicit and/or venal sex has been well established for the *fin-de-siècle* period.[4] In Austria's First Republic, however, "healthy" sex became both a state concern and a popular reform movement that stressed national regeneration, smaller but healthier families, and disease-prevention education. This chapter explores the process of sexual sanitization. Sex was explicitly discussed throughout the creation of Vienna's socialist municipal health and hygiene system.[5] The Municipal Marriage Advice Center, mothers' clinics, venereal disease testing centers, and family support offices that Tandler helped to develop all contributed to an official language of healthy sexuality. Furthermore,

Tandler's failure or refusal to work to change Austria's divorce and abortion laws reveals the limits of Social Democratic investment in sexual reform. In this chapter we shall situate Tandler within a tradition of social reform that increasingly called upon medical doctors to heal entire populations, rather than individual clients. As a doctor and anatomist Tandler diagnosed Vienna's social body and developed municipal policies designed to heal it. Tandler's innovations in the fields of family, maternal, and children's services were manifestations of the sexual hygiene system he created. This chapter mines the discourse of municipal socialism for the seam of sexual responsibility that runs beneath the surface of clinic and welfare development, paying particular attention to the eugenic messages that Julius Tandler and the SDAP used to educate the masses about sexual hygiene. Eugenic thought in Social Democratic welfare practice was an essential element in the creation of SDAP sexual doctrine: personal and civic *Verantwortlichkeit*, or responsibility, that was to begin with an individual's reproductive choices and extend, through the family, outwards to the *polis*.

Social Medicine: Tandler's Early Career

Julius Tandler was born in the Moravian village of Iglau in 1869 and moved to Vienna as a toddler. He attended a poor-relief primary school in the working-class district of Ottakring and prepared for University studies at a *Realgymnasium* in the Leopoldstadt. He attended the University of Vienna's medical school and began teaching anatomy there in 1903. In 1910, he became a full professor, serving eventually as Dean of the Faculty until 1917. From May 1919 to November 1920 he was the Undersecretary of National Health for the new Austrian Republic, while at the same time serving as an elected SDAP representative on the Vienna city council.[6] At the end of this period, he was named City Counselor and Director of the Vienna Welfare Office, a post he maintained for the remainder of the Republic. Along with other leading socialists, he was imprisoned after the civil war of 1934. In 1936, he was released to Moscow, where he had been called to help restructure that city's health system. He died within the year; his ashes were transferred to the Vienna crematorium after World War II.

Tandler first drew attention when he was named the Chair of Anatomy at the University of Vienna. This post had been previously held by the esteemed Emil Zuckerkandl, who died in 1910. Tandler had been Zuckerkandl's assistant even as a medical student and took over teaching obligations for his friend and mentor in 1907. *The Anatomy of the Heart*, Tandler's first book, appeared in 1913, followed by *The Biological Principles of Secondary Sexual Characteristics* that same year, and *The Topographical Anatomy of Emergency Operations* in 1916 (reprinted in 1923). Tandler's magnum opus was a textbook, *Systematic Anatomy*, which he worked on for ten years before publishing it in 1929.[7] Concomitant with his service to the city, Tandler remained the head of the Institute of Anatomy at the university. His anatomy lectures, dissection rooms, and the Institute itself were repeatedly attacked by anti-Semitic student protesters throughout the First Republic.

Tandler did not participate in the war-fever that swept Austria-Hungary in 1914. He spent the war years organizing Lower Austria's medical care system for injured soldiers, beginning in February of 1916 with the creation of a clinic at the University of Vienna for the war wounded. In March, Tandler presented a paper at the Vienna Society of Doctors entitled "War and Population." In it, he identified the current war as a "true war of the peoples," different from preceding European national skirmishes in its size and its causes.[8] The Great War, he told his audience, was "neither a war about races or nations, but was rather, above all, an economic war."[9] His response to this war was as a doctor, and he urged his fellow doctors take a strictly biological approach to what the war would mean for the populations they served. Tandler's apatriotic stance is interesting, but "War and Population" is most useful in establishing Tandler's professional views vis-à-vis population control and eugenic thought before he assumed the responsibilities of Minister of Welfare Services in 1920. Even in 1916, many of the hallmarks of Tandler's interwar welfare and hygiene approaches are present. Furthermore, his pre-war position as University professor allowed him to be more polemical in his formulation of these eugenic themes than his interwar political position allowed. Finally, "War and Population," along with the discussion that followed it, was quickly reprinted and widely disseminated in multiple medical specialty journals.[10] For these reasons, and to allow comparisons with Tandler's later work, "War and Population" deserves a closer look.

In the fall of 1916, after a brutal summer of trench fighting had destroyed any hope of a conclusion to the war, Tandler asked his medical audience to begin planning for the post-war population crises he outlined as inevitable. First and foremost, Tandler identified the cohort presently fighting for the Empire as the most worthy and reproductive of the present population. In a Darwinian sense, Tandler described the war as destructively selecting out the fittest component of society: "Those in danger, those who have fallen, or are injured, are the bravest and the strongest, the best [of the entire population]; those who have stayed at home beyond the reach of danger, who remain alive and are not injured, are those who are the least suitable for the struggle for existence."[11] This is the first, and the gravest, population crisis that Tandler identifies in his work. He organized the remaining crises under two subheadings: quantitative and qualitative. In doing so, Tandler uses for the first time a rhetorical framework popularized by Rudolf Goldscheid, a Viennese sociologist and economist whose work was widely cited by the Social Democratic Party. It is also in "War and Population" that Tandler began referring to the population of a given state as its "organic capital," a term coined by Goldscheid in his 1911 study *The Woman Question and the Economics of Humanity: Laying the Ground for a Social Biology*. We will see Tandler return to the categories of "qualitative" and "quantitative" work later in his career. In 1916, these categories allowed him to highlight the coming post-war population crises.

Tandler focused on the mortality rates of the present generation and what that meant for its ability to produce the next generation. He outlined the quantitative losses of the present war: live births in Vienna were down by 10,000 in the year 1915; 300,000 Austrian men had died in battle, many of whom were too young to have reproduced before they went to the front, and countless soldiers had been effectively sterilized by their exposure to venereal disease.[12] Tandler devoted much more space in his text to the qualitative losses of the Empire's population. The surviving population of the war, he claimed, would be qualitatively marked by a high percentage of veterans rendered invalids by the war, the widespread introduction of venereal disease into the home front, the malnourishment of the population, an increased use of tobacco and alcohol due to stress and depression, and finally, an "increased mixing of races," due to the war's displacement of peoples.[13] The result of these qualitative effects, when combined with the quantitative loss of young men, Tandler warned, would be devastating: "In so far as those recruited young men will have a much higher mortality rate than those who remained free of military duty, the practice of recruitment will allow greater possibilities of reproduction for those who are less able, bodily, to do so … a situation, which carries with it consequences for the degeneration of the *Volk*."[14] Tandler's response to World War I was similar to other eugenic thinkers like Francis Galton, Karl Pearson, and Oswald Spengler. What interests us here is Tandler's specific analysis of the population of Austria-Hungary.

In the conclusion of "War and Population," Tandler outlined three ways for the Empire to "make good on the damages" [*Schadungsgutmachen*] incurred through the present war.[15] Social repair promised to be a long-term project, stretching over many years. To heal the population, Tandler recommended three measures: "(1) The number of children produced by every marriage must be meaningfully increased. (2) The breeding process must also be greatly improved. (3) Emigration must end."[16] Three further actions could be acted upon at once. Tandler requested that the required length of active duty (three years for the Austro-Hungarian Empire in 1916) be shortened, so that the number of young men capable of reproduction returning to society could be increased. He also suggested that society reconsider its position on children born out of wedlock. He blamed the higher infant mortality rate of illegitimate children on the moral stigma that society irrationally placed on such offspring.[17] These children, he argued, were equally valuable to the population as legitimate offspring. Finally, Tandler demanded that treatment of venereal disease be legally required for all that bore it, even though therapy was painful and difficult. He railed against a society that allowed the army to draft young men, and yet prevented doctors, in the name of "medical privacy and personal freedom," from requiring the ill to be treated. Personal freedom, throughout Tandler's essay, had to be subordinate to the health of Austria-Hungary's reproductive population. If social measures—and specifically those that privileged the social body over the individual's—were not taken immediately, he warned, the quality of the coming generation would be sorely diminished. Many of the provisions Tandler outlined in "War and Population" were put into practice during his tenure in Vienna's city hall.

The measures delineated by Tandler as necessary for the repair of popular health were not new within the larger German-speaking discourse of social reform. German and Austrian feminists had begun campaigning for improved *völkisch* health at least ten years earlier. Their work, which responded to a different, yet not unrelated health crisis (state-regulated prostitution and the spread of venereal disease), paved the way for many of Tandler's proposals. The German *Bund für Mutterschutz* and its sister-association in Austria, in particular, supported legally mandated venereal treatment, state subsidization of childcare, and equal rights for all children, regardless of the mother's marital status. Furthermore, initiatives like state standardization of foster care, medicalization of abortion, reduction of illegitimate infant mortality rates, and health testing before marriage were supported by a wide range of feminist organizations in the pre-war period.[18] Tandler was engaged with many of these reforms during his Republican tenure, and, with the exception of legalizing abortion, transformed all of these suggestions into a particular Viennese reality in the interwar period. He, too, used the terms "*völkisch* health" to refer to the people his outreach targeted, eschewing the nationalistic overtones of the words for a progressive directive to serve as wide a population as possible.

Tandler's scientific interests grew out of his anatomy training. In order to provide a wider basis for the study of the human constitution, Tandler founded a medical journal in 1913 entitled *Magazine for Applied Anatomy and Constitutional Research*. The goal of the journal was to transform the human constitution into a scientific category of research and analysis, and Tandler energetically pursued this for the twenty years he remained at the journal's head.[19] *Applied Anatomy and Constitutional Research* featured both specialized medical articles and more general overviews of race hygiene themes, and, by the 1930s, "historical" pieces about the racial development of Germanic peoples. Rather than an anomalous venture into twentieth-century racism, however, the journal represented a well-established scientific and philosophical trend beginning in the 1860s that highlighted the dynamic energy forces of the body and the ways in which they could be conserved and better harnessed to regulate labor power.[20] In his 1913 opening article, "Constitution and Race Hygiene," Tandler argued for the mutability of the human constitution and the uses of social conditioning in changing, over time, the body's ability to withstand disease or hardship. He used the example of an English race horse bred for speed: its inborn capacities further his racing career, but the conditioning and nourishment it receives from its trainer also affect the horse's performance.[21] This imagery was meant to illustrate the differences between inborn dispositions to illnesses, such as lymphoma, and conditional illnesses, such as syphilis and alcoholism, the latter of which could be selected out and fought through social reform.

Tandler did not publish his own work in *Applied Anatomy and Constitutional Research* again, although he remained the editor-in chief until 1933. In that year the journal, which was printed in Germany by Springer-Verlag, was re-organized for political and economic reasons into the *Magazine for Human Inheritance and Constitutional Research*. At that time Tandler was on an extended research trip to China from whence he wrote that the exclusion of anatomy as an organizing category of the journal marked a final division point between his scientific interests and those of the journal.[22] However, the years he spent at its helm coincided with his tenure as Vienna's Welfare minister. Through *Applied Anatomy and Constitutional Research*, scientific research into blood groups, muscle tone, stomach-linings, and epilepsy could be presented and later applied to the kinds of social theories played out in the municipal welfare and hygiene system. Specifically, Tandler's journal served to collect and ground knowledge about the transmission of both human frailties (inherited diseases such as epilepsy) and human strengths (such as the ability to better withstand hunger). Thus, even as he altered the conditions of Vienna's population through welfare reform, Tandler promoted research into the possibility of altering, over generations, the very constitutions of his fellow citizens.

Tandler's career is best understood in the professional context of "social medicine" that developed in Europe at the end of the century and expanded dramatically during and after World War I. As social democracy responded to the population loss and material want in the years following the war, it increasingly called upon doctors to serve and structure society. The SDAP in Vienna saw the medical profession in transition, away from earlier models of "house doctor for those with means to pay," or even the doctor who devoted his life to serving the poor, towards the doctor as health official, who "in the service of all cares for the highest good of the *Volk*, namely, its health."[23] The Welfare ministry identified its primary directives along these lines. Society became a living organism to be cared for:

> The goal of welfare is nothing less than our attempt to provide economically for the thousand-fold emergencies that can befall an individual or a family, and to transform the old practice of poor-relief into a modern one of social services that can encompass every appearance of sickness in the societal organism in order to fight systematically against disease itself.[24]

Such welfare goals demanded professionals who could expand their practices from a struggle against the illnesses of individual patients into a fight against the diseases that threaten society as a whole.

Tandler himself spoke of health officials as transcending specialization and transforming society into an organic whole: "The health official is no longer a doctor who serves himself, and no longer a medical institution, but rather a properly organized part of a larger whole."[25] His definition continued: "Perhaps in no other city as Vienna are the relationships [between social and medical improvements] so clearly recognized and consequently so thoroughly worked through. Here, the health official is a limb in the rich organic construction of the organism that is our city's Welfare Services."[26] Tandler's welfare system changed the way medical knowledge was employed: through public servants rather than private healers. The unusually integrated context of social and medical change in interwar Vienna made possible the organic imagery that Tandler employed, but did not distinguish Austria from an international movement. The creation of the modern health official throughout Europe may be dated to the interwar period. Indeed, within ten years of peacetime activity, health officials in Vienna could recommend more than fifty professional journals from all over Europe devoted to expanding and perfecting social hygiene and welfare, twelve published in Vienna alone.[27]

The professional audience for such public health journals was also growing. The employment roster of Tandler's health empire, in the span of ten years, expanded from 326 health officials (1920) to 544 (1930).[28] Among them were new kinds of city-employed medical professionals: doctors for the central city Health Ministry, city doctors of poor-relief, coroners, tuberculosis care doctors, school doctors and dentists, advice center doctors, ear and eye examination specialists, and doctors who investigated hygiene advancements. Joining them were nurses employed in school clinics, tuberculosis care, sobriety programs, quarantine stations, and disinfection clinics. The genesis of these posts was, in Tandler's mind, the outcome of extreme need. In a 1931 report to the city magistrate, Tandler described his first ten years in office as ones of unrelenting hardship: "In the beginning our path was marked by general need—called out by the war and made stronger through starvation .... We passed milestones of success and marked our buried hopes with tombstones. At the end of this path, [we health officials have found] new suffering, new misfortune, expanded unemployment, economic crisis, growing demands, and increased work."[29] Tandler's somber assessment in 1931 was call to action for the health officials created under him: "So it looks as we glance back after ten years on our path, and so we see the necessity of new work, enough to make us [feel our struggle to be] useless. All of us, doctors, social workers, nurses, care givers, assistants in the service of human needs, we have to work until we make ourselves superfluous ... when suffering and need are no more."[30] The inclusivity of this speech testifies to the firm establishment of the "health official" (rather than simply "the doctor") in Vienna's municipal landscape.

As Tandler's speech suggests, the social powers newly invested in the health official were justified, at least in Vienna, through reference to the great misery that followed World War I. At war's outbreak, Vienna boasted over two million inhabitants. After a post-war spike in population as Imperial soldiers and their families passed through the capital towards the new nations that awaited them, Vienna's population leveled out at 1,824,000. Population experts assessed the losses as critical, claiming, "the growth of Vienna had been violently, catastrophically interrupted by the war and its consequences."[31] The health of the *Volk* was referred to as a work site in the title of *Oberstadtphysikus* Dr. August Böhm's 1929 essay, "The Reconstruction of the People's Health."[32] Before reviewing the hygiene and welfare programs (and their successes) that Vienna developed during the Republic, Böhm reminded his readers of the awful task before medical professionals at the close of World War I. These words opened his essay:

> The wretched war has dealt the health of our people serious wounds. Many of our men were on the field of battle; if they managed to return without having been shot into cripples, then at best they came home with permanent damage to their health. During the war, women and youngsters were forced to take over the hard work of men, to which they were unaccustomed, and through this process buried their own health. Children's development was retarded through malnourishment and privation. Many twelve-year-olds did not meet the normal developmental standards we previously held for eight-year-olds … . Furthermore, the fearful accomplice of war, wartime disease, [could not] be halted, and thus tuberculosis found a particularly fertile ground for its development in the conditions created by war. Venereal diseases also multiplied at alarming rates.[33]

Böhm's descriptions of men "shot into cripples" and women "burying their own health" provided bitter testimony to the destruction of the entire population's welfare. As human organisms broke down or were retarded in their growth, the enemy organisms of tuberculosis and VD flourished. Böhm depicted a biological balance upended by war, unfavorable to humans and their development. Following Böhm's logic, it is the evolutionary danger of this situation that demands intercession by medical professionals. Only they can reconstruct the *Volk* and provide services that will protect the population. The social and biological losses incurred during World War I made professional medical intervention necessary.

It is useful to think of Julius Tandler as a participant in this larger medical shift towards hygiene and welfare authority, but we must also recognize that his singular achievements made him a model for other doctors to emulate. Tandler's career, by the late 1920s, was used as a template for younger doctors to follow. Was it an accident, SDAP proponents of social medicine asked, that "a doctor (Julius Tandler) stood at the pinnacle of the most famous welfare system in the world, namely Vienna's?"[34] In an article for *The Struggle*, the SDAP's monthly theoretical journal, author Ludwig Pollak identified prophylactic planning for general health, rather than simply responding to individual illnesses, as the future for the medical profession. He recommended that young doctors inscribe upon their medical diplomas the following words of Tandler's as "a golden rule": "In the uninterrupted chain of human generations that follow, one after another, the generation that seeks to fulfill its duty cannot do better than to care for the next."³⁵ This kind of holistic approach to improving the coming generation could best be translated into political practice, Pollak argued, by doctors who were devoted to "making sick men once again into useful, productive, machines."³⁶

Although Pollak used mechanistic imagery in his depiction of what doctors could accomplish, he also warned that politically and socially effective doctors would have to recognize that the spirits and souls of their patients were equally worthy sites of healing. Likening the doctor's role in a community to that of a priest, Pollak urged physicians to serve their constituencies as both healers and as politicians. He argued that there was no contradiction in holding both positions at once, and illustrated his point by asking, "Could the Christian Social Party find better members, better agitators, than priests?"³⁷ As priests functioned as the moral authority of the Christian Social Party, so must doctors function as the driving force of reform for the SDAP. The moral system implicit in statements such as Tandler's, that each generation should be responsible for contributing to the health of the next, is guided by biological "science" rather than individual choice. As such, it may be provisionally identified as eugenic, an appellation which will be explored in the final part of this chapter. Regardless of this moral system's name, in many ways it offered a counter-model of scientific truth to that of divine authority (cited by political Catholicism), increasing the influence of doctors in social and moral debates.³⁸

Welfare Innovations: 1920 to 1934

From the beginning of his municipal career, the focus of Tandler's vision for welfare was children. To provide for them was to provide for the nation, he argued: "Our subject is not the welfare of members of a certain age, but rather we are talking about the very firmament of welfare. For the more we care for the youth, the less will we need to do to for them when they come of age; these young people will be healthier, achieve more, and lay ever better claims in the struggle for existence."³⁹ The Vienna welfare office under his direction created a wealth of new services intended to create the kind of young people Tandler envisioned.

The welfare system of interwar Vienna is well documented.⁴⁰ It is instructive to focus on the municipal policies Tandler developed vis-à-vis reproduction and childcare. Within a decade of coming to power, Tandler created the following features of the city's health and hygiene system: the Marriage Advice Center, free venereal disease testing centers and treatment clinics, funding for two civic associations that distributed birth control, advice centers for mothers, a syphilis-testing system for pregnant women, and financial and medical maternity support regardless of marital status.⁴¹ In addition, every mother who gave birth in Vienna after June 1927 received a layette gift of twenty-four diapers, six warm sets of infant clothing, blankets, towels, skin-care items, and a plastic mattress protector, all gift-wrapped in "a tasteful red box" illustrated with municipal images of mother and child.[42] For these children, Tandler created social worker and nurse services dedicated specifically to children's issues, foster care services, city-funded youth homes for those children in families deemed unable to care for them, sixty-one new kindergartens and thirty-five after-school care centers, thirty-one new play places and six summer camps on the edges of the city, free fresh milk programs for children under six, school doctors, dental-care clinics in elementary schools, and periodic testing of school children for tuberculosis.[43] Many of these innovations drew criticism from the Christian Social Party and from the worker constituency that they were designed to serve. Tandler's system of family surveillance, which began when pregnant women sought maternity benefits and extended, through the layette gifts, to all families regardless of need, was seen as an invasive threat to the sanctity of the family.[44]

Of Vienna's welfare services, we will draw special attention to those designed for prospective marriage partners and reproductive adults. The Vienna Municipal Marriage Advice Center (analyzed at length in chapter 4) opened in the summer of 1922 and performed voluntary examinations for prospective marriage partners. The welfare office saw it as crucial to "enlargement of the systematic *Aufklärung* (sexual enlightenment) of the population about the goals and limits of marriage counseling, so that the idea of *medical* marriage counseling could be brought into the widest social circles."[45] In Tandler's own discussion of the Marriage Advice Center, he emphasized it less as a counseling center than as a clearing house for the creation of new citizens: "What we have at hand here [in the Marriage Advice Center] is nothing less than a call to arms for the responsible among us. It is not about getting married or not getting married, but rather about the creation of children and the prediction of the fate before them."[46] The clinic attempted to predict the fate of potential offspring by encouraging citizens to test the reproductive fitness of themselves and their partners. As will be indicated in chapter 4, Viennese adults were less interested in such predictions than Tandler hoped. However, they did use the clinic as an entry-point into the sexual and reproductive health services offered by the city.

Women seeking birth control at the Marriage Advice Center were sent either to the Society Against Forced Motherhood or the Association for the Protection of Mothers, both run by SDAP members with offices in almost every neighborhood of Vienna. Although these associations benefited from annual "donations" from the municipality, they were private. Starting in 1920, pregnant women were referred to an Advice Center for Mothers, where parenting tips and lists of municipal services were dispensed. Thirty-four of these maternity advice centers were in operation by 1928, with expanded services for foster families, widowers, and next of kin who found themselves responsible for young children.[47] Reproductive adults suffering from tuberculosis (TB) could visit one of the twenty-five TB care stations that dotted Vienna, run by the city, private organizations, and health insurance providers.[48] Women without health insurance could sign up for the *Mutterhilfe* program, originally developed to reduce congenital syphilis. In exchange for agreeing to a syphilis test in their first trimester, these women would receive a state subsidy after their children's births in a new municipal maternity ward at Brigittaspital.[49] This three-story wing, built with modernist round corners of floor-to-ceiling windows, was designed to remove poor women in the final stages of pregnancy from their narrow apartments and encourage them to give birth in a sunny, hygienically controlled environment.[50] The SDAP claimed that Vienna's new reproductive policies were responsible for an impressive decline in city infant mortality rates: from 16 percent before World War I to 8 percent in 1925. The municipality described its successes in this realm poetically: "In Vienna's heroic fight against death, the most beautiful victory has been the decline of infant mortality."[51] Once the child was born, a whole new series of programs opened up at the Youth Aid Office. The "almost unbelievable number" of children who tested positive for VD, described as victims of the war-time and post-war epidemic, were sent to a special ward in the city's pediatric hospital starting in 1924.[52]

Finally, adult clients with signs of venereal disease were referred to the Advice Center for Persons with Sexually Transmitted Disease, where they could be tested, receive treatment recommendations, and learn the precautionary measures necessary to avoid further transmission.[53] The SDAP claimed that the Advice Center's greatest service to the public was its ability to "encourage a feeling of responsibility" in the population, a feeling that "was the most valuable aid in the fight against VD."[54] If individuals wished for an anonymous venereal disease test, they could, after 1929, visit one of the sex-segregated "Wassermann Stations" (named for the blood test to determine the presence of syphilis) for a free test that did not require the patients to give their names or addresses. Over a thousand Viennese took advantage of this service in its first year of operation.[55] In fact, many encounters with the municipal government entailed a free Wassermann tests for syphilis: testing was available at all maternity, children's, and general wards, at career counseling centers and district Youth Aid offices, the Mothers' Advice Centers, and of course the clinics that specialized in VD treatment. In addition, every employment applicant to a municipal position also had to be tested and could not be hired until treated.[56] The Welfare Ministry described the Wassermann Stations as inspired by the results of such widespread testing. The Ministry claimed that a "not trifling number of syphilitics, particularly syphilitic women, first learn of their disease via a chance employee blood test."[57] These testing centers should also be understood in the context of medical knowledge about syphilis during this period. Treatment through penicillin was not yet available, and thus doctors' only hope of arresting syphilis and "healing" the patient was to catch the disease before it moved out of its primary site of infection and into the blood.[58]

For adult treatment of gonorrhea, syphilis, or herpes, clients could be sent to one of the Evening Clinics for Venereal Disease, located throughout the city and designed to provide low-cost or free medical care. At their height, twenty-two of these clinics were open Monday through Saturday, from six to seven o'clock every evening.[59] These evening VD clinics were the most highly frequented component of the city's reproductive and sexual health infrastructure, serving at their height ten times as many clients as the Marriage Advice Center.[60] According to municipal reports, 28,174 people were treated at the Evening Clinics during the five-year period spanning 1923 to 1928.[61] These numbers reflect the changed status of venereal disease sufferers after World War I. As Tandler had recommended in his essay "War and Population," the act of seeking treatment for venereal disease during the interwar period was transformed from a personal health choice into a legal obligation. The State Decree of 21 November 1918 required all persons with venereal diseases to be examined, treated, and, if necessary, confined if their behavior or material conditions (such as living in an over-crowded apartment) suggested that they posed a danger to the larger community.[62]

As the previous citations indicate, the municipality's fight against sexually transmitted diseases during the interwar years was intense. Before World War I, there was only one municipal clinic that addressed Vienna's VD problem, even though syphilis was a dominant theme in the medical literature and anti-prostitution campaigns of the *fin-de-siècle*.[63] Private treatment of venereal disease was both expensive and experimental at the turn of the century. Although the salvarsan treatment (an arsenic compound) became widespread during the pre-war years, a cure through private doctors remained expensive throughout the First Republic. What changed after the war was the municipality's willingness to address venereal disease openly as a problem for the general public. All official accounts of the campaign against VD frame the city's responses in terms of World War I and the *Nachkriegszeit*, the years of material hardship directly following the war. Many doctors, including Tandler, had foreseen an explosion of VD in both the military and civilian populations as early as 1915. As predicted, the numbers of VD-infected citizens did jump at the end of the war, and rates of infection did not subside until the 1926.[64] Yet official health reports and reviews well into the 1930s continued to depict the fight against venereal disease as one that was mandated by the "particularly difficult," "unusual," or "terribly destructive" conditions brought on by World War I. In this way, the war opened up a public space for the discussion of sexual responsibility and state interest in sexual hygiene.

The war also provided a rhetorical space for health officials to reframe what they described as the social value of illegitimate children. With post-war Viennese birthrates at their lowest since the cholera year of 1873, doctors and economists combined to entreat the Viennese to regard any child, legitimate or not, as a worthy addition to the community.[65] Thus the mortality rates for all children came under special attention. Before World War I, Vienna's infant mortality rate for children born out of wedlock hovered at 25 percent. Although this mortality rate did decrease to 20 percent in 1920, the SDAP population specialists continued to bemoan the loss of potential manpower.[66] Several reasons were cited for high illegitimate infant mortality rates, including the youth of both mother and potential father, the inability of single women to take time off work during their pregnancy, and the unfavorable nutritional conditions during the years of post-war inflation.[67] During the first Republic, welfare and legal reforms were designed to reduce illegitimate infant mortality rates, support pregnant women regardless of their marital status, and even increase the financial responsibilities for which the fathers of these children could be held responsible.[68] Furthermore, the layette-gifts that the city of Vienna distributed to all newborns, legitimate or not, were intended to reduce infant mortality rates. The municipality explained its program as one designed to encourage motherhood across social strata: "The city of Vienna does this with the particular hope that this program will help awaken and increase the feeling of responsibility among Viennese mothers and also with the expectation that the city will find, in mothers, worthy and powerful coworkers in the battle against high infant mortality rates."[69] At the time of this statement, infant mortality rates among legitimate children had sunk to an impressive 6.69 percent, suggesting that the "high infant mortality rate" cited referred to the illegitimate children. The "worthy and powerful" foot soldiers in the fight for infant health sought by the municipality were unmarried women.[70]

One measure of the increased interest in illegitimate children was the 1930 conference on "The Illegitimate Child" held by the Austrian Society for Population Politics and Welfare Services. At this conference, doctors and administrators pondered Austria's exceptionally high percentage of illegitimate children (25 percent of live births) in relation to other European states and offered a wide range of responses to this situation.[71] Although many applauded the equal civil rights afforded to illegitimate children in Vienna, speakers such as City Councilman Dr. Wilhelm Hecke insisted that children continued to find the best care in *Einehe* ("single-marriage," meaning both parents had never been married before) households. Dr. Franz Hamburger argued that children did not need their parents to be married in a church, but they did deserve a family, and at the very least "a mother's milk and a mother's love," which many (abandoned) illegitimate children lacked.[72] In the name of Julius Tandler, a representative from the Welfare Ministry turned discussion towards the legal status of illegitimate children. He proposed that illegitimate children should bear the name of their fathers, just as did children born in wedlock. Blood testing, he assured, could be completed within the first three months of a child's life, and until the father was medically identified, mother and child were to be provided for by the municipality. The purpose of this law was "to increase men's feeling of responsibility for the child they have created."[73] The overriding theme of the conference was one of support for the mothers who had, despite social stigma, borne children and kept them healthy. These mothers, as reproducing members of a population reduced by war and poverty, were to be judged on biological, rather than moral, principles. Or, as one participant summarized, women bearing children out of wedlock were "more satisfactory citizens than the erstwhile father, and certainly more profitable [to society] than the pleasure-seeking, criminally inclined girls who bore no children at all."[74]

The scope of Julius Tandler's welfare system alone justifies the popular moniker of "medical pope of social democracy." Like the church, Vienna's welfare system could boast of caring for the city's population, literally, from (before) the cradle to the grave.[75] But the name "medical pope" also referred to two social struggles of the period that Tandler was ultimately unwilling to respond to: the attempt to reform Austria's arcane divorce laws and the fight to legalize abortion. Both of these movements are treated more fully in chapter 3, as complements to the subject of adult sexual information and education. However, as popular causes they are also interesting for their failure to mobilize full SDAP support, so I will begin the discussion of divorce and abortion law here, in an attempt to illustrate the limits of Tandler's welfare empire.

The Republic of Austria inherited both its divorce and abortion prohibitions from the Imperial law codes. In the Austro-Hungarian Empire, marriage (and divorce) law was contingent on the religious denomination of the marriage partners. For the majority of German-speakers, this meant that the Roman Catholic Church was able to ban all divorces and most second marriages of divorced people. For interfaith couples who were either unwilling to convert or unable to receive the Church's permission to marry, a special emergency civil marriage procedure was developed by the state in the late Imperial period. Beyond this, there was no civil marriage, nor a legal system to regulate marriage.[76] This complicated system was extended into the first Republic. A wealth of associations devoted to easing divorce laws appealed to the Vienna City Council for reform during the interwar period, but systematic legal reform was never approved. At best, Vienna as a state territory was willing to regulate and rubber-stamp the flood of appeals to the municipal court for recognition of legal separation (defined as separation of *Bett und Tisch*: years spent apart) and second marriage dispensations. However, marriages between Catholics, and thus the majority of marriages celebrated in Vienna, were dissolvable only through the death of one of the celebrants.[77]

In his discussion of marriage, Tandler never referred directly to this limping legal situation. However, the Welfare Ministry literature on the Municipal Marriage Advice Center does show a shift in the Center's willingness to participate in this campaign. Early descriptions of the Center explicitly warned potential advice-seekers that they would not receive help in obtaining a divorce within the Center's walls. Yet in the municipal reports of 1929, the account for the Marriage Advice Center admitted that "ever more cases multiply in which governing bodies require our expertise, above all the Viennese law court in cases of marriage dispensations (when, for example, the first marriage ends in separation on health grounds and the *Dispensehe* is sought for similar reasons), and also for cases of guardianship law, specifically, the question of approving marriages of an underage ward."[78] This passage is unclear, but very exciting. It suggests that Viennese citizens, armed with the rhetoric of national health Tandler had provided for them, ignored the sermonizing they might have received at the Marriage Advice Center and crafted their appeals for divorce, now aimed directly at municipal courts, with an ear for what the SDAP wanted to hear. In these appeals, unhappily married individuals sought to dissolve their unions by arguing that their partner was unfit for reproduction. In turn, the courts hearing the appeals referred back to the Marriage Advice Center, which evidently was more willing to offer expert opinion to the courts than to individual citizens. Although Tandler did not actively support marriage law reform, it seems that individual Viennese used his language to argue for the eugenic equivalent of divorce: "separation on health grounds."

Tandler was much more outspoken on the subject of abortion law reform. Within the SDAP, many feminists and sex reformers agitated for reform of Paragraphs 144 to 148, which made abortion a crime punishable by hard prison sentences. These reformers asked that a trimester system be adopted, which would allow women full choice to abort (abortion on demand) up through the third month of pregnancy. No reform of the laws was ever achieved in the First Republic, despite the constant agitation of private associations and outspoken SDAP members. Beginning in 1920, SDAP representatives Adelheid Popp, Gabrielle Proft, Therese Schlesinger, and Emmy Freundlich used the poverty of Vienna's women and the malnourishment of the city's children to argue for the right of women to limit their household size through abortion. Later that decade, after the city had responded to the immediate effects of the war, SDAP doctors Paul Stein and Karl Kautsky, Jr. (who will reappear in later chapters) shifted this line of argument to claim for the proletariat the right to cleanse their ranks of degeneration through abortion.[79] Whether the arguments were made from the standpoint of women's rights or eugenics, the resulting silence was the same. Any attempt to raise the issue of abortion law reform in parliament was boycotted by the Christian Social Party; these boycotts could sometimes last for a year at a time.[80] However, resistance within the SDAP to abortion law reform was its greatest deterrent. A 1924 SDAP physicians' conference on abortion and population politics rejected the trimester system. Instead, the medical representatives of the SDAP deferred to the position of Julius Tandler, who was also a participant at the conference. Tandler maintained that society, and not the mother, held authority over the life of a child, which he believed began at the moment of conception.[81] He suggested that a panel of medical and legal experts could decide, on a case-by-case basis, whether abortion was in the interests of society. In 1926, the SDAP modified his proposal and included this compromise in its party program: medical abortion was recommended if the birth a) endangered the mother's health, b) might result in an abnormal child, or c) would economically endanger the family.[82] As historians have since pointed out, this proposed solution kept the power of choice in the hands of expert opinion, rather than the women who sought abortions. This decision by the SDAP was greatly influenced by Julius Tandler himself, who utterly rejected abortion on demand. The "medical pope of social democracy," like Pius XI in Rome, wielded great authority over the marital and reproductive lives of the Viennese.

The sexual hygiene directives of Tandler's Welfare Ministry attest to the breadth of city investment in reproductive health. These achievements were all the more impressive when we consider the immense power of the Roman Catholic Church in Austria throughout the interwar period, both in the private lives of individuals and within the political landscape. Tandler energetically defended his health empire from critics. It is in this context that we will now approach his pivotal essay, "Marriage and Population Politics."

Population Politics and Eugenics

In 1923, the Republic of Austria carried out a census that counted just over six and a half million inhabitants.[83] The city of Vienna alone consisted of 1,865,780 souls. Birth rates nationwide had fallen off dramatically since the last complete census of 1910, sinking to within just two points of the death rates for 1923 (15.3 births to 13.7 deaths). In Vienna, this trend was reflected in the contraction of the population cohort of inhabitants under ten years old. In 1910, 16 percent of the population belonged to this cohort. By 1923, that youngest cohort had shrunk to just 10 percent of the population. No other age cohort, including those that could have contained conscripted soldiers, was reduced as much. Furthermore, there were 145,542 more women that men in Vienna in 1923, a number in keeping with the pan-European "woman surplus" following World War I. Annual marriages in Vienna were in decline following a post-war high of 31,164 in 1920. By 1923 this number had sunk to 19,827, a drop SDAP population experts blamed on "suffering during the inflation period, unemployment, and the lasting housing shortage crisis ... [conditions] which have made marriage seem futile even to those who are interested in it."[84]

"Marriage and Population Politics" was a widely distributed synthesis of Tandler's arguments for state interest in and support of sexual hygiene. It was presented first as a lecture in 1923 designed to mark the first anniversary of the Marriage Advice Center, and then appeared as a multi-part article in the prestigious *Viennese Medical Journal* in early 1924. Later that year, it was reprinted in book format by Moritz Perles Press, which specialized in professional and popular medical texts.

Tandler immediately situated his discussion of marriage and reproduction within the welfare of the state. Using the terminology of the Viennese sociologist Rudolf Goldsheid, he explained: "States are not only economic and political creations, but also entities organically contingent upon their human communities, and by organic contingency we mean the dependence of states upon the condition of their organic capital."[85] The people of a state, its "organic capital," must be healthy in order to insure a strong state. Although these people made choices as individuals, Tandler was concerned with the ways in which their choices affected the national community and asked that these choices be informed by responsibility.

Tandler began his construction of responsibility with the responsibility parents feel for their children. Through state organization, this private responsibility could be coordinated into responsibility for the entire next generation. State welfare and sexual hygiene policy, Tandler said, "transform[ed] familial responsibility into population politics, [and elevated] the breeding instinct into a generative ethic."[86] In contrast to the general corpus of Viennese sexology and sexual reform literature, Tandler used the term *Aufzucht*, which connotes the breeding or rearing of animals, throughout his essay. The goal of civilization, Tandler explained, was "not to inhibit the instinct to breed, but rather to enlarge upon it, to make it responsible, and even to rationalize it."[87] Tandler presented the practice of harnessing the breeding instinct as ancient. He traced exogamy and incest taboos through their role in clan formation to their enforcement in the modern state, likewise; he reviewed and rejected "primitive" concepts of male ownership of women in favor of equal rights for man and wife. Tandler's support for the latter development was couched in terms of what is best for society, rather than in terms of rights. He wrote: "Not only in the interest of human dignity, but also in the sense of population politics must we demand the spiritual and ethical equality of husband and wife, because only through equal rights and equal freedom can we foster the feeling of responsibility for creating and rearing life, two most important duties of the family."[88] Creating and rearing life, when elevated to the level of the state, represented the essence of population politics.

Having established his analogy between the family and the state, Tandler then turned to the question of quantity versus quality in population. Again, this theme was well known to Viennese social thinkers and SDAP ideologues, having been popularized by Rudolf Goldsheid in the pre-war period. In Tandler's hands, the comparison between quantity- and quality-oriented population politics was made more provocatively than ever before. He introduced quantitative population politics as an ancient practice, first developed as an imperialistic tool and today employed by the bourgeoisie to keep a plentiful pool of workers to man their factories and soldiers to fight their greed-inspired wars.[89] Population politics based on the quality of offspring, on the contrary, supported and enlarged the sense of responsibility within the family. Tandler presented two levels in which qualitative population politics works: that which is concerned with the present generation (humanitarian), and that which focuses on the coming generation (productive). With this categorization of qualitative population politics, the logic of eugenics entered Tandler's essay. Clearly, Vienna's welfare system under Tandler favored population planning according to quality. Yet even within the realm of quality population politics, he warned, we find inequality, specifically, between the welfare of the present generation and that of the next generation.

Productive population politics, as they appear in Tandler's argument, were those concerned with the reproductive strength of the *Volk*: providing for the health of mothers and children. Productive population politics cared for the body of the reproductive adult, housed the family in a clean and safe environment, and above all valued the welfare of children and of the as-of-yet-unborn.[90] Tandler spent pages outlining the Viennese welfare services devoted to "productive" ends. His pride in these services is palpable. However, he reported that only 42 percent of the total welfare budget for Vienna went towards "productive" services.[91] The majority of funds were used towards humanitarian ends. Accounting totals from the Vienna Welfare office for the years 1925 to 1929 show that this spending trend was never overcome by Tandler: care for adults remained more expensive than children's services despite yearly decreases in the former and budget increases for the latter.[92] The costs of providing medical care and shelter for war veterans alone never peaked, so that by 1931 the Welfare office could report that "in the last few years, not only have these costs failed to recede, but rather we have observed their increase."[93] Furthermore, despite a general decline in population numbers in the interwar period, the absolute number of elderly in Vienna remained even higher than it had been before the war.[94] Tandler assessed this dilemma: "It is our duty to be humane and just, and thus to also care for the old and the criminal, for the weak and the mad. The greater part of this duty is *unproductive*; is purely humanitarian. From the standpoint of population politics, the welfare budget of a state is balanced when its productive spending outweighs its humanitarian spending."[95] Vienna's welfare spending, then, according to Tandler's categories, was faulty: the city was spending too much on the present population at the expense of the coming generation. And because Tandler set "productive" services against "humanitarian" ones, the elision he made between "humanitarian" welfare and "unproductive" welfare barely created a ripple in his logic.

The most important aspect of Tandler's essay "Marriage and Population Politics" was not about marriage (of which he says very little), but rather was the way he reasoned through what it means to base a welfare and health system on population quality over quantity. Quality for the present generation is not as important as quality in the coming generation, according to Tandler. Furthermore "humanitarian" welfare ministrations existed only at the cost to more "productive" services. "Humanitarian" welfare problems could even infect the very children that "productive" population politics sought to protect. In an example drawn from the humanitarian care of the mentally insane, Tandler wrote:

Care of the insane costs the state about 44 million schillings [12 percent of the yearly welfare budget], which is certainly not productive and is about as irrational as the majority of people who spend their lives in insane asylums. Into these places comes every kind of impairment, be it something these people brought upon themselves, through syphilis or alcohol, or be it something their parents, who themselves yielded to drink or contracted syphilis, passed on to them. The mad atone for the sins of their fathers. But it is not only they who must pay the penalty, but rather all the children of Vienna pay for the sins of this father. If, through careful population politics, we could reduce the number of the insane by half … it would be possible to send 70,000 children, and thus close to a third of Vienna's schoolchildren, on a four-week vacation to recuperate. With this money we could ensure the health of our children and offer them joy for at least four weeks out of the year.[96]

In this quotation, Tandler, who as an expert in anatomy and the human constitution would certainly have had strong opinions about the inheritability of disease, displayed little interest in how the insane came to their state. Instead, he presented them as a general burden upon the coming generation. Tandler does not leave his reader without ideas about how the population of "humanitarian" welfare recipients might be reduced, either. He introduced the notion of "destruction of life unworthy of living," as a solution. Tandler did not claim for himself but rather noted that it was "pressing ever more on the consciousness of the *Volk* … because today we in many ways destroy life worthy of living in order to support those unworthy of life."[97] "Marriage and Population Politics" does not contain a definition of "life unworthy of living," but Tandler's usage of the term suggested the terminally ill, criminal, and insane citizens.

Tandler was extremely thorough in his explanations throughout his published work. It is therefore striking that he did not define the term "life unworthy of living" in "Marriage and Population Politics." This fact, combined with the way in which Tandler attributed the term to a vague national feeling, suggests that using negative eugenic arguments, for him, was an experimental rhetorical flourish rather than important part of his vision for social welfare. "Marriage and Population Politics" is overwhelmingly concerned with the right to live and cure. Tandler concluded his article by pointing towards less brutal solutions. Marriage and proper reproduction, in the end, appear in his argument as more rational means of reducing the "humanitarian" drain on the welfare state. He claimed for the state to control marriage, if only in order to control reproduction. He reminded his reader that religion had long held the power to veto marriage and reproduction among certain segments of society, and suggested the welfare state would wield this authority in a more rational manner. Turning the tradition of banning marriage between close relations on its head, Tandler illustrated his point: "In most civilized countries one forbids, for example, the marriage between uncle and niece, even when both are healthy; their union is banned by religion and morality. However, one allows an epileptic man and madwoman to marry, naturally as long as they are not related. This poses no contradiction according to the law nor morality."[98] The contradiction Tandler's argument exposed lay in the product of such marriages. He defined state control of marriage as one of proper reproduction: "Society's input [into prospective marriages] is not simply concerned with those who want to enter into it, but rather is concerned with what the product of this marriage will be."[99] Indeed, determining the prospective quality of offspring was precisely what Vienna's Marriage Advice Center was designed to do, as we shall explore in a later chapter.

Although in "Marriage and Population Politics" Tandler spoke of sterilization as a past, and perhaps future, solution to the problem of population politics, he did not think that the law was presently able to rule fairly on this issue.[100] Until the day that it could—the day in which the creation of sick children was as contrary to the will of the *Volk* as was incest—Tandler limited the welfare state to an advisory role. He closed his eugenic musings with a call to morality: "In my opinion, only one thing will awaken an ethics of procreation, and that is the sexual education of the people, an appeal to the feeling of responsibility within the individual."[101] Certainly the provocative arguments set forth in his essay were intended to engender in his audience just such feelings of individual and civic responsibility.

Conclusions

Vienna's Welfare Ministry was entirely new when Tandler took office at its helm, and his vision shaped it until the Republic ended. Before and during World War I, Vienna did not have its own welfare office; instead, welfare activities were dispersed across an archipelago of private and associational foundations, organized only under the rubric of "poor relief." As in most German-speaking towns in central Europe, availability of welfare services was decided on the parish level and contingent upon being a "hometown" resident.[102] Tandler inherited responsibility for the population of a cosmopolitan capital teeming with refugees and broken families, a capital furthermore locked into an increasing struggle with political Catholicism. Providing welfare in this context required a massive shift in the ways city officials thought about organizing and improving the health of Vienna's citizens. Many of Tandler's welfare innovations were, by any objective measure, salubrious and humane. Within the sub-set of sexual hygiene measures, his successes included turning back the tide of venereal disease by 1926, reducing infant mortality rates, improving maternity health care and social programs, and lessening the legal barriers faced by illegitimate children. Such successes were predicated on a reconfigured message of sexual responsibility that the SDAP launched in the interwar period, founded on the biological authority of evolution and survival. This was the entry-point for eugenics in Tandler's Health Ministry.

Many contemporary critics, and some subsequent historians, have seized upon the most shocking statements by Tandler and other SDAP representatives without considering their larger arguments. Although recent scholarship about eugenic social thought has sought a more nuanced approach to its pre-Holocaust history, it is still considered difficult to reconcile welfare and public health achievements like Tandler's with the frankly eugenic interests that lay behind them.[103] Historians of modern Germany have convincingly argued that eugenics served as a tool with which the early twentieth-century medical profession tried to pry ecclesiastical authority away from the process of reproduction. Yet this viewpoint obscures the greater promise eugenics held for a variety of social reformers during this period. For example, Cornelie Usborne, whose work explores the reproductive policies of Weimar Germany, suggests that the medical community was drawn to eugenics out of professional self-concern, writing, "the fear that theologians, philosophers, or teachers would dislodge [doctors] from their rightful place in reproductive decision-making seems sometimes to have supplied doctors with their motivation for lending support for this doubtful cause."[104] As the Viennese context amply proves, this is not a complete explanation. It neglects the possibility that interwar doctors might have truly believed that sexual and eugenic knowledge could solve the variety of social problems. This was certainly true for Tandler, who made eugenic suggestions in "Marriage and Population Politics" for the proper distribution of welfare resources.

"Marriage and Population Politics" offers useful insights into the balance between Tandler's goals for the immediate present and the racial future. As a doctor, specialist in anatomy, and enthusiast for the science of human constitution building, Tandler responded to the broken social body of Vienna with two related therapies: one based on improving the material and hygienic conditions of individual citizens and another on ensuring that their offspring would fare better than they. Much of the work he did in Vienna fell under the first category. But his heart lay with the latter—the promise of a stronger generation to come. Achieving this goal meant mobilizing a new kind of sexual responsibility, and eugenics provided him with a language with which to appeal to the public.

The eugenic tradition that Tandler participated in had its roots in pre-war Monist, feminist, and sex-reform ideology. "Social radical eugenics" and *Rassenhygiene* are two of the appellations this form of eugenics has recently received.[105] I will not create a new name for the Viennese variant of this eugenic program that Tandler and so many others supported in the interwar years. The content of this form of eugenics, however, is important to delineate. Taking its cue from the Monist tradition, this eugenics assumed that the work of nature, including the individual's satisfaction of "natural" urges, was positive. Sex was released from Christian dogma, yet still constrained by the strictures of heterosexual love, health, and responsibility. Creating, nurturing, and improving life on earth were the highest goals of humanity. Improving life meant, above all, the improvement of life's conditions. As historian Reinhard Mocek has explained, "this mode of eugenics assumed a change in living conditions, or social milieu, to be the key to human betterment."[106] In socialist-run Vienna, this change in living conditions was achieved through public housing, expanded sport and hygiene opportunities, medical subsidies, and, as we have seen in this chapter, extensive sexual, maternal, and family health programs. The class struggle was reinterpreted by the SDAP as a struggle for national health, achievable through a eugenics that required material improvements in the lives of the Viennese working class. A clean bed, healthy sexual partner, and hygienic body were the objects of eugenic reform in Vienna. However, as "Marriage and Population Politics" illustrates, the language of eugenics could be expanded to imagine a reduction of social services to unproductive members of society, sterilization of the reproductively unfit, and destruction of "life unworthy of living." Although these measures are not employed by Tandler's Welfare Ministry, they were well within the limits of the thinkable in interwar Vienna.

In "Marriage and Population Politics," Tandler introduced eugenic principles to a popular audience by talking about sports. In an extended analogy to horse breeding, Tandler spoke of a pedigreed racehorse. His breeder knew that he had a horse with inborn speed, but also that this horse needed a trainer. The trainer attends to the condition of the horse, the breeder to the constitution.[107] In this strange section, Tandler explored the ability of various peoples to withstand disease and hunger, and dreamt of a population that, through its genetic inheritance, is better able to face the struggle for existence. While his arguments are eugenic, he never uses the word. Instead he focuses on the constitution and condition of his hypothetical racehorse, an "organic capital" of a more prosaic sort, which he is able to both train and breed to succeed. This racehorse analogy illustrates the deeds and the dreams of Tandler's hygiene empire. Although he may have dreamt of playing the role of the breeder, he never did. Instead, he took the role of the trainer. He and the city hall he served created new conditions Vienna's population, through housing, health care, and welfare services. These surroundings were intended to, and certainly did, improve the conditions of the present generation. The sexual hygiene system that undergirded these developments, however, was also designed with a future generation in mind, and it was with this generation that Tandler's hopes lay. As a language with which to explore sexual hygiene and future generations, eugenics provided Tandler with a powerful means to appeal to his fellow citizen's sense of responsibility. This responsibility encompassed one's reproductive health, one's children, and one's role in creating the future "organic capital" of Vienna: a thriving population that could overcome the horrors of war and build a more just society.

Notes

1. Helmut Gruber, *Red Vienna: Experiment in Working-Class Culture, 1919–1934* (New York: Oxford University Press, 1991), 160.
2. As reported in Karl Sablik's exhaustive work *Julius Tandler, Mediziner und Sozialreformer: Eine Biographie* (Wien: Verlag A. Schendl, 1983), 127.
3. For psychohistorical approaches to SDAP leaders, see Mark Blum, *The Austro-Marxists 1890–1918: A Psychobiographical Study* (Lexington: University Press of Kentucky, 1985); Peter Lowenberg's chapter "Karl Renner and the Politics of Accommodation," in Peter Lowenberg, *Fantasy and Reality in History* (New York: Oxford University Press, 1995), 119–142; on Otto Bauer in particular, see Hannah S. Decker, *Freud, Dora, and Vienna 1900* (New York: The Free Press, 1991) and Peter Lowenberg, "Otto Bauer as an Ambivalent Party Leader," in Anson Rabinbach (ed.), *The Austrian Social Experiment: Social Democracy and Austromarxism, 1918–1934* (Boulder: Westview Press, 1985), 71–80.
4. Here I think the best approach to "sexualized" Viennese modernity is Edward Timms's *Karl Kraus, Apocalyptic Satirist: Cultural Catastrophe in Habsburg Vienna* (New Haven: Yale University Press, 1986), which posits a principle of displacement: Austrian politics, tragically stymied in parliament, spill out into other channels such as journalism, theater, and language, ideologically saturating Vienna. In particular, Timms suggests that critiques of sexuality and sexual double standards served as coded critiques of Viennese politics. Clearly this is an elaboration upon Carl Schorske's failure of liberalism model in *Fin-de-Siècle Vienna: Politics and Culture* (New York: Vintage Books, 1981). Finally, I also rely upon another critique of/dialogue with Schorske's work: Steven Beller's *Vienna and the Jews, 1867–1938: A Cultural History* (Cambridge: Cambridge University Press, 1989) for the context of assimilation and the race/sex node of anti-Semitism, which plagued the SDAP.
5. Eventually, *Bevölkerungspolitik* ("population politics," the term used by the SDAP to refer to eugenic thought) became the catchphrase for any academic discussion of sexual behavior and reproduction; at the highest level, *Bevölkerungspolitik* entered into SDAP debate for the first time at their 1926 party platform meeting. See Karin Lehner, *Verpönte Eingriffe: sozialdemokratische Reformbestrebungen zu den Abtreibungsbestimmungen in der Zwischenkriegzeit* (Wien: Picus Verlag, 1989), 12.
6. Information on Tandler's early career can be found in "Die Entwicklung des öffentlichen Gesundheitswesen," *Das Österreichische Gesundheitswesen*, Herausgegeben von Volksgesundheitamt der Gemeinde Wien (Wien: Wirtschafts-Zeitungs-Verlag-Gesellschaft, 1930), 80.
7. Publications listed under "Tandler, Julius," *Österreich Lexicon*, Richard Bamberger und Franz Maier-Bruck (hg.), Band II (Wien: Österreichischer Bundesverlag für Unterricht, Wissenschaft, und Kunst, 1966), 1132.
8. Julius Tandler, "Krieg und Bevölkerung," as reprinted in Sablik, *Julius Tandler*, 113–121, 114.
9. Tandler, "Krieg," in Sablik, *Julius Tandler*, 114. Emphasis in original.
10. Sablik, *Julius Tandler*, 123.
11. Tandler, "Krieg," in Sablik, *Julius Tandler*, 114. This argument had already been popularized by the leading German supporter of eugenics Alfred Ploetz in his 1895 book *The Efficiency of Our Race and the Protection of the Weak*. See Michael Burleigh and Wolfgang Wippermann, *The Racial State: Germany 1933–1945* (Cambridge: Cambridge University Press, 1991), 32.
12. Tandler, "Krieg," in Sablik, *Julius Tandler*, 115. It is unclear how Tandler defined "Austrian" men, but the number is high enough to suggest that he was counting the fallen of the entire Empire.
13. Tandler, "Krieg," in Sablik, *Julius Tandler*, 116 and 117.
14. Tandler, "Krieg," in Sablik, *Julius Tandler*, 116.

15. Tandler, "Krieg," in Sablik, *Julius Tandler*, 119.
16. Tandler, "Krieg," in Sablik, *Julius Tandler*, 119.
17. Tandler, "Krieg," in Sablik, *Julius Tandler*, 120.
18. For pre-war German-speaking feminist engagement in sexual and reproductive topics, see Ann Taylor Allen, "Feminism, Venereal Disease, and the State in Germany, 1890–1918," in *The Journal of the History of Sexuality* 4 (1993), 27–50; Harriet Anderson, *Utopian Feminism: Women's Movements in fin-de-siècle* Vienna (New Haven: Yale University Press, 1992); Edward Ross Dickinson, "Reflections on Feminism and Monism in the Kaiserreich," in *Central European History* 3:2 (June 2001), 191–230; and Karin Jusek, *Auf der Suche nach der Verlorenen: Die Prostitutionsdebatten im Wien der Jahrhundertwende* (Wien: Löcker Verlag, 1994).
19. Sablik, *Julius Tandler*, 64.
20. For an excellent summary of this intellectual trend, see Anson Rabinbach, "The Body without Fatigue: A Nineteenth-Century Utopia," in Seymour Drescher, David Sabean, and Allan Sharlin (eds.), *Political Symbolism in Modern Europe* (New Brunswick: Transaction Books, 1982), 42–62.
21. As summarized in Sablik, *Julius Tandler*, 65.
22. Sablik, *Julius Tandler*, 72.
23. Ludwig Pollak, "Der Arzt im Klassenkampf," *Der Kampf* 20/3 (März 1927), 127.
24. "Zehn Jahre Wolfahrtsamt der Stadt Wien," *Blätter für das Wohlfahrtswesen*, 30/286 (Juli-August 1931), 173.
25. Julius Tandler, "Wohlfahrtswesen und Gesundheitsamt," *Das Österreichische Gesundheitswesen*, Herausgegeben von Volksgesundheitamt der Gemeinde Wien (Wien: Wirtschafts-Zeitungs-Verlag-Gesellschaft, 1930), 81.
26. Tandler, "Wohlfahrtswesen," 81.
27. These numbers stem from a section entitled "Zeitschriftenschau" in *Blätter für das Wohlfahrtswesen*, 28:/274 (Juli-August 1929), 288–291.
28. Magistratsrat Dr. Franz Fettinger, "Die Personalstände des städtischen Gesundheitsamtes in den Jahren 1920 bis 1930," *Blätter für das Wohlfahrtswesen*, 29/282 (November-Dezember 1930), 337.
29. Tandler's speech to the magistrate reprinted in "Zehn Jahre Wolfahrtsamt der Stadt Wien,"171.
30. "Zehn Jahre Wohlfahrtsamt," 171–172.
31. "Wiens Bevölkerungsbewegung," *Das Neue Wien*, Städtewerk herausgegeben unter offizieller Mitwirkung der Gemeinde Wien, Band II (Wien: 1927), 602.
32. Oberstadtphysikus Dr. August Böhm, "Wiederaufbauarbiet der Volksgesundheit," *Blätter für das Wohlfahrtswesen*, 28/271 (Jänner-Februar 1929), 9.
33. Böhm, "Wiederaufbauarbeit," 9.
34. Pollak, "Der Arzt," 127.
35. Pollak, "Der Arzt," 127.
36. Pollak, "Der Arzt," 128.
37. Pollak, "Der Arzt," 128. Pollak especially encouraged rural doctors to represent the socialist cause in the (overwhelmingly Catholic) countryside.
38. This replacement of Christian with eugenic morality is well explained in Dickenson, "Reflections on Feminism and Monism," 202–207.
39. Julius Tandler, *Wohltätigkeit oder Fürsorge?* (Wien: Verlag der Organization Wien der sozialdemokratischen Partei, 1925), 5.
40. See chapter XV, "Welfare Work," in Charles Gulick, *Austria from Habsburg to Hitler*, vol. 1, (Berkeley: University of California Press, 1948), 505–543; Michael Hubenstorf, "Sozialmedizin, Menschenökonomie, Volksgesundheit," in Franz Kadrnoska (hg.), *Aufbruch und Unter-*

gang: Österreichischen Kultur zwischen 1918 und 1938 (Wien: Europaverlag, 1981), 247–266; and Gruber, *Red Vienna*, 63–72.

41. This list is culled largely from the Festschrift for Julius Tandler that was printed in the municipally-edited *Blätter für das Wohlfahrtswesen*, 28/271 (Jänner-Februar 1929), 8.
42. "Die Fürsorgeaufgabe der Gemeinde," *Das Neue Wien*, Städtewerk herausgegeben unter offizieller Mitwirkung der Gemeinde Wien, Band IV (Wien: 1927), 215. Lest Viennese women think that they were receiving a poor-relief donation, the following message was posted at advice centers and neighborhood services buildings: "Mothers! The Viennese Municipal Authority wants children to grow up healthy and strong. When we give out practical presents to every child, this is obviously not to be seen as alms for the poor. When we, through unlimited welfare projects, provide for the coming generation, the Municipal Authority works in our own interests."
43. "Wohlfahrtswesen und soziale Verwaltung im Haushaltungsplan der Gemeinde Wien. 1925–1929," reprinted in *Blätter für das Wohlfahrtswesen*, 28/271 (Jänner-Februar 1929), 98.
44. Indeed, Pius XI's 1930 papal encyclical *Casti connubii* was critical of just such state agencies that were perceived as threatening Christian marriage and the family. See chapter 3, "Sexual Knowledge for and about Women".
45. Oberstadtphysikus Dr. Victor Gegenbauer, "Die Tätigkeit des Wiener Gesundheitsamts im letzten Jahrzehnt," *Das Österreichische Gesundheitswesen*, Herausgegeben von Volksgesundheitamt der Gemeinde Wien (Wien: Wirtschafts-Zeitungs-Verlag-Gesellschaft, 1930), 81.
46. Tandler, *Wohltätigkeit oder Fürsorge?*, 7.
47. "Die Fürsorgeaufgabe der Geminde," 215.
48. Gegenbauer, "Wiener Gesundheitsamts," 82.
49. Josef Klar, "Die Mitwirkung der Gemeinde Wien an der Bekämpfung der Geschlechtskrankheiten," *Blätter für das Wohlfahrtswesen*, 28/271 (Jänner/Februar 1929), 26.
50. Böhm, "Wiederaufbauarbeit," 10.
51. "Wiens Bevölkerungsbewegung," *Das Neue Wien*, Städtewerk herausgegeben unter offizieller Mitwirkung der Gemeinde Wien, Band II (Wien: 1927), 604. Despite this report's even-handed way of parsing the socio-economic conditions that have hindered marriage and birth-rates in the post-war period, it ends on a note of supreme hope: "The population history of Vienna teaches us that out of deepest emergency and the desert of [Imperial] collapse, we move forward through revolution and reorganization!", 605.
52. Primarazt Dr. Hilda Ridler, "Die Abteilung für geschlechtskranke Kinder im Zentralkinderheim der Stadt Wien," *Blätter für das Wohlfahrtswesen*, 29/282 (November-Dezember 1930), 268. The actual numbers of children treated for VD appear much milder than Dr. Ridler's language; the ward saw on average 125 children a year in the years 1924 to 1930.
53. "Beratungsstelle für Geschlechtskranke," *Die Verwaltung der Bundeshauptsamt Wien in der Zeit vom 1 Jänner 1923 bis 31 Dezember 1928*. Wiener Stadt- und Landesarchiv Archivbibliothek, M511 2 Ex. 42/1/2, Band II Teil 1, 863.
54. "Bekämpfung der Geschlechtskrankheiten," *Das Neue Wien*, Städtewerk herausgegeben unter offizieller Mitwirkung der Gemeinde Wien, Band II (Wien: 1927), 563.
55. Dr. Josef Klar, "Die Wassermannstationen der Gemeinde Wien," in *Blätter für das Wohlfahrtswesen*, 29/282 (November-Dezember 1930), 268.
56. Dr. Josef Klar, "Die Mitwirkung der Gemeinde Wien an der Bekämpfung der Geschlechtskrankheiten," *Blätter für das Wohlfahrtswesen*, 28/271 (Jänner/Februar 1929), 26.
57. Oberstadtphysikus Dr. Victor Gegenbauer, "Die wichtigsten Einrichten des Wiener Gesundheitsamts," *Blätter für das Wohlfahrtswesen*, 31/290 (März-April 1932), 46.
58. Oberbezirksarzt Dr. Karl Gottlieb, "Geschlechtskrankheiten," *Blätter für das Wohlfahrtswesen*, 30/283 (Jänner/Februar 1931), 16.
59. "Bekämpfung der Geschlechtskrankheiten," *Verwaltung der Bundeshauptstadt Wien*, 561.

60. Here I'm comparing two city reports for the year 1925: 5,464 people visited the evening VD clinics, while 490 new clients visited the Marriage Advice Clinic. "Abendambulatorien für Geschlechtskrankheit," WSLA, 862 and "Eheberatung," *Das Neue Wien*, 570.
61. "Abendambulatorien für Geschlechtskranke," *Die Verwaltung der Bundeshauptsamt Wien in der Zeit vom 1 Jänner 1923 bis 31 Dezember 1928*. Wiener Stadt- und Landesarchiv Archivbibliothek, M511 2 Ex. 42/1/2, Band II Teil 1, 862.
62. Ministerialrat Dr. Wilhelm Eisenschiml, "Die Bekämpfung der Geschlechtskrankheiten in Österreich," *Das Österreichische Gesundheitswesen*, Herausgegeben von Volksgesundheitamt der Gemeinde Wien (Wien: Wirtschafts-Zeitungs-Verlag-Gesellschaft, 1930), 18.
63. For example, the index for the *Wiener medizinische Wochenschrift* for the year 1901 lists syphilis as the most frequent subject for articles and reviews.
64. "Abendambulatorien für Geschlechtskranke," 862.
65. Dr. Siegfried Rosenfeld, "Aus der Gesundheitsstatistik Österreichs," in *Das Österreichische Gesundheitswesen*, Herausgegeben von dem Volksgesundheitamt der Gemeinde Wien (Wien: Wirtschafts-Zeitungs-Verlag-Gesellschaft, 1930), 54.
66. "Wiens Bevölkerungsbewegung," 603.
67. Dr. Wilhelm Hecke, "Fragen der Unehelichenfürsorge," *Blätter für das Wohlfahrtswesen*, 29/272 (Juli-August 1930), 187.
68. For example, the civil suits court in Vienna decided on 19 August 1931 (38 R 1115/31) that even unmarried fathers, who later entered into a marriage with a different woman, were still responsible for paying support to their former sexual partner and the resulting children. See "Gesetze, Vorordnungen, Rechtsfragen," *Blätter für das Wohlfahrtswesen*, 30/287 (September-Oktober 1931), 235.
69. "Die Fürsorgeaufgaben der Gemeinde," 216.
70. This figure for legitimate infant mortality rates comes from "Wiens Bevölkerungsbewegung," 604.
71. The proceedings of this conference are summarized in Hecke's "Fragen der Unehelichenfürsorge," *Blätter für das Wohlfahrtswesen*, 29/272 (Juli-August 1930), 184–188. The speeches of the participants also appeared in *Die Unehelichen in Österreich*, a special issue of the *Jahrbücher für Nationalökonomie und Statistik*.
72. Hecke, "Unehelichenfürsorge," 185.
73. Hecke, "Unehelichenfürsorge," 187.
74. Hecke, "Unehelichenfürsorge," 187.
75. Böhm, "Wiederaufbauarbeit," 9.
76. See Ulrike Harmat, *Ehe auf Widerruf?* (Wien: Klostermann, 1999) for Austrian divorce law and contemporary attempts at marriage law reform, 1918–1938.
77. For a more detailed description, see Paul Pallester, "Eherechtsreform," in Herbert Steiner (hg.), *Sexualnot und Sexualreform: Verhandlung der Weltliga für Sexualreform, IV. Kongress* (Wien: Elbenmühl-Verlag, 1931), 457–459.
78. "Eheberatungstelle," *Die Verwaltung der Bundeshauptsamt Wien in der Zeit vom 1 Jänner 1923 bis 31 Dezember 1928*. Wiener Stadt- und Landesarchiv Archivbibliothek, M511 2 Ex. 42/1/2, Band II Teil 1, 365.
79. Lehner, *Verpönte Eingriffe*, 169. Karl Kautsky suggested that, once legalized, any medical intervention (abortion) should still be reported to the police. See Gruber, *Red Vienna*, 160.
80. Lehner, *Verpönte Eingriffe*, 163.
81. Gruber, *Red Vienna*, 160.
82. Gruber, *Red Vienna*, 160.
83. The figures in this section are cited from Stadtphysikus Dr. Victor Gegenbauer, "Gesundheitsstatistik," *Blätter für das Wohlfahrtswesen*, 29/280 (Juli-August 1930), 161–163.

84. "Wiens Bevölkerungsbewegung," 602. The shrinking number of marriages in Vienna every year is also cited in Rosenfeld's essay "Aus der Gesundheitsstatistik Österreichs." This later article counts "only 51,500 marriages in 1929, and thus 7.7 marriages for every 1,000 inhabitants." Rosenfeld, "Gesundheitsstatistik," 53.
85. Julius Tandler, *Ehe und Bevölkerungspolitik* (Wien: Verlag von Moritz Perles, 1924), 1.
86. Tandler, *Ehe und Bevölkerungspolitik*, 4.
87. Tandler, *Ehe und Bevölkerungspolitik*, 4.
88. Tandler, *Ehe und Bevölkerungspolitik*, 7.
89. Tandler, *Ehe und Bevölkerungspolitik*, 8.
90. Tandler, *Ehe und Bevölkerungspolitik*, 17.
91. Tandler, *Ehe und Bevölkerungspolitik*, 16.
92. "Wohlfahrtswesen und soziale Verwaltung im Haushaltungsplan der Gemeinde Wien. 1925–1929," reprinted in *Blätter für das Wohlfahrtswesen*, 28/271 (Jänner-Februar 1929), 94–98.
93. "Zehn Jahre Wohlfahrtsamt," 188.
94. "Zehn Jahre Wohlfahrtsamt," 176.
95. Tandler, *Ehe und Bevölkerungspolitik*, 16. Emphasis in the original.
96. Tandler, *Ehe und Bevölkerungspolitik*, 16.
97. Tandler, *Ehe und Bevölkerungspolitik*, 17.
98. Tandler, *Ehe und Bevölkerungspolitik*, 21.
99. Tandler, *Ehe und Bevölkerungspolitik*, 21.
100. Later in his career, Tandler's position on sterilization became sharper. In a 1928 presentation to the Austrian Association for the People's Breeding and Inheritance, he called for the sterilization or castration of "master criminals, sexual criminals, idiots, [and] epileptics, who are beginning to endanger human society with the products of their bodies." As quoted in Lehner, *Verpönte Eingriffe*, 91.
101. Tandler, *Ehe und Bevölkerungspolitik*, 22.
102. "Zehn Jahre Wohlfahrtsamt," 172.
103. Here I have found especially helpful Reinhard Mocek's "The Program of Proletarian *Rassenhygiene*" in *Science in Context* 11:3–4 (1998), 609–617. Although some of Mocek's distinctions do not hold for Vienna, he shows that eugenic arguments were made from medical, but also environmental, standpoints. This is a useful way to think about the various eugenic positions defended in interwar Vienna.
104. Cornelie Usborne, *The Politics of the Body in Weimar Germany: Women's Reproductive Rights and Duties* (Ann Arbor: University of Michigan Press, 1992), 147.
105. See Dickenson, "Reflections on Feminism and Monism," 202, and Reinhard Mocek, "Proletarian *Rassenhygiene*," 609.
106. Mocek, "Proletarian *Rassenhygiene*," 609.
107. Tandler, *Ehe und Bevölkerungspolitik*, 19.

Chapter 2

Sexual Education Debates in Late Imperial and Republican Vienna

Sexual education was a central tenet of the international sex reform movement. The question of sexual knowledge for children was in many ways both an impetus and a trial for Viennese sex reformers. It struck deep into the family realm, raising questions about how children learn, what values should be transmitted to them, and when fairy tales and scientific truths were appropriate. In interwar Vienna, socialist and reform-minded educators worked to replace religious authority on sexual matters with a more scientific and publicly distributed discourse of sexual knowledge. Catholic pedagogues, in turn, responded to this trend by developing new approaches to the familiar themes of purity and heavenly love. The result of this collective concern was a wide range of popular and educational publications about sexual *Aufklärung* (literally, "enlightenment") for children.[1] These articles, pamphlets, books, and lecture notes form the backbone of this chapter. In many cases, I demonstrate the popularity of the texts I have chosen through carefully reconstructed reprint histories and the contemporary recommendations of these publications from church and party publications. I have highlighted other sources for their sheer ability to surprise, as I believe the mapping of a horizon of possibility in cultural production to be as fruitful as a study of the average or the popular. Using these texts, I show that sexual education in the interwar period formed, for both Catholics and reformers, the cornerstone of a new social foundation that emphasized the "naturalness" of sexuality, the re-construction of motherhood, and the overwhelming necessity of purity and individual responsibility. Competing visions of how the *neue Menschen* of the first Republic should procreate and replenish the nation are ever present in my sources, just visible behind the pious and/or scientific presentations of concerned priests, socialists, and teachers.

Appropriate sexual knowledge for children was addressed in the popular German-speaking press well before the first Republic. Interest in sex education during the late Imperial period stems from the importance of "making scientific" the business of reproduction within Monist and eugenic groups, the popularity of nature and nudist movements in Germany, and the new vogue of masculine purity literature produced by Catholic authors in Bavaria and Austria.[2] In particular, the leading (Catholic) German pedagogue of the late-nineteenth century, Friedrich Wilhelm Förster, suggested that *Aufklärung* could be a positive addition to school curriculum when formulated as a kind of "willpower training."[3] Finally, the early sexology texts of Krafft-Ebing, Bloch, and Hirschfeld, as well as the work of Freud, all supported the late-nineteenth century hypothesis that sex played a particularly important role in the development of the individual. In the words of Iwan Bloch, from his pre-war masterpiece *The Sexual Life of Our Time*, "sexual love constitutes a part of the very being of man; his sexual life clearly reflects his individual nature, and love influences his development in an enduring manner."[4] This body of scientific and medical knowledge sparked pedagogical and parenting debates, and also directly addressed the need for early *Aufklärung* as a means of combating venereal disease. Sexological research suggested that public and secular sexual education could be a powerful tool in the hygienic improvement of modern urban life.

The series of crises concomitant with the end of World War I—the dissolution of empire, return of wounded veterans, spread of disease, and material distress of Vienna's population—quickly moved sexual education from a sub-topic of hygiene to a subject of municipal debate among teachers and parents of all political backgrounds. Although I stage this debate as part of a larger question of sexual knowledge, in its original reforming moment it was framed within the context of school secularization and reform in Red Vienna. Sexual education was part of an impressive list of city council goals for the Vienna public school system that included the creation of pre-schools and kindergartens, the replacement of rote lessons with self-directed learning, and the abolition of crucifixes in the classroom. After charting and comparing the kinds of sexual education advanced in the pre-war period, I will return to the subject of school reform in a discussion of socialist and reform-oriented sexual education. The task of Viennese municipal socialism vis-à-vis children's education, as my research will show, was to extract sex from the religious and bourgeois structures that controlled children's sexual knowledge. A third section of this chapter presents the range of Catholic responses to *Aufklärung* debates, from papal directives to pedagogical texts that both incorporate and contest sexological knowledge. This section of the chapter illustrates the pressure put on sex reformers by a critical counterforce within Viennese culture: the Roman Catholic Church. I close with an assessment of how these discourses, so polemical in its written form, may have affected the way Viennese families thought about and discussed sex.

Pre-War *Aufklärung*

In general, pre-World War I sexual education literature was written for a young male audience and took as its task the preparation of boys for manhood. After the war, magazines, journal articles, and books began to direct themselves to a female audience, as well. I will present a group of pre-war publications, selected to represent a range of political and religious perspectives that will ground my discussion of the sexual education debates in interwar Vienna. While some of these sources are specifically Viennese, others were written by and for a greater German community.

Taken as a whole, the German-speaking pre-war discussion about sexual education established the following points in common: sexual topics should be discussed in private, with no more than a few children at a time; individual curiosity and differing maturity levels of children means that there is no "right time" for sexual education for all children; the natural world is the easiest bridge into conversations with children about sex; fairy tales about storks and cabbages are, after a certain age, unnecessary and might in fact lead children into distrust and disbelief; and finally, well-educated parents, especially mothers, are best suited to answering the reproductive questions of young children, although male adolescents, plagued by confusing urges and feelings, need reassurance and guidance from strong father figures. These theses were in turn adopted in both the reforming and Catholic *Aufklärung* literature of the interwar period, allowing both sides to expand upon the social and moral implications of educating children about sex.

In 1907, a progressive collective of German-speaking parents and teachers calling itself the *Dürerbund* ("Dürer League": they took an image of the Renaissance artist as their symbol) formed with the goal of encouraging parents to speak openly with their children about sexual reproduction for the health of "the family, the *Volk*, and the race."[5] The alternative, they warned, was that children would learn the facts of life from pernicious school-comrades or bad servants, and that such experiences would put a child's feelings of purity and parental love in jeopardy. After an initial pedagogical journal publication, the *Dürerbund* announced an open call for papers on the topic of talking to children about sex, and received over five hundred essays. As a result, in 1909 the league published *At the Fountain of Life*, a collection of "worthy essays from men and women of all parties, classes and confessions, from teachers and spiritual leaders both Protestant and Catholic, from doctors and judges, from officers and farmers ... and above all from mothers, so many of which share their experiences, the countess answering our call just as often as the worker's wife."[6] They advertised the collection as the first book on the subject of sexual education that was designed as a workbook or series of practical exercises, in which theory and practice could coexist and children and parents alike could find the answers they sought. It was also one of the few books before World War I that included girls in its outreach. During the interwar years, *At the Fountain of Life* was recommended reading for parents and teachers among several groups and publications (often socialist) supportive of sex education. The teaching methods and nature-based science projects within the essays were repeated throughout sex reform literature as appropriate ways to introduce "the wonder of life" to children. Given its enduring popularity, a close reading of *At the Fountain of Life* is in order.

The essays in *At the Fountain of Life* were written in a variety of ways. Some were presented as dialogues between parent and child, teacher and pupil, and parents among themselves; others were written as short stories or letters; a minority was written in essay format in which the author speaks directly to an adult audience. The general guidelines suggested by the *Dürerbund* were for adults to speak out of love for truth and youth, and to ground everything in experience.[7] These ideals of familial love and scientific truth are reflected in the essay collection, submitted by authors from Germany, Austria, and Switzerland.

Perhaps the most popular question repeated throughout *At the Fountain of Life* asked how to introduce the topic of reproduction to children. The overwhelming answer was to build upon observable parallels from the natural world. "The Reproduction of the Human Species," written by a middle-school teacher as an example of what could be achieved in a natural history class, suggests activities such as observing tulip seeds and bulbs under a microscope, studying the reproductive strategies of moss with a full-page diagram taken from Schmeil's *Textbook of Biology* (thoughtfully reproduced in the essay), and starting new growths by placing fruit pits in water. The goal is to guide children through the natural world in such a way that "only a few words are required to lead them to the topic of human sexuality." The author/educator suggests ending the botanical lesson with a terse, "There are single sex plants, like moss, and two-sexed plants. Humans are two-sexed."[8] Less scientific forays into the natural world are offered throughout *At the Fountain of Life*. A walk through the Vienna woods, looking at dandelions and seeds, a dialogue in front of an image of the Madonna holding the Christchild, the birth of puppies in the neighborhood, and, invariably, the pear or apple tree in the courtyard are all presented as opportunities to begin talking about reproduction.[9] Even when the metaphors were unstable, such as the unusual circumstances surrounding the Virgin Mary's pregnancy or the fact that most fruit trees are grafted, the varied authors of *At the Fountain of Life* pressed them upon their readers as the most natural way to educate children. In these cases, the ability to speak from a visible part of the world, be it pollen or a religious painting, was prized above logic. As one rural mother explained: "Show [your boy] some mating chickens. Ask, 'what is the rooster doing? He's putting something in the hen, which is like the seed that we put in the earth.'"[10]

Many of the essays in *At the Fountain of Life* remind parents (and their children) that discussions about sex must remain private. This seems to be both a partial nod to the irregularity of reproductive knowledge among the children's peers and also an extension of the group's belief that *Aufklärung* must be individually tailored and presented only when the audience is mature enough. Several essays modeled ways that parents might express this need for confidentiality. In "Where Do Little Children Come From?" a mother makes keeping quiet a condition for the answer to the child's titular question: "If you pay very close attention and you also promise me that you will speak to no-one but Father and Mother about where small children come from, then I will tell you."[11] Another mother in "An Earnest Hour" ends her frank explanation of the union of germ and seed in her body with a request that her daughter not speak of these things with other adults or children, reasoning that, "only mothers and their children speak of these things together, because it is a topic so entirely dear and secretly beautiful ... [that] we keep it quiet like we keep our prayers to God at night private."[12] In "My Boy," a conversation between mothers about overcoming their embarrassment in order to educate their sons, the holiness of human reproduction is also invoked: "He might ask, 'Did Dad give you something to make me grow inside of you?' Then just explain how wonderful it was when you realized you were pregnant, and that one must only speak of these things as if the dear Lord were right close to you. Stay calm and don't laugh!'"[13] These formulations convey a message of caution without suggesting that the topic of reproduction is improper or shameful. Indeed, they explicitly instruct parents to describe sex as sacred: a divine process that could be profaned through false coyness or laughter.

While many of the essays in *At the Fountain of Life* were directed to girls as well as boys, the majority of pre-war press about children's sexual education was formulated on the premise that boys would be receiving *Aufklärung* alone. There are several implications of writing for an all-male audience. They include an emphasis on the proper hygiene and habits of a student, an inculcation of masculine traits and strengths, and a more explicit call for bodily purity, particularly in regards to the temptation of pre-war state-regulated prostitution. The remaining examples of pre-war attempts at *Aufklärung* elaborate upon these specifically male concerns.

Included in *At the Fountain of Life* are several stories and essays told from the point of view of the father of the family. In these entries his position was especially privileged as the family member best able to explain and present the facts of life to older boys. He also offered clues as to how a young man should feel about sexual matters. In "My Father from Memory," a young father remembers the ways in which his father, an uneducated workingman, encouraged his own curiosity and (sexual) education through biology and the natural world. In "An Episode of Youth," a Viennese man remembers visiting the estate where his father worked as forest master and the fateful day his father explained the birth process while aiding an injured doe in labor. The boy's tears of horror were soothed by his father, who taught him that gratitude and tenderness, in honor of every mother, were more appropriate feelings. The confusions of late adolescence, replete with the pressure to lose one's virginity, are addressed in "Parting Words from a Father to his Son." In this epistolary essay, a father reassures his son that his new emotions, including the "unnamable feeling of desire, that makes you feel as if you must flee from such thoughts, which appear to you to be impure," are nothing more than the natural wishes of a young person for love, a family, and children.[14] However, this father asks his son to save up all of these feelings of desire for his future wife, and to avoid "those unhappy souls, who sell their love, because your modesty [*Scham*, a term that can also mean (female) genitals] dies in their company, and your body can be burdened with terrible ailments for the rest of your life."[15] This combination of emotional reassurance (of the naturalness of sexual feelings) and threats of bodily destruction are repeated throughout popular sex education literature by reformers and Catholics alike.

In order to assure that parents had the right information with which to educate their children about sexual matters, pedagogues focused on presenting information for parents to then re-format in conversations with their young. One such method developed in the pre-war period was the school lecture, delivered in the evening to parents by a teacher or doctor. For example, in 1910 and 1911 the *Schularzt* and *k.k. Gymnasial-Professor Med.-Dr.* Lothar Skalla, in whose person both of these professions were combined, presented lectures on hygiene and sexual education to the parental community of the Währinger middle school. These lectures were published in the *Journal for Austrian Preparatory Schools*, and in a slim book the following year. Skalla's combination of hygiene and sexual knowledge exemplifies the mildly eugenic strain in sexual education that ran throughout the early twentieth century. Purity (*Reinlichkeit*) is stressed throughout Skalla's lectures as a physical imperative: children must learn to wash everywhere, brush their teeth, wear clean, free-fitting clothes, avoid alcohol, caffeine, and tobacco, and get plenty of exercise and sleep. Skalla fit sexual education into this matrix of hygiene as a necessary part of increasing the health of the nation (*Volksgesundheit*) and the struggle against tuberculosis, alcoholism, and venereal disease. These ills, Skalla argued, entered the family through the sexual indiscretions of the father and destroyed marriages, the health of children, and the *Volk* itself.[16]

Skalla's work insisted that children (although Skalla referred only to boys in his text) be educated about sexual matters by their parents at home, because explanations had to be individualized to the age, maturity, and temperament of each child. In order to better equip parents for this duty, Skalla devoted his lecture to debunking popular myths about human sexuality. Beginning with the innocence of the young, Skalla warned that children of a very young age have sexual curiosity and knowledge: through the natural world, by watching younger siblings and listening to older playmates, and above all by reading newspapers and modern novels.[17] Second, Skalla reaffirmed the role of the will in self-control: parents must not believe, as some do, that the sexual drive was irrepressible: this was true for pets, perhaps, but not humans. Skalla in fact suggested that more repression was in order by rejecting the arguments that men were naturally polygamous or that their sexual activity before marriage was harmless on the grounds that such beliefs introduced venereal disease into the family. Most importantly, Skalla separated biological and moral sexual knowledge. True *Aufklärung*, he argued, had nothing to do with likening the human to animal or plant reproduction, but rather concerned itself with teaching every person, women included, how to behave as people and not to believe that "one half of humanity is worth less and exists only to satisfy the lusts of the other!"[18] Here Skalla was clearly reacting against the late nineteenth-century narrative of "natural" male desire and "inherent" female submission, and using the topic of sexual education as a springboard into the inequity of gender relations—a rhetorical trick that was repeated throughout the interwar period. Instead of teaching children to rely upon degenerate cultural stereotypes, Skalla insisted they be taught that willpower made anything achievable and could even overcome "the last and most tyrannical of all natural drives," sexual urges.[19] Although he spoke from a secular point of view, Skalla's separation of biological and moral sexual knowledge was enthusiastically repeated and enlarged upon in the Catholic *Aufklärung* literature of the interwar period.

Skalla's message of hygiene and self-control was tailored and delivered to Viennese parents, but it drew from an established German discourse of *Aufklärung* intended for the educated young man. Skalla's lectures were in many ways condensed versions of Hans Wegner's extremely popular *We Young Men: The Sexual Problem of Educated Young Men Before Marriage*, first published in 1906 and brought out again in 1917 in an effort to combat the loosening morals brought on by war.[20] Wegner's concerns were fourfold: the construction of male honor, the preservation of health and purity, the selection of appropriate women, and the strength of the *Volk*. Because this book was reprinted so often, I want to present Wegner's points clearly. He began with a discussion of what made a (future) man honorable; namely, his strength. This strength was defined as the power to be brave and dauntless, the power to work, and the power to reproduce.[21] In Wegner's book, courage was expressed by refusing to cave into older friends who might goad one into visiting a prostitute, work-power was ensured by avoiding alcohol, tobacco, caffeine, salt, and heated baths, and reproduction, when properly practiced and understood, was the most noble ability that a man possessed. Wegner gave the power of reproduction a thorough discussion. The sex drive or male essence, although difficult to control, was the source of all that was manly in youth, including their ability to work, think, and reason.[22] Its expression was to take place only in marriage to a pure woman. Relationship opportunities for Wegner's young audience were polarized: they might have sex with a syphilitic prostitute, or they might find a pure woman worthy of friendship or respect. The latter was imperative to the health of the *Volk*. Wegner described women's highest ability as their fertility in marriage and grounded women's right to tender consideration in the terrible mortality rate they faced when entering childbirth.[23] Wegner's conception of women was more essentialist than the Viennese presentations of Skalla, but both authors emphasized moral *Aufklärung* over biological sex education in their holistic approach to bodily purity, description of the perniciousness of older comrades and impure literature, and emphasis on the eugenic imperative of healthy reproduction within monogamous marriage.

Although both Wegner and Skalla emphasized moral *Aufklärung*, neither referred to religious dogma in his arguments for sexual restraint and purity. Dr. Jakob Hoffmann's 1915 *Become a Complete Man! Aufklärung and Education for the Growing Male Youngster* is an example of Catholic participation in the growing concern over young people's sexual knowledge. *Become a Complete Man!* was aimed at an audience of 13- to 16-year-old boys who were beginning to question their changing bodies and urges. It was an extremely popular book during World War I, running through six reprints in two years. Hoffmann's work put a positive spin on the serious business of restraint and purity by emphasizing the beauty of mankind and the love of God for his creations while at the same time calling for personal strength and responsibility in the face of sin. Hoffmann, a *Gymnasiam* professor of religion in Munich, designed his book as a series of letters to his young friends that addressed questions about the body and health and suggested ways that his charges might build their spiritual and emotional lives. Essentially, this was a book that told boys how to feel about themselves and the changes that puberty brought. It offered them character-building exercises with which to construct a cohesive, unified self in the face of teenage turmoil.[24] Hoffmann did this by addressing bodily health, love and sexual feelings, and religious life. Religious life in Hoffmann's work, in particular, served as a haven from the confusing feelings of puberty. Like his secular colleagues, Hoffmann counseled sleep, exercise, temperance, and abstention from tobacco in the critical years of bodily development. He was also concerned with middle-school boys' relationships with older students, which he warned could lead to early peer-driven initiation into unhealthy habits like smoking, drinking, reading inappropriate literature, and dancing, activities which "weaken one's nerves, make one a parasite, and can lead to suicide."[25] Intimate friendships with older boys were given a brief discussion. Hoffmann warned that it was unhealthy to be too caught up with one friend—particularly those that wished to exchange letters, gifts, and similar tokens of affection—for such behavior was laughably girlish and could extend into shameful sins.[26] This line of advice was both an oblique reference to the homoerotic practices of schoolboys exposed in *fin-de-siècle* literature like Robert Musil's *Young Törless* and a straightforward reminder that to act in a feminine manner was now unacceptable for young men of this age.[27] Finally, Hoffmann addressed the danger that sexual diseases posed for bodily purity. Like Skalla, he warned that even one encounter with a prostitute could be deadly for his young friends and their future families, and "only one reliable method of protection exist[ed] for the young man who would avoid such a fate: *this was chaste abstinence and purity.*"[28]

Clearly part of Hoffmann's method of outreach involved shaming and scare tactics. Hoffmann's message of hope to young men, on the other hand, was that they were not slaves to their physical conditions, but rather beautiful temples to the Holy Spirit that, with the cooperation of their parents and teachers, would be formed into powerful and sensitive personalities. Again and again Hoffmann related in a familiar tone the story of "a boy I know" who faced the choice between being a shameful slave to his sexual feelings or protecting his body and soul. *Aufklärung*, for Hoffmann, was something that caused young men distress and put them in danger, and as such any proper sexual education demanded clear definition of what was sinful and what was not.[29] In order to do this, Hoffmann framed adolescent bodily changes within the beauty of God's greater plan. He reassured his readers that nothing within young men was inherently sinful; rather, their "natural" sexual feelings were part of God's design. These urges were created by God to lead them into holy matrimony, and it was only when these feelings are acted upon outside of marriage that sin occurred.[30] This naturalized description of adolescent sexual drives later became central to interwar Catholic *Aufklärung* arguments. The strong personalities based on purity and restraint that Hoffmann and other Catholics advised boys to develop were to help them handle their natural sexual feelings appropriately. One way to sublimate sexual feelings according to Hoffmann was to pour one's energies into work; conversely, those who chased after sexual sensations would find themselves without the mental and physical capacities for labor.[31] Like Wegner, Hoffmann equated the ability to work with male honor, and suggested that the respect of society and the love of a pure woman could only be won through labor. This message of sexual sublimation through service and labor was repeated by reforming socialists during the interwar years.

As seen in the above examples, the majority of pre-war *Aufklärung* material was written in an epistolary or dialogical style, literary conceits that allowed parents and children to receive official advice in personal ways. The epistolary style was perhaps most artistically achieved in Lou Andreas-Salomé's *Three Letters to a Young Lad*, which was published during World War I. That the student-muse of Nietzsche, Freud, and Rilke also published an *Aufklärung* book serves to illustrate the widening base of the sexual education movement. Addressed to a young family friend, each of these letters was written to correspond with his growing age and maturity. The first, dated 1907, relates to the boy a revealing conversation Andreas-Salomé claimed to have had with Santa Claus, who exposed the story of the stork bringing babies as a silly fairy tale. The second, dated 1911, was written in response to an imaginary question the young boy had asked about reproduction. Her answer began with a quick review of biology: eggs and sperm, fish and fowl are explained in their biological entirety. Andreas-Salomé was as natural (if poetic) when she comes to human reproduction, describing the woman's "innermost part," the womb, and the man's "precious life-juice," stored in his scrotum.[32] She then turned to what she saw as the young man's more pertinent question, which was reminiscent of many of the conversations in *At the Fountain of Life*: if reproduction were truly beautiful, why was it surrounded by secrecy and shame? Andreas-Salomé answered with pages of romantic meditations on love, tenderness, beauty, and death (replete with verses from Rilke) that assured her young friend that society kept secret not only dirty topics, but also the most heartfelt. All scientific language disappeared from this section of the text. It returned, however, in a final letter from 1913, which cited the psychoanalytic work of Freud in an attempt to explain the changes Andreas-Salomé's young friend felt in his body and soul. The author incorporated the most recent sexological opinions into her text: that urges for union and sexual gratification, including self-gratification, were natural and present from earliest childhood; that the dreams and fantasies experienced by adolescents were part of their development towards monogamous, heterosexual relationships; and that even the incest-taboo had developed from more than simply religious motivations. This was a very advanced and progressive discussion, notable for its complete lack of emphasis on purity. Rather, Andreas-Salomé entreated her young correspondent to resist the temptation to see his body as a dangerous "other" and to accept the stormy disruptions of his physical development as a deep experience that would, in the end, bind his body and soul.[33] Like Hoffmann, Andreas-Salomé did not deny the reality of sex in the lives of young people. Although these two authors approached the problem of sexual education from very different intellectual traditions, both promoted a cohesive self that could accept and appropriately restrain its developing sexual urges. It was Andreas-Salomé's blend of sentimental and scientific language, however, that was more typical of the sex reform and *Aufklärung* movement that found a foothold in Red Vienna.

Reforming Voices, 1919 to 1934

Many of the Viennese proponents of expanded sexual education in the interwar years, both public and private, spoke from a position of alignment with the Social Democratic Worker's Party (SDAP) that held the majority in city council. But the founding fathers of municipal socialism in Vienna said next to nothing on the question of sexual *Aufklärung*, and any attempt to include human reproduction and sexuality in the city school curriculum was abandoned by 1926, as I will explain presently. However, the discussion of appropriate, even prophylactic sexual knowledge for children continued throughout the interwar period among socialist youth group leaders and radical party members concerned with the "sexual misery" [*Sexualnot*, which also connoted emergency] brought on by modern urban life. Their platforms were built upon the same themes we have seen in pre-war sexual education literature: individual or small group initial *Aufklärung*, personally tailored to the needs and maturity of the child(ren) in question; use of the natural world as a template upon which to build; and emphasis on parental, particularly maternal, guidance through these topics. To these theses, socialist reformers also added demands for a more extensive and formal *Aufklärung*—ideally between the ages of eleven and thirteen—and relied upon their influence in youth groups and after-school programs to implement this reform.

While sexual education promoters within the SDAP called for *Aufklärung* to be integrated into high school natural science classes, the realities of school reform in interwar Vienna forced sexual education into the corners of city-organized education. School reform was one of the cornerstones of the SDAP's attempt to reshape the culture of Vienna. In the early, intense months of national restructuring following the war, the SDAP's Otto Glöckel, as Undersecretary of the Ministry of Education in the new Republic, was able to achieve much of the core of the school reform movement: anticlericalism (by removing compulsory religious education from state schools), class mobility (by prolonging the period of uniform compulsory education and postponing career tracking examinations), and greater gender equality (by allowing girls to enter previously all-male state high schools and enlarging the realm of study allowed to women at the university). A former public school teacher and one of the few high-ranking SDAP functionaries that could claim a working class background, Glöckel's early successes made him popular throughout Vienna.

Glöckel had been a member of the pre-war Free School Association, a reform movement that aligned itself with the *Kinderfreunde*, a popular parent association and Austrian modification of the *Wandervogel* movement. The *Kinderfreunde* was created and guided by socialists, but not formally a party organization until 1922. This neighborhood-based scouting group dedicated to "furthering the intellectual and physical welfare of children" developed a network of hostels and camps during World War I for its vacation trips, encouraged former members to become teachers and leaders in schools and after-school programs, and replaced religious celebrations with nonsectarian festivals of truth, beauty, and art.[34] Not surprisingly, in 1922 the Roman Catholic Church labeled the group "a revolutionary socialistic-communistic youth organization" that was "not only totally incompatible with Christianity but directed in fact toward dissolution of the whole present social order."[35] The *Kinderfreunde* served as a laboratory for many of the SDAP reforms pursued in the new Republic. The "Guiding Principles" of school reform outlined by Glöckel included a style of classroom interaction that was based on *Kinderfreunde* innovations, centered in self-activity, use of the natural environment in teaching, and integrated instruction. The city's experimental pedagogical institute at Schönbrunn, where Alfred Adler trained a generation of kindergarten and after-school instructors and where sexual education was part of the curriculum, was run by the *Kinderfreunde*.³⁶ Glöckel's alignment with the movement, combined with the animosity it earned from the Roman Catholic Church, made his position in the Ministry of Education untenable to the Christian Social Party. By 1920, when the socialist/Catholic national coalition broke down, Glöckel's reforms were shelved on the national level by the CSP, and he himself was demoted to Administrative President of the Vienna school board. While in Vienna many of Glöckel's reforms held and were in fact enlarged, the rest of the country's schools returned to Christian Social administration, which rejected secular schooling and viewed SDAP school reforms as part of a plan for Jewish domination.³⁷ This capital/countryside split in education statutes was reinforced in 1927, when a second SDAP push for countrywide school reform was withdrawn as part of a general socialist retreat following the Ministry of Justice fire.³⁸

Due to Vienna's 1919 designation as a *Land*, or state, the city was able to incorporate Glöckel's school reforms and fund its cultural experiments with newly won powers of self-taxation. With declining school enrollment and teaching openings reserved for war veterans, however, the young teachers trained by the city's *Kinderfreunde* pedagogical institute at Schönbrunn were unable to find district positions until 1928. In fact, only a fifth of Vienna's public school teachers supported the SDAP, with the remaining faculty evenly split between the Christian Social and Pan-German parties.³⁹ The young people waiting for teaching positions instead found work as *Horterziehlers*, or after-school instructors, in city day care centers focused on luring youth away from street culture. It was here, in the *Horte*, as well as in youth groups like the *Kinderfreunde, Rote Falkonen,* and Socialist Worker Youth, that education reformers were able to implement their ideas about sexual education. While many of the sources I will present in this section call for sexual education in school curriculum, this remained a goal rather than a reality in Red Vienna. However, the *Aufklärung* debates carried out in pedagogical journals, party publications, and parent-teacher nights throughout the period shaped the way that children were raised both in the household and in city- and party-funded care centers.

The major debate within the *Aufklärung* movement was the site of sexual education: public (at school) or private (at home). Many educational professionals, encouraged by the potential for school reform in the new Republic, argued that children should receive *Aufklärung* at school. This argument was sometimes made as a compromise: parents should speak individually with their children and be prepared to answer basic questions, but the science of reproduction and the message of hygiene should be taught in school. Eduard Golias, whose textbook for parents and educators *At the Doors of Life: On Sexual Aufklärung and Morality* was published by the national schoolbook press as part of a series of home-guides to childhood development, maintained that the schoolroom could prepare children for *Aufklärung* at home by introducing the principles of natural science, including, for seventeen- and eighteen-year-olds, a discussion of human procreation, fertility, and birth.[40] *Kinderfreunde* President Otto Felix Kanitz thought that parents should be prepared to answer initial questions about sex, and he recommended the essays from *At the Fountain of Life*: "Although some of the essays are written from a far too bourgeois or strictly religious standpoint, nonetheless the entire book breathes truth, fresh air, and beauty."[41] Dr. Helene Anderle, writing in the Socialist magazine *The Source*, had less faith in the ability of parents to overcome the false belief that their children lived in sexual ignorance, a delusion that left children to seek sexual information from the Bible, the serving girl, or a schoolmate. Nor could sexual education be taught in books, she maintained, but rather "schoolchildren must learn the basic principles of anatomy and hygiene in their flesh and blood."[42] The basic facts about human reproduction, for Anderle, were only one part of "sexual pedagogy," which she explained as the task of teaching young people "to see sexual things with pure eyes and to learn the responsibilities that a human being has vis-à-vis one's own body and vis-à-vis the next generation."[43] Anderle envisioned a blend of hygiene, eugenic thought, and anatomy being taught at the middle-school level, which was perhaps a reasonable goal when her essay was published in 1925, but certainly impossible to make real after the Christian Social victories of 1926.

    A more moderate path was taken by Dr. Josef Friedjung, a rising star of the city social welfare system and author of the most popular Viennese sexual education manual, *Sexual Aufklärung in Education: A Guide for Parents, Teachers, and Doctors*. Friedjung declared that above all mothers bore the "duty" of sexually educating their children, and provided pre-prepared speeches and scenarios taken from the Dürerbund's *At the Fountain of Life*. However, Friedjung also warned that the majority of parents were incapable of properly explaining either the moral or the scientific aspects of sexuality to their children. Friedjung thus devoted most of his manual to the ways in which schools could aid, supplement, and in some cases correct the *Aufklärung* parents (should have) provided at home, whether through a basic grounding in natural science, an encouragement to sport, or an awakening of "a sense of responsibility for one's own health and the health of others."[44] Friedjung was a passionate advocate of the "Parents' Night," the tradition of bringing sexual education presentations to the parents of school children discussed above for the pre-war period. Between 1920 and 1922, he visited fifty schools to speak at such events, calling parents "to their great duty." The goal, he explained to them, was to build children's knowledge of sexual matters up naturally, so that by ages thirteen to fifteen they were familiar with "the meaning of bodily changes in puberty, the serious responsibility of parenthood, the violation of humanity inherent in prostitution, the dangers of sexually transmitted diseases, and the dangers of early pregnancy for girls."[45] Friedjung's politic blend of parental authority and school supplementation in matters of sexual education was very successful. By 1926, these "Parents' Nights" were organized by the Viennese School Board, and Friedjung had ascended to the title of *Stadtschulrat* and received an appointment at the university medical school in pediatrics.[46]

Dr. Friedjung was not the only educator advocating and leading *Aufklärung* evenings for parents. Otto Felix Kanitz of the *Kinderfreunde* movement wrote in 1922: "It is important that we help parents get in touch with their children. In all [scouting] groups we must institute 'Parents' Nights' that deal with the question of sexual *Aufklärung*, in which we seek to show parents their great responsibility and to tell them that they should let their children grow up naturally."[47] For Kanitz it was essential to convince parents that failing to address their children's sexual questions was like "sticking one's head in the sand."[48] Yet even when parents were cognizant of their duty vis-à-vis sexual education, a "Parents' Night" was sometimes necessary to help them get over their fears and nervousness. In a letter to a socialist women's advice column in 1932, "Hermine T." thanked the party for organizing an evening with a Dr. Rudolf Smola, whose words gave her the courage to talk to her young child:

> Unfortunately, I am also one of those mothers who find it so terribly difficult to enlighten her little daughter and tell her where kids come from. However, Dr. Smola spoke so beautifully and it sounded so easy to tell the truth to children, that I spent a few weeks considering it. I explained to the little one that children grow under their mother's heart until they are big enough to eat for themselves, and that it is truly painful for the mother, when the child frees itself from the mother's body …. With big and meaningful eyes Rosi looked at me, pressing ever closer to me, and as I explained all of it she threw herself in my arms, pressed herself against me and said in my ear: "My dear Mummy, now I love you even more than ever." Since then the child has shown tenderness to me that continues to move me. Only now do I see how much beauty is missed by those parents who don't have the courage to educate their young children themselves about the origins of mankind.[49]

"Hermine T." not only thanked the educators who helped her broach the question of reproduction with her child, but she also testified to a very emotional and tender experience that she could recommend to other parents. Although her formulation of "carrying her child under her heart" and emphasis on the pain of childbirth/separation were textbook reiterations of sexual education advice beginning at least with the *Dürerbund*, "Hermine T." used none of the scare tactics of *Aufklärung* in which socialist literature sometimes indulged. In her arguments for sexual education at home, the fear of precocious sex talk on the street or at school was replaced with the privilege of sharing a loving moment with one's child.

The response "Hermine T." received from the magazine's staff, however, did not limit itself to positive parental reinforcements in its call for early sexual education at home. Although "close bonds of love" were promised to parents who talked to their children about sex in the manner prescribed by Dr. Smola, the wages of silence received even greater attention:

Aufklärung by accident, in the street, or from playmates is a crime committed against one's child. What could have been experienced in purity and beauty with one's parents instead happens amidst filth and depravity, and such a first impression almost never entirely disappears from one's life. He who loves his child will consult a teacher or child specialist to learn how to care for the *Aufklärung* of his child.[50]

To this end, Dr. Joseph Friedjung's sexual education manual was recommended to parents, and the (free) consultation services of Dr. Smola were reprinted; Smola's "Educational- and Sexual-Advice Hour from 8:30 to 9:30 P.M. every Thursday offer[ed] every working person time to seek advice."[51] In a follow-up article that appeared five months later, the same advice column listed fifteen centers for "Youth Advice," promising anonymity and strictest discretion. These consultation hours were available in districts throughout the city from authorities as varied as psychologists, nurses, lawyers, venereal-disease specialists, professors, and even one Catholic priest.[52] The earlier reform concern for the ability of parents to scientifically inform their children about sex had, by 1932, been resolved via emotional testimonies, appeals to parental duty, and counseling centers prepared teach parents how to convey sexual knowledge to their children.

The question of coeducational learning was deeply embedded in the debate between public and private *Aufklärung* as formulated in Vienna. In sharp contrast to Catholic pedagogues, sex reformers of the 1920s and 1930s insisted upon the salutary effects of mixed classrooms and scouting groups. Part of the power of this debate derives from general school reform questions of the period. In response to Glöckel's promise of greater educational opportunities for women, several all-girl middle- and high schools in Vienna were created after World War I. However, in districts without girls' schools, and indeed throughout most of the countryside, girls were to join their brothers in coeducational classrooms.[53] In Vienna, only about 10 percent of the *Volksschulen* were coeducational, although almost half of the girls in middle school were attending mixed (previously boys') schools.[54] Even in these coeducational settings, most girls were taught in separate classrooms from boys. This arrangement, touted as temporary but practiced throughout the First Republic, was never sanctioned by the Church in Austria (coeducational secondary education was in fact explicitly banned in the 1929 papal encyclical *De cristiana inventae educatione* and the 1931 special circular *Decretum de 'educatione sexuali' et de 'eugenica'*) and was a campaigning point among Christian Socials.[55]

The new problem of mixed classrooms was re-read as an opportunity by Socialist pedagogues. Essays in *The Socialistic Education*, the national publication of the *Kinderfreunde* organization, repeatedly defended coeducational learning as a natural setting for children. Andreas Schrott opened his 1921 essay "The Question of Sexual Education in Socialist Teaching" with fiery attack on those who would ban the mixed classroom:

In contrast to the most overwhelming and senselessly cultivated hypocrisy of today's "society," socialistic education has always avowed coeducational instruction in the *Kinderfreunde* as a matter of course. Socialistic education wishes to show the defenders of the present rules of society as guilty of hypocrisy, because they have constructed artificial moral laws and have used them, as they deemed necessary, to separate the two sexes and thus breed lies, prudery, coquetry, and worse.[56]

In his defense of coeducation, Schrott sought to appeal to a working class that was wary of socialist innovation in the classroom. To do this, Schrott evoked an image of single-sex education that was harrowing: "Above all, we must redirect the proletarian family away from the path of lazy bourgeois single sex education, against education that teaches boys to enjoy being brutal and spending money, that teaches girls to be man-ware and marriage-ware, to become living advertisements for frippery, fur, and jewelry."[57] Schrott contrasted these outmoded gendered constructions to the healthy, active children who played and learned together in the *Kinderfreunde*. Throughout his essay, Schrott maintained that girls and boys could and did safely play, swim, do gymnastics, and sunbathe, and that the results were children who trusted each other and were prepared to work together. This was possible, Schrott explained, because children were gender-neutral until roughly age fourteen. Likewise, Eduard Golias's 1925 textbook for sexual education and morality insisted that there were no gendered differences in children before puberty, and that "only the dress makes the girl."[58] Coeducational learning was perfectly natural, according to Golias, because "The child sees in children of the opposite sex simply playmates."[59]

Socialist pedagogues made a limited leap from theorizing gender-neutrality in coeducational learning environments to seeing an opportunity to teach children to regard the opposite sex as equal comrades in the fight for social justice. *Kinderfreunde* President Otto Felix Kanitz's definition of sexual education clearly delineated a medical and a moral side to *Aufklärung*, and separated sex from gender via this divide. The actual explanation of human reproduction, like the sex drive itself, Kanitz claimed, was natural, "beyond good and evil," and relatively easy. It was the moral instruction of children that Kanitz described as the worthy task of socialist education, and the "influence of gender upon the entire life of the individual" that required socialist education to discuss sexual topics with children.[60]

Reform sexual education literature, regardless of its political provenance, used the subject of *Aufklärung* to initiate and justify several conflicting arguments about gender, especially the role of women in the new state. The opportunity to redefine what made a boy masculine, and more often, what feminine qualities were most important in girls, was seized upon by socialist educators immediately after coming to power in Vienna. The promise of female emancipation from purely household activities was touted by *The Socialistic Education*, which described socialism's duty:

> [We are] guiding girls to a socialist land of the future, in which not every woman is a slave of the cooking-stove, the house, and children, but rather where the application of technological advances and communal living will free up untold amounts of female power. The girl should take part in the struggle of socialism, because it can free her from the broom, the dishes, the rinse-water, the iron, and the thousand other things, that today in many ways fills up the entire existence of women.[61]

Beyond this (largely mythical) female escape from the daily grind, socialist education also promised to teach boys to honor women as comrades. Open discussion of sexual morality, combined with coeducational learning, would show boys "that it wasn't really right to treat girls like dolls, or to require them to serve, as a matter of course, as homemakers and servants."[62] In the pages of *The Socialistic Education*, emancipation from "bourgeois" gender and sexual constructions was not a moral imperative, but rather a means of allowing women to be more productive members of the state. This socialist formulation—the modification of sex and gender in society as a means of increasing work power—was also central to the sex-clinic movement in Vienna (see chapter 4).

Most sexual reform literature participated in a limited liberation for young women that was based in reproduction and social motherhood. While arguing for greater female educational opportunities, for example, gynecologist and socialist pedagogue Helene Anderle wrote: "It is particularly important to consider *Aufklärung* in the education of girls, who as women and mothers must have, in particular, basic knowledge of sexual matters as they pertain to hygiene as well as pedagogy."[63] In this line of reasoning, girls were to receive sexual education so that they might better reproduce and teach their own children. At no point in socialist sexual education discourse did girls appear as beings requiring sexual education because they were now free of the moral requirements of respectability previously enforced during the late Imperial period. Instead, advocates of reform bemoaned the hypocrisy that marked both men and women's attitudes about sex. In later editions of his *Aufklärung* guide, Friedjung placed greater emphasis on the evils of the sexual double standard, which suggested to him that certain "bourgeois" ideas about sex were more enduring than reformers imagined. While describing the sexual climate of Vienna in 1926, he wrote: "Everywhere one meets the sexual double-standard, doubled in two directions. On the one side, men are allowed all the freedoms that one denies to women; on the other side one publicly acknowledges moral rules, which in private one laughs at and disobeys without shame."[64]

Golias, despite his claim that "the dress makes the girl," wrote essential differences into his pre-prepared speeches for parents explaining sex to their children. In one soliloquy intended for mothers to deliver to their daughters upon first menstruation, Golias identified motherhood as the acme of female life:

> Come here, my big girl! Don't be afraid of what is happening to you. Look! You are no longer a child, but rather you are beginning to develop into a girl, a young woman. You know, of course, that we women are predetermined by Nature to bring children into this world … . Be joyful, that you grow towards a holy duty, to one day become a mother.[65]

Golias justified sexual education for girls by arguing that women's ignorance of sexual hygiene caused suffering and disease, and that their feelings of shame kept them from seeking medical advice. However, Golias relied upon a traditional conception of women's gendered roles in society to make his argument, concluding that "The female must learn not to be ashamed of her femininity, not to be ashamed of her natural and holy longing for Man and Child, but rather it should be that in marriage and motherhood she sees the highest fulfillment of her existence."[66] Even when Golias encouraged girls to demand respect as individuals, he did so by appealing to the honor of their "natural jobs": "Our girl should not put up with men making certain jokes and trashy comments about women in her presence. She should demand from such men the respect that is due to her as a free person, as future mother and teacher of the coming generation."[67] Golias ended his text with a call for a re-gendered nation, where women serve as moral centers:

> Our time needs genuinely masculine men and genuinely feminine women. Above all, our time needs good mothers because, as the saying goes, "give me better mothers and I'll give you a better world!" The goal of all education on sexual morality should be to teach the female to love and honor being a mother, to remove the female from the filth of degenerate erotica and animalistic carnal desire, to lift her to the position of a luminous being and to make her, what she should be: the free companion of a free man![68]

Golias's "moral *Aufklärung*," designed to free women from the sex-saturated world they inhabited in *fin-de-siècle* culture, also reinforced the socialist tradition of justifying sex reform as a means of increasing social productivity. In this formulation, the dyad of nature and nurture was manipulated so that both were necessary to the alleviation of *Sexualnot*. Women were to be taught to value motherhood; this was the educational component of social change. However, Golias's argument suggested that education alone could not undo the damaged caused by a poisoned environment, and thus women were also to be "removed" from the filth of modern life.

One of the more constant refrains of SDAP and city-sponsored opinion on the sexual trends of modern life, including those involving children, was that human sexuality responded to surrounding living conditions. This viewpoint reflected both a Neo-Lamarckian sexological and anthropological discourse that based differences in human sexuality in climate and geography, as well as the SDAP's investment in Adlerian psychology, which located individual sexual problems, like other developmental processes, as social in origin. This line of reasoning lent itself to a critique of modern urban life (particularly the poverty of the metropolis's inhabitants) and a re-emphasis on the hygienic and pedagogical techniques that could insulate children from disease, bad habits, and sexual misery. However, the environmental argument also allowed socialist reformers to make the alleviation of individual sexual distress contingent upon a far-off, cultural and economic restructuring of society, thus subordinating sexuality to political change.

The fact that children were regularly exposed to the sexual realities of life was a common argument for early and frank *Aufklärung*. Friedjung offered a typically lurid description of urban childhood in his manuals:

> Let us look into the poverty-stricken home of the proletariat! In a narrow, unclean apartment the lives of adults in the family and also foreign bed-renters plays out shamelessly in front of the eyes of children of all ages. Filthy discussions, tendernesses, sexual acts, births—all are openly paraded in front of children; children sleep with their parents, one or more siblings, even those of the opposite sex share the same bed, and the prostitution in the neighboring apartments doesn't even faze the young, but rather passes as a profitable business.[69]

While Friedjung used this imagery to justify sexual education, he also emphasized that the urban environment exposed children to venereal disease. In 1918 alone, he informed his readers, almost 1,800 girls aged thirteen to fifteen were treated for sexually transmitted diseases. This infection rate among young women, which Friedjung attributed to industrialization, rapid urban growth, and the practice of general conscription during the Great War, spread throughout the nation and menaced the *Volk*.

City Welfare Clinician Dr. Siegfried Kraus provided an extreme example of environmental arguments. His essay "The Environmental Conditions of Youth Sexuality" revealed the practical limitations of environmental change in the service of sexual *Aufklärung*, and suggested that only radical changes to the socio-economic system in Vienna could alter the sexual landscape of urban life. Kraus established the specificity of sexuality to climate, culture, and socio-economic structure in his text, and then turned his attention to conditions within the metropolis. He claimed that human sexuality was "primarily determined by social living conditions, whose weight in our system of industrialism overpowers the effects of purely natural [developmental] factors."[70] The housing crisis dominated Kraus's examples. For every fifth child in Vienna between the ages of fourteen and eighteen, Kraus explained, life in the metropolis meant having to share a bed and perhaps be exposed to venereal disease. According to his own investigations into the fate of neglected girls, Kraus claimed that over half of those in his study have begun having sexual intercourse before turning fourteen, most of them experiencing this "fate" in their family's apartment.[71] Rather than assume widespread victimization, Kraus's essay asked why children in the metropolis might be initiating sexual contact at a younger age. He postulated that urban people were homesick for nature, and saw sexuality as central to the eternal rhythms of nature. The modern working-class person also lacked means of relaxation, and used a "flight towards sexuality" as an escape from educational limitations and constant physical proximity to others. Early and increased sexuality, according to Kraus, happened when children turned to sex because other means of enjoyment were closed to them. Such children used sex "as a general substitute for joys in nature and culture that [were] unattainable (joy in work, joy in living in free nature or in quiet contemplation in one's own space)."[72] The only way to combat this, Kraus suggested, was for parents to give their full attention and care to youth: for fathers to spend more time in the household, for mothers to stay at home full time, and for families to break out of the industrialist patterns that keep them atomized and away from the home. Kraus's cultural argument thus ended with a prescription for bourgeois family values and the message that youth sexuality could only be changed via wide-scale economic and social restructuring.

If Viennese youth's "flight towards sexuality" was, as Kraus postulated, a substitute for natural and cultural enjoyments, then would not providing young people with the means to enjoy life inure them to the lures of precocious sex? Indeed, the mirror side of Kraus's logic appeared throughout reform and SDAP *Aufklärung* literature in arguments about sexual sublimation. Golias, representing the Austrian Schoolbook press, called for a "hardening, a steeling of the powers of resistance of the body and will through active sports, gymnastics, hiking, and a joyful life in the fresh air," and held up the *Wandervogel* movement as an ideal means of redirecting children's "energy surplus, which is used up in adults through sexual activity."[73] The task of convincing young adults to sublimate their desires was discussed as a separate, much thornier subject. Otto Felix Kanitz, writing for the *Kinderfreund* journal *Socialistic Education*, reported that asking young people to put off having sex took more than just hikes and hygiene discussions. Although he dismissed the message of Catholicism, Kanitz warned his colleagues against underestimating the means with which the Church provided its adherents to conquer their desires and keep them on the path of morality.[74] Kanitz suggested giving people a new ideal to believe in, one that would help them devote themselves to higher standards of morality. Calling this ideal "the socialistic world view," Kanitz entreated party members:

> Let us seek to anchor in the hearts of man the knowledge that their lives have a great, holy design to them, that they should participate in the upward movement of the human race ... we need such truly ideal people—they alone will keep their bodies and their minds pure, including in sexual matters, for the sake of their ideals, for the sake of Socialism.[75]

Like many socialist approaches to sexuality, Kanitz's vision sold sublimation as a moral imperative and a means of advancing the cause of socialism.

In late 1932, the Central Education Department of the SDAP, together with the leadership of the Socialist Worker Youth, organized a series of evening workshops in which teachers and doctors discussed the question of sexual education for children. Together, they created a document to represent the party's beliefs about what sexual education should fulfill in Viennese culture. Therese Schlesinger, the most radical feminist in the SDAP, and abortion-rights advocate Dr. Paul Stein prepared these findings as "Guidelines for the Sexual *Aufklärung* of the Young" and published them in an education reform journal at the end of that year.[76] The report is a rare example of official SDAP opinion on marriage, sexuality, and the rights of the individual to sexual pleasure: issues to which I will return in the following chapter on adult sexual education.

Children's *Aufklärung*, as envisioned by Schlesinger and Stein, had as its cornerstone coeducation and mixed-sex group activities, which allowed children to develop the same interests, work habits, and enjoyments. Coeducation, according to the SDAP, protected children against the "sexual curiosity, fantasy, and foreignness that hinders their development" in sex-segregated classrooms.[77] Yet even children educated to think about each other naturally, as partners, also had to learn to sublimate their desires once adolescence began. Schlesinger and Stein described the replacement of an adolescent's "increasing [sexual] urges" with worthy energies as a "pressing duty": "Cultural improvement is not possible without spiritualizing and sublimating a part of sexual energy. Culture-creating work and the satisfaction of desires must be brought into a healthy relationship with each other."[78] This world-view was clearly based on a Freudian interpretation of culture as created by sublimated sexual energy. However, the "Guidelines" justify this argument not through reference to the cultural improvements of Red Vienna, but rather with the suggestion that sublimation improved the erotic life of those who practiced it. Giving passion free rein decreased sexual pleasure, in their findings: "Unbridled satisfaction of sexual urges nips every higher development and deepening of the erotic in the bud, and this is even truer, the more sex is liberated from reproduction."[79] The message to youth from the SDAP was one of sexual rights tempered by social and spiritual responsibilities; one had a right to sexual satisfaction, but partnership was one's hope and duty. Schlesinger and Stein appealed to sentiment and responsibility simultaneously: "It is important to concede to youth their right to sexual satisfaction, but [we must] also present the achievement of lasting love from a single sexual partner, who with their love also offers their soul, as the highest joy and also as an earnest duty."[80] These late-Republic guidelines to sexual education, as imagined by the far Left within the SDAP, reflected many of the concerns and constructions that the Roman Catholic Church forwarded throughout the first Republic. Their emphasis on spiritual love and sublimation of sexual urges would be at home in many of the Catholic forays into the sex education discourse.

Catholic Responses

On an official level, many pastoral letters and a papal encyclical from Pius XI rejected any sex education that discussed biological aspects of reproduction. These messages warned that any sexual knowledge would endanger the purity of individual children. However, we can uncover a more interesting and nuanced view of the Church by attending to the plurality of Catholic opinion in this period. Historians' assumptions of a monolithic Church response to the popularization of sexual knowledge in interwar Europe is challenged by the Austrian case, which reveals a degree of convergence between Catholic and Social Democratic approaches to children's sex education.

During the interwar period, Catholic responses to coeducation and sexual *Aufklärung* for children ranged from papal directives, to shrill attacks against reforming teachers and youth counselors, and even to surprisingly frank literature designed to prepare parents for guiding their children through puberty. The prewar Catholic *Aufklärung* literature intended for young boys was replaced by skits, dialogues, and speeches tailored to both sexes and increasingly written for parents. None of the interwar texts I highlight were intended to be studied by young people themselves. It is also important to note from the outset that these voices may not have harmonized with all local, parish-directed messages about children's education. However, the authors identified are priests, theological professors, and other authoritative voices. Furthermore, in keeping with the 1917 Code of Canon Law, a diocesan censor approved each text before it was published.

Like socialist sexual education materials, the Catholic discourse emphasized sublimation via physical exertion with emphasis on outdoor exercise and gymnastics. However, Catholic responses to the interwar *Aufklärung* movement raised several new arguments, all of which supported the central tenet of sex's sanctification only within an indissoluble marriage. The challenge of socialist sexual education during the First Republic prompted the Roman Catholic Church to re-embroider upon familiar themes of purity, heavenly love, and the sanctity of marriage. To this end, Catholic educators and *Seelsorger* (literally, care-givers of the soul) maintained that sex was not a biological necessity, that Catholic teachings of chastity were not at odds with nature, and that an individual's sex-life was not the most important aspect of his or her personality. Catholic sexual education literature affirmed the right of parents to participate in the private *Aufklärung* of their children, and emphasized the role of the Church in the construction of both healthy individuals and healthy marriages.

In response to the interwar pedagogical debate regarding the site of sexual education (home, school, or youth group), Catholic authors argued overwhelmingly for the right of parents to tell their children about sex. Should parents be incapable of educating their children—a situation that Catholic authors described as much rarer than reformist literature suggested—a priest or *Seelsorger* was the only other appropriate provider of sexual knowledge. This was the opening salvo of Cardinal Adolf Bertram's 1929 pamphlet *Reverentia Puero! Catholic Reflections on the Problem of Sexual Pedagogy*. Bertram, Prince-Bishop of Breslau, warned against public-school teachers who "knew no concrete, unchangeable moral norms," and were unfamiliar with the Christian codes of sexual conduct. He asserted that "no teacher and no government [had] the right to undermine the commandments of God."[81] He directly countered the argument used by the supporters of sexual education in schools that parents were unable to properly explain sexual matters at home. To do this, Bertram shifted the emphasis of *Aufklärung* away from reproductive science and towards the realm of feeling, insisting that all parents had to do was simply engender the proper kind of self-respect and a healthy sense of modesty (*Schamgefühl*, or sense of shame) in their children.[82] Likewise, Dr. Rudolf Allers, philosophy lecturer at the University of Vienna, insisted to readers of his 1934 text *Sexual Pedagogy: Foundations and Fundamentals* that only religious answers provided at home (and preferably reinforced at a religious school) could counter the rebellious questions at the heart of any sexual education: "Why should I do what I don't want to do, and why shouldn't I follow my urges?"[83] Allers was a member of the last cohort of psychiatrists trained by Sigmund Freud and by 1934 had worked with Alfred Adler for over a decade; he criticized both mentors for their secular approaches to the human psyche. Allers's larger body of scholarship attempted to synthesize psychoanalytic insight with Catholic teachings. *Sexual Pedagogy* is no exception, and was approved for publication by the Bishop of Salzburg.

Parents were encouraged to trust themselves in their attempts to explain sexual matters to young people. Catholic sex education guides reassured them that neither special anatomical terminology nor teaching techniques were necessary. As the Jesuit theologian Michael Gatterer explained in his 1927 book, *In Faith's Light: Christian Reflections on Sexual Life*: "Even when they have never read a 'teaching guide' and perhaps have never heard the word 'pedagogy,'" parents could deliver a "first-rate education" to their children.[84] *In Faith's Light* was pointedly addressed to adult Christians who sought a faith-based understanding of sexual matters, yet it included empowering messages about parental abilities in the realm of children's sex education.

As in reform sexual education literature, particular emphasis was placed on the mother's role in *Aufklärung*. Father Peter Schmitz, Salzburg priest and member of the Society of the Divine Word, claimed that mothers were usually the first to hear the question, "Where do I come from?" in his 1932 book *At the Pure Source of Life: A Guide Through Children's Sexual Education for the Christian Mother*. He reminded mothers that their response to this question set a child down a permanent sexual path, "determining to a large extent its entire future and enjoyment of life."[85] Like Cardinal Bertram, he explained that *Aufklärung* was not a response to a natural or biological set of questions, but rather was meant to teach young adults their responsibilities as people with sexual urges. Sexual education, in Schmitz's estimation, was the "high duty" of mothers, and as such was completely out of place in a public school setting:

> A few years ago, it was said that children should be taught about sexual matters in school. The results of this method showed its mistakes immediately. The degeneration among the youth increased to such an extent that today this idea, with the exception of certain socialist circles, has been almost entirely discarded. Syphilitic infections among school-age children, which were not only the result of hereditary transmission, served as a particularly crass example of the bankruptcy of these ideas.[86]

In this formulation, sexual education at school, far from preventing disease and personal misery, actually encouraged the spread of venereal disease. Living with the sexual urges that come with puberty required a moral attitude that obviously has not been inculcated by public school *Aufklärung* as Schmitz describes it. He portrayed sexual education in the home, overseen by the child's mother, as an investment that would yield a healthy, happy adulthood.

Daunted perhaps by the wealth of Papal encyclicals issued on sex and the family during the first Republic, some Christian parents were concerned about the very appropriateness of anyone speaking to children about sex, including themselves. In a 1933 pamphlet entitled *How to Teach Your Child*, signed *Von einem Jugendfreund* ("From a Friend of the Youth"), the Salzburg diocese reassured parents that their participation in sexual education was beyond clerical reproach. Parents were encouraged to speak to their children about bodies and reproductive parts in a non-censorial manner. Repeating the familiar refrain that all parts of the body were created by God, the *Jugendfreund* reasoned that it could not be a sin to use any particular part of the body, so long as we use it according to God's will. He concluded: "It is therefore also not a sin to speak to children or young people about these things, not to guide them towards [sexuality], but rather to illuminate the meaning of sexual life and to warn them away from sin."[87] Emphasizing the sacrament of marriage achieved all of these objectives.

Cardinal Bertram defined the goal of Catholic sexual education as preparation for marriage. *Aufklärung* should, in his words, "prepare the path for the fulfillment of this goal [holy matrimony] and, in the middle of all their confusion and weaknesses, guide those without courage towards the sources of strength in our religion."[88] Bertram's emphasis on the necessity of holy matrimony as the framework for sex was repeated throughout Catholic sexual education literature. Catholic authors used the same language of duty and responsibility to describe marriage to children favored by reformist and even socialist educators. In *How to Teach Your Child*, the young person "properly enlightened in sexual life" was described in the following manner:

[H]e will regard marriage and married life from an ideal standpoint and guard himself from misusing this directive from God. He will know that man, in participating in sexual matters, is allowed to take part in God's ability to create .... Thus he will understand sexual activity as an undertaking willed by God and therefore pleasing to God, *so long as this activity takes place within a marriage made legal by God.*[89]

The anonymous author of this text offered several pre-prepared speeches, designed for mothers to deliver to their children according to age and gender, which further described marriage as a set of rights and responsibilities. For the young man finished with school and preparing to enter a larger world, mothers were encouraged to elaborate on the sanctification of marriage by Jesus Christ. The sacrament of marriage, she should explain, was part of a process in which men and women earned the right to participate in creation: "Through this consecration as parents, they earn the right to cooperate with the good Lord in the creation of a child."[90] The author explained that men and women possessed different body parts, and then continued with his description of mortal and divine cooperation in the marriage bed: "In dedicating themselves as fathers and mothers, the marriage partners earn from the good Lord the right to unite themselves in the most intimate love, including by means of their sexual organs. Such relations through sexual organs are called 'sexual relations.'"[91] Only through dedication of oneself as a parent to God (and not to the state or to medical authorities, as will be explored in chapter 4) did the individual earn the right to engage in sex. As Schmitz explained in *At the Pure Source of Life*, this emphasis on the rights and duties of marriage partners was all that separated a successful Christian *Aufklärung* from one that encouraged willful (sexual) behavior. Harnessing sexuality with reproduction in marriage was the key to a successful sexual education according to Schmitz: "thus it is so terribly important to present sexual matters, and above all the sexual drives that come with adult life, as a *purposeful gift from God,* that also comes with *a heavy duty* for mankind."[92] The "heavy duty" alluded to by Schmitz was certainly the burden of child-bearing and, by extension, the responsibility of childrearing. Sexual activity was therefore only justified through reproduction within a Christian family. Yet these restrictions came with a second message of divine generosity, as well. Each of these pedagogical examples taught children that sex within marriage was a source of strength and joy created for humans by God. The "heavy duty" that comes with sexual drives is not merely onerous, but also a privileged opportunity to co-create, with the divine, human life. Interwar Catholic sexual pedagogy thus suggested that sexual urges were intentional, healthy forces within individuals, even as it restricted the expression of these desires to marriage.

All Catholic sex education literature in interwar Austria asked young people to abstain from sexual activity before entering into marriage. As we have seen, this demand stood above any state or social law as a mandate from God; any resulting self-discipline in the abstaining child (such as work ethic, or an ability to sublimate immediate desire for long-term goals) was of tertiary benefit. However, religious pedagogues were sensitive to charges from sexologists and sex reformers that even temporary chastity before marriage was an unnatural and unhealthy demand to make of the individual.[93] Several authors took pains to prove that Catholic teachings of sexual abstinence outside of marriage (and continence within marriage, as discussed in chapter 3) were in fact compatible with the health of the individual. To do this, Catholic authors reframed a popular conception of health and nature and defended Church doctrine against misreading by both reformist opponents and the ill-informed faithful. Two main issues were contested: the idea that sex was a biological necessity and its corollary, the argument that chastity was unhealthy.

Dr. Rudolf Allers reminded his *Sexual Pedagogy* audience that sexual matters belonged in a general framework of the body and mind and therefore should not be singled out for special meaning. Allers defended Catholicism from the popular sex reform criticism that the Church had, through the doctrine of original sin, poisoned man's ability to enjoy and fulfill naturally-occurring sexual feelings. In response, Allers pointed to the example of the Church fathers, who had never separated sexuality from the flesh of man (thus keeping it "natural"), and, contrary to what sex reformers might claim had never referred to sexual matters as inherently "dammed" or "sinful." He repeated and clarified the words of Saint Paul, who "never said that the flesh was in itself sinful, but rather that it was weak."[94] Speaking for Catholic educators, Allers stated: "We want to insist most forcefully that the demands of Catholic morality not only in no way are contrary to nature … but rather that the fulfillment of these challenges is a condition of the perfection of this very nature."[95]

Father Peter Schmitz, responding to sex reformers as a spiritual advisor and educator, took issue with the image of Christianity forwarded in their literature. He directly quoted progressive *Aufklärung* literature in order to characterize sex reformers as a group, "that cannot seem to do enough in the last decade to swamp Christendom with the strongest and ugliest accusations, because 'it has fused the concepts of guilt and sexuality in our Western traditions,' and therefore should be held responsible for modern immorality."[96] Such an opinion could not be further from the Church's teachings, insisted Schmitz, who repeated throughout his work that sexual urges were natural, that they come from God, and that there was nothing debasing or sinful in them. "We seek not to be free of these feelings," Schmitz assured his readers, "but rather to have the will to control them."[97] This control, the ability to abstain from sex when mandated by God, in no way endangered the health of the individual. Directly contradicting a favored reformist analogy, Schmitz asserted: "the satisfaction of sexual urges is not a biological necessity, as is the staying of hunger or thirst. Therefore, one may not place sexual desires on the same level as hunger or thirst."[98] Even more boldly, Schmitz attacked the reformers and medical authorities that have forwarded such notions:

> The youth of today have been persuaded of the biological necessity of sex via the argument that this satisfaction [of sexual drives] is a *human right*, an argument often made with the banal phrase: "one simply cannot deny such things." To this end, irresponsible elements [of society] still claim that sexual abstinence is dangerous to one's health, although the opposite has been established by the most famous medical authorities. A pure, chaste lifestyle, particularly while one is young, has never harmed anyone who was already healthy.[99]

Here, Schmitz's rejoinder to the "irresponsible" literature that saw sexual satisfaction as a human right was based (in this instance) not on the will of God but in the health of the individual. Thus even as Schmitz contradicted the message of "irresponsibility" within reform-based *Aufklärung* he employed its most popular means of establishing morality: the preservation of health.

As an additional incentive to practice sexual abstinence, Catholic *Aufklärung* advertised the special kind of willpower developed by children who had received proper sexual education. Learning to control sexual drives, according to Catholic authors, involved both avoiding temptation and sublimating urges. The education of the will in the service of sexual *Aufklärung*, according to Schmitz, empowered the young individual "to let dirty books fall from his hands, to break with depraved schoolmates, to walk right by theaters and movie houses of ill-repute, to shun pleasures that might cause degeneration, to avoid alcohol, etc. This [discipline] alone can protect him from sexual mistakes."[100] Even a well-disciplined young Catholic, however, had to learn to deal with sexual energies already in his body. In a turn of phrase that could easily be at home in reforming or socialist *Aufklärung* literature, Cardinal Bertram suggested substituting sport, gymnastics, and "hiking through God's green earth" as an aide against the disquieting awakening of sexual urges.[101] He devoted several pages of *Reverentia Pureo!* to the thesis that what children entering puberty really needed in school, rather than sexual education, were more religious exercises to strengthen their wills and bring them joy in a time of emotional confusion.[102] The emotional confusion during adolescence, Catholic educators insisted, was only exacerbated by the false notion that sexuality played the central role in adult character formation.

We have already seen that some Catholic educators blamed the modern practice of separating sexuality out of everyday life for placing undue emphasis on sex's role in the psyche. Allers, in particular, argued that the sudden "sexual crisis," or "sexual question," that had sparked international conferences and inspired countless articles and books was a hoax that led pedagogues and social scientists into a mistaken idea of human development.[103] Because sexuality has been posed as a special and separate condition within man, Allers explained, modern thinkers have wrongly treated it as something relatively independent within human personality.[104] Allers' position allowed individuals to be fully developed people without being sexually active. This was of course important to Catholic educators who were concerned with defending the life-long chastity of nuns, monks, and priests. Peter Schmitz de-emphasized the importance of sex in shaping the individual in plain language: "Displaying one's sexual abilities *is not the be-all and end-all of human life.*"[105] Schmitz admitted to his audience of young Catholics that a healthy sex-life within marriage was one of the most important sources of joy for mankind, but he carefully limited the value of sex in self-development and self-understanding. Insisting on individual completeness, with or without a sexual component in one's life, Schmitz wrote:

> It is an overstatement, a conscious glorification of urges, to place sexual life as the most important aspect of human life. It is totally misleading, and furthermore contradicted a thousand times in history and in daily experience, to suggest that an active sexual life is necessary for the shaping of human personality. Man is a complete person, even when he renounces marriage and sexual love.[106]

Understandably, Schmitz's "complete person" was only complete within the framework of faith. His message is very similar to the wartime Catholic *Aufklärung* text *Become a Complete Man!*. However, Catholic sexual educators writing in the interwar period increasingly responded to the Freudian theories of psychological development that had been popularized by Alfred Adler and the socialist pedagogy he helped to create in Vienna. These new developmental theories prioritized sexual feeling and expression measures of children's progression to maturity. As the above quotation shows, Schmitz met this new challenge by removing sexual activity from the stages of personal development and instead placing sex within concepts of responsibility, reproduction, and spiritual community. Man and wife, in Schmitz's work, were called by God not only to people the earth with their offspring, but also to send new souls to heaven.[107] Sexual joy in marriage was subordinate to this "highest goal" of sex, therefore, "the sexual drive has an extra-individual meaning."[108] Schmitz illustrated the "extra-individual" in sex most dramatically by arguing that, on a mystical level, even our bodies were not individual, but rather extensions of Christ himself. The faithful, he warned, are in some ways never alone with themselves: "In Christians, sexual energies are absorbed into the mystical body of the Lord. Our bodily members no longer belong to ourselves, but rather belong to Christ. Their abuse is therefore desecration of a part of Christ's body."[109]

Although Schmitz believed that the individual was complete even without a sexual component to his life, gender did not appear as optional in Catholic teachings. Schmitz, in opening his popular *Lad and Lassie in God's Hands: A Ministerial and Pedagogical Contribution to the Sex Problem*, invested holy authority in sexual difference, stating: "the polarity between the sexes comes from God."[110] Throughout Catholic literature, gender was reified as an aspect of God's plan, a natural, complementary system that invited man and wife to live together in harmony and, in particular, beaconed women to become mothers. The Innsbruck Jesuit,

Albert Schmitt, provided a common construction: "The two separate genders act as coworkers and representatives of God in this worldly life, just as the priest is the co-worker and representative of God in the supernatural life."[111] Because the sexes must work together as parents and stewards of the earth, women deserved respectful treatment. Again, Schmitt explained: "Woman is so elevated [by this worldview] that Man does not simply see her as a doll with which to satisfy his passions, but rather as an equal partner and the mother of his children."[112]

The crown of motherhood here is the ultimate expression of women's worth, both to her husband and to the world. This is certainly the prevailing message of Catholic sex education materials. Thus, the work of Peter Schmitz, the Salzburg missionary, is especially interesting because he, unlike other Catholic pedagogues, separated girls' supposed natural role as mothers from the changing gendered realities they faced in interwar Austria. While the majority of Catholic *Aufklärung* literature concerned itself with the construction of masculinity via willpower and chastity, Schmitz paused to consider modern forms of femininity.

As did most Catholic sex educators, Schmitz wrote in a voice that is male-inclusive, with frequent breaks that addressed the special needs of girls. *Lad and Lassie* was unusual, however, in that it advocated (sexual) education for girls that could be adjusted to fit a future life without marriage and children. Indeed, in his sex education guide for mothers, Schmitz begged his audience not to send their "daughters out to work in the office or at the serving table" without explaining to them the facts of life.[113] Against all other Catholic voices, and quite a few in the reform literature, Schmitz refuted the idea that (physical) motherhood was girls' eventual vocation and imagined an education that would prepare them for either marriage or a profession:

> The ideal education for girls does not one-sidedly place the main emphasis on preparation for marriage, for the family is not *the* calling, [and] sexual love is not *the* love for women. Rather the goal should be, most importantly, a general development and strengthening of personality for a self-supporting carrier that reflects the soulful nature, the spirit of motherliness, and the feminine ability to love. Our girls must be brought up in a way that they may take not only the path of marriage, but also the path of celibacy. In the latter case a freely chosen profession should replenish their strength and bring them inner satisfaction.[114]

This language was very much in keeping with Catholic justifications of celibacy for nuns or priests who nurtured a wider, spiritual family and thus fulfilled their duties to God and society. However, in unseating the family and reproduction as the highest goals for women, Schmitz's argument reshaped the gendered nature of interwar *Aufklärung*. This may reflect the increasingly impoverished and unemployed status of men and family providers in the late interwar period and/or a delayed acceptance of the kinds of social-motherhood activities and occupations German-speaking feminists and Catholic women's auxiliaries had been demanding since the *fin-de-siècle*. The education Schmitz advocated for girls does not have as its end point fulfillment in holy matrimony as Cardinal Bertram imagined it in *Reverentia Puero!*. Furthermore, although Schmitz's *Lad and Lassie in God's Hands* imagined a future for women outside of marriage, his guide for mothers, *At the Pure Source*, fell back on more traditional roles. For girls experiencing their first period, he claimed the simple comment, "this is a sign that perhaps, in ten years, the good Lord will also make you a mother," often "works wonderfully to soothe them."[115] This message, intended to comfort, surely reinforced girls' belief that their highest calling was motherhood. Yet Schmitz's ability to imagine an education that allowed for different female fates is evidence that Catholic *Aufklärung* authors did not merely repeat Church laws to their audiences, but rather developed their arguments from within the shifting discourse of health, gender, and nation in the interwar period.

Conclusions

In *Red Vienna: Experiment in Working-Class Culture*, historian Helmut Gruber's seminal work on interwar Viennese culture, socialist-controlled Vienna is depicted as an endless (and in many ways fruitless) intrusion into the private sphere.[116] Although city hall had little official opinion about children's sexual education, the *Aufklärung* discourse of the period is an excellent example of the pressure put on private citizens to act in a way that would benefit the public good, whether that vision were determined by religious or political authorities. However, like the SDAP programs that funded healthcare, public housing, and educational reforms, changes in the ways parents were encouraged to talk to their children about sex had real and one might assert positive effects upon the (future) citizens of Vienna. The failure of children's sexual education advocates to create a utopian society of coeducational comrades, or, conversely, to lock into place a Catholic construction of sexual love within marriage, is not an accurate measure of their achievements. Unlike Gruber, my work seeks not to gauge the feasibility or application of sex education, but rather to highlight the common cultural constructions that were used and modified in *Aufklärung* discourse. The question of the "naturalness" of sex, the renewed importance of motherhood during the *fin-de-siècle* and in the wake of World War I, and the overwhelming emphasis placed on purity and responsibility in interwar *Aufklärung* practices made children's sexual education central to the project of reforming sex in Vienna.

It is perhaps ironic that in a book devoted to the cultural production of sexual knowledge there should be so many historical voices arguing for the "naturalness" of sex. What did they mean by this? For SDAP children's sexual education advocates, the naturalness of sexual urges served first and foremost as a contrast to the artificial desires and sexual double standards of the *fin-de-siècle* period. The images of brutal boys and frippery-addicted girls evoked by Andreas Schrott address the effects of this period upon children; by extension, the adult version of this artificiality would highlight an unbridgeable chasm between the interests of men and women, a fetishistic displacement of desire (or worse, homosexual desire), and the emptiness of married life. Indeed, these were precisely the topics popular in pre-war sexological studies and sex reform associations. Emphasizing "natural," heterosexual relations, almost always within the bonds of exclusive partnership, as the principle source of sexual pleasure was in many ways a willful rebuke on the part of the SDAP of Vienna's *fin-de-siècle* legacy of state-regulated prostitution, widely-publicized homosexual scandals, and free-love. The "naturalness" of sex emphasized by reforming educators also denoted the ascendancy of science in the nineteenth century, and their belief that the facts of sexual reproduction could stand outside of morality. The natural world of blooming trees and ripening fruit, far from being a set of euphemisms for sexual activity to be employed by timid parents, was in fact the framework that justified sexual education. Finally, both socialist and Catholic *Aufklärung* advocates used the "naturalness" of sex as a means of reassuring adolescents about distressing bodily and emotional developments. Rather than allow boys to be swayed by their peers, or girls to suffer in ignorance, sexual education literature suggested that puberty could be a transformation guided by scientific knowledge and moral precepts. To this, Catholic authors added the interpretation of sexual urges as "natural" evidence of God's design, comforting pubescent readers with the promise that these new sensations, like the developing bodies that produced them, were in no way sinful.

Nothing appeared more natural in *Aufklärung* literature across the political spectrum than motherhood. Mothers were called upon by all sides to serve as the "natural resources" for their children's first sexual questions, and then exhorted, for the sake of their children's trust in them, to supply simple and natural explanations. In countless pre-prepared speeches, dialogues, and activities, mothers were taught to repeat the phrase, "I loved you so much that I carried you under my heart for nine months" as the first step in explaining a child's provenance. In Catholic texts, and not a few reform-based documents, the unborn child was a gift sent from God, leaving the father's role in conception to be explained at a later date. In socialist literature that built upon the natural world, the mother acted as the warm earth to the child's tiny seed, breathing, feeding, and protecting the child (never fetus) until it was ready to survive on his own. *Aufklärung* thus became not a disclosure of sexual powers but rather a revelation of maternal devotion in an otherwise difficult world. The setting for this monumental celebration of motherhood was a society devastated by war in which families were encouraged by Austromarxist theorists (and, as the previous chapter has shown, the Viennese municipal government) to limit their offspring in an attempt to improve the quality, rather than the quantity, of Viennese *Menschenökonomie*.[117] Simultaneously, across the city, women appealed to the state to help them feed and shelter their young and demanded the right to mitigate the dangers of reproduction through birth control and abortion. Both Catholic and socialist texts, responding to widespread outbreaks of venereal disease and the perceived loosening of sexual morals following the war, instructed mothers to prepare their daughters for reproduction by emphasizing health and purity. Even the most progressive texts portrayed motherhood as the "natural" occupation of women, and encouraged both boys and girls to honor it as a sacred oasis in the profane metropolis.

The language of responsibility that marked *Aufklärung* literature adapted to both religious and political needs. It was foremost directed at parents, who were reminded from all sides that their duty to their children included sexual education. In turn, parents were taught to impart a sense of sexual and gendered responsibilities to their children: to honor mothers, value women as comrades, or resist the temptations of premarital intercourse. Socialist sex education taught that pleasure and self-fulfillment were to be found in cooperation and civic duty rather than sexual affairs. Catholic children were additionally responsible to God and the Church, authorities demanding sexual abstinence outside of marriage. Both Catholic and socialist pedagogues agreed that sexual desire in young people should ultimately be sublimated through physical exertion with emphasis on outdoor exercise and gymnastics. Children's sexual purity, newly defined by Catholic educators as an exercise of the will rather than a state of ignorance, served as proof of their trustworthiness.

Advocates of sexual reform, expressing the eugenic concerns of the early twentieth century, placed similar stress on sexual purity before marriage. Both sides emphasized the importance of sex within the framework of marriage, linking it irrevocably to reproduction and family life. Harnessing sexuality with reproduction in marriage was the key to successful sex education: on this point both Catholics and socialists agreed. Father Schmitz asked Christian mothers to describe sex to their children as a gift that came "with a *heavy duty* for mankind."[118] The "heavy duty" of reproduction, and the importance if securing (healthy) future progeny when choosing one's marriage partner, was also a prominent aspect of socialist sex education for all ages. Socialist pedagogues weighted personal sexual responsibility with that of an even greater duty to one's offspring and the "coming generation." Healthy families were described by Austrian socialist literature as the building blocks of society; they alone could provide the base from which to rebuild war-torn Central European society. Catholic messages about the family were strikingly similar. The Innsbruck theologian, Albert Schmitt, explained in his book *The Catholic Marriage and the Christian Family*: "All virtues are rooted in the family, particularly social virtues and the sense of duty. Thus must children be taught from an early age to work with others and for others."[119] Be this message Jesuit or socialist in origin, interwar Austrian parents were advised to teach their children about sexual matters within the framework of productive family service.

Finally, both Catholic and socialist sex education called for a re-assessment of the role of sex in the individual's life, and thus provided an alternative model of self-formation from that suggested by the interwar world of cinema, radio, and sensationalist print media. Yet importantly, neither Catholic nor socialist sex education in interwar Austria tried to deny that this world of popular culture, replete with sexualized messages, existed. The result was that both kinds of literature rejected the older model of children's purity that demanded sexual ignorance. Instead, both approaches to sex education redefined purity as an informed choice. Father Peter Schmitz, as we have seen, claimed that sexual education, with its attendant emphasis on willpower, would help young boys and girls "walk right by" the temptations of the street and theater, armed as they were with knowledge. In both Catholic and socialist interwar formations for young people sex was thus a powerful force within individuals and society that demanded sober yet compassionate explanation. Furthermore, sex was never separated from the dangerous work of reproduction: mothers suffered patiently, families faced more mouths to feed, and syphilitic prostitutes brought sick babes into the world. Children's purity was described not only as a means of protecting their development, but also as a social investment in a better future. Sexual education as prophylaxis, whether against sin or disease, dominated the Viennese interwar period.

Notes

1. Following its usage in nineteenth- and twentieth-century German-speaking pedagogical literature, I use the term *Aufklärung* throughout this book to refer to sexual education.
2. Monism was a popular scientific and mildly religious movement sparked by Ernst Haeckel and Wilhelm Bölsche's popularizations of Darwinian theory. Monism's widespread appeal to German-speaking audiences is demonstrated in Alfred H. Kelly's "Darwinism and the Working-Class in Wilhelmian Germany," in Seymour Drescher, David Sabean, and Allan Sharlin (eds.), *Political Symbolism in Modern Europe* (New Brunswick: Transaction Books, 1982), 146–167.
3. Lutz D.H. Sauerteig, "Sex Education in Germany from the 18th to the 20th Century," in Franz Eder, Lesley Hall and Gert Hekma (eds.), *Sexual Cultures in Europe: Themes in Sexuality* (Manchester: Manchester University Press, 1999), 18.
4. Iwan Bloch, *The Sexual Life of Our Time*, translated by M. Paul Eden from the sixth German edition (London: Rebman Limited, 1909), 4.
5. Dürerbund, *Am Lebensquell: Ein Hausbuch zur Geschlechtlichen Erziehung. Betrachtungen, Ratschläge und Beispiele als Ergebnisse des Dürerbund* (Dresden: Alexander Köhler Verlag, 1909), vii. After a first printing run of 10,000, the book was brought out again, in equal numbers, in 1917.
6. Dürerbund, *Am Lebensquell*, ix.
7. Dürerbund, *Am Lebensquell*, iv.
8. Dürerbund, *Am Lebensquell*, 358.
9. Dürerbund, *Am Lebensquell*, 86, 260, 61, and 78, respectively.
10. Dürerbund, *Am Lebensquell*, 117.
11. Dürerbund, *Am Lebensquell*, 146.
12. Dürerbund, *Am Lebensquell*, 63.
13. Dürerbund, *Am Lebensquell*, 118. The unmitigated joy at finding oneself pregnant is notably lacking in post-World War I literature on reproduction written for women. See next chapter.
14. Dürerbund, *Am Lebensquell*, 257.
15. Dürerbund, *Am Lebensquell*, 258.

16. Lothar Skalla, *Über Gesundheitspflege der Schüler im Elternhause und Über sexuelle Aufklärung* (Wien: Verlag von Carl Gerold's Sohn, 1912), 22.
17. Skalla, *Über Gesundheitspflege*, 24.
18. Skalla, *Über Gesundheitspflege*, 28.
19. Skalla, *Über Gesundheitspflege*, 30.
20. Hans Wegner, *Wir Jungen Männer: Das Problem des gebildeten jungen Mannes vor der Ehe* (Leipzig: Karl Robert Langwieche Verlag, 1917). In the otherwise exhaustively complete "*literatur*" section that follows the entry for sexual education in Max Marcuse's 1923 *Encyclopedia of Sexual Science*, Wegner's book alone is listed as enjoying "countless editions." See H. E. Timmering, "Erziehung (sexuelle)," in Max Marcuse (hg.), *Hardwörterbuch der Sexualwissenschaft: Enzyklopädie der natur- und kulturwissenschaftlichen Sexualkund des Menschen* (Bonn: A. Marcus & E. Webers Verlag, 1923), 108–111.
21. Wegner, *Jungen Männer*, 9.
22. Wegner, *Jungen Männer*, 14.
23. Wegner, *Jungen Männer*, 31.
24. Yvonne Ivory has argued that one of the clearest late-nineteenth-century markers of male homosexuality, as discussed in sexology texts, was a lack of cohesion between the body (which was male) and the spirit or mind (which was read as feminine, due to intellectual interests, emotionalism, and/or the choice of male sexual partners). I think the emphasis in the sexual education debates placed upon understanding and accepting the changing desires and feelings of puberty was, in an indirect way, an attempt to keep boys' concept of themselves unified: and by extension, an attempt to keep boys straight. From Ivory, "The Urning and His Own: Self-Fashioning and the Fin-de-Siècle Invert," presented at the UCLA Department of Germanic Studies Conference "Sexual States," 22 February 2002.
25. Dr. Jakob Hoffmann, *Werde ein ganzer Mann! Aufklärung und Belehrungen für die heranwachsende männliche Jugend* (Freiburg im Breisgau: Herdersche Verlagshandlung, 1917), 39, 101. On the list of *Schundliteratur* were Schopenhauer, Nietzsche, Darwin, Tolstoy, Ibsen, Zola, and Haeckel.
26. Hoffmann, *Werde ein ganzer Mann!*, 159.
27. *Young Törless* is in fact an interesting counterpoint to the concerns of Hoffmann and other sexual educators who emphasize the emotional turmoil of their audiences. Like Rilke's short story "The Gym Lesson," *Törless* exposes a world within military boarding school that seamlessly accommodates sexual experimentation, abuse, and torture while providing no guidance for the awakening realm of emotion within the male pupils. See Robert Musil, *Die Verwirrungen des Zöglings Törless* (Reinbeck bei Hamburg: Rowohlt Verlag, 1983), 31–34, 126–127.
28. Hoffmann, *Werde ein ganzer Mann!*, 128. Emphasis in the original.
29. Hoffmann, *Werde ein ganzer Mann!*, 115.
30. Hoffmann, *Werde ein ganzer Mann!*, 116. These sentiments are in many ways a repetition of those in "Parting Thoughts from a Father to His Son," albeit rephrased in more overtly religious language.
31. Hoffmann, *Werde ein ganzer Mann!*, 120.
32. Lou Andreas-Salomé, *Drei Briefe an einen Knaben* (Leipzig: Kurt Wolff Verlag, 1917), 31. The romantic language Andreas-Salomé uses to describe sexual functions suggests she was at least familiar with the Monist literature of Haeckel and Bölsche.
33. Andreas-Salomé, *Drei Briefe*, 76–77.
34. Charles Gulick, *Austria from Habsburg to Hitler Volume I: Labor's Workshop of Democracy* (Berkeley: University of California Press, 1948), 585.
35. As quoted in Gulick, *Austria from Habsburg to Hitler*, 599.
36. Josef K. Friedjung speaks of the necessity of keeping sexual education in the curriculum in "Zur Frage der geschlechtlichen Erziehung," in *Die Sozialistische Erziehung* 2/2, (Jänner 1922), 7.

37. Gulick, *Austria from Habsburg to Hitler*, 567. Gulick quotes the Christian Social party platform of 1918 and party papers at the time of Glöckel's 1920 "Guiding Principles."
38. In the summer of 1927 the courts acquitted several right-wing paramilitarists of murder: the protests outside the Ministry of Justice led to a fire, a panicked mob, and a failed general strike.
39. Malachi Hacohen, *Karl Popper – The Formative Years, 1902–1945* (Cambridge: Cambridge University Press, 2000), 109. The year Hacohen quotes for these figures is 1927; it is possible that SDAP percentages went up when new hires were allowed a year later, but unlikely that these would effect a significant change.
40. Eduard Golias, *Am Tore des Lebens: Über sexuelle Aufklärung und Sittlichkeit* (Wien: Österreichischer Bundesverlag für Unterricht, Wissenschaft und Kunst, 1925), 15. Natural history had been introduced to the lower Gymnasium levels in 1848.
41. Kanitz, "Geschlechtliche Erziehung[Third installment]," in *Die Sozialistische Erziehung* 2/3, (März 1922), 61. Like other socialist educators, Kanitz thought home *Aufklärung* should be supplemented with discussions at school and called for teachers to serve as *Seelenärzte*, or doctors of the soul, when answering questions and initiating conversations about sex.
42. Helene Anderle, *Die Sexuelle Aufklärung* (Sonderabdruck aus der Monatschrift "Die Quelle," Wien: Deutscher Verlag für Jugend und Volk, 1925), 10.
43. Anderle, *Aufklärung*, 13.
44. Josef Friedjung, *Die Geschlechtliche Aufklärung im Erziehungswerke: Ein Wegweiser für Eltern, Erzieher und Ärzte* (Wien: Verlag von Josef Safár, 1922), 27.
45. Friedjung, *Aufklärung*, 27.
46. Friedjung, *Die Geschlechtliche Aufklärung im Erziehungswerke: Ein Wegweiser für Eltern, Erzieher und Ärzte* (Vierte, verbesserte und erweiterte Auflage, Wien: Verlag Julius Springer, 1926), 5.
47. Otto Felix Kanitz, "Geschlechtliche Erziehung [Third installment]," in *Die Sozialistische Erziehung* 2/3 (März 1922), 63.
48. Kanitz, "Geschlechtliche Erziehung [Third installment]," 63.
49. "Wie sag' ich's meinem Kinde?," in *Die Unzufriedene* 10/8 (27 Februar 1932), 7.
50. "Wie sag' ich's," 7.
51. "Wie sag' ich's," 7.
52. "Jugendberatung," *Die Unzufriedene* 10/26 (2 Juli 1932), 7. The addresses listed by *Die Unzufriedene* are not simply a reprint of city Jugendberatungstellung, which were legion, but rather represents the work of a cross-denominational group, the Society for Youth Advice.
53. Renata Flich, "'Mütterlich-sozial und hauswirtschaftlich-practktisch': Mädchenbildungswesen nach dem Ersten Weltkrieg bis 1945," in Ilse Brehmer und Gertrud Simon (hg.), *Geschichte der Frauenbildung und Mädchenerziehung in Österreich* (Graz: Leykam Bucherverlagsgesellschaft, 1997), 221.
54. Regina Milkula, "'Die Verweiblichung der Buben und eine Vermännlichung der Mädchen': Die Koeducationsdebatte im 20. Jahrhundert," in Ilse Brehmer und Gertrud Simon (hg.), *Geschichte der Frauenbildung und Mädchenerziehung in Österreich* (Graz: Leykam Bucherverlagsgesellschaft, 1997), 240. These numbers reflect the years 1926 and 1932, respectively.
55. Renata Filch points out that after 1927 the ascendant Christian Socials were able to undo coeducation via the creation of *Hauptschulen*, where all classes were split by gender, and *Frauenoberschulen*, which were designed to help women prepare for household management and described as "like *Realschule*, but not so much [work], and not so hard." Under Austrofascism, schools were reChristianized and more girls' middle schools were built in order to re-separate the sexes. See Filch, "Mädchenbildungswesen," 225.
56. Andreas Schrott, "Die Frage der geschlechtlichen Erziehung in der sozialistischen Erziehung," *Die Sozialistische Erziehung* 1/8 (Dezember 1921), 4.
57. Schrott, "Geschlechtlichen Erziehung in der sozialistische Erzeihung," 5.

58. Eduard Golias, *Am Tore des Lebens: Über sexulle Aufklärung und Sittlichkeit* (Wien: Österreichischer Bundesverlag für Unterricht, Wissenschaft und Kunst, 1925), 24. It is interesting to muse on the literalness of *das Mädchen*'s neutered gender in German grammar in Golias's arguments for coeducation.
59. Golias, *Am Tore*, 24.
60. Otto Felix Kanitz, "Geschlechtliche Erziehung," *Die Sozialistische Erziehung* 2/1 (Jänner 1922), 3.
61. Schrott, "Geschlechtlichen Erziehung in der sozialistische Erziehung," 8.
62. Schrott, "Geschlechtlichen Erziehung in der sozialistische Erziehung," 8.
63. Anderle, *Sexuelle Aufklärung*, 11.
64. Friedjung, *Aufklärung* (4th edition), 9.
65. Golias, *Am Tore*, 36.
66. Golias, *Am Tore*, 38.
67. Golias, *Am Tore*, 43.
68. Golias, *Am Tore*, 47.
69. Josef Friedjung, *Aufklärung*, 7. This description re-appears in all of the editions of this book, moving to the first page of the 1926 edition.
70. Siegfried Kraus, "Die umweltlichen Bedingungen jugendlicher Sexualität," *Blätter für das Wohlfahrtswesen*, 32/296 (März/April 1933), 23.
71. Kraus, "Umweltlichen Bedingungen," 24. Kraus avoids any conclusions about his evidence that suggest incest.
72. Kraus, "Umweltlichen Bedingungen," 26.
73. Golias, *Am Tore*, 30.
74. Otto Felix Kanitz, "Geschlechtliche Erziehung [Fourth installment]," in *Die Sozialistische Erziehung* 2/4 (April 1922), 87.
75. Kanitz, "Geschlechtliche Erziehung [Fourth installment]," 90/91.
76. Therese Schlesinger and Dr. Paul Stein, "Leitsätze für die sexuelle Aufklärung der Jugend," in *Bildungsarbeit* 19 (1932), 234. For the purposes of my research, I have used a reprint of this article, available in its entirety in Hildegard Feistritzer's *Ansätze zur Sexualerziehung in der Sozialdemokratischen Jugendbewegung in der Zeit ihrer Entstehung* (Ph.D. dissertation: Universität Wien, 1978), 129–135.
77. Schelsinger and Stein, "Leitsätze," in Feistritzer, *Sexualerziehung*, 131.
78. Schelsinger and Stein, "Leitsätze," in Feistritzer, *Sexualerziehung*, 133.
79. Schelsinger and Stein, "Leitsätze," in Feistritzer, *Sexualerziehung*, 133.
80. Schelsinger and Stein, "Leitsätze," in Feistritzer, *Sexualerziehung*, 135.
81. Adolf Kardinal Bertram, *Reverentia Puero! Katholische Erwägungen zu Fragen der sexual-Pädagogik* (Freiburg im Breisgau: Herder & Co., 1929), 9 and 11, respectively.
82. Bertram, *Reverentia Pureo!*, 35/36.
83. Dr. Rudolf Allers, *Sexualpädagogik: Grundlagen und Grundlinien* (Salzburg: Verlag Anton Pustet, 1934), 269.
84. Michael Gatterer, *Im Glaubenslicht: Christliche Gedanken über das Geschlechtsleben* (Innsbruck: Felician Rauch, 1927), 2. Gatterer was one of the earliest to work of the theme of sex education within the Church. Extracts of *Im Glaubenslicht* were published separately was pamphlets and translated into many languages.
85. P. Peter Schmitz, *Am reinen Quell des Lebens: Eine Anleitung zur geschlechtlichen Aufklärung der Kinder für die christlichen Mütter* (Mödling: Missionsdruckerei St. Gabriel, 1932), 4. Emphasis in original.
86. Schmitz, *Am reinen Quell*, 10.
87. "Jugendfreund," *So belehrte dein Kind, Ein Schriften für Eltern und Erzieher* (Salzburg: Verlag des Pfarramts Vigaun, 1933), 3.
88. Bertram, *Reverentia Pureo!*, 4.

89. *So belehrte*, 4. Emphasis in original.
90. *So belehrte*, 12.
91. *So belehrte*, 12.
92. Schmitz, *Am reinen Quell*, 29. Emphasis in original.
93. For fuller treatment of debate over the abstinence and its possible dangers, see chapter 3.
94. Allers, *Sexualpädagogik*, 15.
95. Allers, *Sexualpädagogik*, 169.
96. P. Peter Schmitz, S.V.D., *Bursch und Mädel in Gottes Hand. Ein Seelsorglicher und Pädagogischer Beitrag zum Geschlechtlicher Problem* (Innsbruck und Wien: Tyrolia Verlag, 1936), 11/12. Here Schmitz was quoting from an oft-reprinted booklet by G. Manes, *Die Sexuelle Not unserer Jugend*.
97. Schmitz, *Bursch und Mädel*, 12.
98. Schmitz, *Bursch und Mädel*, 14.
99. Schmitz, *Bursch und Mädel*, 14/15. Emphasis in the original.
100. Schmitz, *Am reinen Quell*, 30.
101. Bertram, *Reverentia Pureo!*, 19.
102. Bertram, *Reverentia Pureo!*, 30–33. Bertram's suggestions for sublimation included receiving the sacrament daily and honoring Mary, mother of God.
103. Allers always placed these terms (*Sexualnot, Sexuellefrage*) in quotes, as if to question their strength in the scientific and sexological texts that employed them. I believe he is explicitly mocking the 1930 World League for Sexual Reform Vienna Congress, which took *Sexualnot* as one of its organizing categories (see chapter 6).
104. Allers, *Sexualpädagogik*, 15.
105. Schmitz, *Bursch und Mädel*, 16. Emphasis in the original.
106. Schmitz, *Bursch und Mädel*, 17.
107. Schmitz, *Bursch und Mädel*, 19/20. Schmitz also very clearly states that the use of birth control is against God's will.
108. Schmitz, *Bursch und Mädel*, 20.
109. Schmitz, *Bursch und Mädel*, 22. A looser translation would be: "Our penises no longer belong to ourselves, but rather are Christ's. To abuse them is to desecrate one of Christ's limbs."
110. Schmitz, *Bursch und Mädel*, 11. Not only is Schmitz's language aimed at a popular audience, but also his book was reissued multiple times.
111. Schmitt, *Die katholische Ehe und die christliche Familie* (Innsbruck: Tyrolia), 14.
112. Schmitt, *Die katholische Ehe*, 14.
113. Schmitz, *Am reinen Quell*, 13. Tellingly, his parallel message about boys entering the larger world mentioned "gymnasium and trade school" rather than the low-level service jobs he envisioned for girls.
114. Schmitz, *Bursch und Mädel*, 15.
115. Schmitz, *Am reinen Quell*, 20.
116. Helmut Gruber, *Red Vienna: Experiment in Working-Class Culture, 1919–1934* (New York: Oxford University Press, 1991). Gruber does not discuss sexual education in his work, but does address welfare and cultural programs.
117. See Rudolf Goldscheid, *Frauenfrage und Menschenökonomie* (Wien: Anzengruber Verlag Brüder Suschitzky, 1913); Karl Kautsky, *Der Kampf Gegen den Geburtenrückgang* (Wein: Verlag der Organisation Wien der Sozialdemohratischen Partei, 1924); and Julius Tandler, *Wohltätigkeit oder Fürsorge?* (Wien: Verlag der Organisation Wien der sozialdemokratischen Partei, 1925).
118. Schmitz, *Am reinem Quell*, 29. Emphasis in original.
119. Schmitt, *Die katholishe Ehe*, 27.

Chapter 3

POPULAR SEXUAL KNOWLEDGE FOR AND ABOUT WOMEN

F*in-de-siècle* sexology dedicated much of its scientific investigation and social reform agitation to the homosexual male. Leading sexologists Magnus Hirschfeld, Havelock Ellis, and Richard Krafft-Ebing produced studies that naturalized homosexuality within a wide range of sexual preference and behavior, and drew upon their work to argue for the repeal of anti-homosexual legislation across Europe.[1] In the wake of World War I, the burgeoning sexology discourses of Central Europe were transformed and modified to address the problems of depopulation, venereal disease, and urban misery. This chapter follows the explosion in the public sphere of sexual information intended for adults. In particular, I will show how sexual knowledge in Vienna was transformed from a medical specialty to a popular reform movement in the interwar years, alternately taking "woman" as its subject and its audience. I argue that the main object of sexual reform in interwar Vienna was the heterosexual couple. Popular literature, advice columns, and public clinics all worked to teach women how to determine and safeguard the reproductive capacities of their own bodies, as well as those of their partners. Furthermore, the authors and directors of this new information chose to frame medical and scientific subjects within testimonial confessions, melodramatic themes, and short stories.[2] In this way, narratives of sexual science and reform, leavened with emotion, were repackaged for female audiences.

The Viennese context for this boom in sexual knowledge—an increasingly bitter public debate over marriage reform, abortion rights, and the economic and social place of the New Woman—is crucial to understanding the movement for popular sexual *Aufklärung* (literally "enlightenment"). I want to sketch out what about these issues was particular to interwar Vienna. I will also briefly problematize the two modes of communication that dominated sexual education literature: medical science and melodrama. I then will turn to a selection of Viennese print sources ranging from the period directly before World War I to the end of the Austrian First Republic (1934) and attempt to break down sexual knowledge for and about women into the categories that seem to constitute "healthy" sexuality in my sources: anatomical knowledge, prevention of disease and unwanted pregnancy, and mutual enjoyment of sex within marriage. From popular print materials, I will move into official discourse about adult sexual knowledge, as formulated by the two powers struggling to control Austria during the interwar period: the Roman Catholic Church and the Social Democratic Workers' Party (henceforth, SDAP).[3] Finally, I will conclude with an exploration of melodrama's rising popularity in *Aufklärung* literature and of its strengths and weaknesses as a call to social and sexual action.

Cultural Context

All of the sources I have identified discuss adult sexual education within the context of marriage. This is in keeping with the international explosion of mass-produced and widely translated marriage manuals after World War I. In this literature, healthy and mutually satisfying sex was portrayed as a means of achieving and maintaining a companionate marriage. Such partnership was to be the building block of the civil society envisioned by the Social Democratic Party in control of Vienna's city hall. But what of marriages without love? Did men and women have a right to leave an unhappy union? Interwar Vienna, newly invested with powers as a state province, inherited the marriage code of the Imperial period.[4] This tangle of laws was tightly bound to the Roman Catholic Church, whose refusal to recognize divorce meant that, for most Austrians, a second marriage before the death of one's previous spouse was technically illegal. An arcane system of dispensations from the state courts, as well as an emergency civil marriage for those who declared themselves without religious affiliation (a maneuver often resorted to by interfaith couples) was developed to get around Church law and state bureaucracy. These half-measures sparked increasing controversy and frustration in the Republican period, as expressed by councils, associations, and movements devoted to marriage reform.[5]

Equally contested during this period was the legal status of abortion, which was also inherited from the Imperial period. Most demands for the repeal of anti-abortion legislation (Paragraphs 144 to 148 of the Austrian Code) in the immediate post-war years drew upon the poverty, hunger, and homelessness of wide swaths of the city's citizenry. Women's and family advocates argued that abortion was a rational and responsible option for members of a society unable to feed and shelter its young. Although the radical wing of the SDAP rallied for abortion rights in 1926, the party's leaders responded to this challenge by expanding welfare for women and infants, rather than legalizing first trimester abortion.[6] SDAP ideologues and welfare experts vigorously supported family planning, but did not view abortion as one of its legitimate components. They identified birth control as the rational path to economic and personal freedom, and labeled abortion the irrational answer of an irresponsible woman. This message was repeated throughout Viennese adult sex education literature.

Much of the discourse surrounding sexual knowledge and marriage advice was based in the *Frauenfrage* ("Women's Question"). From the turn of the century to the height of the First Republic, the *Frauenfrage* expanded dramatically; from a question of primarily bourgeois women's access to education and the professions towards a more general question of women working outside the home and thus balancing what feminist historians have identified as the triple burden: wage-earning, housekeeping, and child rearing. In socialist-controlled Red Vienna, the SDAP adopted a position towards wage-earning women that was first suggested by sociologist Rudolf Goldscheid. The working woman, he argued, was a by-product of capitalism: her children and family depended on the wages she earned, and she would remain at her job until the city's ambitious social welfare system expanded enough to offer her the preferred status of helpmeet and mother.[7] Women's rights were recognized as culturally and historically logical, and social theorists from the SDAP expected society to benefit from the extension of voting rights to women in 1919. Yet social democratic support of women's expanded role in the public sphere was not absolute. The party perceived the New Woman as she appeared in fashion, literature, and mass media in the 1920s as potentially dangerous, and this perception was shared by much of the sexual education literature produced at this time. The SDAP was much more interested in creating and supporting a New Mother, rather than the (single and childless) New Woman.[8] The implicitly emancipatory promises made to women through sexual advice—that they could and should fashion their own reproductive and sexual lives—were thus tempered by the often explicit disapproval in advice literature of "selfish" women's non-reproductive sexual practices. Whatever her actual presence in Vienna, the New Woman, with her androgynous style, single status, discretionary income, and liberated sexuality was thought to be on the rise.[9] She appears in many of my sources as a predatory denizen of the metropolis, capable of securing her own happiness by destroying other women's marriages.

It is important to remember, however, that attitudes and knowledge about sex were not only constructed via the popular press at this time. Vienna enjoyed a leading position within the world of medical sexology. Sexual definitions and cultural commentary came from leaders in the field such as Richard von Krafft-Ebing, innovators such as Sigmund Freud, and scandalous gender theorists such as Otto Weininger. Sexual hygiene articles from the prestigious *Wiener medizinische Wochenschrift* were regularly reprinted in special editions for an increasingly scientifically savvy audience.[10] In the texts I will cite in this chapter, there is an underlying shift in the way medical authority is employed. This trajectory within scientific sexual knowledge begins with an attitude of absolute dependence on research doctors for sexual truths before World War I. After the war, practicing physicians and social reformers gained influence through municipal and associational sex clinics and counseling centers, so that by the end of the Republican period a position outside of the medical establishment could serve as a selling point for sex advice literature.

Finally, the much-lauded realm of Viennese theater, operettas, and performing arts also served to mold Viennese citizens' ideas about sex. Much important work has been done exploring the sexual themes of Vienna's elite dramatists, and certainly the wry show reviews of Karl Kraus and daring psychosexual plays of Arthur Schnitzler influenced their fellow citizens.[11] More relevant to my work, however, is the persistence of nineteenth-century melodrama in popular performances and, beginning in the 1920s, film. Melodrama provided a way of telling a story that was stripped of the psychological subtlety that marked much of Vienna's high-culture artistic products and instead presented characters polarized between good and evil, victim and villain. Women played starring roles in melodramas, particularly those that focused on the forces that threatened the family (an important sub-genre). The sympathy and outrage that melodrama was designed to evoke from its audience made it a strong vehicle for messages of social justice, including messages of sexual reform. Melodrama was a forum in which the weak were ultimately protected from the strong, the truth always was revealed, and the forces of oppression were overcome. In short, melodrama promised a happy ending to its audience, in which justice for the downtrodden was a central theme. In the early twentieth-century sources that follow, melodrama combines and even competes with science as the chosen vehicle for adult sexual education. This suggests that sexual knowledge was seen as part of justice for women in the modern, post-war society, an idea I will return to at the end of the chapter.

Women's Sexual Knowledge

What basic sexual knowledge was available to the reading public before and during World War I? The medical response to *fin-de-siècle* social concerns about degeneration emphasized hygiene and education to halt the spread of venereal disease. A broad debate over Vienna's semi-regulated prostitution spilled out from the pages of medical journals and into the mainstream press, carrying with it the beginnings of popular sexual *Aufklärung*. Drawing from experience in private practice and Vienna's public clinics, neurologist Dr. J. Kitaj, for example, produced a guide to sexual life intended to extend medical authority into prospective marriages. The central thesis of his *Normal and Pathological Sexual Life of the Male and Female*, which first appeared in 1909 but was still being reissued in 1921, was that a marriage should be "medically grounded" through examination of the marriage partners before their union was consummated. Indeed, he wrote that he would "see it as a sign of an educated, modern girl, if she refused to be married without a certificate of health from her partner."[12] The pluckiness Kitaj admired in this "modern girl," however, was unusual. Women were more frequently rendered as irrational, over-sexed, and illness-prone patients in his manual. Kitaj's scientific explanation of women's sexual lives portrayed them as victims of their own hormones.[13] His text provides a useful bridge between *fin-de-siècle* portrayals of female sexuality and First Republic attempts at sexual reform.

As he walked his readers through the topics of anatomy, menstruation, masturbation, and homosexuality, Dr. Kitaj illustrated his points with examples drawn from his practice. His sketches varied from voyeuristic and chatty examples of dissolute women to highly professional case studies of impotence, homosexuality, and perversion in men. The case study, readily adapted from medical and psychiatric diagnosis, offered a usable format for lay audiences to absorb sexual knowledge. Kitaj's examples, particularly of female sexual abnormality, created titillating sexual types: the maid who wins children's affection through sexual gratification, the upper-middle class girl whose affairs with famous men land her with a venereal disease that must be hidden from her parents, the student who masturbates compulsively in the library and is disgusted with herself as a result.[14] Kitaj's coverage of "normal" sexuality is far less ardent. Readers looking for anatomical information about the female body found a short paragraph sketch of the reproductive organs and warnings about the effect of masturbation upon the hymen, but no mention of the clitoris. Venereal disease was described as a by-product of prostitution and a danger to young wives, but Kitaj gave no indications of its appearance, varieties, or cycles. And although he allowed that unmarried women might be mentally prepared for sex, he counseled them to remain chaste until marriage, saying simply: "it is well known that plenty of spiritually and morally upstanding girls have the opportunity to have sex. My advice—purely as a scientist and a doctor—don't."[15] The ubiquity of disease, coupled with the inevitability of conception, was the crux of Kitaj's advice to his reader, male or female. The educated public was introduced to the varieties of sexual misery through Kitaj's work, but the text was not concerned with mitigation of such misery. Although Kitaj did extend sexual information to the public, his medical opinion reinforced the late-Imperial cultural imperatives of chastity, silence, or shame for sexually active women.

Kitaj's book was still selling well into the First Republic. After World War I, however, there were new educational options for the Viennese public interested in adult sexuality. Rather than enlarge upon the varieties of abnormal sexuality, interwar texts focused on the creation and maintenance of heterosexual partnerships capable of producing fewer but healthier offspring. The implications of this shift in interest towards "normal" sexuality included an expansion of *Aufklärung* media to include clinics, newspapers, and film, a willingness to feature explicit anatomical diagrams and terms, and an increased possibility of securing female pleasure. Although medical doctors still contributed heavily to the discourse, psychologists, social reformers, and advice columnists entered the fray as advocates of individual happiness and married love.

What information was available to women about their bodies and those of their (always male) partners in interwar Vienna? One of the main goals of the sex reform movement was the popularization of basic anatomical knowledge for adults, which was sometimes justified as preventative social hygiene and more rarely presented as a step towards personal emancipation. For women, who lacked the Latin training many middle class men enjoyed, self-education through medical texts was difficult. In her book *How Woman Experiences Man*, sex reformer Sofie Lazarsfeld declared, "It is in the general interests of mankind to hope that later generations no longer are required to cobble together a knowledge of their own bodies and its important functions from medical-specialty books."[16] Lazarsfeld was a member of Wilhelm Reich's Socialistic Society for Sexual Research (see chapter 4), and her work there was dedicated to ensuring popular, medical self-knowledge for her own generation.

Increasingly explicit tours of the human reproductive system were advocated and provided by sex reformers in the interwar years. In his 1921 guide for girls, *Ripe for Love! A Medical Explanation of Everything Essential about the Love- and Sex-life of the Woman*, Viennese gynecologist Rudolf Glaessner complained that the wealth of *Aufklärung* materials now sitting in the bookstore windows of big cities failed to effectively instruct their readers about the physical facts of life. He wrote:

> The main defect of most of these books in that they either totally discount medical facts and offer their readers only piquant stories, or they mire their readers in purely medical questions and discuss the latest scientific methods of treating venereal disease, pregnancy, and miscarriages, cramming the reader with details.[17]

Ripe for Love! countered this publishing trend by offering young women a frank and folksy tour of their anatomies and of the bodily changes that occur during menstruation, sexual arousal, conception, and disease. The capacity for female orgasm was clearly stated, along with the warning that it could be difficult to achieve through coitus alone.[18] Although Glaessner does not explicitly advise lovers how to overcome this dilemma, other authors openly recommended oral or manual stimulation of the clitoris. The first popular sex advice text to do this was Theodore Van der Velde's 1926 *Ideal Marriage*. Van der Velde diagramed the female genitalia with extensive notes on the clitoris, and advised husbands to satisfy their wives' sexual desires through clitoral stimulation as a preparation for coitus. He recognized women's clitoral orgasms, but insisted that women were renewed through the *élan vital* of their husband's sperm and thus also required penetrative sex for full satisfaction.[19] Viennese sex reformer Lazarsfeld described *Ideal Marriage* as the most widely read sex advice manual in 1930. She praised Van der Velde's attention to the female anatomy and especially the clitoral orgasm, but was critical of what she considered Van der Velde's overall message of feminine weakness and dependency.[20] Lazarsfeld claimed that many of the women she counseled on sexual matters were under the impression that their clitoral, rather than vaginal, sensitivity was a sign of degeneration, and she sermonized that it was only when women gained the courage to talk openly about their bodies that they realized the extent of the misinformation and misery they have suffered through.[21] In further validation of the non-vaginal orgasm, Lazarsfeld augmented her explanation of female sexual organs with a list of erogenous zones for lovers to explore, including the anus, inside and outside the ear, the inner thighs, and the palm of the hand.[22]

Women's curiosity about the male body was applauded as natural and sensible by some sex educators. Socialist pedagogues bemoaned the continuation of Victorian standards of mutual physical ignorance between girls and boys as dangerously outmoded, a refrain that ran through the defense of coeducational learning environments during the First Republic and the appeals for sexual education in public schools.[23] Sexual advice literature was even more outspoken in its critique of men and women's mutual ignorance of each other. In their 1925 book *The Man—A Book for Women*, the Viennese couple Else and Dr. R. Tauber suggested that the curriculum for girls was lacking:

> Only a single subject is scrupulously avoided in girls' upper grades, precisely the one that interests girls and women the most: no-one speaks to them of *Man*, of his physical and mental properties, just as one doesn't enlighten young men in school about women and their peculiarities.[24]

Their book began straight away with a description of human reproduction and a frank discussion of semen, sensitive nerve endings, and ejaculation. Orgasm for both partners was described as necessary to continued health, although the Taubers offered their readers no advice in achieving it.[25] Glaessner's *Ripe for Love!* colloquially discussed the male sex organs in a similar fashion, providing side comments along the way about possible abnormalities resulting from venereal disease.[26]

Educating women to recognize venereal disease in their male sexual partners was a response to social and municipal concerns about syphilis.[27] An important subsection of Vienna's Health Ministry during the interwar period was devoted to combating venereal disease, particularly infections borne by homecoming soldiers. According to the National Decree of 21 November 1918, every individual carrying a venereal disease had the responsibility of securing their own examination and treatment, as well as announcing their illness to others in cases of cramped apartment living or "dangerous personal behavior."[28] The Decree also called for free medical treatment for impoverished VD sufferers, and in the late 1920s anonymous stations offering Wasserman tests for syphilis dotted the city. These services were primarily intended for and used by men. A special center for the care of women carrying venereal disease was set up in nearby Klosterneuberg, but this center seems to have been designed for prostitutes, rather than women infected by their husbands. Admission to this 400-bed clinic was forced, and inmates spent their recovery time engaged in handicrafts intended to help them break the pattern of prostitution once they received a clean bill of health.

Whereas the majority of pre-war warnings about venereal disease were aimed towards a bourgeois male audience, interwar sexual advice explicitly addressed women in an effort to halt the spread of infection and insure healthy offspring for couples. Repeated warnings against both homeopathic home cures and store-bought tonics in adult sexual education literature suggest that a wide range of laymen's solutions to infection existed in Vienna at the time.[29] In a surprising critique of both birth control and marital infidelity, Lazarsfeld suggested that using condoms was a wise precaution even within committed partnerships. Writing late in the period, she exhorted her female readers to demand protection from their partners:

> Many women complain that their husbands cannot bear wearing condoms, as condoms make them impotent. But it often turns out that when these same men visit prostitutes ... in short, when they for any reason want to protect themselves through condom use, suddenly they can bear to wear them. Only when they don't have any interest in the problem, because they believe that it is the responsibility of their wives to take measures against pregnancy, do they refuse to wear condoms.[30]

While this preventative stance was extreme, other sex advice literature suggested a pre-coitus inspection of one's sexual partners for genital abnormalities that could signify disease. In his exhaustively complete *Hygiene of Married Life: The Guide to Love and Marital Bliss*, Josef Carl Schlegel inserted gory illustrations of breasts, gums, genitals, and anuses marked with sores, as well as long text descriptions of syphilis, gonorrhea, and soft chancre.[31]

Even more than venereal disease, pregnancy was presented as the most important physical consideration for women making sexual choices in interwar Vienna. An array of pre- and post-natal services was developed through the city's social welfare system. Most of the advice offered in adult sexual education literature, however, discussed a variety of contraceptive methods for couples. Even the finest public health care and social services system in Europe could not ameliorate the conditions faced by Viennese women when bringing children in the world, and their concerns were acknowledged by sex educators:

> Misery and powerlessness, concern and anxiety over even one's ability to secure one's daily bread cannot provide for children's happiness and our current social conditions

have become, in this matter, worse than ever before. There are plenty of cases in the course of life where the prevention of pregnancy is not only a moral sexual choice, but is also demanded on the grounds of sexual-social hygiene."[32]

Beyond the question of social conditions, some *Aufklärung* manuals for adults argued for birth control as a matter of human rights for women. Speaking to Austrian girls, sex manual author Glaessner insisted that "the human rights of a woman come before her duties as a [reproductive] female" and lamented that "no moral system in the world is willing to admit that woman, in order to create 'children of love' (which are often conceived by accident), must cede her right of self-determination to motherhood."[33]

The right of women to control their fertility was extolled in the pages of the socialist women's weekly magazine *Die Unzufriedene* ("The Unsatisfied"). Most often this was expressed in economic terms that drew upon the hunger and joblessness of the era to explain why couples would want to limit their offspring. The hours for six Viennese birth control advice centers run by the *Bund für Geburtenregelung* (Society for Birth Control) were often printed below questions of fertility regulation that appeared in the magazine's advice column "What Women Speak from their Souls."[34] The emotional testimonies regarding birth control also drew upon an ideal of companionate marriage based in mutual care rather than endless reproduction. As the column's editors put it, "Marriage is not only an institution for the creation of children, but rather should be a life partnership in which two people can belong to each other, without fear of bringing a new being into the world."[35] Such responsibility to each other included birth control, in the pages of this weekly magazine.

The methods of birth control recommended to women in interwar Vienna were either expensive or ineffective, and were sometimes both. Lasting sexual abstinence in marriage was rejected by most sex counselors as destructive to the individual and the marriage.[36] *Die Unzufriedene* warned that marriages were poisoned by the fear of childbirth, which caused "a woman to fear every approach of her husband, who understandably complains of the seeming 'coldness' of his wife, which in turn runs many marriages internally and finally externally into the ground, as neither man nor wife is educated enough in a healthy sexual life."[37] The rejection of abstinence was not new: psychoanalytic experts had begun making the case against it before World War I. In his oft-reprinted essay "The 'Cultural' Sexual Morality and Modern Nervousness," Freud wrote that sexual abstinence was positively unhealthy for young men after their twentieth year, and claimed that young women were only kept chaste through a system of ignorance that would disturb their sexual lives well into marriage.[38] Freud's pupil Wilhelm Stekel, writing to a lay audience in the early 1920s, made an even more dramatic case against marital continence:

> In families in which Malthusianism is practiced, the most remarkable results of relative abstinence may be seen. Apprehension neurosis is fostered by the various methods adopted to prevent pregnancy. Not infrequently ... we find the husband and wife attempting to live in abstinence. Usually this abstinence is a one-sided affair, i.e., the wife fears pregnancy more than a neurosis or her husband's infidelity. Very often one hears the almost unbelievable remark: "let him do what he pleases, if only he leaves me alone." And unquestionably there are naive women who imagine that they have transformed their husbands into asexual beings; women who flatter themselves that their husbands love them even if they do not cohabit with them.[39]

Stekel outlined a series of emotional and physical maladies that haunted the households in which regular marital intercourse is lacking. His critique of women who asked their husbands either to use birth control or abstain from conjugal sex was extreme and at odds with the Neo-Malthusian accounts of impoverished families cited previously. Yet even psychoanalytic theory as mild as that of Alfred Adler disapproved of continence. In an essay entitled "Love and Marriage," he suggested in oblique language that, in order for marital love to be truly companionate, the partners must renounce the selfishness that would keep them from having children.[40] In Adler's opinion, true love could not coexist with marital continence.

Although psychoanalytic authority seemed to equate marital love with reproduction, popular advice manuals and clinics countered this equation by advertising a variety of contraceptive techniques. For women without means or unwilling to visit a doctor, *coitus interruptus* and prolonged nursing periods after birth were commonly endorsed. Pessaries, combined with douching regimes and/or spermicidal preparations, were the safest alternative. English sex reformer Marie Stopes, author of the popular manual *Married Love*, explicitly advised women to use these forms of birth control in her 1918 companion text, *Wise Parenthood*.[41] Many authors dismissed condoms, either out of a concern for male comfort or in the belief that sperm served a special, salubrious function for women, invigorating their body systems.[42] A vocal exception to this was Lazarsfeld, whose professional preference for condoms on both hygienic and contraceptive grounds was noted above. Of course, any barrier method of birth control was forbidden by the Roman Catholic Church, whose cultural authority was by no means unseated by the Socialist city leaders. At the end of the interwar period, however, SDAP sex reformer Dr. Paul Stein was able to announce the discovery of what would become the modern rhythm method, recently revised by an Austrian gynecologist and recommended to women with regular cycles.[43] The recommendation of a "sterile period" within a woman's menstrual cycle predated human ovulation research (simultaneously published in 1932 by Drs. H. Kraus of Graz and K. Ogino of Niigata, Japan), but had unfortunately identified an incorrect one. It is unknown how many women were willing to trust the new rhythm method publicized by reformers like Stein.

A final consideration within literature that encouraged women to use contraception devices was the sobriety of the sexual partners, particularly the male. In her discussion of state-supported birth control, SDAP representative Therese Schlesinger blamed some unplanned pregnancies on alcohol: "All too often, an unwished-for pregnancy is the result of the drunkenness of the husband, who has had his self-discipline so compromised by the alcohol that he neither uses any means of protection nor is able to do without sexual pleasure."[44] Loss of sexual control among working-class men was a major campaigning point for the SDAP's *Arbeiter-Abstinenten Bund* (Worker Temperance Association).[45] The standard *Bund* postcard, developed in 1922, declared "Bring out the Prohibition Law!" and then illustrated why the Republic needed such legislation with a picture of a vicious marital drama.[46] On her knees is a half-dressed woman in a skirt and camisole, her hands clasped in pleading prayer above her head. She is being pulled by her unbound hair to the ground behind her by a man, presumably her husband, who is also stepping on the back hem of her skirt. He has been drinking, and has perhaps just returned from the *Beisl*. His hair is disheveled and his hips are thrust forward. In his free hand, high in the air, he holds an empty bottle by the neck, in preparation of smashing it over his victim's head. The brute sexual force of the drunken husband is at odds with the refined clothes and precarious posture of his victim. In this propagandistic picture, physical and sexual abuse is imminent.

Although the immediate violence upon wives like the one depicted in "Bring out the Prohibition Law!" was deplored by sex advice givers, most literature focused on the possible reproductive outcome of drunken marital rape. Not only was alcoholism seen as an inheritable disease, but also the *Volk* as a whole could be damaged by children conceived in a drunken haze, a condition that reformers recognized as not conducive to careful recognition and use of condoms, pessaries, or safe periods. In a 1931 article entitled "Do You Want a Healthy Marriage?," one concerned doctor reminded Viennese women:

> How many thousands of children must attribute their own "gift" of life to the fact that their parents lost their self-control while under the influence of alcoholic beverages? It's even worse when one half of the parental unit gives itself over to the regular use of alcohol. The healthy half then has the *duty* to prevent reproduction and free the spouse from his addiction. It has been proven among idiots, the weak-willed, and the accident-prone, that the majority of them were conceived while their parents were drinking alcoholic beverages. In wine country [like Vienna], seven years after a good wine year one observes a weak cohort entering school.[47]

In this quotation the drinking spouse is clearly masculine, and it falls to the women in these marital relationships to protect themselves and the *Volk* from conceiving children with alcoholic husbands. The underlying concept of degeneration that supported such warnings could also appear in less anecdotal formats: throughout the interwar period, sex reformers referred back to famous doctor and sexologist August Forel's scientific theories of "Blastodermic Degeneration," which suggested that alcohol altered the cells and sex organs of drinkers.[48] Anti-alcohol propaganda of this period stressed both sexual brutality and eugenic danger, suggesting that bodies of both the wife and the nation were poisoned through drink.

The dire educational warnings about hereditary health that flooded adult *Aufklärung* literature in the interwar years often sat side by side with extremely positive messages about experiencing pleasure in one's body through physical and sexual activity. The massive "body culture" campaigns designed to draw women into the growing public sport movement, particularly socialist-funded gymnastics clubs and municipal swimming pools, are good examples of this. When time was short, a ten-minute morning routine of exercises was recommended to keep modern women feeling strong and looking supple for themselves and their husbands.[49] While the discussion of pleasure in connection to physical activity and sports was more widespread, I will focus on the surprisingly forthright treatment of sexual pleasure within marriage by lifestyle reformers, women's advocates, and *Aufklärung* supporters.

"The Happy Marriage," a ubiquitous sub-heading of any advice or sex manual of the time, was the combination of physical and spiritual connections, rooted in cooperation, between the partners. Most sex advice authors wrote to a married audience, although some were willing to use the euphemism of "love" to write more inclusive sex guides that allowed for single or perhaps engaged readers. For example, throughout his most formal *Aufklärung* text, *Sex-Life Problems*, Glaessner used the terms "love" and "marriage" interchangeably, eventually breaking down towards the end of the book to say "love and marriage" and even "a happy love *or* marriage."[50] Lazarsfeld advised women that marriage was not the only context in which they may enjoy sex, although she dismisses physical pleasure without spiritual connection as masturbation.[51] Free love, or "trial marriage," was dismissed by many writers as preserving individual freedom at the cost of true comradeship and cooperation. Only authors writing from extreme political positions, such as those committed to a socialism more radical than that of City Hall, dispensed with the emphasis of sex within marriage or at the very least within a committed partnership.[52]

Although all of the texts surveyed in this study emphasize the creation of emotionally close, heterosexual partnerships, much of the work of maintaining these unions was described as women's domain. Drawing on the cases she heard as a sex clinic counselor, Lazarsfeld wrote, "often day-to-day life is described as the greatest enemy of love, and in a certain sense this is correct."[53] Winning and keeping a husband required a certain amount of feminine savvy, according to many authors. After devoting a chapter to advising working women with limited schedules and budgets on meeting men, the Taubers' *Man—A Book for Women* covered male behavior within marriage. Here a woman—ostensibly the same one who was looking for a husband between her shifts in the previous chapter—is exhorted to keep the household neat and orderly, to wait on her husband at table, to keep anger out of her voice and be ever patient, and to assume responsibility if he goes to other women for his sexual pleasure, as clearly she has allowed him to grow bored.[54] The one-sidedness of such a partnership apparently did not strike the Taubers. Instead, their model of companionate marriage assumed a certain male antipathy towards his wife. Finally, one Viennese woman writing in to a socialist advice column suggested that her fellow sisters should augment their husbands' sympathy by showing them the realities of female reproductive work. Having attended the educational film *The Human Birth* with her husband, "Rosa V." testified: "I can only advise all women to *go see this film … and to take your husbands, your brothers, and your fiancés with you!* Some men would be milder and more understanding if they knew, and above all *saw*, how much good and loving understanding their wives needed during pregnancy."[55]

Establishing a mutually satisfying sex-life appears as one of the keys to a happy marriage in both marriage and sex advice literature. On a most basic level, happy marriages were also understood to facilitate mutual sexual pleasure, including female orgasm. Here the cultural understanding of men as more sexually experienced than women was exploited by sex reformers, who suggested that ideally the male should guide the couple to marital bliss. In *Hygiene of Married Life*, author Schlegel reasoned:

> Because the sexual satisfaction of both partners is a determining factor for happy progress in the marriage, the man, in the active role of sexual union, must insure that every posture and position in coitus offers the highest possible enjoyment (and thus full satisfaction) for not only himself, but also his wife.[56]

Schlegel suggested basic sexual positions to men, designed to balance the needs of differently sized and sensitized partners. In her work addressed to a female audience, however, Lazarsfeld claimed that creativity was the key to successful sexual positions and dismissed the charts and instructions of other *Aufklärung* manuals with the suggestion that "one minute of inspiration is worth more here than an hour of study."[57]

The unhappy marriage served as an important rallying point for sexual educators and reformers. In this discussion, women appeared in the role of victim, often of a brutal or selfish husband, and responsibility for marital (un)happiness was re-directed towards men. The vast literature portraying the suffering of women in marriage during this period is beyond the scope of my research, but marital strife resulting from sexual misunderstandings was an important subsection of many sex manuals. Schlegel, in his *Hygiene of Married Life*, reminded readers that men should heed their partner's needs, or else face moral consequences:

> Unfortunately, not every husband is tender enough to attend to, in those moments in which he finds his sexual pleasure necessary, the closeness that his wife craves. Brutal physical violence—which for a sensitive man would be impossible—results in a joyless

sacrifice, which, judged by the lasting damage it does to the woman's soul, is not worth the pleasure of the moment.[58]

In order to avoid a sex-life based on marital rape, as portrayed in the above quotation, Schlegel and other sex reformers repeatedly emphasized women's need for tenderness and foreplay. When faced with a truly brutal man, women were encouraged to leave rather than endure violence or, perhaps worse, bear him more children. In the advice pages of *Die Unzufriedene*, a companionate marriage was portrayed as just short of a human right: "Every woman has a duty and a right to make a worthwhile life for herself. It goes against all human and feminine dignity when a woman lets herself be beaten by her husband, or when she stays with him and bears another child every year."[59] In this formulation, private brutality, sexual submission, and relentless reproduction combined to illustrate the suffering of women within non-companionate marriages.

Viennese women were also warned that sexual misery in marriage could occur with the mildest of partners. In a 1929 women's magazine article advertising the Municipal Marriage Advice Centers, director Dr. Karl Kautsky, Jr. itemized the marital unhappiness that sprang from the hidden defects of one's spouse:

> The marriage partners can injure each other in countless ways: health-wise, above all, through the transmission of contagious diseases (tuberculosis, syphilis, gonorrhea), physically and mentally through various sexual abnormalities (homosexuality, malformation, sterility in both sexes, impotence in men and frigidity in women), mentally and materially through mental illness or alcoholism in the other partner.[60]

Here marriage, far from being a site of bliss, is presented as a potentially dangerous undertaking. Kautsky's article stressed the heavy hygienic responsibility married people had toward each other and recommended that all perspective partners undergo medical testing before they committed to an intimate life together.[61] In many ways, the municipal clinic he ran realized the ideals that we first encountered in Kitaj's pre-war text, *Normal and Pathological Sexual Life of the Male and Female*. As Kautsky's article reveals, however, the Municipal Marriage Advice Centers were ill-attended by the Viennese population: in the first seven years of operation, only 2,000 prospective partners had undergone examination.[62]

Women, Sex, and the SDAP

As I will elaborate upon in chapter 4, the eugenic orientation of Kautsky's Marriage Advice Centers overshadowed any role they might have played in counseling women about their private and intimate lives. This orientation is generally true for most of the official Social Democratic texts that discuss women, reproduction, and sexuality. However, the SDAP repeatedly appealed to women voters as mothers, and thus was forced to take a position on adult female sexuality and sexual education.

In a 1923 article entitled "On the Evolution of the Erotic," SDAP feminist Therese Schlesinger reported to fellow party functionaries that the *Frauenfrage* had undergone major expansion, so that "in the last decade, the *Frauenfrage* has been frequently researched from the point of view of population politics and sexual hygiene."[63] The result of this expansion in the *Frauenfrage*, according to Schlesinger, had been to highlight the sexual inequality between the men and women. Citing an evolution from primitive sex drives towards a highly individuated sense of the erotic in humanity, Schlesinger claimed that the social hypocrisy of male jealousy and female sexual shame had kept women from "evolving" [erotically] at the same pace as men.[64] Schlesinger aside, most SDAP theorists did not pursue the question of what women wanted erotically, and focused instead on what they felt their female constituency wanted materially, by highlighting population and hygiene questions in their discussion of women.

The SDAP courted women voters by addressing their spheres of influence, often revealing a highly reproduction-oriented vision of Viennese women. In a 1924 pamphlet entitled *The New Woman*, the party attempted to build upon its October 1923 election success with female voters by outlining the places where Social Democracy was fighting for women.[65] *The New Woman* was arranged so that it addressed women first as housewives, then as mothers, then as workers, and lastly as voters interested in politics. The order of these topics is telling, as is the final section's emphasis on relationships and reproduction. The creation of more housing, the right to limit family size, expansion of maternity and childcare social services, standardization on basic foodstuff costs, reform of divorce and alimony law, and equal rights for illegitimate children were all identified as SDAP policies that benefited women.[66] The "New Woman" addressed by the party is not an intellectual bluestocking or even a hedonistic flapper, but rather a woman very much interested in marriage, reproduction, and the family.

Leading SDAP women theorized marriage as "an erotic-comradely bind between equals," yet party representatives also argued that women could not stand equally at men's side until social services for mothers and children were radically expanded.[67] In many ways, women were asked to subsume their needs to that of the developing social democracy, which could serve them best only when it was stronger. Reproductive issues like abortion law reform and relational issues like divorce statutes fell under this rubric. The arguments of private Viennese organizations that campaigned for abortion and divorce law reform, such as the *Bund gegen Mutterschaftszwang*, the *Bund für Mutterschutz*, and the *Eherechtreformverein* were countered by SDAP ideologues with calls for greater socialization. For example, Therese Schlesinger wrote in "On the Problem of Motherhood" that women who eased their workloads under the "double burden" by limiting their offspring were going about emancipation the wrong way; instead, they should organize and demand communal households and better social welfare.⁶⁸ In a similar vein, party member Heinrich Albert told his readers that only the removal of private property would reform the institution of marriage, and thus dismissed divorce law reform as an ineffective cause.⁶⁹

Interesting exceptions to this logic were the sexual messages for adults embedded in the SDAP's "Guidelines for the Sexual *Aufklärung* of Youth." In this document, men and women were acknowledged as having and exercising sexual agency, although the party asked them to (ideally) sublimate some of their energy to cultural and political production. Guideline 1 stated the political nature of sex: "Sexual relations fulfill a physiological and psychological need, the satisfaction of which, however, also has social consequences. Therefore sexual activity is not simply a private matter."⁷⁰ Guideline 4 reminded advice givers that chastity and abstinence affect each individual differently, and that they may be appropriate options for some men and women. In contrast, overindulgence of the sex drive dulled the erotic palate, and interfered with work ability. However, Guideline 7 clearly denounced the "bourgeois morality" that asked men and women to live without sex until they were married and furthermore turned a blind eye to male extramarital sexual activity while harshly judging women who made the same choices. Guideline 10 furthered this sentiment by announcing that "sexual activity should not be shameful for either partner. Bourgeois morality judged a [sexually active] girl physically, psychically, and socially, although it indulged her male lover, the indignation of which must strike every thinking person."⁷¹ Guidelines 12 and 13 identified recent innovations in contraceptives as a gain to society, because they freed "marital and extramarital erotic life from reproductive anxieties, which very often gave rise to nervous diseases," and protected sexually active people from contracting venereal infections.⁷² Finally, marriage was described as a positive, lasting commitment, although the party was loathe to replay the mistakes made by the Roman Catholic Church in its efforts to regulate marriage. Guideline 16 noted smugly: "The Church failed to eradicate prostitution and divorce." As a result, the SDAP identified "the life-long commitment of a love union as a goal to strive for," with the caveat that this union "must not be attained by any legal, economic, or other pressure."⁷³ In these guidelines, the right to sexual pleasure was consistently linked to the concepts of free will and responsibility. Rather than release Viennese citizens from the sexual shackles of the Church, the SDAP acknowledged their need for sexual satisfaction while asking them to, whenever possible, sublimate their sexual feelings to cultural production or committed partnership.

Catholic Sexual Advice

As suggested earlier, the Social Democratic approach to female sexuality did not simply replace Catholic doctrine in the interwar period. Rather, sex was a contested sphere of influence. Amidst the SDAP's utopian visions of communal households, extra-legal yet committed relationships, birth control opportunities, and sexual satisfaction for adult women, it is important to remember that a majority of the women in Austria were practicing Catholics with at least some sort of allegiance to the Church's forms of sex, marriage and family life. While it is interesting to speculate on the ways in which individual women, and especially SDAP voters, modified and interpreted Church laws for their own use, such research is beyond the scope of this project. Instead, I will present the views of both Austrian Catholic leaders and Papal authority on adult female sexual education and advice. As emphasized in the previous chapter, Catholic doctrine stood firm on the sacrament of one, indissoluble marriage. For unmarried persons, the states of virginity and chastity were defended, and demanded.

Innsbruck Theology professor Michael Glatterer published an advice book for adult Catholics in 1927 entitled *In the Light of Belief: Christian Thoughts on Sexual Life*. Chapter 5 of his manual, "Virginity," was also published as a brochure in the same year. *Virginity* was a mystical meditation on the physical state of purity (in men and women) largely divorced from the social and material conditions of Austria at the time. It reiterated the biblical authority rather than making any kind of contemporary argument, stating succinctly: "Marriage is good, virginity is better."[74] For those who needed a more graduated example of right Catholic sexual behavior, Glatterer provided the following:

> Marriage is a form of purity, because Christian married people deny themselves all forbidden forms of sexual enjoyment. The chastity of widows stands higher still, if following the death of their husband they deny themselves of their own free will the allowed [sexual] satisfaction (in a second marriage). The highest rung belongs to the chastity of the unmarried Christian, because he totally renounces sexual enjoyment for his whole life; this is the complete conquest of the spirit over the flesh; of service over the fallen nature of man.[75]

A sharp hierarchy of purity dominates this quotation. Married people, who renounce all forms of non-procreative sex (including masturbation), are living at the most basic, minimum level of chastity. Widows able to renounce a second marriage, although they presumably enjoyed a chaste married sex-life with their now departed husbands and are allowed by Church law to enter into another sexual union, are even more highly praised than married women still engaging in intercourse. Only life-long virginity, however, can truly claim victory over original sin. There is no description of an adult virgin, male or female, as anxiety-prone or enfeebled.

Glatterer's book, *In the Light of Belief*, expanded the discussion of proper sexual behavior by addressing married life more fully. Citing the *Catholic Guidelines and Instructions on Various Modern Morality Questions* published by German and Austrian bishops in the previous year, Glatterer as a theologian identified the two principal mistakes made by would-be sex reform advocates. First, reformist logic asked people to take Nature as a guide, although the Church clearly asks adults to overcome the base, "natural" sexual drives. Second, sex reformers had responded to post-war material want by twisting "marriage into something immoral and seeing the creation of children as the work of the devil."[76] Natural sexual instincts and difficult living conditions were not new problems, Glatterer implicitly argued, and certainly did not justify the creation of a new morality vis-à-vis marriage. *In the Light of Belief* served as a counterpoint to the faulty logic of sex reformers.

Glatterer's work sought to remind women that, despite recent cultural developments, the Church's views on gender and sexuality remained constant. Nudity, no matter if it should become theorized and celebrated through *Nacktkultur*, was still was a sign of "heathendom."[77] Modern fashion, in so far that it sought to "blur the difference between young men and young women," robbed women of their natural feelings of shame and sorely tested the faith and purity of the men around them.[78] Finally, although virginity was of the highest virtue, Glatterer reminded his readers of the Pauline dictum that it was far better to marry than to burn: "Certainly virginal love for God is gold, and married love is silver. But when one has but little gold, one is poorer than married folk, who possess plenty of silver."[79]

Glatterer's authorial tone stood against the onslaught of modern life and changing sexual attitudes. An illuminating contrast to his attitude is provided by a fellow theologian teaching at the University of Vienna, Dr. Rudolf Allers. In his exhaustive work, *Sexual Pedagogy: Basic Principles and Rules*, Allers showed a willingness to adopt some of the language and concepts made popular by psychoanalysis and lifestyle reformers. The *Ich*, the *Selbst*, and the *Gemeinschaft* peppered his discussion of the role of sex in marriage, and the subsequent role of marriage in the community. Like his socialist counterparts, Allers described marriage as a partnership and a courageous adventure. In an almost Adlerian tone, Allers emphatically recommended cooperation and mutual self-sacrifice as keys to a successful union, in which community was transformed into a sacrament. In his arguments, sex had the ability to extend and prolong sentiment between the partners, yet could not be the basis for the creation, from the household out, of a true community.[80] Proper gender roles, rather, insured that a "We" could be built out of two lives, just as God created humanity (*Menschen*) out of man and woman.[81] Allers recommended "intimate knowledge of the specific gender roles" to those who would be better prepared for marriage, as he claimed that most marital problems arise out of a mutual ignorance of gender particularities.[82] Such intimate knowledge could only be learned in the bosom of a traditional family. Allers thus counseled mothers to teach their children according to their "gender membership," and especially not to poison their daughters with the impression that women's lot in marriage was unfair.[83] To do so would teach girls to see prospective husbands as opponents rather than partners, and thus destroy her chances of creating a sacred partnership.

Writing in 1934, Allers could afford to apply conciliatory psychological approaches to Christian marriage, because he could refer back to the solid rock of Papal authority on the matter. On the final day of 1930, Pope Pius XI announced his Encyclical letter *Casti connubii* (On Christian Marriage). Fulfilling the role of the Church as a teacher, Papal encyclicals were translated immediately into vernacular languages and then published by Catholic Order presses.[84] *Casti connubii* synthesized Catholic thought on marriage, and clearly stated for the first time official doctrine regarding modern developments in divorce, birth control, abortion, and eugenics—all of which received grave proscriptions. In closing this section on Catholic sexual advice, I will mine *Casti connubii* for its depiction of the role of sex within marriage and its implications for Viennese women.

Pius XI opened his letter with the observation that "A great number of men ... either ignorantly or shamelessly decry the great sanctity of Christian wedlock, or relying on the principles of a new and utterly perverse morality, too often trample it under foot."[85] Although this papal letter was addressed to all the world's faithful, surely Viennese readers and listeners must have recognized the attack in terms of local attempts to reform marriage and control reproduction. Pius XI established exclusive jurisdiction over marriage for the Church and identified children as the first and primary blessing of matrimony. Two secondary blessings of matrimony followed: cohabitation (sex) of the married couple and mutual inward molding of the husband and wife. In these blessings, the audience could recognize a companionate marriage cemented by sexual intercourse, similar to those recommended by Christian and socialist sex counselors alike. However, *Casti Connubii* emphasized not the blessings of matrimony, but rather detailed "the evils opposed to each of the benefits of matrimony," which included non-reproductive sexual intercourse and the destruction of unborn offspring.[86]

First priority in all matters of marital relations was to be given to the offspring, and Pius XI thus discussed the fallacy of artificial birth control in dramatic and aggressive language. Pius XI denounced recent arguments for limiting family size and reminded his audience that only virtuous continence and the observance of what were called "safe" or "sterile" periods were allowed to married couples by the Church.[87] If couples were willing to frame all sexual activity within the boundaries of reproduction, however, they could enjoy sex as a natural element of the sacrament of marriage:

> For in matrimony as well as in the use of matrimonial rights there are also secondary ends, such as marital aid, the cultivating of mutual love, and the quieting of concupiscence which husband and wife are not forbidden to consider so long as these are subordinated to the primary end and so long as the intrinsic nature of the act is preserved.[88]

This formulation of the role of sex in marriage allowed men and women to strengthen their emotional ties through physical love. The freedom of women to enjoy sex within marriage was thus also affirmed by the Church. However, this freedom was only available to those whose unions were blessed by the Church. Pius XI explicitly condemned any other kind of lasting relationship:

> Some men go so far as to concoct a new species of unions, suited, as they say, to the present temper of men and of the times, which various new forms of matrimony they presume to label *temporary, experimental,* and *companionate*. These offer all the indulgence of matrimony and its rights without, however, the indissoluble bond, and without offspring, unless the parties alter their cohabitation into a matrimony in the full sense of the [Church] law.[89]

Pius XI condemned such relationships as "hateful abominations" and predicted that their popularity, if unchecked, could "reduce our truly cultured nations to the barbarous standards of savage peoples."[90]

Casti Connubii is a rich source for scholars interested in Catholic responses to birth control and, especially, eugenic state programs. These famous sections of the encyclical have overshadowed the more routine subject that Pius XI chooses as his endpoint: "the honorable and trusting obedience which the woman owes to the man" within matrimony.[91] *Casti connubii* roundly rejected any claim of equality between the sexes, whether in social, economic, or marital. Women were commanded to defer to their husbands' authority in all matters. This deference, the Pope wrote, was necessary maintain the unity of the couple:

> [Unity] forbids that exaggerated liberty which cares not for the good of the family; it forbids that in this body which is the family the heart be separated from the head, to the great detriment of the whole body and the proximate danger of ruin. For if the man is the head, the woman is the heart; and as he occupies the chief place in ruling, so she may and ought to claim for herself the chief place in love.[92]

Casti connubii thus favored the unity of the couple over women's equality within marriage. In doing so, it provides a great contrast with the emancipatory messages for women implicit in other formulations of a companionate, sexually fulfilling marriage.

Conclusions

The materials I have presented in this chapter represent a wide range of sexual advice. The Viennese sex reform movement's means of public outreach are relatively easy to chart: increased published material, journalism, advice columns, clinics, public lectures, film, and hours open to consultation. Catholic authorities spread their sexual advice through papal letter, popular brochures, academic investigations, and sermons. But I would like to comment here on two of the implications of interwar sex advice literature for and about women: the de-medicalization of sex as a topic and the use of melodrama to appeal to public sentiment.

The interwar period represents a shift in the way that medical authority was exercised among sex educators and proponents of sex reform. Although many of the authors I have surveyed still used their medical or academic titles in the front-page, there is a decided movement away from relying upon science alone to make popular *Aufklärung* arguments. As Glaessner, himself a medical doctor, explained in the opening of *Sex-Life Problems*, our understandings of sex are culturally constructed, and "a purely medical inquiry into our sexual lives is not enough to satisfactorily explain or do justice to all of the relationships among humans."[93] He assured his readers that not only medicine, but also sociological, anthropological, and racial-hygienic factors were considered in his study. Yet Glaessner's willingness to dilute medical authority with cultural insights was limited. Although doctors might use sociology or history to understand general sexual behavior, Glaessner still recommended medical intervention on an individual level. In his *Aufklärung* text designed for young women, *Ripe for Love!*, Glaessner exhorted his audience to seek a doctor's care at the slightest suggestion of physical abnormality.[94] In her work, Lazarsfeld suggested that the medical establishment's grip on sex education materials was not the problem, but rather, that the lack of women's input to the study of sex had made it sterile. Even texts written specifically for women had failed to get at the female sexual experience, leaving society with studies "not so much about the sexual life of women as they are campaigns against the sexual life of men."[95] As a member of Wilhelm Reich's Socialistic Society for Sexual Research, Lazarsfeld was deeply committed to her work at sex counseling centers. This meant that she rejected medical discussions of women as a "type," and preferred to offer real-life examples culled from her experience as a care-giver, while still encouraging her readers to seek professional medical and psychiatric help to combat sexual dysfunction and unhappiness. Lazarsfeld also supported the development of sex and marital advice columns in non-medical publications as a means of public outreach, as their question-and-answer format not only addressed an individual crisis, but also added to community knowledge.[96] Finally, the Viennese birth-control advocate Johann Ferch inscribed his paean to romantic sexuality *World of the Erotic* with a promise to lift sex reform away from the bounds of medical knowledge, declaring: "This book was not written with the feather of a doctor, because the entire corpus regarding the pounding, precious joy of love between the sexes should not be represented as a collection of pathological case studies, but rather as the fruit of knowledge for human happiness and *joie de vivre*."[97] Despite its lurid title, Ferch's *World of the Erotic* celebrated sex within marriage as an emotional tie and recommended nothing more suggestive than tendernesses before retiring to a shared bed. Ferch, whose prolific appeals for sex-reform spanned the 1920s, aimed his purple prose at the hearts of his readers rather than their sex-drives.

All respondents in the realm of sexual education in the First Republic agreed upon the necessity of preserving gender differences while expanding women's sexual options and knowledge. This was reflected in a particular gendering of the mode of expression in sexual advice for and about women—away from clinical evidence and towards melodrama. Melodrama, a form of storytelling popularized in the nineteenth century, was well suited to the task of unmasking the secrets of adult sexuality. It abounds in the sources I've presented in this book: the poverty and suffering of women without recourse to birth control, the injustice of marriage laws that bind unsuitable or brutal partners to each other, the lurking diseases of one's marriage partner that indicate an unsavory past, and the emotional testimony of advice-seekers and their erstwhile counselors. Particularly striking in *Aufklärung* literature was the female body's capacity to suffer silently through disease, frequent pregnancies, and marital brutality. Kitaj, Glaessner, and Lazarsfeld, although approaching women's sexuality from very different political positions, all used case studies that illustrated the physical dangers to which sexual activity exposed women. Portraying personal or familial pain within a melodramatic framework was also employed in the widespread anti-alcohol and VD-awareness programs of the period. Although abortion-rights advocates used this same imagery to argue for women's rights to control their own bodies and thus minimize the transmission of hereditary disease, the state and the SDAP itself was unwilling to compromise on this issue.

Melodrama's morally unambiguous world of victims and villains, and particularly its trope of female exploitation, made it an effective medium for the *Aufklärung* movement. For writers and organizers seeking public support and/or municipal funding to alleviate the suffering of Vienna's poor, a melodramatic litany of seduction, abandonment, brutality, rape, hunger and attempted abortions proved more effective than a scientific index of population figures or even a racialized anthropological exploration of the poor. Perhaps most importantly, melodrama as a form highlighted, through extravagant and emotional expression, the persecution of the good and the final triumph of virtue. And virtue was the role of woman: suffering, rebelling, yet ultimately not able to extricate herself from disaster without the help of a loving father or, more often, a sympathetic suitor capable of becoming a companionate husband. Here, certainly, lies the weakness of melodrama from the feminist historian's prospective: melodrama denied women the ability to emancipate themselves. However, this fact did not deter, or perhaps even bother, interwar feminists, sex advice advocates, or the common women of Vienna, all of whom framed their sexual questions and social contexts within melodramatic terms. Perhaps in a time when cooperation and social welfare were deemed so necessary, the need for women to rescue themselves was less felt. Certainly melodrama did extend to women the idea that justice, including sexual justice, was the right of all actors. Threats, lies, and dire situations would be dispelled by the end of the act by the hero, who ultimately protected women from the forces that victimized. In sexual educational materials, these forces might also be faceless villains like ignorance, poverty, or disease. Could not the hero also be anonymous, in the form of an author or sympathetic clinic provider? For educators seeking to convince popular audiences to be sexually responsible, melodramatic testimonies and sketches provided, simply and powerfully, a means to communicate prophylactic sexual knowledge.

Notes

1. See Erwin J. Haeberle, *The Birth of Sexology: A Brief History in Documents* (Washington, DC: Scientific Committee for the Sixth World Congress of Sexology, 1983); Harry Oosterhuis, *Stepchildren of Nature: Krafft-Ebing, Psychiatry, and the Making of Sexual Identity* (Chicago: University of Chicago Press, 2000); Siobhan B. Somerville, "Scientific Racism and the Invention of the Homosexual Body," in Lucy Bland and Laura Doan (eds.), *Sexology in Culture: Labeling Bodies and Desires* (Chicago: University of Chicago Press, 1998), 60–77; and Lucy Bland and Laura Doan, "General Introduction," in Bland and Doan (eds.), *Sexology Uncensored: The Documents of Sexual Science* (Chicago: University of Chicago Press, 1998), 1–9.
2. My definition of melodrama is particularly shaped by Peter Brooks, *The Melodramatic Imagination: Balzac, Henry James, and the Mode of Excess* (New Haven: Yale University Press, 1976), Martha Vicinus, "'Helpless and Unfriended': Nineteenth-Century Domestic Melodrama," *New Literary History* 13:1 (Autumn 1981), 127–143, and Susan Grogan, "Playing the Princess: Flora Tristan, Performance, and Female Moral Authority in the July Monarchy," in Jo Burr Margadant (ed.), *The New Biography: Performing Femininity in Nineteenth-Century France* (Berkeley: University of California Press, 2000).
3. While it would be very interesting to consider German nationalist (right-wing, anti-Semitic) attitudes towards sexuality and advice to women, I did not find sustained published evidence of this kind of material in my research.
4. For an excellent parsing of Imperial divorce law, see Ulrike Harmat, "Divorce and Remarriage in Austria-Hungary: The Second Marriage of Franz Conrad von Hötzendorf," *Austrian Studies Yearbook* 32 (2001), 69–103.
5. See Ulrike Harmat, *Ehe auf Widerruf?* (Wien: Klostermann, 1999) for Austrian divorce law and contemporary attempts at marriage law reform, 1918–1938.
6. See Karin Lehner, *Verpönte Eingriffe: sozialdemokratische Reformbestrebungen zu den Abtreibungsbestimmungen in der Zwischenkriegszeit* (Wien: Picus Verlag, 1989). A woman who attempted abortion could be jailed for up to one year, and a woman who successfully aborted a fetus could be sentenced to one to five years. Assisting midwives and doctors were subject to the same terms. Judges, however, were free to reduce or cancel sentences.
7. Rudolf Goldscheid, *Frauenfrage und Menschenökonomie* (Wien: Anzengruberverlag, 1913), 24–25. The Anzengruberverlag published many of the sex reform texts I've collected, pointing towards a political commitment on their part and/or a clear understanding of the selling power of sex.
8. I take the concept of the New Mother from Katherina von Ankum, who traces her development in interwar German-language culture in "Motherhood and the 'New Woman'": Vicki Baum's *stud. chem. Helene Willfüer* and Irmgard Keun's *Gilgi – eine von uns*, in *Women in Ger-*

many Yearbook 11 (1995), 171–188. See also Gertraud Ratzenböch, "Mutterliebe: Bemerkungen zur gesellschaftlich konstruierten Verknüpfung von Mutterliebe und Familie," in Monika Bernold (Hg.), *Familie: Arbeitsplatz oder Ort des Glücks?* (Wien: Picus Verlag, 1990), 19–50.

9. Ute Frevert has persuasively shown that the German New Woman of interwar imagination was far less free, economically or socially, than she was originally depicted. See Ute Frevert, "Vom Klavier zur Schriebmaschine," in Annete Kuhn und Gerhard Schneider (hg.), *Frauen in der Geschichte* (Düsseldorf: Pädagogischer Verlag Schwann, 1982), 82–112. For a specifically Viennese study, see Helmut Gruber, "The 'New Woman': Realities and Illusions of Gender Equality in Red Vienna," in Helmut Gruber and Pamela Graves (eds.), *Women and Socialism, Socialism and Women: Europe between the Two World Wars* (New York: Berghahn Books, 1998), 56–94.

10. See Ulrike Felt, "'Öffentliche' Wissenschaft: Zur Beziehung von Naturwissenschaften und Gesellschaft in Wien von der Jahrhundertwende bis zum Ende der Ersten Republik," *Österreichischen Zeitgeschichte* 7 (1996), 45–66.

11. See Alfred Pfoser, "Der Wiener 'Reigen-Skandal': Sexualangst als politisches Syndrom der Ersten Republik," in Helmut Konrad (hg.), *Die deutsche und die österreichische Arbeiterbewegung zur Zeit der Zweiten Internationale* (Wien: Europaverlag, 1982), 663–719.

12. J. Kitaj, *Das Normale und das Kranke Sexualleben des Mannes und des Weibs* (Wien: Anzengruberverlag, 1913), 18. This book originally appeared as an article in the *Allgemeinen Wiener Wochenschrift*, and went through at least five editions, with expansions in its sections on male perversion and homosexuality.

13. Kitaj, *Sexualleben*, 6.

14. Kitaj, *Sexualleben*, 13, 9, and 11, respectively.

15. Kitaj, *Sexualleben*, 9.

16. Sofie Lazarsfeld, *Wie die Frau der Mann Erlebt: Fremde Bekenntnisse und eigene Betrachtungen* (Wien: Verlag für Sexualwissenschaft/Schneider & Co., 1931), 17.

17. Rudolf Glaessner, *Rief zur Liebe! Eine ärztliche Aufklärungsschrift über alles Wissenswerte im Liebes- und Geschlechtsleben des Weibes* (Wien: Anzengruberverlag, 1921), 5.

18. Glaessner, *Rief zur Liebe!*, 22–23.

19. Theodore Van der Velde, *Ideal Marriage: Its Physiology and Technique*, translated by Stella Brown (New York: Random House, 1930), 168–169. For a critical reading of Van der Velde's spermatic political economy, see M.E. Melody and Linda M. Peterson, *Teaching America about Sex: Marriage Guides and Sex Manuals from the Late Victorians to Dr. Ruth* (New York: New York University Press, 1999), 93–107.

20. Lazarsfeld, *Wie die Frau der Mann Erlebt*, 150–155.

21. Lazarsfeld, *Wie die Frau der Mann Erlebt*, 297.

22. Lazarsfeld, *Wie die Frau der Mann Erlebt*, 130.

23. This is the subject of chapter 2 of this book.

24. Elsa und Dr. Med. R. Tauber, *Der Mann – Ein Buch für Frauen* (Wien: Rhombus Verlag, 1925), 7.

25. Taubers, *Der Mann*, 46.

26. Glaessner, *Rief zur Liebe!*, 10–12.

27. See chapter 1 of this book.

28. Ministerialrat Dr.Wilhelm Eisenschiml, "Die Bekämpfung der Geschlechtskrankheiten in Österreich," *Das Österreichische Gesundheitswesen*, Hg. Volksgesundheitsamt der Gemeinde Wien (Wien: Wirtschafts-Zeitungs-Verlag-Gesellschaft, 1930), 18.

29. See especially Glaessner, *Rief zur Liebe*, 60–61.

30. Lazarsfeld, *Wie die Frau der Mann Erlebt*, 302.

31. Joseph Carl Schlegel, *Hygiene des Ehelebens: Der Führer zu Liebes- und Eheglücks* (Wien: Verlag Schusdeks, 1929), 123, 127, 129–131.

32. Glaessner, *Rief zur Liebe!*, 42.

33. Glaessner, *Rief zur Liebe!*, 42.
34. It is unclear whether the Society for Birth Control is the same entity as Betty and Johann Ferch's Society Against Forced Motherhood, explored in chapter 4. Maria Mesner suggests that the latter changed its name to the Society for Birth Control in 1925. See Maria Mesner, "Educating Reasonable Lovers: Sex Counseling in Austria in the First Half of the Twentieth Century," in Günter Bischof, Anton Pelinka, and Dagmar Herzog (eds.), *Sexuality in Austria* (New Brunswick: Transaction Publishers, 2007), 48–64, 55.
35. "Was sich Frauen von der Seele reden," *Die Unzufriedene* 10/27 (16 Juli 1932), 7.
36. Johann Ferch, *Die Welt der Erotik* (Leipzig: Parthenon Verlag, 1929), 152; Glaessner, *Rief zur Liebe!*, 45.
37. "Eine Beratungsstelle für Männer," *Die Unzufriedene* 9/40 (10 Oktober 1931), 5.
38. Sigmund Freud, "Die 'kulturelle' Sexualmoral und die moderne Nervosität," *Sexual-Probleme* 1/3 (März 1908), 122.
39. Wilhelm Stekel, "Sexual Abstinence and Health," in *Sexual Continence*, William J. Robinson (ed.), (New York: Eugenics Publishing Co., 1924), 178.
40. Alfred Adler, *What Life Should Mean to You* (Boston: Little, Brown, and Co., 1931), 280.
41. Stopes was translated into German in the immediate post-war period. Lazarsfeld tells us that Stopes's work was popular in Vienna, particularly among women. Stopes's "overnight sensation," *Married Love*, was particularly concerned with women's rights to sexual pleasure in marriage, but reader response led her to argue in her later work that this pleasure could only be secured through birth control. See Angus McLaren, *A History of Contraception: From Antiquity to the Present Day* (Oxford: Blackwell, 1990), 217–221.
42. This theory was widely popularized by Theodore Van der Velde's *Ideal Marriage*.
43. Dr. Paul Stein, "Wann ist die Frau emphängnisfähig?," *Die Unzufriedene* 10/21 (4 Juni 1932), 4.
44. Therese Schlesinger, *Die Frau im sozialdemokratischen Partieprogramm* (Wien: Verlag der organisation Wien der sozialdemokratischen Partei, 1928), 14.
45. For an excellent history of SDAP anti-alcohol activity, see Johanna Gehmacher, "Vom Glück der Nüchternheit: Ein Sozialdemokratischer Entwurf um Alkohol und Familie," in Monika Bernhold (hg.), *Familie: Arbeitsplatz oder Ort des Glücks?* (Wien: Picus Verlag, 1990), 51–79.
46. Sidonie Springer, "Heraus mit dem Alkoholverbot!" (1922), Verein für Geschichte der Arbeiterbewegung, Wien, Lade 6/Mappe 34A.
47. Prof. Dr. R. Fetscher, "Willst du eine gusunde Ehe führen?," *Die Unzufriedene* 9/31 (8 August 1931), 3.
48. Prof. Dr. A. Forel, "Alkohol und Keimzellen (Blastophthorische Entartung)," *Muenschener Medizinische Wochenschrift* 58/49 (5 Dezember 1911), 2596.
49. The socialist woman's weekly *Die Unzufriedene* ran articles suggesting exercise regimes straight through its printing history. See, for example, the letter from Elise Hartmann in the column "Was sich Frauen von der Seele reden," *Die Unzufriedene* 9/32 (15 August 1931), 7; or the essay by Willi Flaschitz, "Leibesübungen und Körperpflege," *Die Unzufriedene* 11/19 (7 Mai 1933), 4, which invited women to attend a mixed gender summer program of gymnastics done to music, taught by a reader of the magazine who also served as a mentor at the "Socialist Lifestyle Reform" advice center.
50. Rudolf Glaessner, *Die Problem des Geschlechteslebens: Die Liebe von Mann und Weib von Liebesglück und Ehe* (Wien: Anzengruber Verlag, 1931 [Drittes Auflage]), 26 and 28, respectively. Emphasis mine.
51. Lazarsfeld, *Wie die Frau der Mann Erlebt*, 107.
52. For example, Wilhelm Reich and some of his colleagues in the Socialistic Society for Sexual Research fall under this category.
53. Lazarsfeld, *Wie die Frau der Mann Erlebt*, 298.
54. Taubers, *Der Mann*, 157–158.

55. "Nehmt auch die Männer mit!," *Die Unzufriedene* 10/25 (25 Juni 1932), 7. Emphasis in original.
56. Schlegel, *Hygiene des Ehelebens*, 84.
57. Lazarsfeld, *Wie die Frau der Mann Erlebt*, 132.
58. Schlegel, *Hygiene des Ehelebens*, 149.
59. "Der Leidensweg der Frau," *Die Unzufriedene* 9/22 (6 Juli 1931), 7.
60. Dr. Karl Kautsky, "Eheberatung," in *Die Frau* 10 (Oktober 1929), 9.
61. See chapter 4 for a more detailed account of Kautsky and the Municipal Marriage Advice Center.
62. Kautsky, "Eheberatung," 11.
63. Therese Schlesinger, "Zur Evolution der Erotik," *Der Kampf* 16/11 (16 November 1923), 368.
64. Schlesinger, "Evolution," 370.
65. In 1923, the SDAP captured a narrow majority of first-time women voters in Vienna.
66. *Die Neue Frau* (Wien: Verlag der Organisation Wien der sozialdemokratischen Partei, 1924), 12–15.
67. Helene Bauer, "Ehe und soziale Schichtung," *Der Kampf* 20/7 (Juli 1927), 332, and Reschy Fischer, "Ehe als soziales Problem," *Der Kampf* 20/8 (August 1927), 390, respectively.
68. Therese Schlesinger, "Zum Problem der Mutterschaft," *Der Kampf* 20/9 (September 1927), 476.
69. Heinrich Albert, "Soziale Entwicklung und Ehe," *Der Kampf* 20/9 (September 1927), 474.
70. Therese Schlesinger and Dr. Paul Stein, "Leitsätze für die sexuelle Aufklärung der Jugend," *Bildungsarbeit* 19 (1932), 234. For the purposes of my research, I have used a reprint of this article, available in its entirety in Hildegard Feistritzer's *Ansätze zur Sexualerziehung in der Sozialdemokratischen Jugendbewegung in der Zeit ihrer Entstehung* (Ph.D. dissertation: Universität Wien, 1978), 129–135.
71. Schlesinger und Stein, "Leitsätze," in Feistritzer, *Sexualerziehung*, 133.
72. Schlesinger und Stein, "Leitsätze," in Feistritzer, *Sexualerziehung*, 134.
73. Schlesinger und Stein, "Leitsätze," in Feistritzer, *Sexualerziehung*, 134.
74. Michael Glatterer, *Die Jungfräulichkeit* (Innsbruck: Verlag von Felician Rauch, 1927), 2.
75. Glatterer, *Jungfräulichkeit*, 1.
76. Michael Glatterer, *Im Glaubenslicht. Christliche Gedanken über das Geschlechtsleben* (Innsbruck: Verlag Felician Rauch, 1927), 3.
77. Glatterer, *Im Glaubenslicht*, 24.
78. Glatterer, *Im Glaubenslicht*, 41–42.
79. Glatterer, *Im Glaubenslicht*, 96.
80. Dr. Rudolf Allers, *Sexualpädagogik: Grundlagen und Grundlinien* (Salzburg: Verlag Anton Pustet, 1934), 249.
81. Allers, *Sexualpädagogik*, 265.
82. Allers, *Sexualpädagogik*, 253 and 264, respectively.
83. Allers, *Sexualpädagogik*, 253.
84. Etienne Lepicard, "Eugenics and Roman Catholicism. An Encyclical Letter in Context: *Casti connubii*, December 31, 1930," *Science in Context* 11:3–4 (1988), 530.
85. As quoted in Alvah Sulloway, *Birth Control and Catholic Doctrine* (Boston: Beacon Hill, 1959), 43.
86. "Pius XI (1930)," as reprinted in Susan Groag Bell and Karen M. Offen, (eds.), *Women, the Family, and Freedom: The Debate in Documents*, vol. II, 1880–1950 (Stanford: Stanford University Press, 1983), 310.
87. "Nor are those considered as acting against nature who, in the married state, use their right in the proper manner although on account of natural reasons either of time or of certain defects, new life cannot be brought forth." It is not clear whether the menstrual cycle here is appearing under "time" or as a "certain defect." See "Pius XI (1930)," in Bell and Offen, 311.

88. "Pius XI (1930)," in Bell and Offen, 311.
89. Pius XI, *On Christian Marriage* (New York: The Barry Vail Corporation, 1931), 25. Emphasis in original.
90. Pius XI, *Christian Marriage*, 25.
91. "Pius XI (1930)," in Bell and Offen, 313.
92. Pius XI, *Christian Marriage*, 13–14.
93. Glaessner, *Problem des Geschlechteslebens*, 4.
94. Glaessner, *Rief zur Liebe!*, 3.
95. Lazarsfeld, *Wie die Frau der Mann Erlebt*, 2.
96. Lazarsfeld, *Wie die Frau der Mann Erlebt*, 12–13.
97. Ferch, *Welt der Erotik*, Vorwort.

Chapter 4

CLINIC CULTURE

"A Piece of Advice for Those Entering into Marriage"

You are about to get married, thus it is of the greatest importance that you heed the following:

The health of the marriage partner is, for the happiness of the marriage, more important than money and property.

Disease in a marriage partner damages their own work-strength, lessens the ability to work, obliges the other partner to increased work, reduces the joy of living, and brings grief and worry into the house.

Diseases, even when they are not hereditary, very often damage the offspring, so that they either are born already weak or sick, or later easily fall ill. A wealth of such diseases can only be detected by a doctor, and by a doctor alone.

Whoever enters into a marriage, without establishing for himself whether or not they are healthy, assumes a heavy responsibility vis-à-vis their marriage partner and their offspring.

Therefore, everyone has the moral duty, before they enter into marriage, to seek the judgment of his state of health from a specialist doctor. The doctor is legally bound to absolute discretion. Should a disease be established, the doctor should be asked if the disease has the ability to harm the marriage. If this is the case, respectability and honor demands that the individual shares this knowledge with his fiancé.

Whoever celebrates a marriage without bringing their disease to the attention of his fiancé infringes on his own well-being and the well-being of his family.

Everyone who enters into marriage should demand medical proof of his future partner's physical and mental health. One must not see it as sign of mistrust, but rather consider it as an important preventative measure that can protect against the greatest unhappiness. For parents or their legal representatives, it is a duty of conscience to have the state of their children's health clarified when these children are applying for marriage.

He who conscientiously follows these warnings spares himself from future self-reproach and remorse.[1]

Vienna Municipal Marriage Advice Center, 1922

Viennese municipal medical care underwent a radical transformation in the first third of the twentieth century. In the late Imperial period, poor-relief clinics funded by charity and staffed by volunteer medical students and doctors attended to individual clients' injuries and illnesses. During the First Republic, this system of emergency care was replaced by a web of highly specialized municipally funded clinics staffed by caregivers who were also civil servants. The goal of these municipal services was to combat disease on a society-wide level, rather than simply to attend to discrete cases of illness. World War I, in particular, changed the way medical care was theorized in Vienna. The city's ability to care for its citizens was strained a variety of factors: its own weakened and malnourished population, injured returning veterans, increased concern that venereal disease would re-enter the home front, and the influenza epidemic of 1918. The resulting new approaches to civic hygiene, and particularly reproductive health, were fore-grounded in chapter 1. In the present chapter, I explore the culture of interwar clinics that administered to the sexual questions and concerns of Vienna's inhabitants.

In the 1920s, sexual information was formatted in a radically new way: the advice clinic. In Scandinavia, the United States, and German-speaking central Europe, individuals (or couples) could come face-to-face with official, medical sexual knowledge that previously might have been found only in books. In interwar Vienna, three types of sexual advice clinics were founded. A municipal center, an independent constellation of reproductive rights clinics, and a series of communist sexual advice offices all offered *Sprechstunden* ("office hours") consultations to the general public. In these *Sprechstunden*, the twin goals of individual aid and social prevention were combined in a dialogical exchange between caregiver and client. The *Sprechstunden* offered by Vienna's sex advice clinics were at the center of what I call "clinic culture": a format of communication somewhere between the doctor's office and the confessional. The confessional mnemonic formula developed by the Roman Catholic Church for priests to use in establishing the character of sin—*quis, quid, ubi, quibus auxiliis, cur, quomodo, quando*—was, perhaps unintentionally, appropriated in the practice of interwar medical counselors seeking to identify the nature of their patient's sexual problems.[2] In the *Sprechstunden*, however, the goal of confession shifted from the remission of individual sexual sin to the establishment of new standards of sexual health. As this chapter will show, clinic culture also opened up a space in which individuals were allowed to initiate and augment their own sexual *Aufklärung*. The sexual education of Viennese men, women, and children was not limited to the printed sexual information, analyzed in the preceding two chapters, available to them. Instead, they were invited to visit centers across the city that promised the explanation of sexual matters and the alleviation of sexual distress. In this chapter, I explore the varying philosophies of the three types of Viennese sex advice clinics, the services they offered, and the limits of their outreach. Using medical forms, associational records, conference proceedings, and advertisements, I analyze the language each type of clinic used to talk about marriage, sexual activity, and procreation.

A wide range of sexual knowledge was dispensed in the clinic culture of interwar Vienna. Before I begin discussion of the clinics themselves, I want to outline the kinds of knowledge imparted within them. As this chapter illustrates, each of the advice clinics answered their clients' sexual questions in different ways. Yet all of the responses were designed to answer the following concerns: what was normal, what was responsible, and what would, if not lead to happiness, at least not cause permanent physical harm. The answers provided to these questions were embedded in discourses based in medical knowledge that stressed social change.

One of the thorniest types of discourse used to convey sexual knowledge in interwar Vienna was eugenic. In chapter 1, eugenic thought was introduced in connection with the Viennese welfare system created by Julius Tandler. The term "eugenics" was rarely used in pre-*Anschluß* Austria; *Menschenökonomie* and *Rassenhygiene* were much more popular ways of identifying social policy in Red Vienna that privileged quality over quantity in the planned generations to come. This local variety of eugenic thought drew its terminology from Viennese sociologist Rudolf Goldscheid, whose pre-World War I publications were widely read among the interwar ideologues of the Social Democratic Workers' Party (SDAP). Goldscheid wrote of a national *Menschenökonomie* ("human economy") that required investment in health services, housing improvements, and welfare reform. Such investment, in return, would yield a stronger and more capable population. Eugenic thought, as understood in Vienna, was used to express sexual knowledge that highlighted the "suitability" of partners for marriage and reproduction. It emphasized the current and familial health records of sexual advice seekers, as well as the responsibility sexually active people bore to their offspring, and by extension, the *Volk*.

Eugenic sexual knowledge was based in medical knowledge. This is also true for the reproductive information that sex advice clinics dispensed to their clients. Reproductive counseling, including anatomical lessons, techniques for spacing births, and instructions for the use of birth control devices, was a major component of interwar sex advice. As the following cases will illustrate, reproductive knowledge was most often delivered to women during the interwar period. A third kind of medically based sexual knowledge provided in clinical *Sprechstun-*

den, sexological information, was largely reserved for men. Sexological knowledge drew upon the range of sexual experience and diagnoses documented in the works of Alfred Moll, Iwan Bloch, Havelock Ellis, Richard Krafft-Ebing, Wilhelm Fleiss, and Sigmund Freud. This research categorized sexual dysfunctions and perversions that then could be referenced by the interwar sex advice giver who in turn imparted fragments of this medical knowledge to clients, and especially to men experiencing impotence or homoerotic feelings.

Not all kinds of knowledge offered by Vienna's interwar clinic culture were medical or anatomical in origin. Some advice centers offered mental health counseling, and addressed the feelings of their clients vis-à-vis sexual experience (or lack thereof). Others provided clients with referrals to social support services and/or sympathetic private doctors. At least one clinic dispensed legal advice in relation to sexual behavior. Finally, in most clinics, the sexual knowledge offered was also accompanied by a moral message of responsibility: to oneself, one's partner, children, and society in general. As my analysis of sexual *Aufklärung* literature in chapters 2 and 3 suggests, interwar sex reformers placed great emphasis on personal responsibility in sexual matters.[3] The sexual knowledge available in Vienna's clinics reflected and modified this ethos in important ways, as the following three cases will show.

The Municipal Marriage Advice Center

In the summer of 1922, Vienna's Social Democratic city administration opened a Marriage Advice Center, the first of its kind in Europe. The Center was housed in the sprawling city-hall complex off of the Ringstrasse, in the offices of the Health Ministry. It was founded as part of a "concentrated attack from all sides" on the "deplorable state of affairs brought on by the war and the following years" that endangered the health of the people.[4] Marriage posed a special set of health problems, according to the Advice Center, that needed to be aired before an individual committed him or herself to it. These problems ranged from the strictly medical to the highly social and most often highlighted the relationship of the diseased individual's body to the social body.

The Marriage Advice Center was opened as a resource for people preparing to enter into marriage, but quickly was forced to change its range of treatment to include people already married, single people with no immediate plans for marriage who nevertheless wanted to inquire about their suitability for reproduction, and young people in *Sexualnot* ("sexual crisis," with connotations of emergency and misery).[5] The clinic was open for consultation two evenings a week, in hour-blocks from five to six. All questions regarding the "hygiene of sexual life" were welcome there, with the exception of how to best obtain a divorce.[6]

In an extended review article that appeared in the *Arbeiter-Zeitung* after a year of service, the Marriage Advice Center was described as a place where tough decisions and compromises were made. The article outlined the public's dire need for marriage advice via a series of harrowing vignettes about the clients within. One young man waited in vain for the second time for his fiancée, who has agreed to be examined but is too ashamed to go through with it. He wanted to know if she were healthy, and would not, "as he put it somewhat plainly, 'buy a pig in a poke.'"[7] Another citizen in the waiting room was a no-longer entirely young woman, whose face was already wrinkled and whose body was beginning to droop. She was with a fat, wheezing man described as "ugly, truly repulsive ... but a man nonetheless."[8] Unfortunately he was also unhealthy, and so she sat in worry waiting to hear the doctor's pronouncement on him, presumably the best prospective husband she could find. Next to her waited a young worker whose father, a mean drunk, had tormented his mother for twenty-four years. He wanted to know how to keep his father sober and whether or not his parents' marriage could be saved. Next waited a very nice young girl, who was completely alone in the world and had found a misshapen cripple who wanted to marry her. His condition and her misplaced desire to marry him was described caustically: "He has a pronounced crooked spine and apparently a lung disease, if not open tuberculosis. But the girl wants to have a man to take care of."[9] Should she act on her emotions? Finally, a young couple waited patiently, having already fully disclosed each other's illnesses and full of compassion for one another and their weaknesses. They seem like the picture of responsibility, but he has suffered from depression in the past and was institutionalized more than once. He is recovered now, but may have been "therapeutically" sterilized at the state hospital. Should they marry?

Outside of the young man whose alcoholic father could be referred to the city sanitarium's "Drinker Care Center," the answers given by the Marriage Advice Center in these melodramatic cases were all negative. The more interesting question posed by these vignettes is why a powerful socialist daily would choose to review, and in some sense advertise, a Social Democratic city service through such emotional short stories. On the one hand, these cases succeed in portraying the limited choices and dire physical circumstances that the Viennese working-class contended with when constructing their personal lives. However, the dramatic elements of the stories—disappointments, surprising information revealed by the doctor, diagnoses revealed only in later paragraphs—seem at odds with the mission of the Center: that of *Aufklärung*, or bringing light to sexual questions that had previously festered in ignorance. In medical journals and city welfare records, the Center represented itself with tables, graphs, percentages, and total numbers cured. Yet, to introduce the Center and its work to the public, its founders approved of melodramatic case studies written for the layman. The crossroads of medicine and marriage provided doctors with an entry into the sexual and emotional lives of their patients, and the Center's sometimes florid language reflects this. In the Center's words: "Getting married can certainly become the source of the highest human happiness, but it can just as easily be the starting point of the most shattering tragedies that those of us in the medical profession treat."[10]

The clientele of the Marriage Advice Center was made up overwhelmingly of workers, clerks, and low-level employees. However, the clinic was quick to point out that people from all walks of life used it, "even those people who could afford a private doctor."[11] The utility of a public clinic, the city argued, was that a civil-servant doctor would deliver the whole truth, whereas a private doctor might be influenced by his fear of losing or betraying a regular patient. Karl Kautsky, Jr., the Center's director and chief publicist, repeatedly addressed the benefit of honest, complete assessments available from the municipal doctors at the advice center. He warned of the shortcuts taken by private doctors: "Over and over we have seen it happen, that the private doctor of a man with syphilis granted him the consent to marry at a time when the man was admittedly free of symptoms and tested negative, but did not yet satisfy all the strict demands concerning the length of infection, how long he has been free of symptoms, and the thoroughness of the examination (such as the omission of examining bodily fluids!)."[12] The debate over public versus private marriage advice was important to Kautsky, and he touted the "fairness" of public advising in almost every write-up produced about the clinic. In this constant depiction of the "security" of public health doctors, marriage was described as an investment. As the case of the young man unwilling to "buy a pig in a poke" suggests, marriage in interwar Vienna had become an anxious transaction best completed with the help of the Center's doctor, who would be more trustworthy than a private doctor in his examination of a future partner. The contractual nature of marriage, and the danger of entering into partnership with an ill-suited person, was emphasized by the network of official forms that dominated a visit to the Center.

Whatever the larger social and reforming aims of the Marriage Advice Center, the official activities of the attending doctor consisted largely of filling out and collecting paperwork. The "Official Manual for the Advice Doctor" describes a world in which the findings of the clinician were carefully backed with a complex system of recommendations from outside doctors, letters from specialists, and (if necessary) the review of a special District Commission for Public Health. The manual is unusual in its complete lack of description of possible clients, their social problems, or the services that might alleviate them, all aspects of the Center that were stressed in its municipal write-ups. Instead, the manual walked its doctor-reader through a series of questions and forms necessary to establish an official medical opinion about the proposed union between man and woman. Here, the professionalization of marriage advice is played out in a series of medical forms. The tone of the "Official Manual" is cautious, curt, and impersonal. It counsels the physician as to which questions to pose, but says nothing about answering the sexual hygiene concerns of his clients.

The only real educational exchange between doctor and client(s) outlined in the manual occurred in the beginning of the visit, when the doctor was instructed to impress upon his clients the seriousness of the examination and the complete disclosure it would require from the prospective marriage partners. The language is one of limitation and intimidation: "The doctor must make it clear to the clients that a medical marriage consultation only fulfills its purpose when both marriage partners submit to examination, answer the questions posed to them to the best of their knowledge and conscience, and undergo the necessary tests."[13] After delivering this message, the doctor began his examination by taking *Anamnesen*—"histories of disease"—of the families of the clients and the clients themselves. These histories were especially attuned to sicknesses that could be transmitted to the other marriage partner, inherited diseases, and any illness that could affect the coming generation.[14] The client was asked about the marriages of their grandparents and parents, the numbers of suicides in their extended family, and any cases of hearing loss or deafness in the family. Then a series of questions were posed that required answer for both for the patients themselves and their families. Many of the questions outlined in the "Guide for Taking Histories of Disease" reflected a concern with "suitability" of genes: there were special sections for alcoholism and other addictions, venereal disease, and several types of vision and hearing problems. Under venereal disease, the doctor was instructed to ask the patient if they had any sores on their genitals, discharge, or burning during urination, what kind of medical treatment they had received in the past, and whether they had ever been given the Wassermann test for syphilis.[15] There was also a special section for "Signs of Degeneration and Pronounced Deformities," under which congenital abnormalities such as dwarfism, giantism, albinism, hermaphrodism, and abnormalities of the genitals and reproductive organs are listed. Questions regarding the mental health of the client made up the longest section of the two columns' worth of illnesses. The patient was required to answer, for himself and his family, questions about mental disturbances based on organic problems, madness, epilepsy, hysteria, neurasthenia, addiction, nervous illnesses (including the treatment, place of treatment, and blood test results), convulsions, and severe and violent psychic attacks. Women were asked an extra set of questions regarding their reproductive capacities: whether they had experienced any disturbances in their menstrual cycles, the courses of their pregnancies, any premature births or miscarriages, and any illnesses they suffered after giving birth.[16]

The "Guide for Taking Histories of Disease" ended on a set of questions that were specific to the individual client. Here, the doctor was instructed to ask about the physical and mental development of the patient, including the point at which he learned to walk and speak, when he got his adult teeth, his progress in school, and the psychic and physical progress of puberty. After these developmental questions, the clients were asked about their "sex-life behavior" and then finally if they were related to the intended marriage partner, and if so how closely.[17] This last section of questions, after the numbing inventory of disease that precedes it, is the most interesting. The inclusion of developmental questions is curious: would, for example, the "truly repulsive," wheezing man described above be able to discuss when he lost his baby teeth? Would his prospective partner recognize such a conversation as critical to her decision to marry him? Finally, the vague inquiry into the sexual experiences of the clients was so brief, compared with the attention paid to venereal and degenerative diseases, as to suggest that the illnesses one carried determined one's sexual behavior. Reproductive and eugenic health dominated the exchange of knowledge at the Marriage Advice Center.

After completing his survey of illness, the doctor was instructed by the "Official Manual" to fill out a series of forms confirming the relative health of his client. These forms required the participation of the client, who (ideally) filled out the first half, which featured three prompts:

> Those inheritable diseases and tendencies to disease, as well as diseases that could change the constitution of my offspring, that are present in my family:_____
>
> I suffer, or have suffered, from the following diseases:_____
>
> Marriages between blood relatives:_____ [18]

After declaring his or her own knowledge about genetic suitability for marriage, the client signed. The form was completed by the doctor, who noted any possible abnormalities in the general constitution of the client and then wrote his expert opinion at the bottom. Next the patient and advice doctor filled out a second form, this one a letter to the client's regular doctor. Again the patient filled in his or her request for a review of personal and family health, and again the advice doctor completed the bottom half, identifying his office, attaching a questionnaire, and including a special return envelope.[19] The advice doctor then sealed these papers and turned them over to the patient, who was to deliver them to his or her primary care doctor. A similar form could be prepared in the event that the advice doctor should require the opinion of a specialist.[20] The patient approved the transfer of findings with his prepared statement and signature, and then the doctor noted the required tests and requested them in the name of the city. In this pattern of dual signatures and input on official forms, the Center's forms emphasized the process of sexual responsibility to the patient. He or she was participating, in partnership with the municipality as represented by the advice doctor, in a moral, hygienic program to promote healthy and happy marriages.

The questions sent to the primary care doctor of clients were largely repeated ones from the Advice doctor's assessment, as if the truthfulness of the clients were at stake. The additions to these questions revolve around syphilis and gonorrhea. Primary care doctors were asked how long they have treated their patient, when they last saw the patient, and then immediately whether or not they examined the patient's urine. Then came a series of questions:

Do you know if and when the prospective marriage partner has survived syphilis or gonorrhea, or if he is currently suffering from one of these diseases? Have you treated the prospective marriage partner for syphilis or gonorrhea? If yes, when and how? Do you consider the prospective marriage partner healed? Was a Wassermann test taken, and if so when and with what results?[21]

The form then moved on to other illnesses, only to return to VD once again in the middle ("Are there any kind of signs [that the patient has] *survived* syphilis or gonorrhea?") and at the end, where the final question was whether or not the patients' family had experienced syphilis. Besides establishing the venereal health of the patient, the primary care doctor was also asked to describe mental health carefully, including whether the patient had "any sort of moral defect or urges."[22] This exhaustive inquiry into the inheritable weaknesses of the patient was returned to the Center in a special envelope by post, to be kept in the locked files of the Center doctor for posterity. The client received the verdict as to his or her suitability for marriage in consultation with the doctor alone or with a prospective marriage partner. Despite this marathon of paperwork production, the Center was not prepared to issue written proofs of the medical investigations, fearing that the public would see it as a possible legal barrier to marriage or a requirement that could be used for racial-purity purposes. The doctor was allowed to provide a written certificate of health only in special cases, and then only after obtaining the permission of the Commission of the Ministry of Sanitation.[23] Instead of a certificate, participants in the Marriage Advice Center could leave with a sense of responsibility fulfilled. Voluntary, non-compulsory marriage advice was meant to illuminate more than just the bodily fitness of reproduction; as Kautsky framed it, informed marriage brought with it a sense of responsibility to "one's own body, to one's partner and progeny, and finally to society."[24]

The Center's greatest difficulty and limitation, according to its creators, lay in its inability to treat on-site any medical problems brought to it; it provided counsel to those who sought it, and in cases requiring treatment made referrals to other city health projects and clinics. As shown in chapter 1, Vienna's municipal projects for public health were wide ranging. The Center's work tied in most closely with programs for sobriety, motherhood, and sexually transmitted diseases. For example, clients with alcoholic husbands were informed about the Drinker Care Clinic at the municipal sanitarium. If said husband were then to have problems finding work again, he could be sent to the municipal Office for Career Counseling. Starting in 1924, pregnant women were referred to the Advice Center for Mothers, where parenting tips and lists of municipal services were dispensed. Finally, clients with signs of venereal disease were referred to the Advice Center for Persons with Sexually Transmitted Disease, where they could be tested, receive treatment recommendations, and learn the precautionary measures necessary to stop the spread of disease.[25] For actual treatment of gonorrhea, syphilis, or herpes, clients could be sent to one of the Evening Clinics for Venereal Disease, located throughout the city and designed to provide low-cost or free medical care. These evening VD clinics were the most highly frequented component of the city's reproductive and sexual health infrastructure, serving at their height ten times as many clients as the Marriage Advice Center.[26]

This outline of the services recommended by the Marriage Advice Center represents, I think, a large part of the practical services provided there.[27] The medical paperwork created for perspective marriage partners could not have been an educational experience for the clients visiting, nor is there any suggestion that birth control devices were available. Although its literature refers to the "sexual emergencies" of Viennese life, sex at the Center seems to be discussed only through the lens of the children it might produce or the diseases it might transmit. Notice the role of sex in the following description of the power one has over a marriage partner:

> The marriage partner can be endangered hygienically through direct exposure to infectious diseases (tuberculosis, syphilis, gonorrhea), socially through a spouse's inability to work, or through the squandering of wealth caused by the drive to drink or mental illness, publicly through the spouse's illegal behavior (homosexuality, alcoholism), emotionally through the sterility, frigidity, or impotence of a spouse, and in countless other ways as well.[28]

In such a formulation of marriage, sex served to infect, to publicly embarrass, and to emotionally cripple the individual. Sex put the individual's body, and eventually the social body, at risk. It was the most dangerous component in a marriage, and could be disarmed only through Center-reinforced concepts of health and responsibility. The power of sex within marriage was such that it demanded public education, in the form of the Advice Center, in order to secure health and happiness for the population. Individuals were not the only beneficiaries of this knowledge; rather, the Center openly embraced its roll in qualitative *Bevölkerungspolitik* for the people of Vienna.[29]

Responsibility was the key message of the Center. It introduced responsibility into its patients' lives both through the practice of medical examination before marriage and through the health-service referrals the Center provided. Marriage, as defined by the Center, entailed a set of responsibilities to oneself, one's partner, and the coming generation. Its official leaflet excerpted parts of the City Hall message quoted in its entirety at the opening of this chapter:

> The health of the marriage partners is more important to the happiness of the marriage than money or property [*geld und gut*] ... whoever enters into a marriage, without establishing for themselves whether or not they are healthy, assumes a *heavy responsibility* to their marriage partner and their offspring. Therefore, everyone has the *moral duty* to seek the judgment of an experienced doctor.[30]

This moral duty was in many ways all that the Center had to recommend its services. Throughout its literature, the Center defined its goal as that of helping people become more responsible for their health, and repeatedly stated that its findings should not become legal barriers to marriage.[31] Instead, the Municipal Marriage Center seems to have been an attempt to refocus the act of marriage as a question of health, for both the spouses involved and the community that supported them. In doing so, the Center inserted itself into a cultural niche still very much inhabited by the Roman Catholic Church in interwar Austria. Traditional Christian concepts of purity were altered through the Center's work, but not entirely dismissed. Fears of sin and spiritual pollution, at the Center, were replaced by biological dangers that demanded a very similar level of personal watchfulness and responsibility.

The League Against Forced Motherhood

In November 1922, the League Against Forced Motherhood opened a new clinic in the 6th district, a few streetcar stops away from the Municipal Marriage Advice Center on the Ringstrasse. This association was headed by the husband-and-wife team of Johann and Betty Ferch, members of the international birth control movement centered around Margaret Sanger.[32] Founded in 1919, the League described itself as a non-political group devoted to "raising the collective feeling of responsibility vis-à-vis children, achieving the right of self-determination for mothers, and increasing the protection of mother and child."[33] In its first years, this meant making legal and parliamentary appeals that demanded the repeal of Paragraphs 144 to 148, which banned abortion in Austria. This legal goal, one shared with feminist groups and the radical wing of the Social Democrats, was never achieved in interwar Austria. Starting in 1922, the League began addressing the self-determination of mothers by organizing birth-control information centers set up throughout Vienna and eventually penetrating into the Catholic countryside.

The League's early literature focused on the dire living circumstances of Viennese families after the war. Laws had to bend to fit the relationships of the times, it argued, and the inability of women to terminate a pregnancy was at odds with the new world they faced in 1918. The language of the League, like that of the municipal Marriage Advice Center, emphasized responsibility. Parents, unable to secure the health of their children, were right to fear and avoid reproduction:

> The joy of childbearing is today, in the days of most pressing emergency, a bitter experience for parents. It has become a terrible martyrdom, because one cannot give children that which safeguards their life, which guarantees [*gewährleistet*] their physical development, and which guards them from the cradle until they have a healthy body,

which is a requirement for the hard struggle for existence. Where a home is lacking, where newborns must go without milk and nourishment—here a sense of responsibility must disavow the creation of a child.[34]

In this passage, Viennese parents are portrayed as pragmatic social Darwinists, only too aware of what will be required of their offspring in life and of their own (in)ability to provide it. The personal responsibility of such parents is then contrasted with the irrational demands of a state that makes forces women to be mothers, but does nothing to secure the lives of the children born to them. The result, implied the League, was hypocrisy: "many today say that the termination of pregnancy cannot be a crime in a state that is not capable of nourishing these children."[35]

An early League brochure by Johann Ferch entitled "Dungeon or Enforced Motherhood" made it clear that women's options under Paragraph 144, one to five years in prison for the crime of abortion or carrying a child to term, were equally unreasonable. By reducing women to "birth machines" and not recognizing the conditions in which they functioned, the state condemned the next generation to being nothing more than "deliveries for tuberculosis and rickets, [diseases] which always need new victims."[36] In this regard the League participated in the same sorts of social hygiene messages delivered by the Municipal Marriage Advice Center. Ferch employed a series of Neo-Malthusian arguments against "forced motherhood," many of which echoed the socialist city council's call for quality over quantity in their *Menschenökonomie*.[37] Ferch described it as "only love" that motivated parents of modest means to desire only one or two children, and claimed "public opinion has changed so much that one now sooner condemns the immorality of unscrupulous parents with many children."[38] Even without the housing and food shortages that defined post-war Vienna, Ferch continued, the state of health of Austria's homecoming soldiers had to be considered before asking women to bear children. Many of his news articles assumed that veterans of the World War, exposed to venereal disease while at the front, would reintroduce disease into the home population. He asked: "Is it really desirable for the state that children of syphilitics should come into the world at any price?"[39] Ferch's willingness to label the children of syphilitics as weak or undesirable is franker than most, but still in keeping with the eugenic logic employed by the SDAP. What set these early arguments for the right of abortion apart is Ferch's admission that unhealthy people still have sex and that appealing to a sense of eugenic responsibility alone will not alter the landscape of Viennese health. Ferch argues for what he calls "humane" realism:

> To condemn all [soldiers] infected with syphilis to celibacy is impracticable, but the requirement that the children of such fathers must be born is inhumane. The case is similar with alcoholics, the tubercular, and those people with scrofula. Under this terrible compulsion to reproduce, crippled criminals and fertilizer for cemetery weeds

will be born, who will torment and burden their families and, in the best cases, be useful only to doctors and gravediggers.[40]

It is worthwhile to note that the League's harsh assessment of the sick offspring revolves around the burden such children place on families, and in particular, women. Indeed, the League's newspaper often depicted the struggle against Paragraph 144 with imagery of a woman being held back or chained. Perhaps the most vivid example of this was the cover drawing from January 1923. Titled "Reduce the Suffering of Mothers," it shows a woman in a flowing dress straining to pull a plow. The yoke to which she's hitched reads "Compulsory Motherhood," and the figure behind the plow is a degenerate, simian-looking child with "Ignorance" written across his shirt.[41] This striking sketch well illustrates Ferch's warnings to women about burdensome children. It also carries an implicit warning to the state. If Vienna wanted to harness female labor power in its effort to rebuild itself in the Republic, Ferch suggested, the municipality must free women from the biological burdens that sap their productivity.

Although clearly critical of the social cost of unwanted pregnancies and unhealthy children, the League's literature most often emphasized the ways in which women privately bore such expenses. That the production of unhealthy children was above all a private burden for women and families, rather than for society, was one of the characteristics of the League's message. This emphasis might be a result of the League's non-affiliation with any political party, but I think it also points to their focus on women's bodies and lives as the loci of both suffering and possible change. A list of visitors to the League's Center for the Protection and Advising of Women, reprinted in the League's newspaper *Sexual Reform*, enumerates the misery of reproduction, and by extension, marriage in Vienna:

—32 years old, 7 children, lives in one room and kitchen

—3 children, youngest 5 months old, lives in a kitchen

—8 births, 4 living children, 6 miscarriages

—7 births, 8 miscarriages, the last self-induced, serious infection

—17 births, 3 living children

—4 children, 4 self-induced miscarriages, without dwelling, husband lives with 1 child at relatives' place, wife lives with 3 children at mother's apartment.[42]

Like the stories of visitors to the municipal Marriage Advice Center reprinted in the *Arbeiter-Zeitung*, this list serves to both situate sexual misery in a language of dire social and medical conditions and to justify the League's work on behalf of women. Although the League never gave up on its goal of legalized abortion, the centers opened in 1922 re-focused League attention on curbing female misery through the dissemination of birth control methods and devices. Like the need for legalized abortion, this more attainable means of limiting unwanted children was also justified through sorrowful vignettes. Witness a reprinted letter from a Viennese client, who wished to thank the League for the improvements the pessary they provided has brought to her life:

> If I had known of the League two years earlier, I would still be a healthy and joyful woman today ... I have given birth twice, the one child is very anemic and the second is deaf, dumb, rickety and mentally ill. Then I miscarried three times in 18 months, most recently in June 1923, at which time I had a violent hemorrhage and I lay for three months with a fever of 39 degrees, could not and was not allowed to work, and my husband is a [war-wounded] invalid. I was close to tears every month with the fear of being pregnant, then I heard of the League against Forced Motherhood, and it was for me like a gift from heaven.[43]

This tribute stands in stark contrast with the list of women reprinted in *Sexual-Reform*. In the latter, women's reproductive misery was reduced to a list of ages, numbers of live and interrupted births, and living conditions in an effort to de-sentimentalize marriage. The woman who received birth control information from the League, however, uses emotional language to appeal to the League's readers. Regret and fear dominate her testimonial as she describes her life before visiting the League. This combination of medical practicality (in the form of legal abortion and birth control) as the answer to the emotional suffering of women typifies the League's approach to marriage and sexuality. Indeed, the League's motto was "Those who would decrease suffering and sorrow must help women and mothers."[44]

The League broadcasted its messages in its quarterly journal, *Sexual-Reform*, in advertisements placed in Social Democratic women's journals, and in the hundreds of speeches and slide shows delivered throughout Vienna by Johann Ferch. These presentations, shown for a small entrance fee that funded League's activities, offered sexual knowledge as entertainment and education. Many viewers would have been familiar with Ferch, having read his popular *Dreigroschen-Romanen* ("penny dreadfuls"), inexpensive melodramas that thematized free union, anti-clericalism, and pacifism.[45] Ferch also was responsible for the dramatic tone of the League's brochures, which attacked any authority, including the Roman Catholic Church, which limited women's marital and reproductive freedom.[46] Ferch's slide-show presentations, like his literature, were both titillating and politically engaging. For example, in 1925 Ferch capitalized upon his return from a birth control conference in America by offering lectures on "Moral, Romantic, and Sexual Concepts in America."[47] His "Family Planning" slide show was especially popular. It ran for ten months and was presented to 140 different audiences.[48]

By 1930, there were seven Information Centers in Vienna, each serving a different district, open six evenings a week for consultation. These offices were staffed by nurses; the birth control method taught was the combined use of pessaries and chemical tablets, which the League preferred over "masculine precautions."[49] The vaginal pessary (what we would call a diaphragm) was a circular rubber cap with a spring that would allow it to be collapsed for insertion. It required a gynecological examination and sizing by a doctor, and even then was not appropriate for all women, depending upon the curvature of the vaginal walls. There was also disagreement within the birth control movement about how the vaginal pessary should fit, with a minority prescribing a circular fit covering the cervix, rather than the more popular diagonal fit across the vagina (as the League prescribed).[50] Semori, a foaming suppository tablet, was the chemical contraceptive of choice. This tablet produced carbon dioxide in the presence of moisture and was one of the most effective chemicals available for birth control, but because it contained chinosol it was very expensive.[51] It was also difficult to store during Vienna's humid summer months, when temperatures inside apartments could trigger the release of the chemical.

Access to both of these devices required a doctor's prescription. By 1930, the League could provide listings for Neo-Malthusian-minded doctors (meaning those who supported limiting family size through birth control) for most of Austria. Within Vienna, the Ferchs had a two-tier system for securing birth control in place by 1923. "Clients with means" could write to the League for a listing of doctors willing to provide protection. In this sense the League served only as an information center, although women who received devices in this way were free to follow-up at the League if they had technical questions about insertion, storage, or care. For poorer clients, the League offered to provide any woman, regardless of marriage status, with a free examination, pessary, and fitting demonstration at one of forty affiliated citywide doctors' offices.[52] Betty Ferch estimated in 1930 that the League had about 250 applicants a week for birth control.[53] That the League was able to provide so many women with birth control in interwar Catholic Austria was a major achievement; in other Catholic countries such as France and Poland, this work would have been illegal. Yet the ability to provide free pessaries to the needy was only a partial solution. Unlike her sisters "of means," it seems highly unlikely that most working class women could use the pessary in the manner prescribed. To do so, she would have to insert it in the evening and leave it in until morning, douche with plain or soapy water before and after its removal, wash the pessary with soap and water, dry it, powder it with talc, and then store it in a special container. For women without running water or a toilet in their homes, or those in cramped spaces without privacy, surely using a pessary would prove difficult. Indeed, birth control advocates across Europe admitted that a large percentage of women either did not use their pessaries or only used them infrequently.[54]

At the 1930 International Conference for Birth Control, Betty Ferch drew from her experiences at the Information Center to outline a series of optimal conditions for women and the Neo-Malthusian groups that sought to help them. These conditions reflect the problems that the League faced across Austria, but also speak to the difficulties they encountered in Vienna. Ferch was especially concerned with the price of contraceptives, their categorization as medicaments, and with the persistence of contraception and abortion techniques among the population that were both ineffective and dangerous.⁵⁵ Her concerns combined both social and individual responsibility, and suggested that neither one was effective alone. The sexual knowledge provided in the League's *Sprechstunden* differed from that provided by the Municipal Marriage Advice Center. Both clinics delivered *Aufklärung* in language that stressed responsibility and identified unplanned reproduction as dangerous. However, the clinics approached these tenets from opposite directions. The Municipal Marriage Advice Center sought to convince Viennese citizens of their abstract reproductive responsibilities and, where possible, facilitate responsible choices through social service referrals. In contrast, the League Against Forced Motherhood suggested to its clients that reproductive responsibility could be secured specifically through the use of birth control. Rather than asking its clients to abstain from marriages or sexual activity, the League provided them with immediate means to control reproduction. Furthermore, the League fought to create long-term change via socio-economic conditions they felt would secure the health of sexually active women: cheap, non-medical birth control devices and legal access to (medical) abortion.

The Socialist Society for Sexual Advice and Research

In January 1929, Vienna's communist press ran advertisements for a new set of clinics devoted to fighting the "rising sexual distress [*Sexualnot*] of the broad masses of the working population."⁵⁶ Six clinics in three different districts offered advice to the general public, including specialized clinics for teenagers and women, and a seventh clinic designed for those seeking legal advice. Here, advice for all questions of sexual hygiene, puberty, marriage, and contraception was offered in an attempt to combat the "ignorance of the working class regarding the most primitive questions of sexuality."⁵⁷ This sexual ignorance, and the living conditions in which it festered, was blamed on the "bourgeois capitalist social order."⁵⁸

The Proletarian Sexual Advice Centers were the creation of the Socialist Society for Sexual Advice and Research, founded in late 1928 by Wilhelm Reich and Marie Frischauf.⁵⁹ Their society consisted largely of reform-minded doctors, psychiatrists, and lawyers, all committed to social change through the improvement of worker sexuality and reproductive health. Sexual misery, the society contended, expressed itself in a deplorable percentage of teenage and adult suicides, in unhappy marriages, and in the rising incapacity of Vienna's citizens for work or practical daily life.⁶⁰ The goal of the society was to uncover and combat sexual misery, for which it proposed individual counsel in cases of sexual conflict and public education about sexual hygiene. In addition, the society identified scientific research on sexuality as a weapon in its struggle.

The Proletarian Advice Center advertised itself as an alternative to municipal counseling, setting itself in comparison with the Municipal Marriage Advice Center. We would do well to question why a person seeking sexual knowledge might visit Reich's clinics rather than the city's Center. Perhaps the most basic deciding factor was accessibility. The society's clinics were located in various districts, kept later hours at night for those visiting after work, and, between the seven of them, held consultation hours every day of the workweek. It is also possible that people saw the society's clinics as an extension of the overcrowded municipal Psychoanalytic Care Center, a project undertaken by Freud and run by Reich in the early 1920s. Indeed, Reich traced his involvement in sexual reform to his years working in Freud's Care Center. Reich's assessment of the cases heard by the society in its first six months of service suggests that most of the clients were, in fact, suffering from psychological problems that could not be ameliorated through sexual education alone. His findings were reported in a 1929 journal article he wrote for *The Socialist Doctor* entitled "Experiences and Problems from Sex Advice Clinics for Workers and Employees in Vienna."[61] Reich separated Proletarian Advice Center clients into two main groups: those that found themselves in a difficult sexual situation and needed advice, and those who suffered from sexual dysfunctions or neuroses. The former group, about 30 percent of the Proletarian Advice Center's patients, included people who were either conflicted about masturbation, suffered from mild cases of erectile dysfunction or frigidity, were in the middle of a common sexual conflict with their partner, or were seeking birth control advice (the society prescribed cervical caps and recommended condoms).[62] One or more consultations, Reich claimed, helped such patients get over their actual difficulties and prevented possible future illnesses to a certain degree. However, 70 percent of the people who visited the Reich's clinics fell under his second category of patients: those who suffered from sexual dysfunctions or neuroses. Almost all of these people came from the working class, and had suffered for long enough to have tried all possible forms of suggestive and physical treatment. Reich describes these people, the majority of visitors to the Advice Centers, as being beyond the help of the clinic doctors:

> Many neurotic people come to the clinic for sexual advice, to whom the relationship between their sufferings and their destroyed sexual lives is perfectly clear, even without having ever heard of Freud's discoveries. The worker has a strangely fine sense of natural sexual requirements and of the shamefulness taught by bourgeois sexual education . . . . When one seeks to find an escape for this group one runs up against the hopeless social situation, against the real impossibility of supplying even a portion of the ill with an appropriate treatment.[63]

It is difficult to tell whether Reich is stereotyping the working class as inherently earthy in its sexuality, or projecting his own psychoanalytic beliefs onto his clients. Either way, he identified 70 percent of the cases he sees as requiring such extensive psychotherapy that "the clinician gets the very depressing impression of sexual and neurotic suffering as endemic to the proletariat, and yet only the bourgeoisie can afford individual treatment."[64] The extent of *Sexualnot* in Vienna, as described by Reich in 1929, was much greater than first suggested by the Municipal Marriage Advice Center in 1922.

The frustration Reich describes in his inability to treat the deeply entrenched and socially reinforced sexual misery of his clientele was doubtless part of the society's commitment to public speaking. In this respect the society, like the League Against Forced Motherhood or the municipal Center, participated in a sustained attempt to present a new form of sexual morality to the public. Reich repeatedly advertised the society's speakers as frank and direct about sexual activity. He assured the Viennese that "Naturally, we do not speak, or do not only speak, about the construction of the reproductive organs or how one should wash oneself, but rather we publicly discuss the most intimate questions."[65] At issue in these advertisements was the kind of sexual knowledge offered by the society, which promised sexological and emotional information rather than the merely hygienic lessons offered in other clinics. The society's lecture offerings for the year 1929 to 1930 suggest a more programmatic approach to sexuality: "The Sexual Question of Youth in Bourgeois Society," "Married Morality and Married Happiness," "Sexual Disturbances and Productivity at Work," "Abortion and Contraception," "Sexual Misery of the Masses and Socialist Sexual Reform," and "Paragraph 144 and the Elections."[66] Of these topics, only the lecture on contraception seems to have had immediate, practical application to the Proletarian Sexual Advice Center's clientele. Discussing birth control to large audiences was important to the society for two reasons: birth control both allowed workers to better control their material existence, and public discussion of it was "necessary morally to aid all those who are still imbued with the official viewpoint that sexual intercourse is permissible only for the production of children."[67] The society complemented these advantages of birth control in their public engagements by highlighting the dangers of home-remedies for inducing abortion. Furthermore, the society declared, "to all those who inquire[d]" that, "coitus interruptus and abstinence are injurious."[68]

The Society's public stance on the naturalness of masturbation and the dangers of abstinence stemmed largely from the psychoanalytic philosophy of Reich himself, who began developing his theory of "orgiastic satisfaction" soon after his break with Freud in 1927. Rejecting the cultural need for sexual sublimation, Reich argued that the lack of sexual release led to a reduced capacity for work, the fixation on non-genital sexual gratification, and sadistic concepts of the sex act itself. In 1930, Reich challenged the Freudian belief that sexuality must be repressed in order to make civilized life possible. Reich's *Critique of Bourgeois Sexual Reform* claimed that sexual repression only secured the existing class structure, and suggested that a liberated sexuality was a revolutionary force.[69] These beliefs certainly influenced the kind of sexual advice provided by the society. Masturbation was taught to be a sensible substitute for sex, particularly for the young, the misshapen, or anyone else for whom sexual activity could be "socially difficult."[70] In order to separate the act of sex from reproduction, birth control was advertised at every clinic, where "Every man and woman without consideration of age and position [was] taught the fact that prevention is necessary so long as the desire for a child and the material possibility of providing for it does not exist."[71] Abstinence was vilified as causing people to fixate on infantile and unconscious sexual mechanisms that then become ingrained and impossible to treat without long-term psychiatric care. The bourgeois roots of marriage and their stress on the total possession of a partner are exposed in order to soothe conflict and jealousy between married people. Such tenets did not leave much room for the discussion of marriage and procreation, other than as difficult situations and structures that cause pain. In private consultation, printed material, and public presentations, the society promoted an ideal of sexual health that corresponded with Reich's orgasm-centered psychoanalytic beliefs. The sexual knowledge provided by the Proletarian Advice Center emphasized individual psychological development and valued the fulfillment of sexual drives over social responsibility.

Conclusions

In 1929, Wilhelm Reich published a set of fifty commonly asked questions from his Proletarian Sexual Advice Center and public lectures. Although doubtless chosen for their pedagogical potential, the questions represent a valuable cross-section of the kinds of sexual knowledge Viennese people were requesting and receiving from the clinic culture of the interwar period. Reich separates the questions into the categories of general knowledge, masturbation, the sexual activity of teenagers, impotence and frigidity, sexual activity and abstinence, and homosexuality. A sampling of the questions follows:

> (15) Comrade K. said in a speech to socialist middle-schoolers that a young person might only have sexual relations after he or she had finished growing. Is this true?
>
> (19) Please, how is it possible that a man of forty-two should already be impotent?
>
> (23) What is to be done if a two-year-old boy plays with himself? Also, I've been married three years and my wife claims that she has yet to be satisfied. I should mention that my wife has masturbated since her earliest childhood. Does this explain the problem? Can this be cured?

(33) What should ugly people do, who can't find a boyfriend or girlfriend?

(35) Is it possible that a man who lives like an ascetic can go without sexual activity by taking daily cold baths, doing gymnastics or sport, etc.?

(44) What influence does partaking in nudism have on one's sexuality?[72]

These direct questions seem very far from the labyrinth of medical questionnaires produced at the Municipal Marriage Advice Center, but I would suggest that this is a trick of tone. It is exciting to hear the common speech and be immersed in the sexual confusion of these queries, but at their base they revolve around the same questions pondered at the Municipal Center and the League Against Forced Motherhood's birth control clinics: what is normal, what is responsible, and what will, if not lead to happiness, at least not cause permanent physical harm.

Marriage and procreation were described throughout this new clinic culture as potentially dangerous undertakings. They endangered the health of the individuals involved, be it physically, as the Marriage Advice Center and League Against Forced Motherhood stressed, or psychologically, as the Proletarian Sexual Advice Centers suggested. In response, the clinics helped to create an expanding culture of medical, reproductive, and sexual responsibility for Vienna's interwar citizenry. If we return to the opening quotation of this chapter, the "Advice for Those Entering Marriage" offered by the Municipal Marriage Advice Center, we can analyze this culture of responsibility more fully. Two languages of marriage guidance, medical and moral, combine in "Advice for Those Entering Marriage." The former dominates the piece, medicalizing marriage partner selection through reference to health, disease, work-capacity, illness of offspring, and specialized medical care. Yet moral concerns are rife throughout "Advice for Those Entering Marriage"; judgment, discretion, conscience and responsibility are described in connection to emotional states like well-being, joy, mistrust, grief, self-reproach, and remorse. "Advice for Those Entering Marriage" provides us with an unusually dense but not uncharacteristic example of the ways sexual advice was dispensed in interwar Vienna. The sexual knowledge provided in advice clinics drew from both medical and moral vocabularies in order to create a new ethics of sexual activity, marriage, and reproduction. In doing so, it encroached upon the authority of the Roman Catholic Church.

In 1931, Pope Pius XI published an encyclical letter on the subject of Christian marriage entitled *Casti connubii*. I have already looked at this document at length in chapter 3 of this book, in relation to its views on women's roles within marriage. Because *Casti connubii* speaks directly to some of the sexual knowledge provide by Vienna's clinic culture, I want to return to it and treat it as a response to the developments traced in this chapter. Pius XI explained the need for his encyclical by referring to "the most pernicious errors and depraved morals [that were] gradually gaining ground" since the last encyclical on marriage, issued by

Leo XIII fifty years earlier.[73] These errors were based in a fundamental misevaluation of marriage present, the Pope warned, in all legal and social reforms that failed to recognize the Church's sole authority in the realm of marriage and reproduction. In *Casti connubii*, the Church roundly rejected divorce, birth control, abortion, and unsanctioned (mixed) union. Furthermore, earthly governing bodies were asked to "take account of what is prescribed by divine and ecclesiastical law," and reminded that the Church and its marital order brought dignity and peace to the state.[74]

Pope Pius XI thus condemned many of the practices discussed in the *Sprechstunden* of Vienna's sexual advice clinic. The birth control methods offered by the League Against Forced Motherhood, as well as the League's campaign to repeal Austria's anti-abortion laws, obviously fell outside of Church-sanctioned action. *Casti connubii* also contradicted the messages of individual sexual fulfillment outside of marriage regularly delivered by the Socialistic Society for Sexual Advice and Research. These judgments, in many ways, had already been made and publicized by Pope Leo XIII in the late nineteenth century, and pre-dated the development of Viennese clinic culture. What was new about *Casti connubii* was that it addressed the young science of eugenics, as well. Pius XI explained the Church's position:

> There are some who, over-solicitous for the cause of *eugenics*, not only give salutary counsel for more certainly procuring the strength and health of the future child—which, indeed, is not contrary to right reason—but put *eugenics* before aims of a higher order, and by public authority wish to prevent from marrying all those who, even though naturally fit for marriage, they consider, according to the norms and conjectures of their investigations, would, through hereditary transmission, bring forth defective offspring.[75]

This passage provides an interesting response to the social hygiene messages delivered at Vienna's Municipal Marriage Advice Center. Its allows for gradations of censure; "salutary counsel" for the strength of the future child is not condemned, but valuing the health of offspring over individuals' right to (Christian) marriage and its attendant blessings is in violation of Church doctrine. Children are identified by *Casti connubii* as the first and most important blessing of marriage, and as such any state hindrance to their production within Christian marriage is condemned, including abortion and involuntary sterilization.[76]

When we take into account the Roman Catholic Church's defense of its marital authority, the sexual knowledge provided in Vienna's interwar advice clinics is thrown into even greater relief. All of the advice clinics in Vienna participated in kinds of knowledge production and distribution that were explicitly condemned by *Casti connubii*. The "temporary unions" that Wilhelm Reich's Society tolerated and encouraged were explicitly rejected as pernicious, as was the practice of abortion. The League Against Forced Motherhood's repeated descriptions of reproduction as dangerous to women's health were identified, in *Casti connubii*, as invalid arguments for abortion, even when the mother's life was at risk.[77] Finally, the Municipal Marriage Advice Center's attempt to dissuade eugenically unfit couples from marriage and reproduction constituted an infringement upon ecclesiastical and divine law, which defended the right to Christian marriage for all people, regardless of their genetic qualifications. *Casti connubii* clearly described eugenic principles such as those espoused by the municipal Center as attempts by "the civil authority to arrogate to itself a power which it never had and can never legitimately possess."[78] In doing so, *Casti connubii* provided ammunition for religious and political leaders who opposed Vienna's sexual hygiene system.

The quotation that opened this chapter, the SDAP's official "Piece of Advice for Those Entering Marriage" has interesting parallels with a section of *Casti connubii* devoted to marital advice. This section counsels Christians to take care in their selection of a marriage partner:

> To the proximate preparation of a good married life belongs very specially the care in choosing a partner; on that depends a great deal whether the forthcoming marriage will be happy or not, since one may be to the other either a great help in leading a Christian life or a great danger and hindrance. And so that they may not deplore for the rest of their lives the sorrows arising from an indiscreet marriage, those about to enter into wedlock should carefully deliberate in choosing the person with whom henceforward they must live continually; they should in so deliberating keep before their minds the thought first of God and the true religion of Christ, then of themselves, of their partner, of their children to come, as also of human and civil society, for which wedlock is a fountain-head.[79]

This section of *Casti connubii* echoes in important ways the "Piece of Advice for Those Entering Marriage" provided by Vienna's Municipal Center in 1922. Both passages are concerned with the process of choosing a marriage partner. Both warn that one's emotional future, in the forms of happiness or sorrow, rests upon the proper selection of a marriage partner. Both passages warn readers that marriage can be dangerous, and ask them to consider the children that might issue from their marriage. Finally, both pieces stress health as the factor at risk in marriage: spiritual health in *Casti connubii*, and physical health in the "Advice for Those Entering Marriage." Marriage with the wrong partner, according to Pius XI, could hinder one's ability to "lead a Christian life." According to the Vienna Municipal Marriage Advice Center, we might safely say, marriage with the wrong partner would hinder one's ability to lead a Socialist life as envisioned by the SDAP; one's ability to produce and reproduce well could be compromised by their partner's health.

This comparison of religious and secular marriage advice provides us with a timely reminder of the ways in which sexual knowledge in Vienna's clinic culture was delivered within a moral message. All of the Viennese clinics I have discussed pointedly omitted (or, in some cases, challenged) any reference to Catholic morality in the sexual advice they dispensed. This clinic-based process of secularization was denounced on principle by Pius XI in *Casti connubii*, and, locally, bitterly contested by the Christian Social Party in Vienna. Yet Christian values were not completely dismissed by interwar clinic culture; instead, they were replaced with concepts of social health and personal responsibility. If we re-read "A Piece of Advice for Those Entering into Marriage" with this process in mind, much of the passage's strangeness dissipates. The piece's strict, moralizing tone and emphasis on honor and conscience were appropriate to the task of convincing Viennese adults that one's suitability for marriage depended upon one's physical health. The Municipal Center was, after all, asking its clients to confess their physical and sexual weaknesses. As this chapter has shown, not all of the forms of sexual knowledge available in Vienna's advice clinics were as eugenically driven as that dispensed at the Municipal Marriage Advice Center. However, all forms of sexual knowledge available through the clinic culture that flourished in interwar Vienna carried with them highly charged political and religious implications. How one conducted one's life, how one enjoyed sexual activity or suffered from its results, were given new meanings by the various sexual advice centers of interwar Vienna. These meanings placed an intensely political valence on the sexual lives of Viennese men and women.

Notes

1. "Ein Rat für Eheschließende," *Das Neue Wien*. Städtewerk herausgegeben unter offizieller Mitwirkung der Gemeinde Wien, Band III (Wien: 1927), 578.
2. "Who, what, where, with whom, why, in what manner, when." My conceptualization of the process of Catholic confession is inspired by Peter Brook's *Troubling Confessions: Speaking Guilt in Law and Literature* (Chicago: University of Chicago Press, 2000).
3. For a Foucaultian reading of these three clinics that emphasized bio-power and gender over responsibility, see Maria Mesner, "Educating Reasonable Lovers: Sex Counseling in Austria in the First Half of the Twentieth Century," in Günter Bischof, Anton Pelinka, and Dagmar Herzog (eds.), *Sexuality in Austria* (New Brunswick: Transaction Publishers, 2007), 48–64.
4. "Eheberatung," *Das Neue Wien*. Städtewerk herausgegeben unter offizieller Mitwirkung der Gemeinde Wien, Band III (Wien: 1927), 569.
5. "Die Eheberatungstelle," *Die Verwaltung der Bundeshauptsamt Wien in der Zeit vom 1 Jänner 1923 bis 31 Dezember 1928*. Wiener Stadt- und Landesarchiv Archivbibliothek, M511 2 Ex. 42/1/2, Band II Teil 1, 864/865.
6. The Marriage Advice Center's unwillingness to be involved in divorce cases weakened as the decade progressed; by 1927 it was receiving requests for health inspections from the state courts.
7. Laurenz Genner, "Was man vor der Ehe wissen muß," *Arbeiter-Zeitung* 336 (8 December 1923), 15. The German version of this idiomatically expressed logic is even more negative: "er will nicht die Katze im Sack kaufen."
8. "Was man vor der Ehe wissen muß," *Arbeiter-Zeitung*, 15.

9. "Was man vor der Ehe wissen muß," *Arbeiter-Zeitung,* 16.
10. "Eheberatung," 569.
11. "Was man vor der Ehe wissen muß," *Arbeiter-Zeitung,* 15.
12. Karl Kautsky, "Oeffentliche oder private Eheberatung?," *Blätter für das Wohlfahrtswesen,* 28/271 (Jänner/Februar 1929), 30–31.
13. "Dienstvorschrift für den Beratungsarzt," *Das Neue Wien.* Städtewerk herausgegeben unter offizieller Mitwirkung der Gemeinde Wien, Band III (Wien: 1927), 571.
14. "Dienstvorschrift für den Beratungsarzt," 571.
15. "Anleitung zur Aufnahme der Anamnese," *Das Neue Wien.* Städtewerk herausgegeben unter offizieller Mitwirkung der Gemeinde Wien, Band III (Wien: 1927), 573. The Wassermann blood test for syphilis was the most modern method of testing, able to detect the disease even when it was between visible stages. The city eventually opened up neighborhood stations for free and confidential testing, which were heavily frequented until the end of the 1930s.
16. "Anleitung zur Aufnahme der Anamnese," 573. It is unclear why these questions presume that the clinic's female clients have had children before, as the rest of the clinic instruction sheets describe the clients as people thinking about entering into marriage. These questions suggest that second marriages for women, perhaps especially in the wake of World War I, were part of the planning of the clinics.
17. "Anleitung zur Aufnahme der Anamnese," 573.
18. "Die Formularien der Eheberatungstelle, Formular 1," *Das Neue Wien.* Städtewerk herausgegeben unter offizieller Mitwirkung der Gemeinde Wien, Band III (Wien: 1927), 572.
19. "Die Formularien der Eheberatungstelle, Formular 3," *Das Neue Wien.* Städtewerk herausgegeben unter offizieller Mitwirkung der Gemeinde Wien, Band III (Wien: 1927), 574.
20. "Die Formularien der Eheberatungstelle, Formular 4," *Das Neue Wien.* Städtewerk herausgegeben unter offizieller Mitwirkung der Gemeinde Wien, Band III (Wien: 1927), 576.
21. "Die Formularien der Eheberatungstelle, Formular 1," 575.
22. "Die Formularien der Eheberatungstelle, Formular 1," 575.
23. "Dienstvorschrift für den Beratungsarzt," *Das Neue Wien.* Städtewerk herausgegeben unter offizieller Mitwirkung der Gemeinde Wien, Band III (Wien: 1927), 571.
24. Karl Kautsky, "Eheberatung," *Die Frau* 10 (1 Oktober 1929), 11.
25. "Beratungstelle für Geschlechtskranke," *Die Verwaltung des Bundeshauptsamt Wien in der Zeit vom 1 Jänner 1923 bis 31 Dezember 1928.* Wiener Stadt- und Landesarchiv Archivbibliothek, M511 2 Ex. 42/1/2, Band II Teil 1, 863.
26. Here I am comparing two city reports for the year 1925: 5,464 people visited the evening VD clinics, while 490 new clients visited the Marriage Advice Clinic. See "Abendambulatorien für Geschlechtskrankheit," *Die Verwaltung des Bundeshauptsamt Wien in der Zeit vom 1 Jänner 1923 bis 31 Dezember 1928.* Wiener Stadt- und Landesarchiv Archivbibliothek, M511 2 Ex. 42/1/2, Band II Teil 1, 862, and "Eheberatung," 570.
27. For a more complete discussion of Vienna's municipal health system, see chapter 1.
28. "Eheberatung," 569.
29. Kaustky, "Eheberating," 11.
30. "Was man vor der Ehe wissen muß," *Arbeiter-Zeitung,* 15. Emphasis in original.
31. "Eheberatung," 570.
32. In late 1925, the League Against Forced Motherhood was absorbed into the League for Regulated Births, headed by Dr. Leo Fischmann. For the purposes of this chapter, I will refer to it throughout as the "League." Betty Ferch remained a guiding force of the League until it was dissolved in early 1934.
33. "Bund gegen den Mutterschaftszwang." Wiener Stadt- und Landesarchiv, police report R. 17 Reg 110 Sch. A32–125, gel. Vereine 1440/23.

34. "Die Angst vor dem Kinde," in "Bund gegen den Mutterschaftszwang," Wiener Stadt- und Landesarchiv, Vereine 1440/23. The German word for guarantee in this passage, *gewährleisten*, can also be translated as an acceptance of responsibility.
35. "Die Angst," BgM, WSL. The League used the formulation *die Flucht vor dem Kinde* to denote the desire for an abortion or an abortion itself. The literal translation would be "the flight from the child," but I have opted for looser translations.
36. Reviewed in "Die Flucht vor dem Kinde: Ein Bund gegen den Mutterchaftszwang," *Neuen Wiener Journal* (7 Oktober 1919), and reprinted for "Bund gegen den Mutterschaftszwang," Wiener Stadt- und Landesarchiv, Vereine 1440/23.
37. In keeping with the historiography, I use "Neo-Malthusian" to indicate concepts of sexuality that divorce sexual activity from reproduction: a stance first adopted by middle-class sex reformers in the late nineteenth century.
38. "Die Flucht," BgM, WSL.
39. "Die Flucht," BgM, WSL.
40. "Die Flucht," BgM, WSL.
41. "Mindert das Leid der Mütter," *Sexual-Reform, Zeitschrift für Sexualreform und Neomalthusianismus* 13 (Jänner 1923), 1.
42. "Einige Schutz- und Ratsuchende der Frauenschutz-Beratungstelle," *Sexual-Reform* 13 (Jänner 1923), 1. Interestingly, the German used for "self-induced abortion" is *selbst-hilfe*, which carries with it connotations of self-defense.
43. "Aus einem Brief an die Weiner Frauenschutzberatungstelle," *Sexual-Reform* 17 (Jänner 1924), 5.
44. "Wer Leid mindern will, helfe den Frauen, den Müttern." This motto was used to advertise the League's provincial advice centers. As quoted in Karin Lehner, *Verpönte Eingriffe: sozialdemokratisch Reformbestrebungen zu den Abtreibungsbestimmungen in der Zwischenkriegzeit* (Wien: Picus Verlag, 1989), 39.
45. Ferch published a number of best-selling novels (sometimes using the pseudonyms J. Ferro, Joh. Freiner, or J. Ferron) in the interwar period, including *Kaserne, Zölibat, Mutter, Am Kreuzweg der Liebe, Triumph des Brautkusses,* and *Der Liebesnest*. Ferch's entire publishing history is fascinating, but clearly beyond the scope of this project.
46. For example, see Ferch's literal call to arms in *Kulturkampf* (Wien: Verlagsbuchhandlung Rudolf Cerny, 1922), 13.
47. "Amerikanische Sitten-, Liebes,- und Sexualbegriffe," Bund gegen den Mutterschaftzwang lecture advertisement, 1925. Reprinted in Lehner, *Verpönte Eingriffe*, 35.
48. Lehner, *Verpönte Eingriffe*, 39.
49. Betti (sic) Ferch, "The Birth Control Association of Austria," in Margaret Sanger and Hannah M. Stone (eds.), *The Practice of Contraception: An International Symposium and Survey* (Baltimore: The Williams and Wilkins Company, 1931), 270.
50. Hannah M. Stone, "The Vaginal Occlusive Pessary," in Margaret Sanger and Hannah M. Stone (eds.), *The Practice of Contraception: An International Symposium and Survey* (Baltimore: The Williams and Wilkins Company, 1931), 7.
51. Cecil Voge, "Future Research upon Sterilization and Contraception," in Margaret Sanger and Hannah M. Stone (eds.), *The Practice of Contraception: An International Symposium and Survey* (Baltimore: The Williams and Wilkins Company, 1931), 85–86.
52. "Notizen: Unsere Frauen-Beratungstellen, Für Wien," *Sexual-Reform* 15 (Juli 1923), 2. This notice ran in every edition of *Sexual-Reform*, expanding to list provincial League centers as the decade progressed. It continues with the assurance that all women whose husbands were without work and all poor mothers with large families could receive free pessaries indefinitely, and ends with the highlighted reminder that the Centers will not give advice on how to obtain an abortion or self-induce a miscarriage.
53. Ferch, "The Birth Control Association of Austria," 269.

54. Stone, "The Vaginal Occlusive Pessary," 13.
55. Ferch, "The Birth Control Association of Austria," 270.
56. "Proletarische Sexualberatungsstellen in Wien," *Die Rote Fahne* [27 Jänner 1929], 4.
57. "Proletarische Sexualberatungstellen," *Rote Fahne*, 4.
58. "Proletarische Sexualberatungstellen," *Rote Fahne*, 4.
59. Wilhelm Reich's later involvement with sexual counseling movements in Berlin is beyond the scope of this project. For his career outside Vienna, see Wilhelm Reich, *The Function of the Orgasm: Sex-Economic Problems of Biological Energy*, translated by Theodore P. Wolfe (New York: Noonday Press, 1942); Lee Baxendall (ed.), *Sex-Pol: Essays, 1929–1934* (New York: Random House, 1972); Karl Fallend und Bernd Nitzschke (hg.), *Der "Fall" Wilhelm Reich: Beiträge zum Verhältnis von Psychoanalyse und Politik* (Frankfurt am Main: Suhrkamp, 1997); and especially Atina Grossmann, *Reforming Sex: The German Movement for Birth Control and Abortion Reform, 1920–1950* (New York: Oxford University Press, 1995), which offers healthy skepticism in the face of Reich's own myth-making. For the purposes of this chapter, I have found Karl Fallend's biography of Reich, which focuses on his work in Vienna, to be most useful. See Karl Fallend, *Wilhelm Reich in Wien: Psychoanalyse und Politik* (Wien: Ludwig-Boltzmann-Instituut für Geschichte der Gesellschaftswissenschaften, 1988).
60. Statuten des Vereines "Sozialistische Gesellschaft für Sexualberatung and Sexualforschung," Wiener Stadt- und Landesarchiv, Vereine 1440/23.
61. Wilhelm Reich, "Erfahrungen und Probleme der Sexualberatungstellen für Arbeiter und Angestellte in Wien," *Der Sozialistische Arzt* 5 (Mai 1929), 98–103.
62. Reich, "Erfahrungen," 98.
63. Reich, "Erfahrungen," 100.
64. Reich, "Erfahrungen," 101.
65. Wilhelm Reich, *Sexualerregung und Sexualbefriedigung* (Wien: Münster-Verlag, 1929), 63. This statement comes as an answer to "commonly asked question" number 48, "In what way does the Sexual Advice Center combat sexual misery?"
66. Reprinted in Karl Fallend, *Wilhelm Reich*, 125.
67. Wilhelm Reich, "The Socialistic Society for Sexual Advice and Sexual Research," in Margaret Sanger and Hannah M. Stone (eds.), *The Practice of Contraception: An International Symposium and Survey* (Baltimore: The Williams and Wilkins Company, 1931), 271.
68. Reich, "Socialistic Society," 271.
69. Wilhelm Reich, *Geschlechtsreife, Enthaltsamkeit, Ehemoral: Eine Kritik der bürgerlichen Sexual-Reform* (Wien: Münster Verlag, 1931).
70. Reich, "Erfahrungen," 99.
71. Reich, "Socialistic Society," 271.
72. Reich, *Sexualerregung*, 42–58.
73. Pius XI, *On Christian Marriage: The English Translation* (New York: The Barry Vail Corporation, 1931), 2.
74. Pius XI, *Christian Marriage*, 63.
75. Pius XI, *Christian Marriage*, 31–32. Emphasis in original.
76. Pius XI, *Christian Marriage*, 32. Voluntary sterilization is also condemned, on the grounds that "private individuals have no other power over the members of their bodies than that which pertains to their natural ends." Pius XI, *Christian Marriage*, 33.
77. Pius XI, *Christian Marriage*, 29.
78. Pius XI, *Christian Marriage*, 32.
79. Pius XI, *Christian Marriage*, 58.

Chapter 5

EMOTIONAL RESPONSES
Hugo Bettauer's Vienna Weeklies

The range of sexual knowledge described thus far in this book has been bound by science. Sexual knowledge production in Vienna began with medicine and sexology in the nineteenth century. In turn, the social scientific traditions of sociology, psychology, and economics prompted state and medical authorities to expand popular sexual knowledge and shaped the ways that this knowledge was expressed. Popular advice manuals for children and adults mirrored these changes. The present chapter, however, looks at the ways erotica sold sexual knowledge to the reading (or looking) public of Vienna. It focuses on the weekly newspapers published by Hugo Bettauer, a successful author whose journals featured sexual information, including knowledge drawn from science, for a non-elite audience. The popular, unofficial *Aufklärung* provided by Bettauer was more sensational and emotional and yet very similar to the reform directives of feminists, socialists, and supporters of sexual education.

In the 1920s, Hugo Bettauer's life and death were publicized in the Viennese press. A broad spectrum of Vienna's politicians, journalists, and ravenous newspaper readers championed and reviled Bettauer. This life, in turn, has been chronicled in a single biography written in 1978: *Der Fall Bettauer* ("The Case of Bettauer"), by Murray C. Hall. Hall reconstructs Bettauer's life using records from the Viennese press and the Austrian justice system.[1] He argues that Bettauer was the first victim of a climate of political polarization and anti-Semitism that fed upon itself until the Republic itself was broken.[2] Hall's assessments are correct, but they tell a scandalous story rather than a complicated one. Hall does not analyze the ostensible source of the Bettauer controversy, that is, the weekly newspapers Bettauer edited. Because Hall argues that the pornography charges brought against Bettauer were ruses that hid political hatred, the content, style, and unusual emotional tenor of Bettauer's publications goes unnoticed. Clearly, Bettauer's Jewishness made him a target for many groups in interwar Vienna. Jews played critical roles in creating psychoanalysis and sexual science, and Bettauer publicized both of these forms of knowledge to a popular audience. Yet rather than a simple case of anti-Semitism, the attacks on Bettauer were linked to his campaign for greater sexual knowledge and erotic freedom.

Hugo Bettauer's career as a controversial journalist who published information about sex in non-scientific genres has been overshadowed by his success as a novelist and by the spectacular way in which he died. This chapter establishes his place in the city's popular cultural landscape by studying publishing runs, press coverage, pornography charges, and finally, his assassination in 1925. Bettauer was committed to a kind of society-wide economic and political reform that was highly critical of "bourgeois morality" and the Roman Catholic Church, and yet did not fit within the boundaries of the Social Democratic Worker's Party (henceforth SDAP) that challenged these traditions in the interwar period. His journals focused on the personal consequences of sexual behavior, and used emotional language to convey a new approach to popular sexual knowledge that was sold by book copies and subscription rates. Two newspapers brought him fame: *Er und Sie* ("He and She") and *Bettauers Wochenschrift* ("Bettauer's Weekly"). Using concepts drawn from recent work on the history of emotion, I highlight the political messages embedded within Bettauer's journalism. I then turn to Bettauer's murderer, Otto Rothstock, to show that these political beliefs were the primary motivation for Bettauer's assassination.

Hugo Bettauer and the *Prozeß* of Pornography

Maximilian Hugo Bettauer was born in Baden, a town just outside of Vienna, in 1872.[3] He attended the Franz-Josef Gymnasium in Vienna, where he was the classmate of Karl Kraus. In 1890, on his eighteenth birthday, Bettauer formally registered his departure from the Jewish community and was baptized in a Viennese Lutheran church. Soon afterwards, he enlisted for one year of service in the army, and was stationed in Tyrol. After five months, Bettauer deserted and, with the help of his mother, fled to Zurich. There he married his childhood sweetheart and began a peripatetic existence between New York, Berlin, and Hamburg that lasted until 1910, when he returned to Vienna. In this twenty-year period, he divorced, remarried, and became an American citizen. Bettauer worked in New York as a correspondent to several German newspapers and wrote crime serials published in the local German-language press. Once he returned to Vienna, Bettauer worked as a writer and editor for *Die Zeit*, a small daily newspaper. During the war years, he was on the editing team of the much more prestigious *Neue Freie Press*, and was eventually sent to cover the Polish front.[4] In 1918, while at the front, he was charged with stealing an Underwood typewriter and fired. Briefly styling himself as Hugo von Bettauer, he returned to Vienna and served as the correspondent to two New York newspapers, covering the worsening post-war conditions in the city. In 1920, his journalistic efforts led to a position as the press representative of an American relief fund that provided foodstuffs to the Austrian population.

Bettauer's engagement with the living conditions in Vienna was reflected in the novels he produced in the immediate post-war period. Homelessness, hunger, poverty, sexual exploitation, inflation, blackmail, and anti-Semitism marked the daily struggles of his characters. His most famous works, *The City Without Jews* (1922) and *The Joyless Street* (1924) date from this period. It was through the former novel that he first drew criticism from the Christian Social Party (CSP), whose party newspaper reported that *City Without Jews* advocated Jewish husbands for virgin Christian girls.[5] Bettauer published twelve other novels in these four years, whose titles reflect a specialization in murder mysteries and what were called *Sittenromanen* ("morality stories"): melodramatic romances with a social message or moral commentary.[6] These *Sittenromanen* were set in contemporary, post-war Vienna and featured current political, religious, and cultural leaders as background characters. In these novels, Catholic and Socialist forces battled, financial collapse loomed, and characters and readers alike shared a world that seemed poised to shift and rip apart at any moment.[7] Bettauer's *Sittenromanen*, many of which were serialized, were also extremely successful. By 1924, *City Without Jews* had sold more than 250,000 copies, had been developed into a three-act play, and was in the process of being filmed by director Hans Karl Breslauer.[8] That same year, *The Joyless Street* appeared in book form, immediately sold 30,000 copies, and was filmed by P.W. Pabst.[9]

Drawing from the acclaim and financial success of his novels, Bettauer founded a newspaper in early 1924 entitled *Er und Sie: Wochenschrift für Lebenskultur und Erotik* ("He and She: Weekly Newspaper of Lifestyle Reform and the Erotic"). As editor of the weekly, Bettauer wrote front-page essays and also answered advice questions in a column called "Life's Problems." Each issue printed chapters from Bettauer's latest novel-in-progress, "The Merry Women of Vienna." The paper also serialized a melodramatic first-person testimony to poverty, marital unhappiness, and abortion attempts "told" by an anonymous Viennese midwife. There was a section for personal ads, a medical column that alternated weekly between a psychiatrist and a specialist in women's health, and a section devoted to "Erotica from around the World." This last column featured historical and scientific examples of the diversity of sexual experience. It reprinted individual cases first studied by sexologists Havelock Ellis and Iwan Bloch, mused on the cultural differences that led different peoples to view aspects of the body or sexual activity as shameful, and illustrated Darwin's principals of sexual selection with reference to butterflies, birds, and frogs. As the paper's title suggested, *Er und Sie* concerned itself primarily with heterosexual lifestyles.

On the front page of each issue, the title *Er und Sie* was set over a stylized rising sun, flanked by a reclining couple sketched as artist's models—flat, faceless, and nude. Beginning in the second issue, each front page also featured a black-and-white reproduction of an Old Masters painting that took love as its theme and usually included a nude female form. This front-cover reproduction was the major pictorial relief to an otherwise text-dominated newspaper. Small sketches were incorporated into the titles of serial-novel columns, rather like illuminated letters. However, any human figures in these sketches were fully clothed. The use of the term "erotica" in the paper's title and columns was somewhat misleading. Erotica is sexually explicit material intended to provoke sexual arousal.[10] *Er und Sie* featured sexually explicit material that was presented within a sexological format. Readers were exposed to non-procreative sexual practices, but these practices were not packaged as fantasies or "scenes," but rather embedded within medical and sociological reporting. I will explore this topic latter in the chapter, in relation to the pornography charges brought against *Er und Sie*. For now, I simply want to forewarn modern readers that Bettauer's erotica was at times titillating but largely tame.[11]

Er und Sie first appeared on Valentine's Day, 1924. The first issue, twelve pages long, was funded entirely by Hugo Bettauer and his business partner Rudolf Olden. Twenty thousand copies were printed and sold at 2,000 Kronen each.[12] The second and all subsequent issues were sixteen pages each, and printed in larger batches of 60,000 copies. Advertising and a personals section (for which people paid 1,200 Kronen per word, with a rough average of 15 words per blurb) both expanded during *Er and Sie*'s run. Hall estimates that the second issue of *Er und Sie* reached about 200,000 readers.[13] This would mean that every copy was read by at least three people, which is in keeping with reading practices reported slightly later in the interwar period, especially among women's magazines.[14] However, the popular success of the newspaper can also be established by its expansion in length and printing batch, both of which were expensive undertakings and would have been financially foolish without reader support and acclaim.

On 29 February, after three issues of *Er und Sie* had appeared, Dr. Julius Tandler wrote to the Vienna police division in charge of the press. Tandler and his lead role in the development of interwar Vienna's sexual hygiene system have been discussed at length in the opening chapter of this work. Tandler, as director of the municipal Welfare Office, and thus of Youth Welfare, criticized Bettauer for knowingly spreading dangerous concepts to young readers, who were exposed to the paper on street corners and in public places. Tandler argued in his letter that *Er und Sie* should be removed from the public. He wrote that only a particular section of the population was "ripe" for Bettauer's revolutionary thoughts on love and that his newspaper "must surely be misunderstood by most, because the paper itself does not offer the required moral and aesthetic *Aufklärung* and explanation [of sexual matters]."¹⁵ He continued: "In the absence of a properly aligned feeling of responsibility [*Verantwortlichkeitsgefühls*], this unrestrained propaganda represents a great danger to society in terms of health, population politics, and moral relationships (venereal diseases, divorce without regard for the children, etc.)."¹⁶ Tandler closed his argument by suggesting that the editor and publisher of the newspaper were surely aware of the "adverse effects" of their paper, and that its contents "at the very least consciously exploited, above all, a youthful urge."¹⁷ By identifying sexual urges as youthful and suggesting that young people were exposed to *Er und Sie* in public places, Tandler signaled that the magazine was suitable for censorship.

There was no governmental censor in the Austrian First Republic, but Tandler's letter indicated that that *Er und Sie*'s content qualified for the application of Paragraph 12 of Vienna's press laws, which allowed materials posing a danger to the moral well-being of youths to be seized upon recommendation by a school authority or a Youth Welfare officer. As the ultimate Youth Welfare authority, Tandler was within his legal rights when he wrote to the Viennese police. Yet it is curious that he chose to do so. Tandler and the SDAP supported sexual education for both children and adults as part of a society-wide attempt to prevent venereal disease and promote the creation of orderly (and thus smaller) working-class families. Tandler may have felt genuinely concerned about the open discussion of sexological issues in *Er und Sie*, particularly the reprinted case studies, which were reported as news. It is also clear that Tandler's concepts of sexual responsibility were at odds with the messages of personal sexual and romantic freedom that *Er und Sie* promulgated. However, I think that politics played a major role in this decision. Tandler and the Social Democratic powers he represented enjoyed complete control of the Welfare Office in Vienna. Yet the SDAP was engaged in a bitter struggle for dominance in the Ministry for Education throughout the interwar period. As historian Malachi Hacohen has recently shown, SDAP education reforms were repeatedly blocked by the Christian Social Party, and throughout the period the majority of teachers in Vienna remained staunchly Catholic politically.¹⁸ Thus, of the two authorities that could conceivably demand censorship of Bettauer's magazine, only one was reliably aligned with city hall. In this light, Tandler's move appears as a preemptory strike, designed to shut down the newspaper before any teacher-based group could draw attention to the "unrestrained" sexual *Aufklärung* Bettauer's weekly magazine offered. A Catholic Social attack on *Er und Sie* would certainly use the magazine as ammunition with which to argue against any form of public sexual education, be it in schools, counseling centers, or popular magazines. By denouncing the style in which Bettauer offered sexual information, Tandler left room for more controlled, morally secure forms of *Aufklärung* to be approved by the municipal government.

Tandler complained that *Er und Sie* lacked a "properly aligned feeling of responsibility."[19] It is not clear from his denunciation whether Tandler was referring to a political alignment or a more general sense of sexual morality. However, Tandler's reference to the paper's "far-reaching 'revolutionary' notions of love" suggests that he had both read and taken exception to Bettauer's first editorial, "The Erotic Revolution."[20] This essay combined the emotional, the sexual, and the political in ways designed to provoke any city authority. Bettauer began with a long list of what was wrong in the Vienna of 1924, including inflation, housing shortages, "racial and nationalistic hate," and the increasing assertions of capitalism.[21] He then identified the hidden stirrings of a new cultural force:

> These daily worries so terribly confuse and drown us that we hardly know or feel that we are in fact living through a powerful revolution, the most decisive of all times. We are in the middle of a revolution accomplished without leaders and trends, without public notices and unrestricted by power bases or demagogy. This revolution, more than any political one, will surely alter the lives of the coming generation. It is the erotic revolution![22]

As shown in chapter 1 of this book, "the coming generation" was a topic of great import to Tandler, who explained his hygiene and welfare reforms explicitly in terms of what would be best for the next Viennese generation. In Bettauer's hands, the coming generation stood to inherit a radically altered sexual landscape. Erotic feelings would be liberated from the Christian concept of a single, eternal marriage. Divorce and illegitimacy would be freed of moral approbation. Prostitutes would be given the vote, and women would cease to be objects and become actors in all arenas, including sexual ones.[23] Bettauer claimed that erotic relationships had become jumbled in the aftermath of the war, and that the youth and working class were already dispensing with previous sexual hypocrisies and getting on with new lives. "The erotic revolution," he promised, would "create free people, more joyful people."[24] Obligation of any kind, much less that aligned with a political party's goals, was absent in Bettauer's manifesto. Whatever his personal feelings, Tandler must have been professionally appalled by the text.

Bettauer never saw Tandler's letter to the police, nor knew who had begun the proceedings against his newspaper. On 4 March 1924, he was notified that *Er und Sie* was henceforth pulled from magazine stands and street-vendors and that its sale to minors (anyone under eighteen) was now illegal. The Vienna police press-bureau also made it clear to Bettauer that they had nothing to do with the case, but rather that the complaint had come from within the Youth Authority.[25] This knowledge may have prompted Bettauer's response to the case, which was to write a letter of appeal to the Social Democratic mayor of Vienna, Karl Seitz, asking him to lift all barriers to *Er und Sie*'s publication. This letter is worth quoting at length for the logic of Bettauer's argument. Bettauer grounded his request by explaining his own goal as publisher:

> It would strike the editors of *Er und Sie* as entirely improper to establish a purely commercial undertaking. Rather, the paper is saturated by the idea that precisely our time demands advice and *Aufklärung* for the most difficult problems in life. Not only would we never intend any kind of unhealthy influence on youth, but rather we are convinced that a paper that, among other things, concerns itself with sexual problems and handles them in a serious manner can only be of use to young people. The two to three hundred letters that we receive daily from our readers are the best evidence that this paper serves a purpose. Even the most rigorous examination of our previously appearing issues will not reveal even a fragment of a racy remark or anything that would be suitable for arousing sexual fantasies. Nevertheless, we are entirely ready to take even greater regard for young readers than our editing team has already done, and to wipe out everything in word and picture that could somehow have an adverse affect on youthful fantasies.[26]

Bettauer's letter to Seitz contains a mixture of self-righteousness and willingness to compromise with city authorities. Bettauer situated himself among the sexual reformers who have populated earlier chapters of this book: people who sought to "be of use" by bringing scientific knowledge to a general public through sexual education. His emphasis upon the timeliness of the sexual advice *Er und Sie* provided, and of the number of inquiries and reader responses that poured back into the editing office, wove the young weekly into the fabric of the city. Bettauer's pride in offering such a service to his readers, via *Aufklärung*, is checked only by the willingness he expressed to modify the newspaper in any way city hall saw fit. Such a stance further supported his description of *Er und Sie* as a teaching tool rather than a money-making scheme.

As the Christian Social President of the Viennese Police, Johann Schober, and the Social Democratic vice-president of the Viennese School Council, Otto Glöckel, squared off over the appropriateness of applying Paragraph 12 to *Er und Sie*, Bettauer's case was taken up in even wider circles. On 14 March 1925, the CSP's *Reichspost* reprinted a speech made by Chancellor Ignaz Seipel at a party congress two days earlier. Seipel was respected as a priest, Professor of Theology in Salzburg, and the leader of the Christian Social Party since 1921. In this speech, Seipel attacked pornography and social democracy with one blow and named the SDAP responsible for the spread of soul-damaging materials like *Er und Sie*. Explaining that the amount of pornographic materials available in the typical Viennese corner *Tabak* was such that he had all of his newspapers delivered to his home, Chancellor Seipel claimed that "until now, such a flood of pornography had never existed in our Vienna before."[27] He placed the blame for this upon the SDAP in control of city hall and especially upon the *Landeshauptmann* and mayor of Vienna, Karl Seitz. He charged: "Often it has been reported to me that the police will move to censure [plays, forms of art, or newspapers], but that censorship in Vienna will then regularly be rescinded in the name of the *Landeshauptmann*."²⁸ Seipel then referred to Bettauer's weekly. He re-narrated the political situation for his audience:

> I seem to remember that in one of these cases the municipal Youth Welfare Office protested against the spread of certain obscene publications [*Schmutzschriften*] and notified the police, but even this was' not enough. The police, who wanted to step in, were detained, apparently by a report that came from the municipal School Board. I believe that the mayor, as *Landeshauptmann*, will have to choose a side.

Seipel's feigned tone of distance from the case ("I believe I remember …," "apparently by a report …") only sharpened the critique he leveled. His speech hinted at the tensions within the SDAP regarding pornography. In it, Seipel set Tandler, as final authority within the Youth Welfare Office, against Glöckel, a School Board leader and SDAP representative who enjoyed great popularity. In Seipel's story, the Viennese police were merely caught in the middle, unable to do their job. By calling Seitz out, Seipel hoped to make public the private rift within the SDAP over Bettauer's newspaper.

Seitz's response came three days later, on 15 March 1924, at the Austrian Representative Assembly. His attack was personal and divisive:

> The Chancellor must come to terms with the fact that one cannot judge the civilized life of a world capital from the perspective of church views … but rather that certain sections of a big city's population naturally judge the erotic differently from the simple population of the countryside or some monk in his cloistered isolation.²⁹

Seitz went on to challenge Seipel to produce any evidence that the SDAP was acting in ways that increased public immorality. He suggested that the Christian Social furor over papers like Bettauer's was a ruse, and that Seipel himself misunderstood the Vienna constituency he claimed to serve:

> The facts of this case are clear: that Professor Seipel has set out not to protect the morality of the public or even that of youth from certain excesses of the press, but rather, as he has shown from this entire discourse, that he wants to open up a *Kulturkampf* against a great party and against the great majority of the Viennese population. I say with complete confidence: "There is not one Social Democrat who does not have the courage to take up this battle, if the Chancellor wants it. When Professor Seipel came to Vienna so many years ago, perhaps he did not imagine that he would someday feel himself called to instruct the Viennese about which party has no business on Viennese soil, and which party has been called to lead the city."³⁰

Seitz thus warned that any action Seipel might take in the censorship debate would only further reveal the gap between Christian Social ideals and Viennese realities. Seitz's suggestion that the Chancellor was a stranger to the capital and out of touch with the common people must have been personally galling to Seipel, who was born in Vienna, and whose father was a *Fiaker* (carriage taxi) driver.[31]

Seitz ended his speech with a vow. Whenever the Christian Socials wanted to pursue their interests in city government, he counseled, they would find an SDAP representative willing to stand up to them and defend what was important, including free artistic and journalistic expression. "Naturally," assures Seitz, "we will defend the right of young people to protection from moral dangers with the same energy ... . This protection can be provided without endangering the freedom of the press or the freedom of any art form."[32] With this speech, Seitz committed himself and the SDAP to *Er und Sie*, despite the obvious lack of consensus within his party. Along the way, he derided the most powerful Christian Social statesman of the First Republic, personally and politically.

Seitz's speech was reprinted in both the municipal *Wiener Zeitung* and the Catholic daily *Reichspost*. Other papers merely commented on the acid exchange between Seipel and Seitz, charging the former with "prelate-scolding," and "perfidious political tactics" (*Arbeiter-Zeitung*) and the latter with "answering [serious charges] with cheap scorn and superficial little jokes" (*Wiener Stimmen*).[33] The sniping continued. On 21 March, Christian Social City Councilman Anton Orel sidelined a report by Julius Tandler on proposed municipally funded after-school day care by bringing up the Bettauer scandal. Orel interrupted the debate with a series of questions on what might be taught in the centers. Implying that the Social Democrats would allow children to read inappropriate material, Orel's speech incited a shouting match between SDAP and Christian Social representatives. He addressed Seitz directly:

> If the Mayor doesn't know what is allowed to appear before children's eyes, then I will have to tell him! (Stormy applause) If the Mayor knew what he had done [in defending Bettauer], then he would have had to give this Jew a swift kick and thrown him out the door! (Stormy applause.) Emphatically, I can say that we categorically oppose the fact that the mayor is forcing a dirty Jewish commercialist upon us, who wants to soil our children with Jewish poison and Jewish swinishness![34]

Orel was unable to curb his passionate speech. When Seitz eventually reprimanded Orel for breaking parliamentary procedure, Orel refused, claiming that Seitz was unworthy of his position as mayor. The Social Democratic bench broke out of turn and cried that they would not allow "their mayor" to be insulted by such an "idiot."[35] Orel then cried out, "Go home, Bettauer-Party!," and his phrase was picked up and chanted throughout the room.[36] A fistfight broke out in council chambers. The scene was reported immediately by a spectrum of newspapers, from the *Arbeiter-Zeitung* on the left to the *Volkssturm* on the right. The latter newspaper's headlines for that week were: "Seitz on the run. Mayor called to responsibility for the Bettauer Scandal. Big defeat for the Red-Jewish terrorists in City Hall."[37]

The "Bettauer Scandal" revealed the widening chasm between Social Democratic and Christian Social approaches to civic culture. As the above speeches show, the debate turned on the issue of what kinds of knowledge should be available to the Viennese public. Sexual knowledge, especially when accessible by children, was deemed by many too dangerous to be a component of the city's cultural landscape. Those opposed to its dissemination could identify along party lines, but the subject also made allies out of political opposites. The Bettauer case provoked both the anti-Semitic councilman Orel and the Jewish head of the city's welfare program, Julius Tandler, into arguing the same point: that the presence of *Er und Sie* on city sidewalks endangered Viennese children. Indeed it is likely that Orel chose for his outburst a city council meeting in which Tandler was presenting precisely because Tandler had moved to censure *Er und Sie*. Perhaps Orel had hoped that Tandler would join him in denouncing Bettauer before the mayor and the rest of the SDAP in office. Certainly the topic of that day's debate, municipal care of children, was a meaningful component of Orel's attack. In this spectacular instance, the Bettauer case expanded very quickly from a political contestation over the right to censorship into a public debate over pornography, broadcast in newspapers across the city. The media storm surrounding Bettauer, which erupted immediately after the scene in city council chambers, continued for the next two years. During this time, Bettauer would be identified as a friend of the common man, a vile profiteer, a Jewish swine, a martyr, and a traitor.[38] It was as if he had entered the pages of his own Viennese *Sittenromanen* as hero, villain, and victim all at once.

Meanwhile, in response to Seipel's initial public complaint, the Vienna District Attorney began preparing a suit. On 14 March, one month after the first edition appeared, *Er und Sie*'s editors were charged with breaking four separate laws involving public obscenity, degradation of marriage and of the family, and procurement.[39] Bettauer responded by bringing a countersuit for illegal seizure against the city courts. Perhaps optimistically, he then sent the plans for *Er und Sie*'s sixth issue to the city press attorney, who, in his role as "preventative censor," objected to a psychological article that explicated sexual problems.[40] Five days later, Bettauer resigned from his post as editor and began dissolving the journal.

Although the sixth issue of *Er und Sie* never went to print, we can surmise the style of the offending article from the format of previous editions. The anonymous *Nervenarzt* who wrote for Bettauer's newspaper provided a bimonthly column that drew from his professional practice and occasionally addressed readers' anatomical, medical, and psychiatric questions. *Er und Sie*'s in-house psychiatrist signed himself as Dr. Werner.[41] He had last written for the March 6th issue, when he addressed the problem of impotence in young people. Werner took as his starting point two letters that had been sent for publication in *Er und Sie*'s "Life's Problems" column. In a style that combined the formats of an advice column and a case study, the *Nervenarzt* diagnosed both letters, now titled "Case I and II." His explication made reference to Adlerian inferiority complexes and cited Wilhelm Steckel's *Impotence in Men* and *Masturbation and Homosexuality*. Nothing about the article would be unusual, were it appearing in a professional journal. What was daring about the piece was that it was not an abstract case study intended for a medical audience, but rather a series of direct messages to common men suffering from impotence: pills and shock treatments were useless, masturbation was safe, and marriage was no cure.[42] It is most likely that the "preventative censor's" objections to Dr. Werner's column stemmed from its presentation of the daily lives of Viennese people as sexological case studies. Such studies were acceptable in specialist texts and medical journals, but not, as the Bettauer case shows, in the popular press. *Er und Sie* forced political authorities to declare precisely what kinds of sexual information were appropriate for whom. Apparently, sexological insights and case studies, when set in contemporary Vienna, were inappropriate for a general audience.

On 21 March, Bettauer's countersuit against the city of Vienna was thrown out of court. The Vienna Police received a second warrant to confiscate copies of *Er und Sie* on 1 April 1924. Only three unsold copies of the first issue were found in Vienna; two copies of the second issue were confiscated.[43] The by now two-week old fifth issue yielded 4,570 copies, less than 10 percent of the printing. There was no sixth issue to seize. The legal argument against Bettauer and his partner, Rudolf Olden, posited that the newspaper was marketed to young readers. It also increasingly focused on procurement, claiming that *Er und Sie* had published, for profit, singles' ads that were in fact advertisements for sexual services. Their trial began in September and was widely covered in the press.

At the trial, both men pleaded not guilty to all charges. Bettauer explained his newspaper's purpose as that of mitigating the sexual misery of modern urban people, especially young people. Responding to the term "sexual misery" [*Sexualnot*], the district attorney immediately suggested that the room be cleared, perhaps in deference to the fact that the majority of people who had lined up to attend the trial were women.[44] The defense lawyers representing Bettauer and Olden successfully argued to keep the trial public. Bettauer then went on to testify that the incriminating singles' ads that had appeared in *Er und Sie* had been placed by his layout team and that he himself never was in the habit of reading them. Olden told a similar story, explaining that his role was entirely administrative. Two witnesses from the paper confirmed their accounts. Late that evening, the district attorney withdrew the charges of procurement, and the case against Olden was thrown out. The next day, the jury was presented with a list of sixteen counts, and asked to judge if any of them showed Bettauer to be in conflict with Paragraph 516 of the legal code: violation of public morality or modesty through images or lewd stories.[45] After a three-hour deliberation, they found him not guilty on all counts.[46]

Emotion in *Er und Sie*

What was it about *Er und Sie* that shook Vienna in 1924? Bettauer's biographer and subsequent historians have answered this question by emphasizing Bettauer's person, and especially his Jewishness, rather than the content of his publications.[47] Obviously, Bettauer was a colorful character—deserter, converter, divorcé, thief, and self-titled aristocrat, all before his publishing career in Vienna took off. I agree that Bettauer's colorful past may have brought attention his publications. Nor do I want to argue that his publications were, or were not, indecent. As I have already suggested, the newspaper was not formatted in ways that lent themselves to fantasy or sexual stimulation, but I hesitate to rule out the imaginative readings it may have received from Viennese consumers. Instead, I assert that the line between erotica and pornography would not illuminate Bettauer's case. Rather than delimit the boundaries of taste, I want to look at the emotional messages within *Er und Sie*. Bettauer's paper did not merely offer knowledge about sexual matters, it also offered a model for how to feel about sexual matters. Sex, in *Er und Sie*, was a function of strong emotion and physical attraction combined. Even as the magazine enumerated the global variations of object choice and activity, it provided a local language of love and loneliness that made sex talk possible. Using this emotional language, *Er und Sie* instructed its readers to find and enjoy satisfaction through (physical) love.

The layout of *Er und Sie* provided a map of various emotional models for its readers to emulate. Bettauer's front-page editorials and responses to "Life's Problems," dominated by his open talk about sexual and social matters, formed the largest continent of this map. As we will see, Bettauer often asked his readers directly to feel a certain way about a sexual situation. In contrast, the medical columns and "Erotica from Around the World" presented sexual information in a neutral tone, but also offered psychoanalytical insight into emotional states. Bettauer's serial melodrama, "The Merry Women of Vienna," was an entirely different landscape. Set amidst the high life of Vienna, its characters moved through grand hotels, train stations, and five o'clock teas with emotions consistent with their roles. The static nature of its victims and villains was enlivened by plot twists, which may have excited the readers but did not offer insight into the characters' psychological lives. Similarly, the singles' ads run in the newspaper under the title "People Seeking One Another" did not offer emotional flexibility or show changes in feeling states. People rarely described themselves or their ideal partners in emotional terms, but rather quickly sketched themselves as "types." Finally, *Er und Sie* also gave considerable space to first-person testimonies, which came in the form of letters to the editor ("Life's Problems") and the autobiography of a midwife, which was printed in installments. Whether or not these testimonies were actually first-person, as opposed to the creation of the editorial team, is irrelevant to the argument I want to make. In the letters and testimonies, individuals struggled with sexual problems and cogently explained their related feelings. This process provided yet another way for readers to see emotion experienced, explained, and managed.

As this map of *Er und Sie* suggests, three sections of the paper deserve close attention to the emotions expressed therein: the editorial essays and responses of Hugo Bettauer, the scientific information provided within medical columns and "Erotica from Around the Word," and the first-person life stories that dominated both "Memoirs of a Midwife" and "Life's Problems." Instead of analyzing each section individually, I will compare their messages within the framework of emotions. By this I mean the ways in which certain feelings were discussed, but also the social attitudes and personal attributes that combined to make a desired (or undesired) emotion possible. In thinking about emotion, in *Er und Sie*, I have drawn from William Reddy's concept of "emotional regimes" or the systems within a society that govern the ways in which its citizens are asked to feel.[48] It seems to me that the truly remarkable thing about *Er und Sie* was not the content of the magazine, but rather the emotional regime that it created for its readers. This emotional regime, while not necessarily at odds with some of the political causes of the First Republic (particularly socialist sexual education), illuminated the instability of the Republic' through reference to individual pain and personal injustice. *Er und Sie* revealed the interconnectedness of social conditions, personal freedom, and the ability to satisfactorily find and retain a sexual, loving relationship.

Inclination. The term "inclination" is difficult to translate into a modern emotion, but was central to the construction of love in *Er und Sie*. Bettauer defined love through mutual inclination in his editorials. He wrote: "I allow every human the right to fulfill himself erotically ... and am free from any kind of sexual prejudice. There is only one rule in my book: the relationship between man and woman must be based upon understanding, free will, and deep, inner inclination!" Using this logic, Bettauer reversed the official morality of union, claiming that union for inclination was justified even outside of marriage, but that marriage without free will and inclination was "immoral prostitution in the worst sense of the word."[49]

Following one's inclination might entail making a difficult choice. One reader, "Anny," received a response from *Er und Sie* to a problem either so specific or so grave that the question was not reprinted. She was advised to search her own complex feelings and consult her heart. *Er und Sie* wrote: "Your feelings are twofold. You are making yourself sick over a man/husband who neglects you, but another part of you is ready to seek a new partner. Think the matter over carefully and then do that which your will urges."[50] Without the original letter, it is impossible to know whether the neglectful man is "Anny's" husband or lover. The indeterminacy of her relationship to the man makes the letter slightly piquant. That an individual should consult her own desires, rather than abide by the will of her parents, her husband, or her church, is a surprising response to be delivered by a popular magazine in 1925. What is especially interesting about this message is the way inclination is decided by personal feelings, or "will," alone.

In *Er und Sie*, inclination was linked to loyalty as well as choice. "Lore" wrote to the magazine seeking advice about a married man she felt inclination for. He offered to divorce his wife and apply for a *Dispensehe*, and thus the right to remarry "Lore." She questioned, though, whether it was better to remain his lover, writing: "Should I enter into a *Dispensehe*, provoking a struggle with [his current] wife, who sees me as her mortal enemy, or should I continue to live as his mistress, scorned by the world?"[51] The response she received valued loyalty in love over any legal action:

> Hold your head up and remain a true companion to the man who has, through love for you, surely suffered enough. Remain a true companion, with or without the *Dispensehe*. And don't concern yourself with the talk of others. People who throw stones at a girl because she is true to the man who loves her cannot be held in high regard.[52]

In this example, following one's inclination meant staying loyal to a love, regardless of its legality. Like "Anny," "Lore" is advised to value her inclination above what others might say about her sexual behavior. *Er und Sie*'s response to "Lore" was at once supportive and subversive. Her lover's friends, her own family, and perhaps even the Roman Catholic Church (whose opposition to divorce had necessitated the legal category of the *Dispensehe*, as explained in chapter 3), might "throw stones," but "Lore" and any *Er und Sie* subscribers sympathizing with her were free to disregard them.

Inclination appeared in Bettauer's editorials as something that should be allowed to direct people's sexual practices. Here it served as a drive. However, this use of inclination was equally tied to emotional well-being. In his essay "Sadism, Children, and Obscenity," Bettauer argued that sexual inclination should be freely acted upon so long as it was consensual. He wrote: "Acting out sadistic, masochistic, flagellistic ... homosexual, and fetishistic urges is a private matter."[53] Were one inclined to look at pornographic material, Bettauer would also judge it to be a private matter. It is important to note that Bettauer did not categorize homosexual and non-procreative sexual practices together in order to pathologize them, as did Krafft-Ebing and most other medical and legal authorities. Instead, he was making a much more radical claim the private enjoyment of sexual activity. The only consideration Bettauer believed should trump an individual's sexual inclinations was that of children's safety. Perhaps coyly, he challenged would-be censors:

> When the District Attorney's office sues a book handler for selling or producing pornographic books, I find it laughable, stupid, beastly. Even the creation and enjoyment

of pornography is a private matter [for the individual], which since the time of Maria Theresa has been nobody else's business. However, if I knew of a case in which someone offered such a book ... to a pre-pubescent boy or girl, I would be in favor of the strictest prosecution of this man. For it is a crime to brutally influence the sex life of a person whose concepts are only just being formed, to force open the senses at that age in which nature has not yet awakened such impulses.[54]

What is interesting about Bettauer's example of children exposed to pornography is that it illustrates the limits of inclination in free sexual activity. Those who do not yet possess overt sexual drives, children, are not inclined to pornography. Without clear urges to follow, they cannot consciously choose to consume pornography, which would "force open" their senses. Like any forced sexual situation in Bettauer's editorials, to make a choice for someone else, against their will, is criminal. Bettauer goes on to lampoon attempts made by the police to regulate sexual inclination, which he sees as "nothing less that brutal attacks upon private life."[55] In their inability to honor the free expression of sexual inclination, he suggests, the police fail to protect anyone. Instead, they "serve blackmailers, hypocrites ... [and] swindlers, greasing the way for bribes, hunts, and denunciations."[56]

Guilt. The feeling of guilt was referred to in both Bettauer's editorials and in the advice-seeking letters of "Life's Problems." Guilt was approached from two different levels in these columns: it could stem from a personal (often sexual) action, or it could originate in a general condition.

In the "Mailbox" section of *Er und Sie*'s advice column, a reader identified as "Helene" was told to dispense with her feelings of guilt. The response stands without a letter, but implies sexual dysfunction: "Any guilt should lie less with you, and more with the man that doesn't understand how to awaken you and apparently doesn't complement you physically. There are no grounds for concern, but visit a woman's doctor anyway."[57] This tantalizing answer totally bypasses any question of guilt stemming from sexual activity, and instead hints at the negative effects of unpleasurable or painful sex on a woman's psyche. In another response, a woman identifying herself as frigid is told that she is not alone, and that "shame should play no role here."[58] She also is referred to a doctor, "or better, a psychoanalyst," who can assure her that her "sufferings are not inborn, but rather acquired, and can be healed."[59] These two examples are especially interesting because they show female readers who feel guilty for not enjoying sex, rather than more traditional cases in which sexual activity or pleasure is the impetus for feelings of guilt.

Guilt was also described in relation to reproductive choices. This is clear in examples culled from the anonymous "Memoirs of a Midwife." In this testimony, the narrator is asked by her childhood friend Kathi to perform an abortion. The midwife is torn: "The guilt that no one spoke aloud and yet everyone secretly whispered, that no one wanted to hear about and yet everyone knew about, this guilt, that meant disgrace, imprisonment, and misery, should I take it upon myself?"[60] In this first example, guilt is the inevitable result of social mores. A woman like Kathi will be guilty either of getting an illegal abortion, or shamed by raising an illegitimate child. However, the story also illustrates the way generalized guilt plays out in an individual's body. The midwife refuses her friend, but then finds herself wracked by the physical consequences of guilt. She is unable to sleep, and describes her state: "Over and over, like a bodily pain, [I experienced] thoughts of Kathi."[61] The midwife questions the morality of refusing to help her friend, who will surely seek a dangerous solution to her problem. When Kathi drowns herself in the Danube, the narrator spends days haunted by "the feeling of a serious, treacherous illness … that so altered me, that I sometimes felt I did not know myself."[62] In this serialized testimony, very immediate feelings of personal guilt are combined with a kind of society-wide guilt that accompanies the shamefulness of abortion. "Memoirs of a Midwife" thus instructed readers about how to feel vis-à-vis abortion, suggesting that all citizens were implicated, even "guilty," when the Kathis of Vienna were driven to suicide.

Bettauer also addressed guilt stemming from a general social condition in his editorial "Eros in Chains." The housing shortage of Vienna provided the stage for this emotional lesson. Bettauer described an overcrowded apartment filled with family members from various corners of the former Empire who have come to Vienna in search of work, housing, and possibility. In the poverty of shared beds, incest ensues. The family is miserable, but unable to identify a source, crying, "No one is guilty for the terrible things that happen to us!"[63] Bettauer, as narrator, claims that society is guilty for the emotional and sexual distress within his hypothetical tenement: "What bread-cards, the lack of meat, and inflation don't contrive to do, lack of housing manages: it allows people to become animals, it causes murder and suicide, hate and poison, and creates circumstances more gruesome than the most perverted fantasy could come up with."[64] Lack of housing, Bettauer argues, leads to "sexual relationships against a person's will."[65] As suggested by the discussion of inclination above, forced sexual relationships were described as inherently immoral throughout Bettauer's editorials. In this instance of incest, however, Bettauer did not hold the overcrowded apartment's inhabitants as guilty, but rather blamed the socioeconomic conditions that engendered the incestuous behavior.

Hope. Many of the letters reprinted in "Life's Problems" expressed hope that love would deliver them from personal pain. "Heinrich G." wrote a long testimony to the abuse he had suffered as a child. He was so scarred that he found himself almost unable to feel happiness as a young adult. He concluded: "I know that only a [warm-hearted] girl can lift the sentence upon me, can bring me joy, can fill me with true happiness, and I will love her like nothing else on earth."[66] The editing team approved of his attitude: "The picture that you paint of your childhood makes us shudder. But do not give up! You are young and the woman that you seek will come!"[67] A similar message was delivered to a lonely young doctor, who wrote that he had for some time "been looking for a woman who would marry me, who could care with me and for me, who could be my all … ."[68] The applicant begged: "Publish this letter, esteemed editor of *Er und Sie*, and perhaps among the great number of your female readers I will find a *Sie* who has a heart for me."[69] His request was granted and his letter was published, followed by a short message of encouragement from the editor.

Sometimes, however, the responses to reader letters in *Er und Sie* saw hope that their applicants clearly lacked. One young widow living with her mother wrote to complain that she had not had any relationships with men for four years. She described her loneliness as unbearable: "I am already entertaining suicidal thoughts, as it would be better to die than to live like this."[70] "Lonely Woman" received the following curt reassurance: "The advertisement (*Annonce*, also the word used for singles' ads) you have provided will surely fulfill your goal. At any rate, you should join an association or club that can provide you with social contact. Perhaps there you will find a relationship!"[71] Such advice was sound but perhaps incommensurate with the severity of "Lonely's" distress. The editing team at *Er und Sie* treated "Lonely Woman's" desperate plea as another listing in their "People Seeking One Another" column, perhaps optimistically hoping that she might receive letters from gentlemen with a penchant for the depressed.

"Ernst" opened his testimony with an even darker disclaimer: "I expect no help nor consolation from you; rather, I only mean to exculpate myself, because I feel that something terrible is going to happen."[72] He is concerned that his loneliness and suffering, brought on by childhood blindness, temporary deafness, and an unidentified foot problem, will drive him to crime. He has never had a girlfriend, and is repulsed by the pity people express for his disabilities. This pity evokes scorn, mistrust, and hate within him. He closes by asking the editor why he writes so often about the agonies of adults, paying no head to the tortured lives of those whose sexual drives are not yet ripe. *Er und Sie*'s response to "Ernst" is strangely upbeat:

> Your letter shows you to be an intelligent, thoughtful person. Try to overcome yourself! Sink yourself entirely into a course of study, relinquish yourself! And later on, a woman might even cross your path who is made of stern enough stuff that she might treasure you and be your companion.[73]

The desperation of "Ernst" is thus met with hope. Although the young man is physically scarred, evinces disgust for himself, and feels hate for all around him, *Er und Sie* counsels that if he can only forget himself, then he might hope to meet a woman who can care for him.

Compassion. Perhaps the most common emotional response to sexual situations cited in *Er und Sie* was compassion, which was discussed as an affective state and an attitude. The German word for compassion, *Mitleid,* literally calls for a "suffering with" someone. Because so much of *Er und Sie* was devoted to narratives of individual lives, it provided countless occasions for its readers to "suffer with" their fellow citizens.

Within the medical columns, readers were provided with knowledge of varied forms of sexual activity. Whatever the practice, they were asked to respond to individual sexual misery with compassion. In "One Beset by Release," readers were introduced to the case of a student so frightened by his own sadistic fantasies that he begins to use his dog as a sexual object. The author demands of his reader: "Who stands before the gigantic struggle in the heart of this unhappy young man; who will throw the first stone at him?"[74] When a psychiatrist describes a case of autoerotic asphyxiation gone fatally wrong in "Unusual Love Accident," readers are cued to respond with educated tolerance:

> Whoever is familiar with the way the human psyche hangs together, whoever knows the way the isolated Ego within cries out, will look upon the image of this tied and chained self-tormentor with only the deepest compassion and ask themselves why this person couldn't find the path to a doctor ... who could help him solve the puzzle of his Ego ... .[75]

In this instance, the compassion required to think about such a young man is called for again at the end of the article, when the author ponders how to assess such an individual. He muses: "This is one of the fates of man! Who can judge it?"[76] According to the author, this man could have been spared if someone had helped him understand his true sexual urges, which in this case are diagnosed (*post mortem*) as homosexual and masochistic. Judging him by Christian or legal national standards would be beside the point, the author implies. Instead, readers are asked to suspend any discomfort they might have with the victim's sexual proclivities and regard him with tolerance and mercy.

In an editorial titled "The Turning Point," Bettauer illustrated the compassion he had for homosexuals with an example from his own life. In an extreme example of "suffering with," Bettauer told his readers that he, too, "could have become a homosexual."[77] He described the loving feelings and tenderness that passed between him and a fellow classmate at the age of fifteen. Their relationship was chaste, but Bettauer attributed this only to the fact that one day, while waiting in the *Volksgarten* for his friend, he noticed a beautiful girl and for the first time began having sexual feelings. In this story of the road not taken, the key to sexual orientation lies not in instinct of biology but rather in reciprocal feeling, which Bettauer by chance found with a girl. Bettauer instructs his readers to evaluate homosexuality in terms of personal happiness, asking, "When will people be brought up to believe that everyone has the right to be themselves, the right to be happy in their own way, so long as they do not cause suffering in others?"[78]

The emotional regime suggested by *Er und Sie* had clear political consequences. Compassion, in particular, threw injustice into clear relief. The sexological case of thwarted homoeroticism that resulted in fatal self-strangulation described above implied that the victim's life would have been spared, had he been free to act upon same-sex physical attraction. Indeed, were all citizens allowed union on the basis of inclination and mutual free choice, Bettauer maintained in his editorials, such cases would not exist. Similarly, the guilt that wracked the midwife who refused her friend an abortion would be senseless in a society that allowed women to thus regulate their births. *Er und Sie* reported on abortion rights in its first issue and found both the SDAP and the CSP's positions untenable. Bettauer's essay "The Pressure to Bear Children" weighed the suffering of impoverished women and found it too heavy to justify a ban on abortion. Legal scholars might identify seeking an abortion as illegal activity, the editorial said, but within the *Volk*, "no one held such women as criminals," because common people empathized with them.[79] As Bettauer attested in "The Turning Point," compassionate feelings transformed into passionate politics in his own life. He held up his own experience as a model for readers to use in drawing their own conclusions about sexual freedom and self-fulfillment. Being able to feel supra-political compassion for individual cases of unwanted pregnancy or frustrated homosexuality, in the emotional world of *Er und Sie*, led to political positions against the legal Paragraphs outlawing abortion or same-sex intercourse.

The terms of *Er und Sie*'s "Life's Problems" column are instructive. "Life's Problems" promises responses from "a modern person, who is familiar with the relationships in modern life, who wears no blinders, who isn't a narrow-minded moralist, and who will use this column to speak to people who have something difficult to bear."[80] The passage suggests that compassion will dominate any advice given, rather than any concern for official morality. It is worth noting that the appellation "narrow-minded," (*engherziger*) in the original, would translate exactly as "narrow-hearted," implying that prejudice marked emotional responses rather than just intellectual beliefs. This dichotomy between the heart and mind is continued in the next sentence: "'Life's Problems' will be discussed here without reference to political affiliation, without prejudice, with a cool head but also with a warm heart."[81] The column thus outlines a space in which readers may discuss their romantic and sexual problems (and all of the problems cited in the first issue stem from these areas) without reference to the reigning political or social systems. Such a promise, however, is in itself very political, as it implies that sexual matters can be judged via emotion, and especially compassion, alone. Bettauer's magazine created an ethics of love that used the very imagery of the New Testament ("who will throw the first stone?") to demand humble tolerance of sexual diversity from its readers.

The emotions or attitudinal states that dominated *Er und Sie*'s descriptions of love and sex were not new to public discussion. The branch of German feminism led by Helene Stöcker had advocated free union and equal rights for illegitimate children since 1905.[82] In addition to a local branch of Stöcker's *Bund Fur Mutterschutz*, interwar Vienna was also home to the far-reaching propagandizing and clinical work of Johann and Betty Ferch, whose distribution of birth control information and devices was analyzed in chapter 4. In addition, Johann Ferch wrote over twenty popular, widely-circulating melodramas during this period, all of which pitted heroes and heroines against poverty and sexual hypocrisy in situations very similar to the pages of "Life's Problems." Official municipal culture, dominated by the SDAP, likewise argued for some of the same things as *Er und Sie:* municipal housing, widespread testing for venereal disease, and welfare support for pregnant women and mothers. Finally, as I have shown in chapter 2, sectors within the SDAP even supported sexual *Aufklärung* for children: a topic championed in both Bettauer's editorials and the medical columns of *Er und Sie*.

What was new about the way these subjects were treated in *Er und Sie* was the concept that emotional responses like compassion should take precedence over the received legal and religious traditions governing sexual knowledge and behavior in interwar Vienna. Perhaps even more relevant to *Er und Sie*'s censorship, the newspaper formatted this stance from within scenes of Viennese daily life. Rather than argue for compassion on a philosophical level, *Er und Sie* illustrated the need for compassion through personal testimony, fiery editorials, and medical examples. It showed its readers what their fellow citizens thought and felt. In its pages, the consequences of sexual action or lack of sexual knowledge affected individuals, and personal tragedies set within the city's cultural landscape played out in real time. By depicting the variety of experience, *Er und Sie* implicitly argued against any universal law that could regulate sexual relationships or sexual knowledge. Instead, it created an emotional regime of personal erotic freedom and deep compassion for those whose lives had been stunted by a lack of such freedom.

Bettauer's Message

The dramatic conclusion to Bettauer's pornography trial did not occasion much change in his professional schedule. In fact, since mid-May, he and Olden had been publishing a second newspaper, *Bettauer's Wochenschrift*. Even as the case against his style of journalism was argued in the courts and the press, Bettauer had continued to publish, albeit under a different title, essentially the same magazine. Furthermore, he had used the front-page editorials appearing every week in *Bettauer's Wochenschrift* as platforms from which to defend his work in *Er und Sie*. *Bettauer's Wochenschrift* was printed in weekly batches of 60,000 and sold at the same price as *Er und Sie*. It quickly expanded from sixteen to twenty-four pages and augmented traditional pen-and-ink sketches with photospreads. Instead of an erotic Old Masters reproduction on the cover, *Bettauer's Wochenschrift* ran a series of drawings and photos of women from history, the Viennese stage, film, and exotic places. All were fully clothed. Madame de Pompadour, a local ballerina appearing in the *Staatsoper*, and an Umatilla (Native American) maiden might appear one after another, as weekly examples of beautiful and unusual women. New features were added to the magazine, including a "Foreign" serialized story, a "Story of the Week," (usually by Bettauer himself), and a fashion page. Movie house ads were expanded, and photo-essays about upcoming film adaptations of Bettauer's novels were added. Yet the layout and structure of the newspaper remained the same. Bettauer's front-page editorials, the singles' ads, the multi-part confessional essays revealing seamy sides of Viennese life, and the advice column "Life's Problems" were unchanged. Like *Er und Sie*, Bettauer's new magazine featured a title-piece sketched around a rising sun. The nude cartoon couple that had framed *Er und Sie*'s title now turned their backs to the viewer and looked towards a silhouette of the Viennese skyline. The male figure protectively held his partner's waist, below which the drawing faded out. The name of *Er und Sie*'s most famous column, "Life's Problems," ran below the sketch, acting as a sub-title to the new *Bettauer's Wochenschrift*.

Perhaps the most meaningful difference between *Er und Sie* and *Bettauer's Wochenschrift* was that the latter was clearly a magazine oriented towards women. This fact has gone unnoticed in the historiography, perhaps because Bettauer's name is so closely associated with the pornography trial he endured. What is interesting about thinking about *Bettauer's Wochenschrift* in this light is just how little modification *Er und Sie* required to become a women's weekly. The column "Erotica from Around the World" was dropped, as were the articles written by medical professionals. Advice about the body was now limited to hygiene and sports articles, and the sexological case studies were removed entirely. Movie-reviews, photo-essays, fashion pages, additional serialized stories, and even occasional housekeeping tips were eventually added. *Bettauer's Wochenschrift* still addressed sexuality, yet increasingly this was done through social justice issues (limiting family size, legalizing abortion, recognizing the burdens of working women) rather than via explicit information that illustrated a wide variety of sexual experience, as had been the case in *Er und Sie*. The transition was surprisingly smooth.

Bettauer presented himself as a friend of the people in his new magazine. He showed special concern for the unemployed and for women who lived in poverty, either alone or with children. Two of the informational formats in *Bettauer's Wochenschrift* attest to this. The first was an outgrowth of the "Life's Problems" column. *Bettauer's Wochenschrift*, like other women's magazine's later in the period, provided its readers with weekly "office hours."[83] As shown in chapter 4, sex advice clinics and birth control centers across Vienna began this trend in 1922. Bettauer's "office hours" were advertised as an additional option for advice-seekers when his new magazine came out. For two hours every Tuesday and Friday, readers were shown into the editor's office and allowed to air their problems.[84] These personal crises often revolved around romantic problems, but some also included economic, familial, professional, and legal aspects that could not easily be solved in an advice column. In *Er und Sie*, Bettauer occasionally responded to reader's letters by asking them to visit his offices so that the matter could be addressed more fully or privately.[85] This certainly could have been a literary device divorced from any real correspondence—an attempt to pique readers' curiosity or to make Bettauer appear compassionate—but it may also have been the impetus for *Bettauer's Wochenschrift*'s "office hours." The system of "office hours" suggests that Bettauer was in fact responding to an actual public, and that he was committed to helping them.

Although Bettauer could not offer material relief to those who visited him, he could suggest municipal and charitable services to alleviate some kinds of suffering. That he served as a guide for such services is suggested by the Almanac he published for 1925: the second informational format that highlighted his role as "friend of the people." This was sold separately at magazine stands and may have come with subscriptions to *Bettauer's Wochenschrift*. The Almanac included a very simple calendar, a short biography of Bettauer, a series of his stories, fashion and beauty tips, and a section entitled "Where I Can Find Help?" The latter was composed of twenty-six densely packed pages of referrals organized by subject: childcare, clinics, maternity services, educational opportunities, vocational training, legal advice, emergency services, etc., all for Vienna and the surrounding province of Lower Austria. Unlike such directories put out by the city administration, "Where Can I Find Help?" listed municipal, Catholic, and private organizations side-by-side. This chapter of *Bettauer's Almanac* was introduced with the following statement:

> This presentation ... was created by the editing team of *Bettauer's Wochenschrift* in response to the necessity, expressed in dozens of daily inquiries, of knowing where to turn when one is in dire need. Here is an attempt to spare many of you a trip or a letter [to our offices]. From the child, even the unborn, who prepares to enter life; to the adults who seeks to know his rights, or is sick, or just unlucky; to those who have grown weak with age and tire of their existence: here all kinds of difficult circumstances are listed, along with the public and private means of assistance that address them. We have striven to bring together the widest possible list of such organizations.[86]

Indeed, *Bettauers Almanac* did offer a service listing unparalleled in the period. Even the recommendation system of the Municipal Marriage Advice Center, a clearinghouse for city services, was dwarfed by *Bettauer's Almanac*, largely because municipal service indices excluded Catholic charity organizations. *Bettauer's Al-*

manac may have stemmed from a desire to augment an image of Bettauer as a "friend of the people," or to dispel associations of his name with pornography. However, providing this listing was also a service in itself. It also worked to further weave Bettauer into the fabric of the city, and the city into the fabric of *Bettauer's Wochenschrift*.

As in *Er und Sie*, Bettauer used the front page of his second journal as a personal editorial page. Many of the causes he defended were similar to those promoted by the SDAP: better support for the poor, full legal rights for illegitimate children, and expanded municipal housing. His essays at times directly commented on current political crises. For example, Bettauer criticized the President of the Republic, Dr. Michael Hainisch, for using his office to open art exhibits and make decorative speeches, rather than working to improve the lives of citizens.[87] In "Nine Viennese Men," Bettauer compared the inability of current politicians to compromise with each other to an evening he had recently spent with several gentlemen of varying political persuasions. Why was it, he asked, that Christian Social Party members, Social Democrats, Jews, and Nazis could speak productively and civilly about political issues around a *Beisl* table, but not in Parliament?[88] Finally, when power struggles over the right to taxation erupted in 1924, Bettauer energetically defended the SDAP Financial Officer for Vienna, Hugo Breitner.[89] By repeatedly using the poverty and want of Viennese citizens as the primary basis for political action, Bettauer's editorials engaged in current debate without regularly endorsing a single party.

Bettauer also called attention to social problems that fell through the cracks of political platforms. The loneliness of single people in the city, the frustration of married couples who remained childless because they were unable to support even themselves, and the daily lives of prostitutes all appeared in the front pages of *Bettauer's Wochenschrift*, told from the perspectives of emotional pain rather than political injustice.[90] Indeed, the emotionality of these topics obscured any political valence they might have. The issues championed by Bettauer in his later editorials were often identified as "women's issues" by political parties, yet were absorbed into Bettauer's general *Weltanschauung* in his editorials. On the front pages of *Bettauer's Wochenschrift*, Bettauer self-identified as a feminist, called for the repeal of anti-abortion laws, raised questions about the increasing pressure for women to be beautiful and athletic, and sympathized with those making the difficult decision to divorce their partners.[91] As had been the case in *Er und Sie*, *Bettauer's Wochenschrift* redefined what was political by emphasizing what affected its readers' emotional lives.

Assassination

On 10 March 1925, a young man named Otto Rothstock exploited Bettauer's "office hours" practice to gain access to the busy editor. On that Tuesday, perhaps unfamiliar with the exact schedule, Rothstock appeared before lunch and was asked to return at three that afternoon, when "office hours" began.[92] Upon return, Rothstock entered Bettauer's office and shot him five times. Bettauer managed to counterattack with a desk lamp, and then stumbled out of his office. Rothstock shut the door behind him, ripped up the contents of Bettauer's desk, and waited for the police to arrive.[93] He was taken into custody and there began a letter campaign to national officials. He identified his actions as morally and politically driven, and asked that he be allowed to explain himself in the Senate. Meanwhile, Bettauer spent two weeks in the hospital, where he was able to narrate the event for the press, the police, and his own editing team. On 26 March, he died of his wounds.

Rothstock was not allowed to explain himself before any legislative body. However, his testimony was reprinted in the press, and his case received great attention in Austria and Germany. His family, he explained, had come to Vienna from the Sudetenland in 1915, when he was eleven years old. He eventually found work as a dental assistant. He had joined a National Socialist group in 1922, but left it two years later. He claimed that this was around the same time that he first thought of "doing something about pornography," and that he didn't want to implicate the party in his actions.[94] An unidentified book by Bettauer had caught his attention, and he had heard of Bettauer's journalistic erotica via the press coverage of Bettauer's censorship trial. Rothstock maintained that his motive for shooting Bettauer was to protect fellow young people from being lured into crime by smutty novels and newspapers. A letter written by Rothstock in July and republished in several national socialist magazines explained his logic in targeting Bettauer, the "great traitor to my people [*Volksgenossen*]."[95] Bettauer's literature "led to perverse sexual intercourse and perversity led to degeneration—infection of the body and mind—and the German people will be turned into animals within a generation."[96] When asked to comment on Bettauer's journalism, Rothstock only mentioned the "Bettauerish magazine" *Ich und Du*, with which Bettauer had no association.[97] The ideas represented by Bettauer, rather than the man himself, were Rothstock's target. In Rothstock's statement, the kinds of stories and information Bettauer printed made him a traitor, if not to the Austrian nation, then at least to the Germanic people. They thus not only represented a *Lebensphilosophie*, but also were of political import. Furthermore, sexual information led directly to perverse sexual activity and infection.[98] Rothstock read the consequences of this as physical and moral, and thus dangerous to the nationalist causes to which he was committed.

At his trial in October 1925, Rothstock refused to plead either innocent or guilty to the charge of murder. Instead, he explained:

> If it pleases the court, two thousand years ago ... the son of God came to this world in order to lead the battle against these Jewish publishers and know-it-alls, because they are the sons of Lies and of Satan. I came into this world to continue this struggle. What I have committed is not an assassination. It is a call to arms, [intended] to awaken all people and especially the German Nation, to lead forth the battle, brutal and relentless, in order to protect [the people], before it is too late. Hugo Bettauer mocked all that was German. I have no guilt.[99]

A jury found Rothstock guilty of murder and illegal possession of a weapon. However, his defense team successfully argued that Rothstock was mentally ill, and thus the defendant was sentenced to the municipal mental hospital "Am Steinhof." A year later, a panel of psychiatrists judged him sane. At his request, Rothstock was released to an army battalion. He served for two years before returning to Vienna and opening a dentist's office. He resumed a stormy relationship with the Austrian National Socialist Party, and briefly published his own newspaper, *Rothstock's Monthly Political Magazine*. In 1938, Rothstock unsuccessfully applied to city of Vienna for 100,000 *Reichsmarks* as restitution for the period he was "institutionalized against his will by Jewish power."[100] Rothstock served in the *Waffen SS* during World War II, survived wounds incurred in 1944, and became a German citizen in the post-war years. As an older man, he practiced dentistry in Hanover.[101]

Conclusions

The unusual history of Hugo Bettauer—his publications, censorship trial, and assassination—provide the historian with a highly publicized cultural crisis within the crisis that was interwar Vienna. From the close of World War I, when the city endured severe famine and want, through the collapse of the SDAP/CSP coalition in 1920, to the Palace of Justice Fire in 1927, and finally in the February Civil War of 1934, Vienna was a place of endless contestation. It witnessed two major political shifts: the peaceful transition from Empire and Monarchy to Republic in 1918 and the bloody street-fighting that ushered in a Church-aligned form of fascism in 1934. The city was rocked by financial collapse in 1924, and again by world-wide depression in 1931. Both Ignaz Seipel and Karl Seitz, whom we saw so bitterly opposed to each other in the debate over *Er und Sie*, survived assassination attempts in the 1920s. By the year Bettauer was assassinated in 1925, two separate militias, the Christian Social *Heimwehr* and the SDAP *Schutzbund*, were drilling in competition against each other. The first fatalities from militia street fighting came just two years later. These militias in turn were joined that of the Austrian National Socialists, whose party was technically illegal but whose presence was already felt in Vienna by the mid-1920s. Because the First Republic was at all times unstable, it has been difficult for historians of Vienna to focus on anything other than the socialist-controlled city's demise at the hands of its more conservative countrymen.[102]

The "doomed Atlantis" narrative of Viennese interwar history pits a courageous Social Democratic Party against the forces of the Roman Catholic Church. When the Red city finally went under the waves in 1934, little was left but for Hitler to make his triumphal entrance four years later during the *Anschluß*. One of the benefits of close attention to the history and journalism of Hugo Bettauer is that they challenge the narrative of a unified SDAP vision for their Atlantis. Bettauer's magazine *Er und Sie* served as a lightning rod for Vienna in 1924, drawing storms of protest that can not be classified simply along party lines. It posed dramatic questions about what kinds of sexual information should be available for whom in Vienna. *Er und Sie* revealed an SDAP divided by the question of erotica censorship, setting Mayor Karl Seitz and School Board Vice-president Otto Glöckel against the powerful head of the city's Welfare Bureau, Julius Tandler. It literally provoked a brawl in city council chambers between the Christian Social and Social Democratic benches. The censorship trial of Hugo Bettauer and his partner, Rudolf Olden, was covered by papers of every conceivable political orientation. Bettauer was popular enough to hold his own "office hours" every week, and reviled enough that his assassin pleaded (successfully, given his sentence) that he was guilty of murder but innocent of crime. Seen through the lens of Hugo Bettauer, interwar Vienna ceases to appear as a monolithic citadel of socialist reform. Instead, the city is restored to the daily vicissitudes of urban life in early twentieth-century central Europe—the scandals, strikes, harsh winters, housing shortages, and family dramas that Bettauer's weekly papers reported.

Notes

1. Murray C. Hall, *Der Fall Bettauer* (Wien: Löcker Verlag, 1978).
2. See Gerhard Botz, *Gewalt in der Politik: Attentate, Zusammenstöße, Putschversuche, Unruhen in Österreich, 1918–1938* (München: Wilhelm Fink Verlag, 1983) for a more complex history of the climate of political violence during the First Republic.
3. The bibliographic information in this paragraph is culled from Hall, *Der Fall Bettauer*, 9–18.
4. For characterizations of the major Viennese newspapers during this period, see Fritz Csoklich, "Press und Rundfunk," in Erika Weinzierl und Kurt Skalnik (hg.), *Österreich 1918–1938: Geschichte der Ersten Republik* Band II (Graz: Styria Verlag, 1983), 715–730.
5. In *The City Without Jews*, post-war Vienna expels its Jewish population only to find itself a sleepy backwater without business, culture, or urbanity. After much melodrama and political machination, the Jews are invited to return, and the (Jewish) hero marries his (Gentile) sweetheart. The party organ of the CSP, *Reichspost*, read the novel as a threat, and wrote: "In *The City*

Without Jews ... the Christian population happily buys back Jews at the price of the virginity of Christian girls." As quoted in Hall, *Der Fall Bettauer,* 25.
6. The list of publications from this period includes four crime-novels and six romances. A complete accounting of Bettauer's publishing record, including helpful notes regarding serialized novels, novellas, and adaptations for the stage, can be found in Hall, *Der Fall Bettauer,* 212–213. For the context of *Sittenromanen* and their challenges to the gender roles in Vienna, see Alfred Pfoser, "Verstörte Männer und emanzipierte Frauen: Zur Sitten- und Literaturgeschichte der Ersten Republik," in Franz Kadrnoska (hg.), *Aufbruch und Untergang: Österreichische Kultur zwischen 1918 und 1938* (Wien: Europaverlag, 1981), 205–222.
7. This is especially true for *The City Without Jews, Vienna Enchained,* and *The Battle of Vienna,* which are essentially novelized versions of the political and financial forces at work in the city at the time they were serialized.
8. Hall, *Der Fall Bettauer,* 24.
9. Hall, *Der Fall Bettauer,* 34. In the film version of *The Joyless Street,* Pabst cast Greta Garbo in her first big role.
10. Today, "erotica" refers to sexually explicit material that either does not use illustrations or does not graphically depict sexual acts, including touching. To use an extreme example, graphic sexual scenes of children touching others and being touched are considered pornographic, and are illegal in many western countries today. However, child erotica—for instance, pictures of children playing outside in the nude—is not prohibited.
11. This was less true for the knock-offs of *Er und Sie* that were published in Vienna in 1925. *Wir beide* ("We Two") featured photos and sketches of scantily clad, and topless, women. After five issues, the newspaper took the title of *Das Rendezvous.* Under this title, it offered a reader survey entitled "Would You Let Yourself Be Photographed Naked?" and began selling a series of posed photographic "scenes" featuring naked women. The most obvious difference between these papers and *Er und Sie* is the depiction of women. *Wir beide* and *Das Rendezvous* sketched flappers as sex objects: women with short hair and shorter skirts drinking, smoking, and dancing with stereotyped Black jazz musicians. *Wir beide: Zeitschrift für Kultur und Erotik* 1 (1925), 1 and 5 for topless images; "Würden Sie sich Nackt photographieren lassen?," *Das Rendezvous* 6 (1925), 8–9; "Blues," *Das Rendezvous* 11 (1925), 1 for sexualized interracial sketch and accompanying poem.
12. *Er und Sie*'s price was standard for the period.
13. Hall, *Der Fall Bettauer,* 41.
14. For example, the reader-response letters in *Die Unzufriedene*'s advice columns from the late 1920s suggest that each copy of the paper might be read by several women (and their husbands) in the neighborhood of a single subscriber. Of course, *Die Unzufriedene* was an "independent" magazine published by the SDAP, and subscribers were probably fulfilling more than just literary tastes when paying for the magazine. I mention this connection only to suggest that, in the crowded apartment communities of the city, multiple people, including those outside the household, often shared reading materials.
15. Juluis Tandler to Polizeidirektion Wien Pressburo, 2/29/25, reprinted in full in Hall, *Der Fall Bettauer,* 43–44.
16. Tandler to Polizeidirektion, in Hall, *Der Fall Bettauer,* 43–44.
17. Tandler to Polizeidirektion, in Hall, *Der Fall Bettauer,* 44.
18. Malachi Hacohen, *Karl Popper – The Formative Years, 1902–1945* (Cambridge: Cambridge University Press, 2000), 107–110. Hacohen's work is especially useful because it highlights the widespread pedagogical innovation the SDAP formulated during the interwar period, yet reminds us that the CSU was able to successfully limit or block the application of these reforms.
19. Tandler to Polizeidirektion, in Hall, *Der Fall Bettauer,* 43–44.
20. Tandler to Polizeidirektion, in Hall, *Der Fall Bettauer,* 43.
21. Hugo Bettauer, "Die erotische Revolution," *Er und Sie* 1 (14 Februar 1924), 1.

22. Hugo Bettauer, "Die erotische Revolution," *Er und Sie* 1 (14 Februar 1924), 1.
23. All of these goals are outlined in the second column. Bettauer, "Revolution," *Er und Sie* 1 (14 Februar 1924), 1. Bettauer's claim that prostitutes were without voting rights in the First Republic was singular: no other text I have found touches upon the subject. As was the case in Germany, Austrian women were given the vote during the heady reorganization of 1918. Whether or not state-registered prostitutes were excluded remains a tantalizing mystery to me.
24. Bettauer, "Revolution," *Er und Sie* 1 (14 Februar 1924), 2.
25. Hall, *Der Fall Bettauer*, 44.
26. Hugo Bettauer und Rudolf Olden to Karl Seitz, 3/6/25, reprinted in Hall, *Der Fall Bettauer*, 45–46.
27. "Auszüge aus einer Rede Bundeskanzler Ignaz Seipels in zwei Massenversammlung der Landstraßer Christlichsozialen am 12. März 1924," in Hall, *Der Fall Bettauer*, 164.
28. "Rede Ignaz Seipel," in Hall, *Der Fall Bettauer*, 164.
29. "Eine unwürdige Antwort des Wiener Bürgermeisters," *Reichspost*, 15 März 1924, as quoted in Hall, *Der Fall Bettauer*, 49.
30. "Auszüge aus einer Rede von Bürgermeister Karl Seitz während einer Debatte über das Kapital 'Soziale Verwaltung' im Finanzausschuß des österreichischen Nationalrates am 15. März 1924," in Hall, *Der Fall Bettauer*, 165.
31. "Seipel, Ignaz," *Österreich Lexikon*, zweiter Band (Wien: Österreichischen Bundesverlag für Unterricht, Wissenschaft, und Kunst, 1966), 1061–1062.
32. "Rede von Karl Seitz," in Hall, *Der Fall Bettauer*, 165–166.
33. Both papers quoted in Hall, *Der Fall Bettauer*, 50.
34. "Seitz auf der Flucht gestellt," *Der Volkssturm* 5/13 (30. März 1924), 1. Orel himself is very interesting. In the pre-war years, he founded a Catholic Social reform movement and a workers' youth group that eventually changed its name to "Austrian Union of Christian Youth" in 1907. He represented the Christian Socialists on City Council from 1923 to 1925, when he was thrown out of the party, apparently for his anti-capitalist beliefs. *Der Volkssturm*, "Weekly Journal of German Christians for a National Christian Culture, against Judaism, Materialism, and Capitalism," gleefully reprinted the proceedings of Orel's attack on Seitz.
35. "Seitz auf der Flucht," *Volkssturm*, 2.
36. "Seitz auf der Flucht," *Volkssturm*, 2.
37. "Seitz auf der Flucht," *Volkssturm*, 1.
38. Because the dizzying amount of media descriptions of Bettauer is precisely chronicled by Hall, I have tried to highlight only the range of responses.
39. Hall, *Der Fall Bettauer*, 58.
40. Hall, *Der Fall Bettauer*, 51.
41. Hall assumes that Dr. Werner was an actual psychiatrist responding to real cases. Certainly Werner referred to some of the most current psychiatric texts available, yet his full name and professional credentials remain unknown to me.
42. "Ueber die Impotenz Jugendlicher, von einem Nervenarzt," *Er und Sie* 4 (6. März 1924), 7 and 8, respectively.
43. Hall, *Der Fall Bettauer*, 59.
44. Hall, *Der Fall Bettauer*, 71, 70.
45. Paragraph 516 as excerpted in Hall, *Der Fall Bettauer*, 48.
46. Hall, *Der Fall Bettauer*, 72. The Austrian justice system did not require unanimous findings from the jury. Hall claims that the jury was split, nine innocent/three guilty, on most counts.
47. See for example Karl Fallend, who even after showing the influence of Bettauer's "erotic revolution" on Wilhelm Reich's work suggests that Bettauer was assassinated because he was Jewish. Karl Fallend, *Wilhelm Reich in Wien: Psychanalyse und Politik* (Wien: Ludwig-Boltzmann-Institut für Geschichte der Gesellschaftswissenschaften, 1998), 109.

48. See chapter 4, "Emotional Liberty," in William M. Reddy, *The Navigation of Feelings: A Framework for the History of Emotions* (Cambridge: Cambridge University Press, 2001). The concept of "emotionology" first outlined by Peter and Carol Stearns has also been useful to this project, because it demands that historians distinguish between an official emotional regime and records of individual emotional expression. However, in the case of *Er und Sie*, it seems clear that Bettauer as editor did not represent any kind of official emotional regime. Furthermore, the individual emotional testimonies in the paper seem to contribute to the tenor of the *Er und Sie* as a whole, rather than contradict it or represent some kind of truer reality. See Peter N. Stearns and Carol Z. Stearns, "Emotionology: Clarifying the History of Emotions," *American Historical Review* 90:4 (October 1985), 813–836.
49. Hugo Bettauer, "Eros in Ketten," *Er und Sie* 4 (6 März 1924), 2.
50. "Probleme des Lebens," *Er und Sie* 4 (6 März 1924), 13. The German word *Mann* means both "man" and "husband." This response lacks the context to decide which translation to use, so I treat both as possibilities.
51. "Probleme des Lebens," *Er und Sie* 4 (6 März 1924), 13.
52. "Probleme des Lebens," *Er und Sie* 4 (6 März 1924), 13.
53. "Sadismus, die Kinder, und die Zote," *Er und Sie* 2 (21 Februar 1924), 1.
54. "Sadismus, die Kinder, und die Zote," *Er und Sie* 2 (21 Februar 1924), 1. I do not think Bettauer is defending himself here, as he did not consider his newspaper pornographic.
55. "Sadismus, die Kinder, und die Zote," *Er und Sie* 2 (21 Februar 1924), 2.
56. "Sadismus, die Kinder, und die Zote," *Er und Sie* 2 (21 Februar 1924), 2. Again, I want to stress that although Bettauer defends the right of the individual to pornography, he did not provide it in his own newspaper.
57. "Probleme des Lebens," *Er und Sie* 5 (13 März 1925), 12.
58. "Probleme des Lebens," *Er und Sie* 5 (13 März 1925), 13.
59. "Probleme des Lebens," *Er und Sie* 5 (13 März 1925), 14.
60. "Errinerungen einer Hebamme, von ihr selbst erzählt," *Er und Sie* 3 (28 Februar 1924), 6.
61. "Errinerungen einer Hebamme, von ihr selbst erzählt," *Er und Sie* 4 (6 März 1924), 5.
62. "Errinerungen einer Hebamme, von ihr selbst erzählt," *Er und Sie* 4 (6 März 1924), 6.
63. Hugo Bettauer, "Eros in Ketten," *Er und Sie* 4 (6 März 1924), 2.
64. Hugo Bettauer, "Eros in Ketten," *Er und Sie* 4 (6 März 1924), 2.
65. Hugo Bettauer, "Eros in Ketten," *Er und Sie* 4 (6 März 1924), 2.
66. "Probleme des Lebens," *Er und Sie* 4 (6 März 1924), 11.
67. "Probleme des Lebens," *Er und Sie* 4 (6 März 1924), 11.
68. "Probleme des Lebens," *Er und Sie* 5 (13 März 1924), 12.
69. "Probleme des Lebens," *Er und Sie* 5 (13 März 1924), 12.
70. "Probleme des Lebens," *Er und Sie* 4 (6 März 1924), 13.
71. "Probleme des Lebens," *Er und Sie* 4 (6 März 1924), 13.
72. "Probleme des Lebens," *Er und Sie* 3 (28 Februar 1924), 13.
73. "Probleme des Lebens," *Er und Sie* 3 (28 Februar 1924), 13.
74. "Von einem, der um Erlösung rang, von einem Nervenarzt," *Er und Sie* 3 (28. Februar 1924), 7.
75. "Seltsame Liebesfälle, von einem Nervenarzt," *Er und Sie* 1 (14 Februar 1924), 5.
76. "Seltsame Liebesfälle, von einem Nervenarzt," *Er und Sie* 1 (14 Februar 1924), 6.
77. Hugo Bettauer, "Der Wendepunkt," 5 (13 März 1924), 2.
78. Hugo Bettauer, "Der Wendepunkt," 5 (13 März 1924), 2.
79. "Die Gebärzwang," *Er und Sie* 1 (14 Februar 1924), 10.
80. "Probleme des Lebens," *Er und Sie* 1 (14 Februar 1924), 5.
81. "Probleme des Lebens," *Er und Sie* 1 (14 Februar 1924), 5.
82. See Ann Taylor Allen's "Feminism, Venereal Disease, and the State in Germany, 1890–1918," *Journal of the History of Sexuality* 4:1 (July 1993), 27–50.

83. Again, I am drawing on my knowledge of *Die Unzufriedene*, which held office hours in conjunction with its advice column, "What Woman Speak from their Souls," in 1927. I would be very surprised if CSP women's magazines did not offer a similar service. The practice of holding office hours appears to take its cues from both medical consultations and religious confession. Indeed, *Die Unzufriedene* explicitly took the Roman Catholic Church as its inspiration to hold office hours, claiming that it had "recognized the deep need of people for regular self-expression from the beginning, and used this knowledge to serve its own purposes." Paula Nowotny, "Beratung in allen Lebenslagen: Aus der Sprechstunde der 'Unzufriedene'," *Die Frau* 11 (1 November 1930), 12.
84. Hall reports that sixty to eighty visitors came every week. If this number is correct, either many were turned away or the individual conversations were very short. Hall, *Der Fall Bettauer*, 80.
85. In some cases Bettauer also invited readers to pick up mail that had been sent to the offices in response to a question posed in earlier issues. See "Probleme des Lebens," *Er und Sie* 3 (28 Februar 1924), 15. Such notices and invitations to private consultation eventually were organized into a "Mailboxes" section at the bottom of "Life's Problems."
86. *Der Bettauer Almanach für 1925* (Wien: Verlag Bettauer's Wochenschrift, 1924), 36.
87. Hugo Bettauer, "Wenn ich Präsident wäre …," *Bettauer's Wochenschrift* 22 (9 Oktober 1924), 2.
88. Hugo Bettauer, "Neun Wiener," *Bettauer's Wochenschrift* 2 (1925), 2.
89. Hugo Bettauer, "Der Kampf gegen Breitner," *Bettauer's Wochenschrift* 26 (6 November 1924), 1.
90. See "Einsame Menschen," *Bettauer's Wochenschrift* (12 Juni 1924, Nr. 5), 1; "Das Fremde Kind," *Bettauer's Wochenschrift* 8 (3 Juli 1924), 1; "Das sanierte Mädel," *Bettauer's Wochenschrift* 7 (1925), 1. All essays by Hugo Bettauer.
91. See "Bin ich Feminist?" *Bettauer's Wochenschrift* 11 (24 Juli 1924), 1; "Der Wahre Grund," *Bettauer's Wochenschrift* 13 (7 August 1924), 1; "Äussere und innere Haltung," *Bettauer's Wochenschrift* 4 (1925), 1; "'Er' und 'Sie'," *Bettauer's Wochenschrift* 1 (1925), 1. All essays by Hugo Bettauer.
92. Or so went the testimony of Bettauer's secretary, quoted in Hall, *Der Fall Bettauer*, 82.
93. Hall, *Der Fall Bettauer*, 84.
94. Hall, *Der Fall Bettauer*, 89.
95. Hall, *Der Fall Bettauer*, 93.
96. Hall, *Der Fall Bettauer*, 93. Apparently all of Rothstock's letters were written in this clause-comma-dash-clause style, without grammatical sentences. Hall reprints a letter of Rothstock's to the Austrian Senate President in the "Document" section that concludes his book, and the style is the same, almost as if he is transcribing hesitant, spoken sentences. Although this could be an emulation of a style I am unfamiliar with (perhaps National Socialist press?), I think it is more likely that Rothstock was poorly educated. Hall, *Der Fall Bettauer*, 179.
97. Hall, *Der Fall Bettauer*, 94. *Ich und Du* and *Wir beide* were journalistic knock-offs of *Er und Sie*. They contained cartoons, sketches of scantily clad women, and less text than *Er und Sie*.
98. "Perverse sexual activity" did not necessarily refer to positions or partner choice. "Non-procreative" was the most widespread interpretation of "perversity" at the period, which could be extended to even married couples that practiced birth control.
99. Hall, *Der Fall Bettauer*, 117. This speech was also reprinted in the daily newspapers. Hall speaks of the Rothstock case as "novelized" in the press. Hall, *Der Fall Bettauer*, 123.
100. Rothstock's letter is reprinted in Gotz, *Gewalt in der Politik*, 408.
101. Hall, *Der Fall Bettauer*, 133. Hall corresponded with Rothstock in 1976 and reprints one of his letters. Rothstock defended his actions: "Then [1925], as now, I was not an outspoken anti-Semite; I merely saw that a Jew wanted to eroticize young people and establish a money-

making business in the process. I also explained at my trial that I acted out of love for my fellow young people, and that my act should be a wake-up call to the peoples' leaders." Otto Rothstock to Murray C. Hall, 6/8/1976, reprinted in *Der Fall Bettauer*, 182.

102. This historical trope of tragedy has been in place since before World War II, stretching from G.E.R. Gedye's *Fallen Bastions* (London: Victor Gollancz Ltd., 1939) to Josef Weidenholzer "Red Vienna: A New Atlantis?," in Anson Rabinbach (ed.), *The Austrian Socialist Experiment* (Boulder: Westview Press, 1984).

Chapter 6

LOCAL REFORM ON AN INTERNATIONAL STAGE
The World League for Sexual Reform in Vienna

On Wednesday, 17 September 1930, the fourth conference of the World League for Sexual Reform (WLSR) opened in the Vienna *Konzerthaus*. The daily newspaper of the Social Democratic Workers' Party, the *Arbeiter-Zeitung*, described the scene:

> Sexual reformers from all civilized countries filled the middle concert hall, along with many famous Viennese doctors, jurists, and educators. In front of the *Konzerthaus* a noticeably large number of policemen were present, and inside the building were countless plain-clothed guards. The police were said to fear disturbances from supporters of "nationalist circles." Apparently these fears were concerned with those elements of society for whom an intellectual meeting is a cross to bear—perhaps even the twisted cross of the swastika—because they always experience the life of the mind as an insulting snub to their individuality. Why, however, they would be so sensitive about the scientific discussion of sexual defects in "German Vienna" (as one correspondent reported) may be left to the reader's imagination.[1]

This quotation richly illustrates the political contestation of sexual knowledge in interwar Vienna. In it, Viennese readers are asked to choose between two attitudes towards sex: support of international scientific research and sex reform or *völkisch*, ignorant fear of intellectual discussion of sexual matters. The piece suggested three parties in Vienna who might take the latter attitude. The police expected "supporters of 'nationalist circles,'" the 11 percent of the Austrian population that voted for the German Nationalist Party, to disturb the proceedings.[2] Although the German Nationalists were strongest in the countryside, their anti-Semitic, anti-Marxist platform and conservative position vis-à-vis women and the family might have drawn protesters to Vienna on that September morning, where Jews, women, and left-leaning intellectuals were scheduled to discuss sexual reform. The reference to those with a "cross to bear" identified the Christian Socials (CSP), who dismissed "scientific" discussion of marriage relations, sexual reform, and non-procreative sexual behavior on the grounds that the Roman Catholic Church's laws on such matters were eternal. However, the CSP's rich intellectual tradition and non-nationalist position suggest that they were not the true targets of the *Arbeiter-Zeitung*'s distain. Those followers of the "twisted cross," those who prized Vienna for its "German-ness" and ran in "nationalist circles," were singled out for special mockery. In 1930, only 3 percent of the nation supported the National Socialist Party of Austria (aligned with Hitler since 1926), but the party was gaining momentum and quickly drawing young voters away from the German Nationalist Party.[3] The *Arbeiter-Zeitung* suggested that National Socialists were incapable of appreciating intellectual debate at all, and were especially sensitive about sexual discussions. In veiled language, the *Arbeiter-Zeitung* implied that Nationalist Socialist supporters would be drawn to protest the World League for Sexual Reform meeting in Vienna out of self-serving fear: because National Socialists were themselves sexual deviants.[4]

The World League for Sexual Reform, as the *Arbeiter-Zeitung* went on to report, was meeting in Vienna to discuss more than "sexual defects." In 1930, the WLSR addressed eight points of debate, ranging from housing shortages to hormonal secretions. The seven-day event was open to the public, as was a book fair, a medical display on birth control, and a special exhibit on loan from the Vienna Museum of Sociological and Economic Sciences.[5] Over 2,000 participants and guests, ten times the size of the previous year's WLSR congress, listened to representatives from Europe, the U.S.S.R., the United States, and South America.[6] Many of the German participants in the congress had traveled to Vienna via Zurich, where they had attended the first International Conference for Birth Control (1 to 5 September 1930). Historian Atina Grossmann has called attention to the striking differences between the two events. In Zurich, the "experts only" participants were asked "to avoid all issues of 'politics, religion, and morality' and to discuss contraception, abortion, sterilization, and further research areas in a strictly medical manner."[7] In contrast, the WLSR congress in Vienna explicitly sought to contextualize scientific advances in sexual research within the political and economic systems that would best serve sexual reform. Grossmann characterizes the journey between the Zurich and Vienna conferences as one to a "different political universe": "The Vienna event was enthusiastically supported by the socialist city government; the local press paid the delegates admiring attention, and the mayor hosted a wonderful banquet. A crowd-pleasing adjoining exhibit showcased every variety of birth control devices."[8] The WLSR meeting in Vienna, far from being an "experts only" conference, was a public event.

Vienna's largest daily newspaper, the *Neue Freie Presse*, praised the general public's interest in and ability to attend the congress:

> The special educational background of the Viennese—intellectuals as well as workers, women as well as men—was evident. The movement to educate the common people of Vienna about the natural sciences [*naturwissenschaftliche Volksaufklärung*], achieved through speeches and publications, has had an important effect upon our citizens. In particular, psychology in Vienna has been popularized to a previously unknown degree by countless associations ... . [Therefore] the public followed the often complicated and deep presentations with comprehension. Not a cynical or lewd comment was to be heard in the *Konzerthall*, which was filled to capacity throughout the entire week. Rather, the meeting was marked by an intellectual excitement and an earnestness that was fitting for a discussion of humanity's problems. That we in Vienna are able to discuss sexual themes in public openly is in no way a sign of 'shamelessness and poor taste,' but rather proof of our emotional maturity and integrity.[9]

This passage suggests that the Viennese citizens attending the WLSR meeting, as both speakers and audience members, were uniquely qualified to discuss sexual science and sexual reform. The author cites several reasons for this: widespread and successful *Volksaufklärung*, the popularization of psychology, private associational work, and "emotional [*seelischer*, also connoting mental and spiritual] maturity." That not everyone in Vienna shared the author's opinion, however, is evidenced by his defense of public sexual discourse from those who thought it "shameless." Clearly, the WLSR's Vienna meeting was a point of both pride and contention within the city.

The above pair of newspaper reports of the WLSR's 1930 Vienna conference brings to life the tensions surrounding sexual knowledge. Both articles supported the WLSR's decision to meet in Vienna, yet they described very different populations within the city. The *Arbeiter-Zeitung* report attacked those segments of the population—nationalistic, Catholic, or National Socialist—expected to contest either the WLSR's format of public sexual discussion or its message of sex reform.[10] The *Neue Freie Presse* article, in contrast, described a respectful, informed, and engaged Viennese citizenry primed for the scientific discussion of sexual matters. In both articles, political affiliation, religion, and education divided those engaged with the WLSR from those enraged by it. How one reacted to sexual reform, particularly during the week that the WLSR met in Vienna, revealed where one stood in the city's political landscape. As Rudolf Goldscheid, the famous Viennese sociologist, announced at the congress, "one could put it simply: 'Tell me what kind of social and class structure you want, and I will tell you with which sexual morals you will be engaged.'"[11] The WLSR's meeting in Vienna made explicit the political implications of sexual reform.

The World League for Sexual Reform's 1930 Vienna conference, although not the last event in the chronology of this book, opens up important avenues for reflection. I have argued that sexual knowledge in Vienna during the years 1900 to 1934 was transformed from a scientific inquiry dominated by medical specialists to a social reform movement pursued by a wide participant base. Furthermore, I have shown throughout the previous chapters that sexual *Aufklärung* ("enlightenment") during this period was radically redirected towards a new audience that included women, workers, and children. No single party in Vienna orchestrated these changes, rather, socialists, Catholics, and reformers of all political persuasions contributed to a highly varied discourse on the scientific and social causes of sexual problems. These problems included reproductive rights, welfare responsibilities, marriage reform, educational standards for children, and the clinical and psychological care of adults. I have established a broad context in which to place the WLSR 1930 congress: one of almost constant sexual science and sex reform discussion in Vienna from the end of the nineteenth century to the dissolution of the First Austrian Republic. For one week in September 1930, however, the discourse on sexual knowledge in Vienna that this book has analyzed became literal; it was performed at a conference at the *Konzerthaus* that featured many of Vienna's leading sexual scientists and reformers. In this final chapter, I review the proceedings of the WLSR's 1930 convention, highlighting the issues and historical characters that have been discussed in the previous five chapters.

The topics discussed in the WLSR 1930 Vienna congress reflected the League's aim to scientifically approach the sexual problems of western society. The "Aims of the League," formulated in Copenhagen in 1928, were diverse:

> At present the happiness of an enormous number of men and women is sacrificed to false sexual standards, to ignorance, and to intolerance. It is therefore urgently necessary that many sexual problems (the Position of Women, Marriage, Divorce, Birth Control, Eugenics, Fitness for Marriage, the Unmarried Mother and the Illegitimate Child, Prostitution, Sexual Abnormality, Sexual Offences, Sexual Education, etc.) should be re-examined from a common-sense and unbiased standpoint and dealt with scientifically.[12]

As this list indicates, a great number of these issues could be illuminated through science, and especially medicine. Sexual abnormalities could be catalogued and psychoanalyzed, prospective marriage partners could be tested for venereal and congenital disease, and better birth control devices and techniques could be developed. Other sexual problems identified by the WLSR could be tackled through social science, particularly welfare and hygiene systems. These included the positive eugenic attempts to secure state support for single mothers, illegitimate children, and sexual education. Yet a good deal of the issues identified by the WLSR could not be resolved through science at all. Marriage, divorce, and the socio-economic position of women were crucial topics for the WLSR that required social reform rather than scientific investigation. These questions, so central to the sexual "happiness" of individuals that the WLSR sought to secure, best illustrate the society-wide and utopian nature of interwar sexual reform.

The central historical process traced in this book has been the transformation of sexual knowledge in early twentieth-century Vienna from a heterogeneous scientific discourse into discrete social reform action. Each of the public figures I have placed along this trajectory of change had particular ideas about the appropriate application of sexual knowledge in order to effect social change. All of them, however, were forced to grapple with a basic question: should widespread sexual knowledge be used to secure and enlarge individual freedom, or should the expansion of sexual knowledge to new sectors of the city instead serve as the cornerstone to greater social responsibility? Hugo Bettauer, for example, reformatted sexological knowledge for a popular audience in order to illustrate the varieties of sexual experience and to demand the erotic freedom for his fellow citizens. Likewise, Wilhelm Reich claimed that sexual and economic repression had crippled, in a distinct psycho-sexual manner, the vast majority of Vienna's population. Conversely, Julius Tandler, whose welfare and sexual hygiene innovations reshaped First Republic municipal culture, used eugenic arguments to communicate the imperative of sexual responsibility to the Viennese. Many of the reformers who participated in the movement for sexual *Aufklärung*, including Josef Friedjung, Johann and Betty Ferch, and Sofie Lazarsfeld, combined concepts of sexual freedom and social responsibility in order to secure state funding or social support for children's sexual education, women's access to birth control, and marital/sexual counseling. The tension between freedom and responsibility that ran through the Viennese sex reform movement was especially evident at the 1930 WLSR congress.

Further questions haunted sexual reformers in the interwar years. If sexuality were to be a concept big enough to include the various activities and subjectivities catalogued during the turn of the century, then perhaps science alone was not sufficient to define it. History, sociology, and anthropology were often drafted into an unequal partnership with science in an attempt to objectively study the experience of sexuality. These disciplines begged the question of whether sexuality was an individual question, or one that must always be studied within the dominant culture. Was sexuality biological, or was it a social issue? Were individual rights the best way to secure freedom from the old norms and strictures, or was a broad educational initiative better able to effect change? And finally, what form of political engagement was required for true sexual reform?[13] Many of the most radical reformers looked to the USSR for guidance, and yet by 1930 the soviet system had become much less progressive. Indeed, plans to hold a WLSR meeting in Moscow were scrapped as the political and economic tensions of western Europe escalated after the Vienna congress. All of these questions animated the debate within the WLSR, and influenced its Viennese participants and audience.

The WLSR had met three times before coming to Vienna. Its first meeting, held in Berlin in 1921, had been a small affair with thirty-nine speakers. Five categories of discussion were laid out for the Berlin meeting, ranging from the purely scientific in "The Meaning of Inner Secretions for Human Sexuality" to largely social questions such as "Population Politics and Birth Control." Two special topics in Berlin were afforded resolutions: "Reform of Penal Legislation" and "Sexual Pedagogy." The participants were overwhelmingly German, although there were also speakers hailing from Prague, Vienna, and Moscow. The next meeting, in Copenhagen in 1928, produced a revision of the League's constitution, the creation of the "Aims of the League," and a ten-point platform of what the League was fighting for. First on the list was the "Political, economic, and sexual equality of men and women"; other planks included sex education, contraception, and decriminalization of sexual acts between consenting adults.[14] The Copenhagen meeting restricted itself to four themes: Sexual Reform, Sexual Pedagogy, Birth Control, and Sexual Legislation. Forty-four speakers and over seventy participants from ten countries took part in the conference, although Germany was again best represented.

The London congress followed a year later, generating even more participation and a wider range of specialists. Over a hundred speakers, using English, French, German, and Esperanto, were drawn from wide-ranging fields, including "education, medicine, science, literature, law, the stage, the church, journalism, [and] art."[15] Although the organizers decried English backwardness when in came to sexual discourse, they were able to arrange a visit to an English birth control center as part of the program. The London congress also featured several new themes of discussion, including Marriage and Divorce, Venereal Disease and Prostitution, Sex and Censorship, and Treatment of Sexual Disorders. The business meeting of the WLSR, which took place at the conference, revealed that a tremendous increase in membership had occurred in the year since the Copenhagen meeting, and that there were now more than 350 world-wide members of the League.

The Vienna congress of the WLSR was opened by Dr. Josef Friedjung, the only Austrian member of the WLSR's working committee and the leader of the Austrian League for Sexual Reform.[16] Friedjung was a rising young Social Democrat within the educational system, and had lectured and published extensively on the subject of children's sexual education (see chapter 2). In his opening address, Friedjung explained how Vienna had been chosen as the WLSR's congress site. Because the previous congresses had taken place in Berlin, London, and Copenhagen, WLSR organizers had sought a venue that would be more convenient to scholars from Southern and Eastern Europe.[17] The greatly expanded platform for discussion in Vienna included eight topics: Housing Shortage and Sexual Reform, Sexual Misery, Sexuality and Inner Life, Inner Secretion (hormonal research), Sexual Morality, the Judicial System, Birth Control and the Economy of the Human Species ("*Menschenökonomie*"), and the Rights of Children. Vienna, however, was much more than a geographical midpoint in Friedjung's address. He cited Vienna's scientific tradition: "this city of *Krafft-Ebing* and *Sigmund Freud* is truly worthy of the honor of receiving such a congress within its walls."[18] Friedjung also made reference to recent political changes to Vienna's social fabric, bringing up the "full equality of women in Austria" and the Vienna's "increased attempts to provide municipal housing for the masses."[19] He explained the latter point with pride: "We Viennese think there is a causal relation between the housing shortage and sexual reform; and the achievements in house-construction here in Vienna have to be mentioned before all others."[20] The deeply social nature of sexuality dominated his address.

Friedjung's speech was followed by a formal opening address from the WLSR's president, German sexologist and sex reformer Magnus Hirschfeld. Hirschfeld admired Vienna as hospitable and beautiful, "a city in which nature, science, and art had combined in a harmonious trinity."[21] He continued: "for our Congress's work I cannot think of a more qualified place than the capital of old and new Austria. For here were active those great researchers of nature and humanity, who we hold as the most important forerunners of our sexual science."[22] After praising the work of Krafft-Ebing, Mendel, and Freud, Hirschfeld singled out four more researchers who were present and active at the Congress: social hygienist Julius Tandler, sexual physiologist Eugen Steinach, sexual ethnographer Siegfried Kraus, and sociologist Rudolf Goldscheid. Hirschfeld then moved to define the work of the Congress, stating that, "our struggle seeks a more just, more humane, scientific morality."[23] He attacked official morality as one that subsumed the "sex- and love-lives of human beings as merely a means to a very particular goal and not as natural needs in and of themselves. This particular goal is married reproduction. Every love act that does not serve this task is more or less imprinted with the stamp of shame."[24] Official morality, he claimed, was responsible for a tissue of lies that blinded society to the needs and rights of individuals. His criticism was scathing: official morality scorned relationships based in freely given love, but tolerated prostitution; it promoted both enforced celibacy and masturbation far beyond the stage of puberty; it saw the sexual act as merely a means of increasing the population, even in times of high unemployment, starvation, and lack of shelter; it forced people to remain married, even in households of hate where children were poisoned by their parents' animosity; it viewed unmarried women and their children as second-class citizens; it legally ruined the lives of those men and women who love members of their own sex, exposing them to blackmail, suicide, and doubt; it saw original sin in hereditary defects and relegated many thousands of people whose actions stemmed from sexual sickness in prisons, without giving them the possibility to be treated and healed by doctors. By enumerating the restrictive positions of official morality, Hirschfeld inveighed, the congress "held a mirror up to the sexual order of our time."[25] His righteous fury may have been intended to unify the divergent positions of WLSR participants, but it also stuck a sincerely indignant, emotional note to ignite the conference.

What did the World League for Sexual Reform propose to do about the "old," official morality? Hirschfeld defined the league as one that would "set against this sexual order a new sexual ethic that takes as its starting point a scientific investigation of human nature."[26] The injustices of the old order would be addressed with compassion: the double morality that condemned prostitutes but excused their male patrons was to be removed, sexual minorities' right to love was embraced, and illegitimate children were to be recognized as living, with their mothers, in equality with others. Yet the focus of the new sexual morality proposed by Hirschfeld was ultimately modest. The morality of the league, he claimed,

> ... builds itself first of all on a rational sexual education, whose pillars are sexual knowledge and a sexual sense of responsibility. Likewise, a sexual morality based in science sees in the union of father, mother, and child the natural center-point of sexual life, whose highest form is embodied in marriage. Yet even in marriage sexual activity must be sanctified through love, and this love through freedom,—holy not in the supernatural sense, as a marriage made in heaven—but rather holy in the sense of the most complete life arrangement through love, marriage, and creation.[27]

Hirschfeld's vision of marriage was spiced with the right to divorce, and he repeated the feminist Ellen Key's formulation that marriage without love was more immoral than love without marriage. Yet by placing monogamous, heterosexual, and even reproductive sex at the center of the League's reform, he slyly suggested that this most basic of relationships was in need of reformulation. What made it new was the insistence on choice and freedom throughout Hirschfeld's speech. Hirschfeld closed by pointing to the congress's threefold purpose: to "give an overview of the current state of scientific knowledge in the service of the human sex- and love-life" by emphasizing sexual biology and sexual sociology, to point the way in the application of this knowledge to daily life, and to bring together "like-minded men and women from all parts of the world" whose engagement with reform would be of use to all countries.[28] He thanked the city of Vienna for its warm reception, and gave his personal rallying cry to the participants: "Through Science to Justice!"[29] With these words, the 1930 WLSR meeting began.

The World League for Sexual Reform's call to justice deserves exploration. Its ten-point platform, formalized at the Copenhagen conference of 1928, demanded far-reaching reform from the individual, family, and society. On a personal basis, the WLSR asked that all people be able to determine their own reproductive schedule, calling for "control of conception, so that procreation may be undertaken only deliberately, and with a due sense of responsibility."[30] The WLSR also asked that individuals feel a certain way about sexuality, promoting "a rational attitude towards sexually abnormal persons, and especially towards homosexuals, both male and female."[31] All other abnormalities were to be treated as illnesses, rather than crimes: the WLSR claimed that the only criminal sexual acts were those that "infringe[d] the sexual rights of another person."[32] Such points required tolerance from the individual, and in the final case, the education of the courts, so that "sexual acts between responsible adults, undertaken by mutual consent, [could] be regarded as the private concern of those adults."[33] These goals emphasized the individual's rights over his or her own sexuality.

Justice on a social level required more far-reaching changes. Several of the WLSR's platforms required social attitudes themselves to modify. "Race betterment by the application of the knowledge of eugenics" was a responsibility for all, as was the "protection of the unmarried mother and the illegitimate child."[34] Local communities might also be able to achieve the "prevention of prostitution and venereal disease."[35] By far the majority of the beliefs of the league, however, could only be achieved through state or national decree, such as the revolution in legal sexual rights described above. These were some of the most radical of the league's positions, including the "political, economic, and sexual equality of men and women," "the liberation of marriage (and especially divorce) from the present Church and State tyranny," and "systematic sexual education."[36] For these goals to be realized, the league would have to petition government rather than simply change the hearts of citizens. Although individual rights were important to the league, these latter goals suggest that sexuality was clearly a social issue for the WLSR.

The Vienna Congress of the WLSR reflected Hirschfeld's call to let rationality and science to lead to social and sexual justice. The relationship between housing and sexual morality was the first point of discussion. Dr. Julius Tandler, head of Vienna's Welfare Office, led the debate, which was dominated by Viennese participants. Tandler's speech was in many ways an extension of the same issues he had treated in "Marriage and Population Politics," analyzed in chapter 1. At the WLSR congress, Tandler argued that economic conditions in general and housing shortages in particular shaped a population's sexual behavior, and that ability of society to support the reproduction of its citizens was the true measure of its sexual morality.[37] Moral sexual behavior was that which encouraged the "generative ethic." Sex was thus subsumed in his discussion to the production of healthy offspring, which could be best provided for in hygienic households with separate beds for parents and children.[38] Tandler vigorously insisted that individuals enter into long-term, monogamous relationships that could economically and emotionally care for children. A society that did not encourage this kind of pairing among its citizens could not achieve a highly developed "generative ethic," which meant that such a society would be immoral.[39] Sexual happiness or satisfaction for the individual went unconsidered in Tandler's speech. Tandler's first concern was consistently the "coming generation." In order to protect this cohort from disease and degeneration, ever-present in urban centers, the conditions in which they lived would have to be altered:

The danger of degeneration, the danger of eventual destruction, brought on by domestication: it rests above all in the absolutely impossible conditions in which people in major metropolitan and industrial centers live, and the question is, what should be done? The only thing to be done in my opinion is the erection of *new* housing. I am convinced that this housing reform will point to true sexual reform. For without these prerequisites, I hold, one would be hard pressed to change anything. All of the current customs are surely related to the housing conditions in which all humans live. He who alters these conditions, he who betters them, if you will, betters morality.[40]

"True sexual reform," in Tandler's hands, was a lasting marriage between biologically fit partners set in a hygienic environment. Tandler proposed to expand and sanitize the environment in which children were conceived through the construction of city housing that made responsible, hygienic sex possible.[41]

Newspaper reports of Tandler's presentation, the first paper of the conference, remarked upon the "lively reception" and "stormy applause" he received.[42] Tandler was the highest-ranking Social Democrat to speak at the Congress, and his presentation had taken a conservative stance towards sexual behavior, emphasizing social responsibility over individual sexual freedom. In the panel discussion following his presentation, however, Tandler was criticized from the audience by the Viennese doctor Rudolf Dreikurs:

> I wish to speak to Professor Tandler's opinion that sexuality should be looked at principally as a generative question. This is essentially the standpoint that we have abandoned and that separates us from our opponents: namely that we no longer see human sexuality as something merely in the service of reproduction, but on the contrary recognize it as having over and above [reproduction] a special meaning in people's lives.[43]

This special meaning, Dreikurs suggested, went beyond simple concern for infection or degeneration among children in tight housing situations. Rather, it included the sensations and meanings that people attributed to sexuality. Dreikurs accepted Tandler's point that close quarters led to dangerous situations between the generations, and was particularly sensitive to the sexual impressions that children received from the adults around them. The most perilous pattern that children might learn, he continued, was that of using women as sexual objects. This lesson, learned early in life, would be hard to eradicate. It also blocked the development of women's sexual consciousness, which Dreikurs extended to a sense of ownership of one's own body.[44] This close attention to the individual's rights in the face of social pressure provided a sharp contrast to Tandler's points. A second respondent to Tandler's speech enlarged on the needs of children trapped in desperate housing situations. Referring to his own sociological study of early sexual activity among "at risk" Viennese girls, Dr, Siegfried Kraus noted that their living conditions often included missing, sick, or unemployed parents who were unable to keep the household together.[45] Kraus recommended that the Congress and society reconsider the meaning of being orphaned to include all children who have seen the dissolution of a living community with their parents. He also insisted that sexual education was the right of all young people, and that "society has no moral right to prosecute children and young people for sexual offences so long as it hasn't provided for an adequate *sexual pedagogy as a social duty.*"[46]

Tandler's message of hygiene and eugenic duty was most forcefully countered by Wilhelm Reich, who spoke the following day on a panel devoted to *Sexualnot* ("sexual misery," with connotations of emergency and suffering). Reich defined *Sexualnot*, a term that has appeared in materials throughout this book, as a two-part problem. External *Sexualnot* was social in origin and could be addressed through improvements to the material conditions of humanity. Such improvements were in keeping with the previous day's panel on Housing Reform. But Reich's paper, titled "The Sexual Misery of the Working Masses and the Difficulties of Sexual Reform," stressed the internal component of *Sexualnot*, which he called "the sexual-psychological structure of suffering."[47] Reich explicitly critiqued Tandler's presentation, arguing that the construction of new apartments in Vienna "not only helped a mere fraction of those suffering from the housing shortage, but also entirely ignored the question of such people's sexual solitude."[48] What the city of Vienna actually should be building, Reich argued, were homes designed to attend to the sexual needs of the masses, who, without private bedrooms of their own, were presently relegated to coupling in parks and dark doorways. Instead of relying upon tropes of disease and degeneration to argue for public housing as Tandler had, Reich described the greatest danger of Vienna's housing shortage to be that of individual sexual frustration. Claiming that 80 to 90 percent of working people lacked a room of their own in which their sexual life could play out in an undisturbed manner, Reich told his audience that a great proportion of this population "performed the sex act fully clothed," in fear of being discovered by fellow dwellers.[49] Where a romantic pair could not truly be alone, he warned, shame and sexual dysfunction reigned. True sexual reform on the state level, according to him, would not prioritize a "generative ethic," but rather would provide municipal rendezvous points for the satisfaction of its citizens' sexual needs. Reich further criticized the WLSR position on venereal disease prevention, marriage and prostitution, calling it an "old recipe that never worked."[50] Asking people to remain abstinent before marriage and faithful within marriage, Reich explained, had never been successful in combating venereal disease. Moreover, he claimed, the practice of prostitution (and the attendant spread of venereal disease) could only be altered through changes to the bourgeois economic order; until proletarian women had enough to eat, and until bourgeois men no longer demanded virginal brides from their own classes, prostitution would remain a source of sexual misery within society. So too would unwanted pregnancies, until abortion was legalized and a broad propaganda initiative brought contraceptive devices into everyday life. Healthy sexuality was a biological need and right, according to his logic, yet so deeply embedded in social realities as to be beyond the means of much of the population.

When Reich spoke at the 1930 WLSR, he had almost two years of experience in his Viennese Proletarian Sexual Advice Centers to draw from. His message to the Congress was concomitant with the general demands of the Socialistic Society for Sexual Advice and Research, which were outlined in chapter 4. Rather than request "scientific papers" on sexual knowledge, Reich told the WLSR, the congress should ask about the relation of social structures to mass sexual misery:

> One certainly must be clear that science has prepared the way for sexual reform. However, the real question regards establishing which political relationships or social systems allow scientific knowledge to be put into practice; in other words, which political formats make possible sexual reform based on scientific discoveries.[51]

Reich argued that the praxis of sexual reform had become a more pressing issue than the creation of scientific sexual knowledge. Speaking for the members of his Society for Sexual Advice, Reich warned that sexual reform could never be entirely brought about within bourgeois society, but rather that the WLSR should look to Soviet Russia, where divorce and abortion had been legalized following the communist revolution. Only a revolutionary political engagement would bring about the desired sexual reforms of the League, according to Reich.

As a psychoanalyst, Reich spoke to the sexual irregularities that troubled his Viennese clients. The sexually disturbed household, he warned, was by far the norm amongst the working poor. Among one case study of youth groups, he claimed, fully 50 percent of the men and 70 percent of the women showed evidence of sexual neuroses. Furthermore, Reich drew upon his work at the Society for Sexual Advice to highlight the intractability of these disruptions in healthy sexual function. Of the roughly seven hundred sick clients seen in the past year and a half, only about 30 percent were treatable, leaving a great number of his patients without the possibility of healing, until "institutions and interest for their diseases" increased.[52] Indeed, Reich's speech stood as a frank assessment of the limits of psychoanalysis, particularly among the masses. Individual treatment of sexual neuroses, the very means of healing in which Reich was trained, was failing both the discrete sufferers and society itself. His central question thus became:

> Is the production of neuroses just an accidental byproduct, so to say an act of negligence by our sexual order, or is it something more: does the production of neuroses belong together with this sexual order specifically to the continued existence of society as we know it…? In the first case, we are justified in having great hopes that decisive measures could already be found from within this [sexual] order. In the second scenario, the question becomes as hopeless in our society as those of the housing crisis or birth control.[53]

As a doctor, Reich continued, it was his difficult duty to pronounce the second option to be the case, proclaiming that the neuroses and sexual disturbances of his clients were not byproducts, but rather essential to the ruling middle-class sexual order. He identified three causal stages in the social creation of sexual neuroses: childhood, puberty, and the preparation for marriage. In each, he argued against abstinence, sexual repression, and the conflation of familial love with social and economic order.

Reich's speech, taken as a whole, argued for radical sexual freedoms the likes of which Vienna had only seen supported in the pages of Hugo Bettauer's erotic newspapers.[54] Few speakers at the 1930 convention, however, were willing to support Reich's political claims, much less his suggestion that the city of Vienna build municipal trysting-rooms. Although the WLSR welcomed discussion of social effectiveness within sexual reform, it was, at base, a league of middle-class doctors, jurists, and social reformers. How disappointing it must have been for these reformers to hear the pronouncements of Reich on the efficacy of change. Indeed, their very Congress was attacked when he warned that the experiences of the post-war years had taught that it was not enough to form committees and associations designed to help the working classes out of sexual misery, but rather that social reformers would only find solutions in extreme revolution.[55]

Nevertheless, many of the Viennese speakers at the WLSR conference dealt implicitly with Reich's questions about liberation and the praxis of sexual reform within society, particularly in relation to children. Dr. Felix Kanitz questioned the pattern of adult dominion over children and counseled solidarity, instead. He outlined three rights that children should enjoy. The first was the right not to be born until their parents (or their community) could secure their physical and cultural needs. Second, he demanded what was necessary to meet children's developmental needs: "the *right* to nourishment, clothes, education, play, and joy!"[56] The final right of children he delineated was "the right of children to be taken seriously," which included their emotions, hopes, and fears. It was within this third category that Kanitz introduced the problem of sexual education for children. He argued that the lack of trust between children and parents had painful results, for the child and for society at large:

> This lack of serious consideration of children, this lack of attention to the child personality, bears the greatest responsibility for the wretched *sexual education* of the present day. Adults, especially parents, fail to take pains to heed the expressions of childlike sexuality; they have no idea of the meaningful sexual urges and distresses in children. For them masturbation is a black vice; for them making children acquainted with the processes of conception and birth are a grave offence against "childlike innocence." They do not take seriously children's friendships, which are erotically determined, but rather make them the object of scorn or pedagogical inquisition. They have no understanding for the miseries and joys of puberty … that so often fill this segment of life![57]

Kanitz transformed the question of sexual education into the larger issue of recognizing children's humanity. In doing so, he explicitly framed sexual pedagogy within the larger rubric of what he called "the new social pedagogy," which would "build itself upon a new reorganization of the relationships between the generations, which must itself be built upon the principle of *solidarity*."[58] This sweeping solidarity between adults and children would recognize children's sexualities and take seriously their sexual questions and concerns. It also demanded greater responsibility on the part of adults.

Helene Anderle, whose demands that children's sexual education take place in public schools were analyzed in chapter 2, argued at the WLSR that sexual *Aufklärung* was not a decision that parents had any right over, but rather was a right of children themselves, and should be guaranteed by society.[59] Josef Friedjung, the Viennese educator and author of the most widely-used sexual education manual in the First Republic, outlined the need for social reform vis-à-vis the rights of children. Arguing that children had heretofore been treated as objects by legal structures, Friedjung demanded at the WLSR that they become the subjects of social institutions. Children's rights, according to Friedjung, included the right to healthy parents (who should consult medical experts before marrying), the right to social welfare support, the right to be educated in public schools (parents were "objectively and subjectively not properly qualified") and the right to sexual knowledge.[60] Both Anderle and Friedjung argued that children should no longer be considered the "property" of their parents, but subjects protected and educated by the state. These educators' presentations were based not in scientific exploration, but rather on social organization principles that demanded fundamental change of and intervention into family life: social changes similar to the scale that Reich had argued was necessary for true sexual reform.

At the WLSR 1930 Congress, and indeed throughout this period covered in this book, the family was viewed as central to discussion of sexual reform within society. As we have seen from Hirschfeld's introduction and Tandler's paper, reproduction within the family was a popular starting point for the construction of sexual morality. However, the construction of the family and its right to self-determination were hotly debated at the congress. Many Viennese participants argued for sexual reforms that combined Tandler's call to sexual responsibility with a Reichian insistence upon greater individual freedom. Rudolf Goldscheid, whose theory of *Menschenökonomie* was central to Julius Tandler's Vienna welfare policy (see chapter 1), argued that economic exploitation of workers had always also extended to proletarian women and their families. His presentation, "Towards a History of Sexual Morals," was a long look at the ways the "generative ethic" of sexuality had been harnessed in the service of society. He claimed that the large families demanded of proletarian women were "the foundation of all reactionary domination," and that their freedom could be best secured through self-selective fertility regulation.[61] The modern state, according to Goldscheid, should encourage smaller families that could draw upon social welfare services for support: something he called "the rationalization and democratization of reproduction."[62]

Although Goldscheid emphasized responsibility throughout his presentation, he also warned that society was changing far more quickly than sexual morals, and that sexual rights lagged behind both. This imbalance begged for immediate reform. "We reformers are not destroyers of morality, but in reality are rather those who seek above all the breathing room for a healthy, effective morality," he explained.[63] As such, he called upon the League to formulate and proclaim a new constitution of sexual rights that could illuminate with clarity the manifold injustices of the present morality, including the following:

> The sexual and generative right to self-determination for every full grown and competent person; the rights over one's own body and the limits of these rights; the sexual and generative responsibilities of individuals and society; the rights of mothers, unmarried just as much as married; the culturally necessary legal formulation of marriage and divorce; the possibility of legal protection for free love, the legal assumption of equality between the genders; the rights of children, beginning with human rights before birth; the extent of rights to satisfy the natural sexual needs, by children and adults, including outside of marriage; the rights of sexual minorities ... and much more.[64]

These rights, although framed within responsibility, were some of the most far-reaching formulations of the convention. They synthesized the work of the League into a concrete set of reforms that, while perhaps in part inspired by science, fell entirely to the realm of culture to enact.

Several speakers engaged in Goldscheid's essential right to generative self-determination from their positions on the Birth Control panel. Viennese feminist and SDAP Senator Adelheid Popp used Goldscheid's arguments at the WLSR to make claims for women's right to birth control and abortion. Her presentation summarized many of the demands made by the *Bund gegen Mutterschaftzwang*, detailed in chapter 4. Popp demanded the inclusion of "social indications" (such as poverty) to the current law that provided exceptions based on medical danger to the mother and eugenic considerations. She proposed a motto for those who would fight for abortion rights: *"No woman should be required to carry more than she can bear, out of respect for her dignity and enjoyment of life."*[65] Challenging the idea that women chose abortion because they simply did not want any children, she suggested that women and men should be able to call upon the community and welfare organizations to help them raise the children they desired. Popp was joined on her panel by Dr. Sigismund Peller of Vienna, who emphasized the high costs of illegal abortion to women's health, longevity, and productivity. Decrying Paragraphs 144 to 148 of the Austrian penal code, he declared the law "cruel, dangerous to health, socially unjust, ineffective, and absurd."[66] Until it could be revoked, he asked his colleagues to work with him "between the shadows of the law" by promoting extensive birth control information, legally protecting the rights of those who had undergone an illegal abortion to hospital treatment, and increasing the effort to find better, safer, and more palatable contraceptive devices.[67] Illegal abortion, in this panel, was clearly characterized as punishing the individual (woman) for her sexuality.

Several panelists joined Popp and Peller in their call for birth control information. However, the technologies of birth control and their weaknesses were also frankly aired. Pessaries and intrauterine rings (the Gräfenburg method) were discussed as effective only most of the time and as potentially dangerous to a woman's health if left in the body too long.[68] Temporary X-ray sterilization of women was rejected as inadvisable, yet discussed as a possible (if costly) treatment for male partners.[69] Dr. Herbert Steiner of Vienna, while decrying the state's unwillingness to legalize safe, medical abortions, criticized the lack of attractive contraceptive alternatives available to the common woman. His solution was to make pessaries available to all and to ask doctors in community-run clinics to administer them on a weekly basis free of charge. Steiner insisted that the problem of effective birth control could not be solved in a merely scientific sense, but rather that it would require the social engagement of medical professionals.[70]

Sidonie Furst drew attention to the sexual rights of the single woman and mother who she claimed "was punished, in Austria and elsewhere, by societal contempt when she dared to fulfill her sexual and maternal needs."[71] Furst's inclusion of single mothers in her defense countered the many presentations that explicitly based family structure within marriage. Paul Pallester, representing the Austrian Marriage Reform Society, described Austria's arcane and ecclesiastically-controlled divorce law, which he suggested was responsible for the sexual misery of many adults trapped in loveless marriages, as well as the distress of children caught in such artificial unions.[72] The freedom to divorce, his presentation suggested, would alleviate great social unhappiness. All of the presentations called for the reform of the social structures in which reproduction took place and suggested that marriage, as traditionally understood, was not an analytical category large enough to meet the realities—including impoverished worker families, single mothers, and broken marital bonds—encompassed by sex reform.

Also in the *Konzerthaus* during the WLSR's conference was an exhibition on loan from the Museum for Sociological and Economic Sciences in Vienna. This museum, located in City Hall, was devoted to social hygiene *Aufklärung* and used socio-economic charts and graphs in an attempt to educate the masses. Using the so-called "Viennese Method," these tables illustrated population patterns of birth, work, and death using sharp relief graphics and very few words. An excellent example of this was the chart entitled "Graduation of Ages of the Austrian People for 1923."[73] This vividly represented the age cohorts for Austria, divided by gender with the youngest Austrians at the bottom. The war years feature a drastically reduced cohort, and many of the branches above this group show a distinct shortfall in male members. The resulting effect is of a tree poorly pruned, having lost its symmetry in all but the very oldest members of the population.

Of the seventeen tables on loan, eleven expressed statistics specific to Vienna. Tables proudly documented the number of marriages in the city, as well as the distribution of infant layette sets to a wide variety of households. Yet many tables warned of the bitterest sides of recent city life. Three tables examined suicide in Vienna according to profession, gender, motive (including broken hearts), and method. Even more alarming were the many charts devoted to infant and child mortality. Although "Decline of Infant Mortality Rates in Vienna" clearly shows that infant mortality for the years 1926 to 1927 had been almost halved since its wartime high, the graphics still bore outlines of infants in the fetal position being transformed into tiny coffins.[74] This image was repeated in several other tables, including "Infant Mortality and Social Conditions" and "Infant Mortality and Annual Income."[75] In these, the cruelty of poverty was expressed explicitly through children's survival rates of their first year of life.

How was such information intended to complement a congress devoted to sexual reform? War, economic distress, and employment rates certainly were beyond the scope of the WLSR's concerns. But if we look to the charts regarding marriage, mortality, and the family, we see the outlines of what Julius Tandler would have called *Menschenökonomie*: the management of a city's organic capital. Facing the suicide and infant mortality rates of the city were part of the Museum for Sociological and Economic Sciences' charge to educate the people in the realities of their material and social existence. Celebrating the marriages and means of welcoming new babies to the city was likewise a way to advertise to conference-goers the sexual health of Vienna.

The president of the World League for Sexual Reform, Magnus Hirschfeld, made the closing remarks at the 1930 Vienna congress. Hirschfeld thanked all of the participants for their "efforts and devotion to a great cause," and then declared:

> I must make some special remarks in reference to the three moments which all of us will consider as the highpoints of our seven-day congress. These were the reports of Professor Tandler, Rudolf Goldscheid, and Assistant Professor Friedjung. It is no accident that the other papers gravitated towards and interacted with their clear, spiritual, and searching presentations. Rather, it springs from the *genius loci* to which we sexual reformers have particular reason to pay tribute.[76]

The papers that Hirschfeld identified as pivotal to the WLSR were those that most strongly emphasized the need for scientific state intervention into private sexual behavior. In these papers, sexual knowledge was to be transmitted to the widest possible population, including women, children, and the working class. This sexual knowledge was intended to convey both the scientific facts of human reproduction and a new sense of social responsibility to the health of the nation.

It liberated the individual from traditional and religious sexual interdictions even as it bound him or her to a larger community of sexually responsible citizens. Hirschfeld attributed this kind of sex reform to the *genius loci* of Vienna. This book has argued that Vienna's distinct intellectual, political, and religious traditions shaped the transformation of sexual knowledge from a science of sexology into a social movement for sexual reform in the early twentieth century. Vienna's *genius loci*, which produced sexological, psychoanalytic, and eugenic theories during the period analyzed by this book, was central not only to the historiography of modern Austria, but also to the creation of sexual knowledge today.

The sexual reforms proposed at the WLSR Vienna conference were international in scale, but, as this book has shown, also profoundly local. This was not simply a question of Viennese presenters dominating the roster. All of the issues identified as crucial to sexual reform by the WLSR—family, marriage, divorce, sexual education, eugenics, the position of women, and the rights of illegitimate children—had already been addressed (with varying degrees of success) in Vienna by 1930. Yet, as has been suggested at many points in this work, none of the changes attempted or effected by Viennese sex reformers were permanent. As the historiography of early twentieth-century Austria amply demonstrates, the particular political and cultural conditions of Vienna made it a laboratory for radical social and sexual change. The unstable amalgam of national crisis, socialist politics, and Catholic tradition in Vienna made possible the application of sexual knowledge in the innovative, but ultimately fleeting, ways explored by this book.

Notes

1. "Wohnungsbau und Sexualreform," *Arbeiter-Zeitung* (18 September 1930), 6. Ellipsis in original.
2. The Austrian German Nationalist Party (*Grossdeutsches Volkspartei*) received 11.61 percent of the national vote in 1930. See Thomas Dostal, "Die Großdeutsches Volkspartei," in Emmerich Tálos, Herbert Dachs et al. (hg.), *Handbuch des Politischen Systems Österreiches: Erste Republik, 1918–1938* (Wien: Manzsche Verlags- und Universitätsbuchhandlung, 1995), 197.
3. Gerhard Jagschitz, "Die Nationalsozialistische Partei," in Emmerich Tálos, Herbert Dachs et al. (hg.), *Handbuch des Politischen Systems Österreiches: Erste Republik, 1918–1938* (Wien: Manzsche Verlags- und Universitätsbuchhandlung, 1995), 235. In 1932, the Austrian German Nationalist Party dissolved, and most of its members were absorbed into the Austrian Nationalist Socialist Party. For the role of the Austrian National Socialist Party in city violence, see Bruce F. Pauly, *From Prejudice to Persecution: A History of Austrian Anti/Semitism* (Chapel Hill: University of North Carolina Press, 1992), 102–116 and 190–209.
4. The *Arbeiter-Zeitung* leaves it to their readers to make this connection, but clearly hints that National Socialist disapproval of sex discussion is due to their own sexual imperfections. The "experience of scientific sexual discussion as a snub to their individuality" (*ihrer Eigenart*, which might also be translated as "their particularity") that National Socialists felt may also be a play on words. The leading (non-scientific) German journal of homosexuality was called *Der Eigenen*, which celebrated homosexuals' ability to resist conventionality.

5. The Vienna Museum of Sociological and Economic Sciences was an organization that created several international exhibits, although their "home gallery" was in Vienna's City Hall, through the Department of Social Hygiene and Social Security. See Otto Neurath, "Die Sozialhygieneische Ausstellung des Gesellschafts- und Wirtschaftsmuseums in Wien," in Herbert Steiner (hg.), *Sexualnot und Sexualreform: Verhandlung der Weltliga für Sexualreform, IV. Kongress* (Wien: Elbenmühl-Verlag, 1931), 655.
6. Herbert Steiner, "Vorwort," in Herbert Steiner (hg.), *Sexualnot und Sexualreform: Verhandlung der Weltliga für Sexualreform, IV. Kongress* (Wien: Elbenmühl-Verlag, 1931), xv.
7. Atina Grossmann, *Reforming Sex: The German Movement for Birth Control and Abortion Reform, 1920–1950* (New York: Oxford University Press, 1995), 41.
8. Grossmann, *Reforming Sex*, 43.
9. Paul Federn, "Der Wiener Kongress der Weltliga für Sexualreform," *Neue Freie Presse* Nr. 23,723 (28 September 1930), 13.
10. In fact, the *Arbeiter-Zeitung* attacks National Socialist demonstrators in implicitly sexual ways, which compromises the sexually progressive position the newspaper appears to speak from.
11. Rudolf Goldscheid, "Zur Geschichte der Sexualmoral," in Herbert Steiner (hg.), *Sexualnot und Sexualreform: Verhandlung der Weltliga für Sexualreform, IV. Kongress* (Wien: Elbenmühl-Verlag, 1931), 279–300, 280.
12. "Aims of the League," in Hertha Reise (hg.), *Verhandlung der Weltliga für Sexualreform, II. Congress* (Copenhagen: Leven & Munksgaard, 1929), ii.
13. Many of these analytical categories are suggested by Nicholas Matte's excellent article on the WLSR: "International Sexual Reform and Sexology in Europe, 1897–1933," in *Canadian Bulletin of Medical History* 22:2 (2005), 253–270.
14. Herha Reise and J.H. Leunbach, eds., *Sexual Reform Congress, Copenhagen 1–5. VII. 1928*. *WLSR World League for Sexual Reform, Proceedings of the Second Congress* (Copenhagen: Levin & Munksgaard, 1929), 10.
15. Norman Haire, "Welcome," in Norman Haire, ed., *Sexual Reform Congress, London 8–14. IX. 1929. WLSR World League for Sexual Reform, Proceedings from the Third Congress* (London: Kegan Paul, Trench, Trubner & Co., Ltd., 1930), xvi.
16. Herbert Steiner (hg.), *Sexualnot und Sexualreform: Verhandlung der Weltliga für Sexualreform, IV. Kongress* (Wien: Elbenmühl-Verlag, 1931), xxii–xxiii.
17. Previous WLSR congresses had taken place in Berlin (1921), Copenhagen (1928), and London (1929). The next conferences were scheduled for Moscow (1932) and Paris (1933). In actuality, the last WLSR congress was held in Brno, Czechoslovakia in 1932, where a subsequent conference in Moscow was planned, but never came to fruition. In 1933, the offices of WLSR President Magnus Hirschfeld were sacked in Berlin. The destruction of Hirschfeld's Institute of Sexual Science, combined with political differences between League members, seems to have destroyed the WLSR, making the 1930 Vienna congress its highest achievement. See Grossmann, *Reforming Sex*, 135.
18. Josef Friedjung, "Eröffnung des IV. Kongresses der Weltliga für Sexualreform in Wien," in Herbert Steiner (hg.), *Sexualnot und Sexualreform: Verhandlung der Weltliga für Sexualreform, IV. Kongress* (Wien: Elbenmühl-Verlag, 1931), xxxi–xxxii. Emphasis in original. Neither scientific luminary attended the congress; Krafft-Ebing had died in 1902, and Freud was "unable to be present" (Friedjung, "Eröffnung," xxxii).
19. Friedjung, "Eröffnung," in Steiner, *Sexualnot und Sexualreform*, xxxi.
20. Friedjung, "Eröffnung," in Steiner, *Sexualnot und Sexualreform*, xxxi.
21. Magnus Hirschfeld, "Einführungswort des Vorsitzenden," in Herbert Steiner (hg.), *Sexualnot und Sexualreform: Verhandlung der Weltliga für Sexualreform, IV. Kongress* (Wien: Elbenmühl-Verlag, 1931), xxxvii–xliii, xxxvii.
22. Hirschfeld, "Einführungswort," in Steiner, *Sexualnot und Sexualreform*, xxxvii.

23. Hirschfeld, "Einführungswort," in Steiner, *Sexualnot und Sexualreform*, xxxix.
24. Hirschfeld, "Einführungswort," in Steiner, *Sexualnot und Sexualreform*, xxxix.
25. Hirschfeld, "Einführungswort," in Steiner, *Sexualnot und Sexualreform*, xli.
26. Hirschfeld, "Einführungswort," in Steiner, *Sexualnot und Sexualreform*, xli.
27. Hirschfeld, "Einführungswort," in Steiner, *Sexualnot und Sexualreform*, xli.
28. Hirschfeld, "Einführungswort," in Steiner, *Sexualnot und Sexualreform*, xlii–xliii.
29. Hirschfeld, "Einführungswort," in Steiner, *Sexualnot und Sexualreform*, xliii.
30. "The Chief Planks of the League's Platform," in Hertha Reise (hg.), *Verhandlung der Weltliga für Sexualreform, II. Congress* (Copenhagen: Leven & Munksgaard, 1929), 11.
31. "The Chief Planks of the League's Platform," in Reise, *Verhandlung der Weltliga*, 11.
32. "The Chief Planks of the League's Platform," in Reise, *Verhandlung der Weltliga*, 11.
33. "The Chief Planks of the League's Platform," in Reise, *Verhandlung der Weltliga*, 11.
34. "The Chief Planks of the League's Platform," in Reise, *Verhandlung der Weltliga*, 11.
35. "The Chief Planks of the League's Platform," in Reise, *Verhandlung der Weltliga*, 11.
36. "The Chief Planks of the League's Platform," in Reise, *Verhandlung der Weltliga*, 11.
37. Julius Tandler, "Wohnungsnot und Sexualreform," in Herbert Steiner (hg.), *Sexualnot und Sexualreform: Verhandlung der Weltliga für Sexualreform, IV. Kongress* (Wien: Elbenmühl-Verlag, 1931), 5–15, 6–7.
38. Tandler, "Wohnungsnot," in Steiner, *Sexualnot und Sexualreform*, 12–13.
39. Tandler, "Wohnungsnot," in Steiner, *Sexualnot und Sexualreform*, 8.
40. Tandler, "Wohnungsnot," in Steiner, *Sexualnot und Sexualreform*, 14. Emphasis in original.
41. Tandler, "Wohnungsnot," in Steiner, *Sexualnot und Sexualreform*, 14.
42. "Wohnungsbau und Sexualreform," *Arbeiter-Zeitung*, 6.
43. "Diskussion zu den Vorträgen 1–4," in Herbert Steiner (hg.), *Sexualnot und Sexualreform: Verhandlung der Weltliga für Sexualreform, IV. Kongress* (Wien: Elbenmühl-Verlag, 1931), 39–42, 39.
44. "Diskussion zu den Vorträgen 1–4," in Steiner, *Sexualnot und Sexualreform*, 40.
45. "Diskussion zu den Vorträgen 1–4," in Steiner, *Sexualnot und Sexualreform*, 42.
46. "Diskussion zu den Vorträgen 1–4," in Steiner, *Sexualnot und Sexualreform*, 42.
47. Wilhelm Reich, "Die Sexualnot der werktätigen Massen und die Schwerigkeiten der Sexualreform," in Herbert Steiner (hg.), *Sexualnot und Sexualreform: Verhandlung der Weltliga für Sexualreform, IV. Kongress* (Wien: Elbenmühl-Verlag, 1931), 72–86, 72.
48. Reich, "Sexualnot," in Steiner, *Sexualnot und Sexualreform*, 75.
49. Reich, "Sexualnot," in Steiner, *Sexualnot und Sexualreform*, 74.
50. Reich, "Sexualnot," in Steiner, *Sexualnot und Sexualreform*, 76.
51. Reich, "Sexualnot," in Steiner, *Sexualnot und Sexualreform*, 72–73.
52. Reich, "Sexualnot," in Steiner, *Sexualnot und Sexualreform*, 79.
53. Reich, "Sexualnot," in Steiner, *Sexualnot und Sexualreform*, 80.
54. There are interesting similarities between the sexual systems imagined by Bettauer and Reich. Historian Karl Fallend has recently hypothesized that Bettauer's advice column was one of cultural stimuli for Reich's Proletarian Sexual Advice Centers. See Karl Fallend, *Wilhelm Reich in Wien: Psychoanalyse und Politik* (Wien: Ludwig-Boltzmann-Institut für Geschichte der Gesellschaftswissenschaften, 1998), 109–111.
55. Reich, "Sexualnot," in Steiner, *Sexualnot und Sexualreform*, 85–86.
56. Felix Kanitz, "Das Recht des Kindes," in Herbert Steiner (hg.), *Sexualnot und Sexualreform: Verhandlung der Weltliga für Sexualreform, IV. Kongress* (Wien: Elbenmühl-Verlag, 1931), 627–629, 627. Emphasis in original.
57. Kanitz, "Das Recht des Kindes," in Steiner, *Sexualnot und Sexualreform*, 628–629. Emphasis in original.
58. Kanitz, "Das Recht des Kindes," in Steiner, *Sexualnot und Sexualreform*, 629.

59. Helene Stourzh-Anderle, "Die sexuelle Aufklärung," in Herbert Steiner (hg.), *Sexualnot und Sexualreform: Verhandlung der Weltliga für Sexualreform, IV. Kongress* (Wien: Elbenmühl-Verlag, 1931), 630.
60. Josef K. Friedjung, "Das Recht des Kindes," in Herbert Steiner (hg.), *Sexualnot und Sexualreform: Verhandlung der Weltliga für Sexualreform, IV. Kongress* (Wien: Elbenmühl-Verlag, 1931), 589–592, 590–592.
61. Goldscheid, "Zur Geschichte der Sexualmoral," in Steiner, *Sexualnot und Sexualreform*, 289.
62. Goldscheid, "Zur Geschichte der Sexualmoral," in Steiner, *Sexualnot und Sexualreform*, 296.
63. Goldscheid, "Zur Geschichte der Sexualmoral," in Steiner, *Sexualnot und Sexualreform*, 282.
64. Goldscheid, "Zur Geschichte der Sexualmoral," in Steiner, *Sexualnot und Sexualreform*, 299.
65. Adelheid Popp, "Geburtenregelung und Menschenökonomie," in Herbert Steiner (hg.), *Sexualnot und Sexualreform: Verhandlung der Weltliga für Sexualreform, IV. Kongress* (Wien: Elbenmühl-Verlag, 1931), 498–502, 501. Emphasis in original.
66. Sigismund Peller, "Der Abortus im Rahmen des menschlichen Reproduktionsproblems," in Herbert Steiner (hg.), *Sexualnot und Sexualreform: Verhandlung der Weltliga für Sexualreform, IV. Kongress* (Wien: Elbenmühl-Verlag, 1931), 487–496, 495.
67. Peller, "Der Abortus," in Steiner, *Sexualnot und Sexualreform*, 495.
68. Norman Haire, "A Preliminary Note on Haire's Pessary and the Intrauterine Silver Ring of Gräfenberg," in Herbert Steiner (hg.), *Sexualnot und Sexualreform: Verhandlung der Weltliga für Sexualreform, IV. Kongress* (Wien: Elbenmühl-Verlag, 1931), 512–513.
69. Dr. J. Borak, "Über die temporäre Röntgensterilisierung," in Herbert Steiner (hg.), *Sexualnot und Sexualreform: Verhandlung der Weltliga für Sexualreform, IV. Kongress* (Wien: Elbenmühl-Verlag, 1931), 543–549, 543.
70. Herbert Steiner, "Kritik antikonzeptioneller Methoden und praktische Wege der Geburtenregelung," in Herbert Steiner (hg.), *Sexualnot und Sexualreform: Verhandlung der Weltliga für Sexualreform, IV. Kongress* (Wien: Elbenmühl-Verlag, 1931), 550–557, 550.
71. Sidonie Furst, "Das Problem der alleinstehenden Frau," in Herbert Steiner (hg.), *Sexualnot und Sexualreform: Verhandlung der Weltliga für Sexualreform, IV. Kongress* (Wien: Elbenmühl-Verlag, 1931), 92–93, 92.
72. Paul Pallaster, "Eherechtsreform," in Herbert Steiner (hg.), *Sexualnot und Sexualreform: Verhandlung der Weltliga für Sexualreform, IV. Kongress* (Wien: Elbenmühl-Verlag, 1931), 457–459, 457–458.
73. Otto Neurath, "The Social Hygiene Exhibition of the Museum for Sociological and Economic Sciences in Vienna," in Herbert Steiner (hg.), *Sexualnot und Sexualreform: Verhandlung der Weltliga für Sexualreform, IV. Kongress* (Wien: Elbenmühl-Verlag, 1931), 655–670, 659.
74. Otto Neurath, "The Social Hygiene Exhibition," in Steiner, *Sexualnot und Sexualreform*, 666.
75. Otto Neurath, "The Social Hygiene Exhibition," in Steiner, *Sexualnot und Sexualreform*, 661 and 662.
76. Magnus Hirschfeld, "Schlusswort," in Herbert Steiner (hg.), *Sexualnot und Sexualreform: Verhandlung der Weltliga für Sexualreform, IV. Kongress* (Wien: Elbenmühl-Verlag, 1931), 679–680.

Conclusion

SEXUAL KNOWLEDGE BETWEEN SCIENCE AND SOCIAL REFORM

The fall of Austrian Social Democracy ended in February of 1934. Already besieged in government, SDAP leadership was ousted from Vienna's city hall in a violent coup led by what would become known as the Fatherland Front: an authoritarian regime aligned closely with the Roman Catholic Church. While the production of sexual knowledge in Vienna did not end in 1934, it certainly lost its innovative drive. Many of the personages in this book had already left the stage. Hugo Bettauer had been dead almost a decade; Wilhelm Reich had left for Berlin and then exile in Scandinavia; Johann and Betty Ferch had dissolved the *Bund gegen Mutterschaftzwang* and along with it popular access to cheap contraceptives. Julius Tandler moved to Moscow to begin reorganizing Soviet hospital systems, dying two years later. In many ways, the moment of reform through sexual knowledge passed in Vienna, replaced by a return to the family values promoted by the Church. Although racial science and eugenics flourished in Vienna during the Nazi years, the city never again enjoyed a reputation as a hub of sexology, a science that itself died out under fascist regimes in Central Europe.

What was it about Vienna that had allowed for such a creative moment of transition between sexual knowledge as a science, presided over by doctors and professors, and sexual knowledge as a social reform movement that targeted women, children, and workers? Certainly the rich medical community surrounding the university, combined with the social problems inherent in Vienna's dense urban population at the turn of the century, made commentary about and research into population problems likely. Fear of disease, especially syphilis, drove many individuals to organize against prostitution and illicit sex. But these factors were common for many European capitals in the years leading up to World War I. The war itself played a crucial role in transforming the city, as refugees crowded the streets and soldiers returned from the front only to find privation and misery had remade Vienna into a restive capital of an unwanted state. The perceived emergency in population planning and terrible loss of life during and after the war encouraged innovative new sexual systems within the city's expanding welfare structure, as well as private associations who devoted themselves to meeting the contraceptive needs of the women of Vienna. Yet it was the years after the war, in the democratic Republic, that were the most creative in the expansion of public sexual knowledge. In the realms of policy, publishing, and activism, Viennese individuals expressed a dedication to re-establishing a heterosexual norm for the city that emphasized health and family planning.

The purpose of sexual knowledge shifted subtly over the period 1900 to 1934. Hygiene, which was so crucial to the *fin-de-siècle* fight against syphilis, remained a watchword throughout the interwar years. But added to this imperative was a new emphasis on personal responsibility, a kind of positive spin that afforded the individual a measure of control through rational decision-making, even in the realm of sexuality. Rationalizing reproduction was central to the position of responsibility, as was living a sober, upright lifestyle that mirrored Social Democratic ideals for the citizens of the city. Information devoted to eugenically sound reproduction as well as birth control for all levels of society helped to define and enable responsibility. But responsibility also had an emotional component: an attitude towards sex and love that combined clean living with personal fulfillment. This is especially clear in the rise of literature extolling a companionate marriage, in which both partners were sexually satisfied within the bounds of a lasting commitment that may or may not yield children. This literature sometimes engaged in the discourse of reproductive responsibility, but more often highlighted the emotional benefits of monogamy for the individual, rather than the good of the collective or of future offspring.

The discourse of sexual danger in Vienna, which was well developed at the turn of the century in terms of vice, homosexuality, and disease, only intensified during the aftermath of war. Returning soldiers were characterized as carriers of venereal disease, spreading sexual misery as they reentered society. But by far the newest danger to threaten the population in the interwar years was that of unregulated reproduction, which threatened individual women's health and led to city-wide poverty and suffering. The threat of unregulated reproduction was used on a local level to argue for eugenics as well as the right to abortion, although neither movement found traction among the Austrian government. Much more successful were the attempts to secure access to birth control throughout the city and especially in working-class districts. That this was achieved in a profoundly Catholic nation in the interwar period remains a major achievement. Birth control access was justified through emotionally fraught and at times melodramatic representations of women's capacity to suffer—from pain, disease, hunger, and the injustice of not being able to feed one's children—which proved to be extremely successful campaign images. At the same time, these images and stories emphasized the danger of sexual activity and the personal misery that could result from it.

Emotionality itself was an increasing presence in sexual information throughout the interwar years. The dispassionate medical doctor as ultimate authority in sexual matters was displaced, in part, by the sympathetic layperson. In popular magazines, how-to guides, and children's sexual education materials, we see a rise in informal, non-specialist voices guiding people towards sexual knowledge. Pleasure, compassion, and both familial and romantic love were championed as integral parts of this knowledge. These feeling states encouraged readers to "suffer with" one another as they moved from ignorance to wisdom.

Leavening sexual knowledge with emotional testimonies was a way to reassert the private even as it was discussed in public forums. The individual was faced with a bewildering set of messages about sex in the interwar period, ranging from calls to chastity to celebrations of (hetero)sexuality in print and film. Perhaps the emotional valence of these messages was meant to access the personal in an increasingly mass society, or perhaps it was coolly injected into anatomical and biological information merely to appeal to less-educated audiences. Whatever its genesis, the result is striking: a transition away from sexological literature (with its taxonomies of perversion) and towards opportunities for self-care and self-reliance, mediated by a new set of educators, social workers, clinicians, and authors. The culture of confession was crucial to this shift. Individuals were encouraged to confess their health, their desires, and their histories in order to be better "diagnosed" by the attending care-giver, whether he or she be a professional doctor or a self-help columnist. By accessing this Catholic process, laypeople and authorities alike in Vienna could better order the sexual information they needed to receive from and convey to individuals.

The innovations of the interwar years brought sex education and advice to a wider public than ever before. By 1934, women, children, and workers were the intended audience of publicly shared sexual knowledge that was formatted specifically for them. What they did with this knowledge belongs to another story. We may hope, along with contemporary Viennese educators, that they used it to safeguard their health, plan their families, and enjoy their bodies.

BIBLIOGRAPHY

Archival Sources

Wiener Stadt- und Landesarchiv. Vienna, Austria.
  Bund für Mutterschutz, Vereine 3644/21
  Bund gegen den Mutterschaftszwang, Vereine 1440/23
  Bundes für Geburtenregelung, Vereine 1440/23
  Eherechtsreformverine, Vereine 2154/26
  Societas, Vereine 3936/21
  Sozialistische Gesellschaft für Sexualberatung and Sexualforschung, Vereine 1440/23
  Die Verwaltung der Bundeshauptsamt Wien in der Zeit vom 1 Jänner 1923 bis 31 Dezember 1928, Band I und II. Wiener Stadt- und Landesarchiv Archivbibliothek, Material 511 2 Exemplar 42/1/2
  Die Verwaltung der Bundeshauptsamt Wien in der Zeit vom 1 Jänner 1929 bis 31 Dezember 1931, Band I und II. Wiener Stadt- und Landesarchiv Archivbibliothek, Material 511 2 Exemplar 42/1/2
Verein für Geschichte der Arbeiterbewegung. Vienna, Austria.
  Arbeiter-Abstinenten Bund, Lade 6/Mappe 34A.

Published Primary Sources: Newspapers and Journals

Arbeiter-Zeitung
Bettauers Wochenschift: Probleme des Lebens
Bildungsarbeit
Blätter für das Wohlfahrtswesen
Er und Sie: Wochenschrift für Lebenskultur und Erotik
Die Frau
Ich und Du
Jahrbuch für Nationalökonomie und Statistik
Der Kampf

Muenschener medizinische Wochenschrift
Neue Freie Presse
Neuen Wiener Journal
Die Quelle
Reichspost
Das Rendezvous
Die Rote Fahne
Sexual-Probleme
Sexual-Reform, Zeitschrift für Sexualreform und Neomalthusianismus
Der Sozialistische Arzt
Die Sozialistische Erziehung
Die Unzufriedene
Der Volkssturm
Wiener medizinische Wochenschrift
Wir beide: Zeitschrift für Kultur und Erotik

Published Primary Sources

Adler, Alfred. *What Life Should Mean to You*. Boston: Little, Brown, and Co., 1931.
Allers, Rudolf. *Sexualpädagogik: Grundlagen und Grundlinien*. Salzburg: Verlag Anton Pustet, 1934.
Anderle, Helene. *Die Sexuelle Aufklärung*. Wien: Deutscher Verlag für Jugend und Volk, 1925.
Andreas-Salomé, Lou. *Drei Briefe an einen Knaben*. Leipzig: Kurt Wolff Verlag, 1917.
"Anleitung zur Aufnahme der Anamnese." In *Das Neue Wien*, Band III, Städtewerk herausgegeben unter offizieller Mitwirkung der Gemeinde Wien, 573. Wien: 1927.
"Bekämpfung der Geschlechtskrankheiten." In *Das Neue Wien*, Band II, Städtewerk herausgegeben unter offizieller Mitwirkung der Gemeinde Wien, 563. Wien: 1927.
Bertram, Adolf Kardinal. *Reverentia Puero! Katholische Erwägungen zu Fragen der sexual-Pädagogik*. Freiburg im Breisgau: Herder & Co., 1929.
Der Bettauer Almanach für 1925. Wien: Verlag Bettauers Wochenschrift, 1924.
Bloch, Iwan. *The Sexual Life of Our Time*. Translated by M. Paul Eden. London: Rebman Limited, 1909.
Borak, Dr. J. "Über die temporäre Röntgensterilisierung." In *Sexualnot und Sexualreform: Verhandlung der Weltliga für Sexualreform, IV. Kongress*, herausgegeben von Herbert Steiner, 543–549. Wien: Elbenmühl-Verlag, 1931.
"Dienstvorschrift für den Beratungsarzt." *Das Neue Wien*, Band III, Städtewerk herausgegeben unter offizieller Mitwirkung der Gemeinde Wien, 571. Wien: 1927.
Dürerbund. *Am Lebensquell: Ein Hausbuch zur Geschlechtlichen Erziehung. Betrachtungen, Ratschläge und Beispiele als Ergebnisse des Dürerbund*. Dresden: Alexander Köhler Verlag, 1909.

"Eheberatung." *Das Neue Wien*, Band III, Städtewerk herausgegeben unter offizieller Mitwirkung der Gemeinde Wien, 569–570. Wien: 1927.

Eisenschiml, Wilhelm. "Die Bekämpfung der Geschlechtskrankheiten in Österreich." In *Das Österreichische Gesundheitswesen*, Herausgegeben von Volksgesundheitamt der Gemeinde Wien, 18–19. Wien: Wirtschafts-Zeitungs-Verlag-Gesellschaft, 1930.

"Die Entwicklung des öffentlichen Gesundheitswesen." In *Das Österreichische Gesundheitswesen*, Herausgegeben von Volksgesundheitamt der Gemeinde Wien. Wien: Wirtschafts-Zeitungs-Verlag-Gesellschaft, 1930: 80–82.

Ferch, Betti [sic]. "The Birth Control Association of Austria." In *The Practice of Contraception: An International Symposium and Survey*, edited by Margaret Sanger and Hannah M. Stone, 270–271. Baltimore: The Williams and Wilkins Company, 1931.

Ferch, Johann. *Kulturkampf*. Wien: Verlagsbuchhandlung Rudolf Cerny, 1922.

———. *Die Welt der Erotik*. Leipzig: Parthenon Verlag, 1929.

Forel, August. *The Sexual Question: A Scientific, Psychological, Hygienic and Sociological Study*. Translated by C.F. Marshall. Brooklyn: Physicians and Surgeons Book Company, 1936.

"Die Formularien der Eheberatungstelle, Formular 1." In *Das Neue Wien*, Band III, Städtewerk herausgegeben unter offizieller Mitwirkung der Gemeinde Wien, 572. Wien: 1927.

"Die Formularien der Eheberatungstelle, Formular 3." In *Das Neue Wien*, Band III, Städtewerk herausgegeben unter offizieller Mitwirkung der Gemeinde Wien, 574. Wien: 1927.

"Die Formularien der Eheberatungstelle, Formular 4." In *Das Neue Wien*, Band III, Städtewerk herausgegeben unter offizieller Mitwirkung der Gemeinde Wien, 576. Wien: 1927.

Freud, Sigmund. "Die 'kulturelle' Sexualmoral und die moderne Nervosität," *Sexual-Probleme* 1/3 (März 1908): 121–130.

———. *The Freud Reader*, edited by Peter Gay. New York: W.W. Norton & Company, 1989.

———. *Dora: An Analysis of a Case of Hysteria*. New York: Simon and Schuster, 1997.

Friedjung, Josef. *Die Geschlechtliche Aufklärung im Erziehungswerke: Ein Wegweiser für Eltern, Erzieher und Ärzte*. Wien: Verlag von Josef Safár, 1922.

———. *Die Geschlechtliche Aufklärung im Erziehungswerke: Ein Wegweiser für Eltern, Erzieher und Ärzte* (Vierte, verbesserte und erweiterte Auflage). Wien: Verlag Julius Springer, 1926.

———. "Das Recht des Kindes." In *Sexualnot und Sexualreform: Verhandlung der Weltliga für Sexualreform, IV. Kongress*, herausgegeben von Herbert Steiner, 590–592. Wien: Elbenmühl-Verlag, 1931.

———. "Eröffnung des IV. Kongresses der Weltliga für Sexualreform in Wien." In *Sexualnot und Sexualreform: Verhandlung der Weltliga für Sexualreform, IV. Kongress*, herausgegeben von in Herbert Steiner, xxxi–xxxiii. Wien: Elbenmühl-Verlag, 1931.

"Die Fürsorgeaufgabe der Gemeinde." In *Das Neue Wien* Band IV, Städtewerk herausgegeben unter offizieller Mitwirkung der Gemeinde Wien, 215. Wien: 1927.

Furst, Sidonie. "Das Problem der alleinstehenden Frau." In *Sexualnot und Sexualreform: Verhandlung der Weltliga für Sexualreform, IV. Kongress*, herausgegeben von Herbert Steiner, 92–93. Wien: Elbenmühl-Verlag, 1931.

Gegenbauer, Victor. "Die Tätigkeit des Wiener Gesundheitsamts im letzten Jahrzehnt." *Das Österreichische Gesundheitswesen*, herausgegeben von Volksgesundheitamt der Gemeinde Wien, 81. Wien: Wirtschafts-Zeitungs-Verlag-Gesellschaft, 1930.

Glaessner, Rudolf. *Rief zur Liebe! Eine ärztliche Aufklärungsshrift über alles Wissenswerte im Liebes- und Geschlechtsleben des Weibes*. Wien: Anzengruberverlag, 1921.

———. *Die Problem des Geschlechtslebens: Die Liebe von Mann und Weib von Liebesglück und Ehe*. Wien: Anzengruber Verlag, 1931.

Glatterer, Michael. *Im Glaubenslicht. Christliche Gedanken über das Geschlechtsleben*. Innsbruck: Verlag Felician Rauch, 1927.

———. *Die Jungfräulichkeit*. Innsbruck: Verlag von Felician Rauch, 1927.

Goldscheid, Rudolf. *Frauenfrage und Menschenökonomie*. Wien: Anzengruber Verlag Brüder Suschitzky, 1913.

———. "Zur Geschichte der Sexualmoral." In *Sexualnot und Sexualreform: Verhandlung der Weltliga für Sexualreform, IV. Kongress*, herausgegeben von in Herbert Steiner, 279–300. Wien: Elbenmühl-Verlag, 1931.

Golias, Eduard. *Am Tore des Lebens: Über sexuelle Aufklärung und Sittlichkeit*. Wien: Österreichischer Bundesverlag für Unterricht, Wissenschaft und Kunst, 1925.

Haire, Norman. "A Preliminary Note on Haire's Pessary and the Intrauterine Silver Ring of Gräfenberg." In *Sexualnot und Sexualreform: Verhandlung der Weltliga für Sexualreform, IV. Kongress*, herausgegeben von Herbert Steiner, 512–513. Wien: Elbenmühl-Verlag, 1931.

Hirschfeld, Magnus. "Einführungswort des Vorsitzenden." In *Sexualnot und Sexualreform: Verhandlung der Weltliga für Sexualreform, IV. Kongress*, herausgegeben von Herbert Steiner, xxxvii–xliii. Wien: Elbenmühl-Verlag, 1931.

———. "Schlusswort." In *Sexualnot und Sexualreform: Verhandlung der Weltliga für Sexualreform, IV. Kongress*, herausgegeben von Herbert Steiner, 681–682. Wien: Elbenmühl-Verlag, 1931.

Hoffmann, Jakob. *Werde ein ganzer Mann! Aufklärung und Belehrungen für die heranwachsende männliche Jugend*. Freiburg im Breisgau: Herdersche Verlagshandlung, 1917.

Kammerer, Paul. *Lebensbeherrschung: Grundsteinlegung zur organischen Technik*. München: Geschäftsstelle des Deutschen Monistenbundes, 1919.

Kanitz, Felix. "Das Recht des Kindes." In *Sexualnot und Sexualreform: Verhandlung der Weltliga für Sexualreform, IV. Kongress*, herausgegeben von Herbert Steiner, 627–629. Wien: Elbenmühl-Verlag, 1931.

Kautsky, Karl Jr. *Der Kampf Gegen den Geburtenrückgang*. Wein: Verlag der Organisation Wien der Sozialdemohratischen Partei, 1924.

Kitaj, J. *Das Normale und das Kranke Sexualleben des Mannes und des Weibs*. Wien: Anzengruberverlag, 1913.

Krafft-Ebing, Richard. *Psychopathia Sexualis: With Especial Reference to the Antipathic Sexual Instinct, A Medico-Forensic Study*. Translated by F.J. Rebman. New York: Physicians and Surgeons Book Company, 1924.

Lazarsfeld, Sofie. *Erziehung zur Ehe*. Wien: Verlag von Moritz Perles, 1928.

———. *Wie die Frau der Mann Erlebt: Fremde Bekenntnisse und eigene Betrachtungen*. Wien: Verlag für Sexualwissenschaft / Schneider & Co., 1931.

Meisel-Hess, Grete. *Der Sexuelle Krise.* Jena: 1909.
Musil, Robert. *Die Verwirrungen des Zöglings Törless.* Reinbeck bei Hamburg: Rowohlt Verlag, 1983.
Die Neue Frau. Wien: Verlag der Organisation Wien der sozialdemokratischen Partei, 1924.
Otto Neurath. "Die Sozialhygieneische Ausstellung des Gesellschafts- und Wirtschaftsmuseums in Wien." In *Sexualnot und Sexualreform: Verhandlung der Weltliga für Sexualreform, IV. Kongress,* herausgegeben von in Herbert Steiner, 655–670. Wien: Elbenmühl-Verlag, 1931.
Pallester, Paul. "Eherechtsreform." In *Sexualnot und Sexualreform: Verhandlung der Weltliga für Sexualreform, IV. Kongress,* herausgegeben von Herbert Steiner, 457–459. Wien: Elbenmühl-Verlag, 1931.
Peller, Sigismund. "Der Abortus im Rahmen des menschlichen Reproduktionsproblems." In *Sexualnot und Sexualreform: Verhandlung der Weltliga für Sexualreform, IV. Kongress,* herausgegeben von Herbert Steiner, 487–496. Wien: Elbenmühl-Verlag, 1931.
"Pius XI (1930)." Reprinted in *Women, the Family, and Freedom: The Debate in Documents,* volume II, edited by Susan Groag Bell and Karen M. Offen, 210–316. Stanford: Stanford University Press, 1983.
Pius XI. *On Christian Marriage.* New York: The Barry Vail Corporation, 1931.
Popp, Adelheid. "Geburtenregelung und Menschenökonomie." In *Sexualnot und Sexualreform: Verhandlung der Weltliga für Sexualreform, IV. Kongress,* herausgegeben von Herbert Steiner, 498–502. Wien: Elbenmühl-Verlag, 1931.
"Ein Rat für Eheschließende." In *Das Neue Wien,* Band III, Städtewerk herausgegeben unter offizieller Mitwirkung der Gemeinde Wien, 578. Wien: 1927.
Reich, Wilhelm. *Sexualerregung und Sexualbefriedigung.* Wien: Münster-Verlag, 1929.
———. "Die Sexualnot der werktätigen Massen und die Schwerigkeiten der Sexualreform." In *Sexualnot und Sexualreform: Verhandlung der Weltliga für Sexualreform, IV. Kongress,* herausgegeben von Herbert Steiner, 72–86. Wien: Elbenmühl-Verlag, 1931.
———. *Geschlechtsreife, Enthaltsamkeit, Ehemoral: Eine Kritik der bürgerlichen Sexual-Reform.* Wien: Münster Verlag, 1931.
———. "The Socialistic Society for Sexual Advice and Sexual Research." In *The Practice of Contraception: An International Symposium and Survey,* edited by Margaret Sanger and Hannah M. Stone, 271. Baltimore: The Williams and Wilkins Company, 1931.
———.*Der Einbruch der Sexualmoral: Zur Geschichte der Sexuelle Ökonomie.* Kopenhagen: Verlag für Sexualpolitik, 1935.
———. *The Function of the Orgasm: Sex-Economic Problems of Biological Energy.* Translated by Theodore P. Wolfe. New York: Noonday Press, 1942.
———. *The Sexual Revolution: Toward a Self-Governing Character Structure.* Translated by Theodore P. Wolfe. New York: Orgone Institute Press, 1945.
———. *The Invasion of Compulsory Sex-Morality.* New York: Farrar, Straus, and Giroux, 1971.
Reise, Hertha. "Aims of the League." In *Verhandlung der Weltliga für Sexualreform, II. Congress,* herausgegeben von Hertha Reise, ii–iii. Copenhagen: Leven & Munksgaard, 1929.

Rosenfeld, Siegfried. "Aus der Gesundheitsstatistik Österreichs." In *Das Österreichische Gesundheitswesen*, herausgegeben von dem Volksgesundheitsamt der Gemeinde Wien, 54–60. Wien: Wirtschafts-Zeitungs-Verlag-Gesellschaft, 1930.

Schlegel, Joseph Carl. *Hygiene des Ehelebens: Der Führer zu Liebes- und Eheglücks*. Wien: Verlag Schusdeks, 1929.

Schlesinger, Therese. *Die Frau im sozialdemokratischen Partieprogramm*. Wien: Verlag der organisation Wien der sozialdemokratischen Partei, 1928.

Schlesinger, Therese and Paul Stein. "Leitsätze für die sexuelle Aufklärung der Jugend." Reprinted in *Ansätze zur Sexualerziehung in der Sozialdemokratischen Jugendbewegung in der Zeit ihrer Entstehung*, von Hildegard Feistritzer, 129–135. Wien: Universität Wien (Ph.D. Dissertation), 1978.

Schmitt, Albert. *Die katholische Ehe und die christliche Familie: Die Grundelemente der Kultur*. Innsbruck: Tyrolia Verlag.

Schmitz, P. Peter. *Am reinen Quell des Lebens: Eine Anleitung zur geschlechtlichen Aufklärung der Kinder für die christlichen Mütter*. Mödling: Missionsdruckerei St. Gabriel, 1932.

———. *Bursch und Mädel in Gottes Hand. Ein Seelsorglicher und Pädagogischer Beitrag zum Geschlechtlicher Problem*. Innsbruck und Wien: Tyrolia Verlag, 1936.

Skalla, Lothar. *Über Gesundheitspflege der Schüler im Elternhause und Über sexuelle Aufklärung*. Wien: Verlag von Carl Gerold's Sohn, 1912.

So belehrte dein Kind, Ein Schriften für Eltern und Erzieher, von einem Jugendfreund. Salzburg: Verlag des Pfarramts Vigaun, 1933.

Steiner, Herbert. "Kritik antikonzeptioneller Methoden und praktische Wege der Geburtenregelung." In *Sexualnot und Sexualreform: Verhandlung der Weltliga für Sexualreform, IV. Kongress*, herausgegeben von Herbert Steiner, 550–557. Wien: Elbenmühl-Verlag, 1931.

———. "Vorwort." In *Sexualnot und Sexualreform: Verhandlung der Weltliga für Sexualreform, IV. Kongress*, herausgegeben von Herbert Steiner, xv–xvi. Wien: Elbenmühl-Verlag, 1931.

Stekel, Wilhelm. "Sexual Abstinence and Health." In *Sexual Continence*, edited by William J. Robinson. New York: Eugenics Publishing Co., 1924.

Stone, Hannah M. "The Vaginal Occlusive Pessary." In *The Practice of Contraception: An International Symposium and Survey*, edited by Margaret Sanger and Hannah M. Stone. Baltimore: The Williams and Wilkins Company, 1931.

Stourzh-Anderle, Helene. "Die sexuelle Aufklärung." In *Sexualnot und Sexualreform: Verhandlung der Weltliga für Sexualreform, IV. Kongress*, herausgegeben von Herbert Steiner, 630. Wien: Elbenmühl-Verlag, 1931.

Tandler, Julius. "Konstitution und Rassenhygiene," *Zeitschrift für angewandete Anatomie und Konstitutionslehre* 1 (1913): 11–26.

———. *Ehe und Bevölkerungspolitik*. Wien: Verlag von Moritz Perles, 1924.

———. *Wohltätigkeit oder Fürsorge?* Wien: Verlag der Organization Wien der sozialdemokratischen Partei, 1925.

———. *Gefahren der Minderwertigkeit*. Wien: Verlag des Wiener Jugendhilfswerks, 1929.

———. Psychiatrische Kliniken und Siechenhäuser," *Zeitschrift für das gesamte Krankenhauswesen* 25 (3 Dezember 1929), 718–722.

———. "Wohlfahrtswesen und Gesundheitsamt." In *Das Österreichische Gesundheitswesen*, herausgegeben von Volksgesundheitamt der Gemeinde Wien, 81–82. Wien: Wirtschafts-Zeitungs-Verlag-Gesellschaft, 1930.

———. "Wohnungsnot und Sexualreform." In *Sexualnot und Sexualreform: Verhandlung der Weltliga für Sexualreform, IV. Kongress*, herausgegeben von Herbert Steiner, 5–14. Wien: Elbenmühl-Verlag, 1931.

———."Krieg und Bevölkerung." Reprinted in *Julius Tandler, Mediziner und Sozialreformer: Eine Biographie*, by Karl Sablik, 113–121. Wien: Verlag A. Schendl, 1983.

Tauber, Elsa und R. *Der Mann — Ein Buch für Frauen*. Wien: Rhombus Verlag, 1925.

Timmering, H.E. "Erziehung (sexuelle)." In *Handwörterbuch der Sexualwissenschaft: Enzyklopädie der natur- und kulturwissenschaftlichen Sexualkund des Menschen*, herausgegeben von Max Marcuse, 108–111. Bonn: A. Marcus & E. Webers Verlag, 1923.

Voge, Cecil. "Future Research upon Sterilization and Contraception," in *The Practice of Contraception: An International Symposium and Survey*, edited by Margaret Sanger and Hannah M. Stone, 76–90. Baltimore: The Williams and Wilkins Company, 1931.

Wegner, Hans. *Wir Jungen Männer: Das Problem des gebildeten jungen Mannes vor der Ehe*. Leipzig: Karl Robert Langwieche Verlag, 1917.

Weininger, Otto. "Curriculum Vitae." In *Otto Weininger: Eros und Psyche. Studien und Briefe, 1899–1902*, herausgegeben von Hannah Rodlauer, 210–211. Wien: Österreichische Akademie der Wissenschaften, 1990.

———. *Sex and Character*. Authorized translation from the 6th German edition. London: William Heinemann, 1906.

"Wiens Bevölkerungsbewegung." In *Das Neue Wien* Band II, 602. Städtewerk herausgeben unter offizieller Mitwirkung der Gemeinde Wien. Wien: 1927.

Selected Secondary Sources

Allen, Anne Taylor. "Feminism, Venereal Disease, and the State in Germany, 1890–1918." *Journal of the History of Sexuality* 4/1 (July 1993): 27–50.

———. *Motherhood and Feminism in Germany, 1870–1914*. New Brunswick: Rutgers University Press, 1991.

Anderson, Harriet. *Utopian Feminism: Women's Movements in fin-de-siècle Vienna*. New Haven: Yale University Press, 1992.

Ankum, Katherina von. "Motherhood and the 'New Woman': Vicki Baum's *stud. chem. Helene Willfüer* and Irmgard Keun's *Gilgi – eine von uns*." *Women in Germany Yearbook* 11(1995): 171–188.

Baader, Gerhard. "Eugenische Programme in der sozialistischen Parteienlandschaft in Deutschland und Österreich im Vergleich." In *Eugenik in Österriech: Biopolitische Strukturen von 1900–1945*, herausgegeben von Gerhard Baader, Veronika Hofer, und Thomas Mayer, 66–139. Wien: Czernin Verlag, 2007.

Baxendall, Lee. *Sex-Pol: Essays, 1929–1934*. New York: Random House, 1972.

Beller, Steven. *Vienna and the Jews, 1867–1938: A Cultural History*. Cambridge: Cambridge University Press, 1989.

Bernheimer, Charles and Claire Kahane, editors. *In Dora's Case: Freud—Hysteria—Feminism*. New York: Columbia University Press, 1985.

Beyer, Doris. *'Die Strategen des Lebens': Rassenhygiene und Wohlfahrtswesen – zur Entstehung eines sozialdemokratischen Machtdiapositivs in Österriech bis 1934*. Wein: Universität Wien (Diplomarbeit), 1986.

Bland, Lucy and Laura Doan. "General Introduction." In *Sexology Uncensored: The Documents of Sexual Science*, edited by Bland and Doan, 1–9. Chicago: University of Chicago Press, 1998.

Blau, Eve. *The Architecture of Red Vienna, 1919–1934*. Cambridge: The MIT Press, 1999.

Blum, Mark. *The Austro-Marxists 1890–1918: A Psychobiographical Study*. Lexington: University Press of Kentucky, 1985.

Botz, Gerhard. *Gewalt in der Politik: Attentate, Zusammenstöße, Putschversuche, Unruhen in Österreich, 1918–1938*. München: Wilhelm Fink Verlag, 1983.

Boyer, John W. *Political Radicalism in Late Imperial Vienna: Origins of the Christian Social Movement, 1848–1887*. Chicago: University of Chicago Press, 1981.

———. *Culture and Political Crisis in Vienna: Christian Socialism in Power, 1997–1918*. Chicago: University of Chicago Press, 1995.

Brooks, Peter. *The Melodramatic Imagination: Balzac, Henry James, and the Mode of Excess*. New Haven: Yale University Press, 1976.

———. *Troubling Confessions: Speaking Guilt in Law and Literature*. Chicago: University of Chicago Press, 2000.

Bukey, Evan Burr. *Hitler's Austria: Popular Sentiment in the Nazi Era, 1938–1945*. Chapel Hill: University of North Carolina Press, 2000.

Burleigh, Michael and Wolfgang Wippermann. *The Racial State: Germany 1933–1945*. Cambridge: Cambridge University Press, 1991.

Csoklich, Fritz. "Press und Rundfunk." In *Österreich 1918–1938: Geschichte der Ersten Republik*, Band II, herausgegeben von Erika Weinzierl und Kurt Skalnik, 715–730. Graz: Styria Verlag, 1983.

Dean, Carolyn J. *The Frail Social Body: Pornography, Homosexuality, and Other Fantasies in Interwar France*. Berkeley: University of California Press, 2000.

———. *Sexuality and Modern Western Culture*. New York: Twayne Publishers, 1996.

Decker, Hannah S. *Freud, Dora, and Vienna 1900*. New York: The Free Press, 1991.

Dickinson, Edward Ross. "Reflections on Feminism and Monism in the Kaiserreich." *Central European History* 34:2 (June 2001): 191–230.

Dose, Ralf. "The World League for Sexual Reform: Some Possible Approaches." In *Sexual Cultures in Europe: National Histories*, edited by Franz X. Eder, Lesley Hall, and Gert Hekma, 221–241. Manchester: Manchester University Press, 1999.

Dostal, Thomas. "Die Großdeutsches Volkspartei." In *Handbuch des politischen Systems Österreich*, herausgegeben von Emmerich Tálos, Herbert Dachs, Ernst Hänisch, und Anton Staudinger, 195–206. Wien: Manzsche Verlags- und Universitätsbuchhandlung, 1995.

Eder, Franz X. "Erotisierendes Wissen. Zur Geschichte der 'Sexualisierung' im Wiener Fin de Siècle." In *Erotik, Versuch einer Annährung. Ausstellungskatalog des Historisches Museum der Stadt Wien*, 20–28. Wien: Historisches Museum, 1990.

———. "Sexual Cultures in Germany and Austria." In *Sexual Cultures in Europe: National Histories*, edited by Franz X. Eder, Lesley Hall, and Gert Hekma, 138–172. Manchester: Manchester University Press, 1999.

Ehmer, Joseph. *Familienstruktur und Arbeitsorganisation im frühindustriellen Wien*. München: R. Oldenbourg Verlag, 1980.

———. "Vaterlandslose Gestellen und respecktable Familienväter: Entwicklungsformen der Arbeiterfamilie im internationalen Vergleich, 1850–1930." In *Die deutsche und die österreichischen Arbeiterbewegung zur Zeit der Zweiten Internationale*, herausgegeben von Helmut Konrad. Wien: Europaverlag, 1982.

Ekel, Martha. *Körperkulture und 'proletarische Weiblichkeit,' 1918–1934*. Wein: Universität Wien (Diplomarbeit), 1986.

Embacher, Helga. "Der Krieg hat die 'göttliche Ordnung' zerstört! Konzepte und Familienmodelle zur lösung von Alltagsproblemen nach dem ersten Weltkrieg." *Zeitgeschichte* 15 (1988): 347–361.

Faderman, Lillian and Brigitte Eriksson. *Lesbians in Germany: 1890's-1920's*. Tallahassee: Naiad Press, 1990.

Fallend, Karl. *Wilhelm Reich in Wien: Psychoanalyse und Politik*. Wien: Ludwig-Boltzmann-Instituut für Geschichte der Gesellschaftswissenschaften, 1988.

Fallend, Karl und Bernd Nitzschke. *Der "Fall" Wilhelm Reich: Beiträge zum Verhältnis von Psychoanalyse und Politik*. Frankfurt am Main: Suhrkamp, 1997.

Febvre, Lucien. *The Problem of Unbelief in the Sixteenth Century*. Translated by Beatrice Gottlieb. Cambridge: Harvard University Press, 1982.

Felski, Rita. "Introduction." In *Sexology in Culture: Labeling Bodies and Desires*, edited by Lucy Bland and Laura Doan, 1–8. Chicago: University of Chicago Press, 1998.

Felt, Ulrike. "'Öffentliche' Wissenschaft: Zur Beziehung von Naturwissenschaften und Gesellschaft in Wien von der Jahrhundertwende bis zum Ende der Ersten Republik." *Österreichischen Zeitgeschichte* 7 (1996): 45–66.

Filch, Renata. "'Mütterlich-sozial und hauswirtschaftlich-pracktisch': Mädchenbildungswesen nach dem Ersten Weltkrieg bis 1945." In *Geschichte der Frauenbildung und Mädchenerziehung in Österreich*, herausgegeben von in Ilse Brehmer und Gertrud Simon, 220–234. Graz: Leykam Bucherverlagsgesellschaft, 1997.

Foucault, Michael. *A History of Sexuality*. New York: Vintage Books, 1978.

Frevert, Ute. "Vom Klavier zur Schriebmaschine." In *Frauen in der Geschichte*, herausgegeben von Annette Kuhn und Gerhard Schneider, 82–112. Düsseldorf: Pädagogischer Verlag Schwann, 1982.

Gabriel, Heinz Eberhard and Wolfgang Neugebauer, editors. *Vorreiter der Vernichtung? Eugenik, Rassenhygiene und Euthanasie in der österreichischen Diskussion vor 1938*. Wien: Böhlau, 2005.

Gasman, Daniel. *The Scientific Origins of National Socialism: Social Darwinism and the German Monist League*. London: MacDonald & Co., 1971.

Gedye, G.E.R. *Fallen Bastions*. London: Victor Gollancz Ltd., 1939.
Gehmacher, Johanna. "Vom Glück der Nüchternheit: Ein Sozialdemokratischer Entwurf um Alkohol und Familie." In *Familie: Arbeitsplatz oder Ort des Glücks?*, herausgegeben von Monika Bernhold, 51–79. Wien: Picus Verlag, 1990.
Gilman, Sander. "Sigmund Freud and the Sexologists: A Second Reading." In *Sexual Knowledge, Sexual Science: A History of Attitudes to Sexuality*, edited by Roy Porter and Mikulás Teich, 323–347. Cambridge: Cambridge University Press, 1994.
Ginzburg, Carlo. *The Cheese and the Worms: The Cosmos of a Sixteenth-Century Miller*. Translated by John and Anne Tedeschi. Baltimore: Johns Hopkins Press, 1976.
Goldstein, Jan. *Foucault and the Writing of History*. Oxford: Blackwell, 1994.
Grogan, Susan. "Playing the Princess: Flora Tristan, Performance, and Female Moral Authority in the July Monarchy." In *The New Biography: Performing Femininity in Nineteenth-Century France*, edited by Jo Burr Margadant. Berkeley: University of California Press, 2000.
Grossman, Atina. *Reforming Sex: The German Movement for Birth Control and Abortion Reform, 1920–1950*. New York: Oxford University Press, 1995.
Gruber, Helmut. "Reflections on the Problematique of Socialist Party Culture and the Realities of Working-Class Life in Red Vienna." In *Die deutsche und die österriechische Arbeiterbewegung zur Zeit der Zweiten Internationale*, herausgegeben von Helmut Konrad, 647–661. Wien: Europaverlag, 1982.

———. *Red Vienna: Experiment in Working-Class Culture*. New York: Oxford University Press, 1991.

———. "The 'New Woman': Realities and Illusions of Gender Equality in Red Vienna." In *Women and Socialism, Socialism and Women: Europe Between the Two World Wars*, edited by Helmut Gruber and Pamela Graves, 57–94. New York: Berghahn Books, 1998.

Gulick, Charles. *Austria from Habsburg to Hitler*, volumes I and II. Berkeley: University of California Press, 1948.
Hacohen, Malachi. *Karl Popper – The Formative Years, 1902–1945*. Cambridge: Cambridge University Press, 2000.
Haeberle, Erwin J. *The Birth of Sexology: A Brief History in Documents*. Washington, DC, 1983.
Hall, Murray C. *Der Fall Bettauer*. Wien: Löcker Verlag, 1978.
Hänisch, Ernst. "Das System und die Lebenswelt des Katholizismus." In *Handbuch des politischen Systems Österreich*, herausgegeben von Emmerich Tálos, Herbert Dachs, Ernst Hänisch, und Anton Staudinger, 444–453. Wien: Manzsche Verlags- und Universitätsbuchhandlung, 1995.
Hardy, Charles O. *The Housing Program of the City of Vienna*. Washington, DC: The Brookings Institution, 1934.
Harmat, Ulrike. *Ehe auf Widerruf?* Wien: Klostermann, 1999.

———. "Divorce and Remarriage in Austria-Hungary: The Second Marriage of Franz Conrad von Hötzendorf." *Austrian Studies Yearbook* 32 (2001): 69–103.

Hauser, Renate. "Krafft-Ebing's Psychological Understanding of Sexual Behavior." In *Sexual Knowledge, Sexual Science: The History of Attitudes to Sexuality*, edited by Roy Porter and Mikulás Teich, 210–227. Cambridge: Cambridge University Press, 1994.

Healy, Maureen. *Vienna and the Fall of the Habsburg Empire: Total War and Everyday Life in World War I*. Cambridge: Cambridge University Press, 2004.

Herzog, Dagmar. "Sexuality in Twentieth Century Austria." In *Sexuality in Austria*, edited by Günter Bischof, Anton Pelinka, and Dagmar Herzog, 7–20. New Brunswick, NJ: Transaction Publishers, 2007.

Hubenstorf, Michael. "Sozialmedizin, Menschenökonomie, Volksgesundheit." In *Aufbruch und Untergang: Österreichischen Kultur zwischen 1918 und 1938*, herausgegeben von Franz Kadrnoska, 247–266. Wien: Europaverlag, 1981.

Hugo Breitner, Julius Tandler: Architekten des Roten Wien. Wien: Verein für Geschichte der Arbeiterbewegung, 1997.

Hull, Isabel V. *Sexuality, State, and Civil Society in Germany, 1700–1815*. Ithaca: Cornell University Press, 1996.

Hunt, Lynn. "Foucault's Subject in *The History of Sexuality*." In *Discourses of Sexuality from Aristotle to Freud*, edited by Domna C. Stanton, 78–93. Ann Arbor: University of Michigan Press, 1992.

Hyams, Barbara and Nancy A. Harrowitz. "A Critical Introduction to the History of Weininger Reception." In *Jews and Gender: Responses to Otto Weininger*, edited by Nancy A. Harrowitz and Barbara Hyams, 3–20. Philadelphia: Temple University Press, 1995.

Ivory, Yvonne. "The Urning and His Own: Self-Fashioning and the Fin-de-Siècle Invert." Paper presented at the UCLA Department of Germanic Studies Conference *Sexual States*, 22 February 2002.

Jagschitz, Gerhard. "Die Nationalsozialistische Partei." In *Handbuch des politischen Systems Österreich*, herausgegeben von Emmerich Tálos, Herbert Dachs, Ernst Hänisch, und Anton Staudinger, 231–244. Wien: Manzsche Verlags- und Universitätsbuchhandlung, 1995.

Janik, Allen and Stephen Toulmin. *Wittgenstein's Vienna*. New York: Simon and Schuster, 1973.

Jusek, Karin J. *Auf der Suche nach der Verlorenen: Die Prostitutionsdebatten im Wien der Jahrhundertwende*. Wien: Löcker Verlag, 1994.

Kapner, Gerhardt. "Der Wiener kommunale Wohnbau," in *Aufbruch und Untergang: Österrichische Kultur zwischen 1918 und 1938*, herausgegeben von Franz Kadrnoska, 135–166. Wien: Europaverlag, 1981.

Kelly, Alfred H. "Darwinism and the Working Class in Wilhelmine Germany." In *Political Symbolism in Modern Europe*, edited by Seymour Drescher, David Sabean, and Allan Sharlin, 146–167. New Brunswick: Transaction Books, 1982.

Kreissel, Claudia. *Wohnungspolitik und Arbeiterwohnhäuser in Wien, 1919–1934*. Wien: Universität Wien Diplomarbeit, 1993.

Laqueur, Thomas. *Making Sex: Body and Gender from the Greeks to Freud*. Cambridge: Harvard University Press, 1990.

Lehner, Karin. *Verpönte Eingriffe: sozialdemokratische Reformbestrebungen zu den Abtreibungsbestimmungen in der Zwischenkriegseit*. Wien: Picus Verlag, 1989.

Lehnert, Detlef. "Politisch-kulturelle Integrationsmilieus und Orientierungslager in einer polarisierten Massengesellschaft." In *Handbuch des politischen Systems Österreich*, herausgegeben von Emmerich Tálos, Herbert Dachs, Ernst Hänisch, und Anton Staudinger, 431–443. Wien: Manzsche Verlags- und Universitätsbuchhandlung, 1995.

Lepicard, Etienne. "Eugenics and Roman Catholicism. An Encyclical Letter in Context: *Casti connubii*, December 31, 1930." *Science in Context* 11/3–4 (1988): 527–544.

Le Rider, Jacques. *Le cas Otto Weininger*. Paris: Presses Universitaires de France, 1982.

———. *Modernity and Crises of Identity: Culture and Society in Fin-de-Siècle Vienna*. Translated by Rosemary Morris. New York: Continuum, 1993.

Lesky, Erna. *The Vienna Medical School of the 19th Century*. Baltimore: The Johns Hopkins University Press, 1976.

Lessing, Theodor. *Der jüdische Selbsthaß*. Berlin: Jüdischer Verlag, 1930.

Löscher, Monika. "Zur Popularizierung von Eugenik und Rassenhygiene in Wien." In *Wissenschaft, Politik, und Öffentlichkeit: Von der Wiener Moderne bis zur Gegenwart*, herausgegeben von Mitchell Ash und Christian Stifter, 233–266. Wien: WUV-Universitätsverlag, 2002.

———. *"...der gesunden Vernuft nicht zuwider..." Katholizismus und Eugenik in Österreich vor 1938*. Innsbruck: Studien Verlag, 2009.

Lowenberg, Peter. "Otto Bauer as an Ambivalent Party Leader." In *The Austrian Social Experiment: Social Democracy and Austromarxism, 1918–1934*, edited by Anson Rabinbach, 71–80. Boulder: Westview Press, 1985.

———. *Fantasy and Reality in History*. New York: Oxford University Press, 1995.

Luft, David. *Eros and Inwardness: Weininger, Musil, Doderer*. Chicago: University of Chicago Press, 2003.

———. "Thinking about Sexuality and Gender in Vienna." In *Sexuality in Austria*, edited by Günter Bischof, Anton Pelinka, and Dagmar Herzog, 21–30. New Brunswick, NJ: Transaction Publishers, 2007.

Maderthaner, Wolfgang and Lutz Musner. "Kirche und Sozialdemokratie. Aspekte des Verhältnisses von politischem Klerikalismus und sozialistischer Arbeiterschaft bis zum Jahre 1938." In *Neuere Studien zur Arbeitergeschichte*, Band III, herausgegeben von Helmut Konrad und Wofgang Maderthaner, 527–558. Wien: Europaverlag, 1984.

———. *Die Anarchie der Vorstadt: Das andere Wien um 1900*. Frankfurt am Main: Campus Verlag, 1999.

Mattl, Siegfried. "Geschlecht und Volkscharacter: Austria Engendered." *Österreichische Zeitschrift für Geschichte* 7 (1996): 499–515.

Matysik, Tracie. *Reforming the Moral Subject: Ethics and Sexuality in Central Europe, 1890–1930*. Ithaca: Cornell University Press, 2008.

McGrath, William J. *Freud's Discovery of Psychoanalysis: The Politics of Hysteria*. Ithaca: Cornell University Press, 1986.

McGuire, Kristin. "Helene Stöcker's 'neue Ethik' from 1905–1915." Paper presented at the German Historical Institute Conference *Sexuality in Modern German History* (October 2002).

McLaren, Angus. *A History of Contraception, from Antiquity to the Present Day*. Oxford: Blackwell, 1990.

Melander, Ellinor. "Toward the Sexual and Economic Emancipation of Women: The Philosophy of Grete Meisel-Hess." *History of European Ideas* 14:5 (1992): 695–713.

Melody, M.E. and Linda M. Peterson. *Teaching America about Sex: Marriage Guides and Sex Manuals from the Late Victorians to Dr. Ruth.* New York: New York University Press, 1999.

Mesner, Maria. "Educating Reasonable Lovers: Sex Counseling in Austria in the First Half of the Twentieth Century." In *Sexuality in Austria,* edited by Günter Bischof, Anton Pelinka, and Dagmar Herzog, 48–64. New Brunswick, NJ: Transaction Publishers, 2007.

Milkula, Regina. "'Die Verweiblichung der Buben und eine Vermännlichung der Mädchen': Die Koeducationsdebatte im 20. Jahrhundert." In *Geschichte der Frauenbildung und Mädchenerziehung in Österreich,* herausgegeben von Ilse Brehmer und Gertrud Simon, 236–245. Graz: Leykam Bucherverlagsgesellschaft, 1997.

Mocek, Reinhard. "The Program of Proletarian *Rassenhygiene.*" *Science in Context* 11:3–4 (1998): 609–617.

Mosse, George. *Nationalism and Sexuality: Middle-Class Morality and Sexual Norms in Modern Europe.* Madison: University of Wisconsin Press, 1985.

Naiman, Eric. *Sex in Public: The Incarnation of Early Soviet Ideology.* Princeton: Princeton University Press, 1997.

Oosterhuis, Harry. *Stepchildren of Nature: Krafft-Ebing, Psychiatry, and the Making of Sexual Identity.* Chicago: University of Chicago Press, 2000.

Oxaal, Ivar. "Editor's Introduction: Perspectives and Problems." In *Jews, Antisemitism, and Culture in Vienna,* edited by Ivar Oxall, 2–11. New York: Routledge and Kegan Paul Ltd., 1987.

Pauley, Bruce F. *From Prejudice to Persecution: A History of Austrian Anti-Semitism.* Chapel Hill: University of North Carolina Press, 1992.

Pelinka, Anton. *Austria: Out of the Shadow of the Past.* Boulder: Westview Press, 1998.

Pfoser, Alfred. "Verstörte Männer und emanzipierte Frauen: Zur Sitten- und Literaturgeschichte der Ersten Republik." In *Aufbruch und Untergang: Österreichische Kultur zwischen 1918 und 1938,* herausgegeben von Franz Kadrnoska, 205–222. Wien: Europaverlag, 1981.

———. "Der Wiener 'Reigen-Skandal': Sexualangst als politisches Syndrom der Ersten Republik." In *Die deutsche und die österreichische Arbeiterbewegung zur Zeit der Zweiten Internationale,* herausgegeben von Helmut Konrad, 663–719. Wien: Europaverlag, 1982.

Pick, Daniel. *Faces of Degeneration: A European Disorder, 1948–1918.* Cambridge: Cambridge University Press, 1989.

Pollard, Miranda. *Reign of Virtue: Mobilizing Gender in Vichy France.* Chicago: University of Chicago Press, 1998.

Pollok, Michael. "Cultural Innovation and Social Identity in Fin-de-Siècle Vienna." In *Jews, Antisemitism, and Culture in Vienna,* edited by Ivar Oxall, 59–74. New York: Routledge and Kegan Paul Ltd., 1987.

Rabinbach, Anson. "The Body without Fatigue: A Nineteenth-Century Utopia." In *Political Symbolism in Modern Europe,* edited by Seymour Drescher, David Sabean, and Allan Sharlin, 42–62. New Brunswick: Transaction Books, 1982.

———. *The Crisis of Austrian Socialism: From Red Vienna to Civil War, 1927–1934.* Chicago: University of Chicago Press, 1983.

Ratzenböck, Gertraud. "Mutterliebe: Bemerkungen zur gesellschaftlich konstruierten Verknüpfung von Mutterliebe und Familie." In *Familie: Arbeitsplatz oder Ort des Glücks?*, edited by Monika Bernold, 19–50. Wien: Picus Verlag, 1990.

Reddy, William M. *The Navigation of Feelings: A Framework for the History of Emotions.* Cambridge: Cambridge University Press, 2001.

Roberts, Mary Louise. *Civilization without Sexes: Reconstructing Gender in Postwar France, 1917–1927.* Chicago: University of Chicago Press, 1994.

Rodlauer, Hannelore. "Fragments from Weininger's Education (1895–1902)." In *Jews and Gender: Responses to Otto Weininger*, edited by Nancy A. Harrowitz and Barbara Hyams, 35–58. Philadelphia: Temple University Press, 1995.

Rosenwein, Barbara H. "Worrying about Emotions in History." *American Historical Review* 107 (June 2002): 821–845.

Sablik, Karl. *Julius Tandler, Mediziner und Sozialreformer: Eine Biographie.* Wien: Verlag A. Schendl, 1983.

Sauerteig, Lutz D.H. "Sex Education in Germany from the 18th to the 20th Century." In *Sexual Cultures in Europe: Themes in Sexuality*, edited by Franz Eder, Lesley Hall and Gert Hekma, 9–33. Manchester: Manchester University Press, 1999.

———. "Sex, Medicine, and Morality During the First World War." In *War, Medicine, and Modernity*, edited by Roger Cooter and Mark Harrison, 167–188. London: Sutton Publishing, 1998.

Singer, Peter. *Pushing Time Away: My Grandfather and the Tragedy of Jewish Vienna.* New York: Harper Collins, 2003.

Somerville, Siobhan B. "Scientific Racism and the Invention of the Homosexual Body." In *Sexology in Culture: Labeling Bodies and Desires*, edited by Lucy Bland and Laura Doan, 60–77. Chicago: University of Chicago Press, 1998.

Steakley, James D. *The Homosexual Emancipation Movement in Germany.* New York: Arno Press, 1975.

Stearns, Peter N. and Carol Z. Stearns. "Emotionology: Clarifying the History of Emotions." *American Historical Review* 90 (October 1985): 813–836.

Steininger, Rolf. "12. November 1918 bis 13 März 1938: Stationen auf dem Weg zum 'Anschluß.'" In *Österreich im 20. Jahrhundert: Von der Monarchie bis zum Zweiten Weltkreig*, herausgegeben von Rolf Steininger und Michael Gehler, 99–152. Wien: Bòhlau, 1997.

Sulloway, Alvah. *Birth Control and Catholic Doctrine.* Boston: Beacon Hill, 1959.

Sully, Melanie A. *Continuity and Change in Austrian Socialism: The Eternal Quest for the Third Way.* Boulder: East European Monographs, 1982.

———. "Social Democracy and the Political Culture of the First Republic." In *The Austrian Socialist Experiment: Social Democracy and Austromarxism, 1918–1934*, edited by Anson Rabinbach, 57–70. Boulder: Westview Press, 1985.

"Tandler, Julius." In *Österreich Lexicon Band II*, herausgegeben von Richard Bamberger und Franz Maier-Bruck, 1132. Wien: Österreichischer Bundesverlag für Unterricht, Wissenschaft, und Kunst, 1966.

Timm, Edward. *Karl Kraus, Apocalyptic Satirist: Cultural Catastrophe in Habsburg Vienna.* New Haven: Yale University Press, 1986.

Toews, John E. "Foucault and the Freudian Subject: Archeology, Genealogy, and the Historicization of Psychoanalysis." In *Foucault and the Writing of History*, edited by Jan Goldstein. Oxford: Blackwell, 1994.

———. "Historicizing Pyschoanalysis: Freud in His Time and for Our Time." *Journal of Modern History* 63 (September 1991): 503–545.

Turda, Marius and Paul J. Weindling, eds. *Blood and Homeland: Eugenics and Racial Nationalism in Central and Southeast Europe, 1900–1940.* Budapest: Central European University Press, 2007.

Usborne, Cornelie. *The Politics of the Body in Weimar Germany: Women's Reproductive Rights and Duties.* Ann Arbor: The University of Michigan Press, 1992.

Van der Velde, Theodore. *Ideal Marriage: Its Physiology and Technique.* Translated by Stella Brown. New York: Random House, 1930.

Vicinus, Martha. "'Helpless and Unfriended': Nineteenth-Century Domestic Melodrama." *New Literary History* 13:1 (Autumn 1981): 127–143.

Walkowitz, Judith R. *City of Dreadful Delight: Narratives of Sexual Danger in Late-Victorian London.* Chicago: University of Chicago Press, 1992.

Weber, Fritz. "Hauptprobleme der wirtschaftlichen und sozialen Entwicklung Österreichs in der Zwischenkriegszeit." In *Aufbruch und Untergang: Österreichische Kultur Zwischen 1918 und 1938,* herausgegeben von Franz Kadrnoska, 593–622. Wien: Europaverlag, 1981.

Weeks, Jeffery. *Sex, Politics, and Society: The Regulation of Sexuality since 1800.* London: Longman, 1989.

Weidenholzer, Josef. *Auf dem Weg zum 'Neuen Menschen': Bildungs- und Kulturarbeiter österreichischen Sozialdemokratie in der Ersten Republik.* Wien: Europaverlag, 1981.

———. "Red Vienna: A New Atlantis?" In *The Austrian Socialist Experiment: Social Democracy and Austromarxism, 1919–1934,* edited by Anson Rabinbach, 195–200. Boulder: Westview Press, 1984.

Ziche, Paul. *Monismus um 1900: Wissenschaftskultur und Weltanschauung.* Berlin: Verlag für Wissenschaft und Bildung, 2000.

Zweig, Stephan. *The World of Yesterday.* New York: Viking Press, 1943.

INDEX

abortion
    divorce and abortion prohibitions in Austria 40–41
    law reform in Austria 41–2
    legal status of 92–3
Adler, Alfred 12, 13, 64–5, 76, 81, 100, 115n40
Adler, Victor 27
adolescence, confusions of 58–9
advice clinics, advent of 119–20
    see also clinical sexual advice
"Advice for Those Entering into Marriage" (Vienna Municipal Marriage Advice Center, 1922) 118–19
Albert, Heinrich 106, 116n69
Allen, Anne T. 23–4n45, 25n62, 50n18, 172n82
Allers, Rudolf 76, 79, 80–81, 89n83, 90n94, 90n103, 108–9, 116n80
anatomical knowledge, sex reform and 96–7
The Anatomy of the Heart (Tandler, J.) 28
Anderle, Helene 66, 70, 88n42, 188
    see also Stourzh-Anderle, Helene
Anderson, Harriet 7, 22n21, 50n18
Andreas-Salomé, Lou 62–3, 87n32
von Ankum, Katherina 113–14n8
anti-Semitism 15, 29, 49n4, 144–5, 146, 153, 173n101, 175–6
    history in Austria of 7–8, 29

ideas of sexual knowledge and 12–13, 14, 113n3
Arbeiter-Zeitung (SDAP daily) 122, 130, 140n7, 141n9, 152, 175, 176, 177, 192n1, 192n4, 193n10
assassination of Bettauer 167–8
At the Doors of Life: On Sexual Aufklärung and Morality (Golias, E.) 65
Atlantis narrative in interwar Vienna 169, 174n102
Aufklärung ("enlightenment")
    sexual education and 54, 55, 56, 58, 60–89
    sexual knowledge and 91, 92, 94–5, 96, 99, 102, 103, 106, 111, 112
Austria, First Republic
    censorship in 148, 151, 153, 163, 167, 168, 169
Austria, First Republic in 2–4, 5, 18–19, 92, 95, 152, 156, 171n23
    abortion law reform 41–2
    anti-Semitism in 29
    coeducation and mixed classrooms in 68–9, 97
    divorce and abortion prohibitions in 40–41
    emergency health system 119
    Frauenfrage ("Women's Question"), expansion of 93

instability and political violence 8–9, 168–9, 169n2
political culture, *Lager System* in 7–8
sexual education in 112, 188
sexual knowledge, dissemination (and creation) of 8, 9
socialist sexual education, challenge of 75
state concern for "healthy" sex 27–8
welfare and sexual hygiene innovations 179
Austrian German Nationalist Party 175, 176, 192n2, 192n3
Austrian League for the Protection of Mothers *(Österreichischer Bund für Mutterschutz)* 15–16, 25n61, 31, 105, 163
Austrian Women's Association *(Allgemeine Österreichischen Frauenvereins)* 15, 16, 24n59
Austro-Hungarian Empire 2, 4
dismantling of, post World War I 4–5
Austromarxism 8, 27, 84

Bamberger, R. and Maier-Bruck, F. 49n7
Bauer, Helene 116n67
Bauer, Ida 1–2, 2–3, 11–12, 18, 20n1, 23n39
Bauer, Otto 2, 27
Baum, Vicki 113–14n8
Becoming a Complete Man! Aufklärung and Education for the Growing Male Youngster (Hoffmann, J.) 61, 81
Bei, N., Förster, W. et al. 25n67
Beller, Steven 7, 22n23, 49n4
Bernheimer, C. and Kahane, C. 20n5
Bertram, Cardinal Adolf 76, 77, 80, 83, 89n81, 90n101
Bettauer, Hugo 144–5, 168–9, 179, 187, 196
appeal to Seitz 149–50
censorship, challenge to 157–8
message from 163–6
Sittenromanen ("morality tales") of 146, 153, 170n6
Bettauer's Almanac 165–6, 173n86
Bettauer's Vienna Weeklies 19, 144–69
assassination of Bettauer 167–8
Bettauers Wochenschrift ("Bettauer's Weekly") 145, 163–4, 165–6, 173n86
compassion, emotion and 161–3
countersuit from Bettauer against city, dismissal of 154
dangerous concepts, criticism for spread of 147–8
emotion in *Er und Sie* 155–63
Er und Sie ("He and She: Weekly Newspaper of Lifestyle Reform and the Erotic") 145, 146, 147–50, 152, 153, 154, 155–63, 164, 165, 166, 168, 169, 170n11, 171n22, 172n48, 173n97
"Eros in Chains" *(Er und Sie)* 159
"The Erotic Revolution" *(Er und Sie)* 149
"Erotica from Around the World" *(Bettauer's Wochenschrift)* 146, 156, 164
exchange between Seipel and Seitz over 151–2
front-cover appearance 147
goal of Bettauer as publisher 150
guilt, emotion and 158–9
homoeroticism thwarted 162
hope, emotion and 159–60
inclination, emotion and 156–8
"Life's Problems" *(Er und Sie)* 146, 155–6, 158, 159–60, 162, 163, 164
"Lonely Woman" *(Er und Sie)* 160
"Mailbox" *(Er und Sie)* 169
"Memoirs of a Midwife" *(Er und Sie)* 156, 158–9
"The Merry Women of Vienna" *(Er und Sie)* 146, 155

message from Bettauer 163–6
moral well-being of youth, danger to 148
Nervenarzt (anonymous columnist) 153–4, 171n42, 172n74
"office hours," system of 164–5
"One Beset by Release" *(Er und Sie)* 161
"People Seeking One Another" *(Er und Sie)* 155, 160
pornography, Bettauer and the *Prozeß* (trial) of 145–55
responsibility, charges of lack of 148–9
Social Democratic and Christian Social approaches to, chasm between 153
tensions within SDAP regarding pornography and 150–51
"The Pressure to Bear Children" *(Er und Sie)* 162
"The Turning Point" *(Er und Sie)* 161
"Unusual Love Accident" *(Er und Sie)* 161
"Where Can I Find Help?" *(Bettauer's Almanac)* 165
"women's issues" 166
The Biological Principles of Secondary Sexual Characteristics (Tandler, J.) 28
birth control
 access in Vienna to 197
 dissemination of methods and advice on 130–32
 information on, call by WLSR for 190
 League Against Forced Motherhood clinics 128, 137
 municipal policies for 36–7
 pregnancy and 98–9
 sexual knowledge and 98–100
Bland, L. and Doan, L. 113n1
"Blastodermic Degeneration" (Forel, A.) 101–2
Bloch, Iwan 55, 86n4, 146–7
Blum, Mark 49n3

Böhm, August 34, 50n32
Bölsche, Wilhelm 86n2
Borak, J. 195n69
Botz, Gerhard 22n24, 169n2
Boyer, John W. 7, 22n19
Breitner, Hugo 27, 166
Breuer, Josef 10
Brooks, Peter 113n2
Bukey, Evan B. 22n23
Burleigh, M. and Wippermann, W. 25n66, 49n11
Butler, Josephine 15, 25n60

Canon Law, 1917 Code of 75
The Case of Bettauer (Hall, M.C.) 144–5, 169–70n5, 169n1, 170n6, 173n84, 173n96
Casti connubii (On Christian Marriage, Encyclical of Pius XI, 1930) 109–10
The Catholic Marriage and the Christian Family (Schmitt, A.) 85
Catholicism 4, 5, 17, 19, 22n29
 cultural legacy of 7
 Guidelines and Instructions on Various Modern Morality Questions 108
 literature on sexual education 78–9
 responses to reform agenda on sexual education 75–83
 Seelsorger (care-givers of the soul) 75–6
 sexual advice form Catholic Church 107–10
 sexual forms of knowledge, structuration of 8
 struggle of modernizers with politics of 35, 40, 42, 46
celibacy 82, 129–30, 181
censorship 148, 151, 153, 163, 167, 168, 169
 Bettauer's challenge to 157–8
change, trajectories of 94, 178–9
childcare, municipal policies for 35–6
children
 exposure to sexual realities 71–2

humanity of, sexual education and 187–8
illegitimate children, municipal interest in 39–40
responsibility for, state organization and 43
SDAP workshops on sexual education for 74
sexual knowledge, appropriateness for 55
urban environment and exposure to venereal disease (VD) 72
Christian League of Viennese Women *(Christlicher Weiner Frauenbund)* 15
Christian Social Party (CSP) 7, 17, 35, 36, 41, 146, 148, 162, 166, 176
   Heimwehr 168–9
   Kulturkampf with SDAP 2
   Reichspost 150, 152
Christliche Ständestaat ("Christian Corporate State") 8
The City Without Jews (Bettauer, H.) 146, 169–70n5, 170n7
clinical sexual advice 19, 118–140
   advice clinics, advent of 119–20
   "Advice for Those Entering into Marriage" (Vienna Municipal Marriage Advice Center, 1922) 118–19
   birth control, dissemination of methods and advice on 130–32
   congenital abnormalities in families 124
   "Drinker Care Center" 122
   eugenic sexual knowledge, discourse of 120–21
   Evening Clinics for Venereal Disease 127
   "Experiences and Problems from Sex Advice Clinics for Workers and Employees in Vienna" (Reich, W.) 134–5
   genetic suitability for marriage 125
   gonorrhea, questions about 125–6
   "histories of disease" in families 124–5
   humane realism, argument for 129–30
   International Conference for Birth Control (1930) 132–3
   League Against Forced Motherhood 128–33
   marriage and procreation, dangers of 137
   medical problems, difficulties of on-site treatment of 126–7
   Municipal Marriage Advice Center 26, 27, 40–41, 104, 116n61, 119, 121, 128–9, 133, 134–5, 137, 138, 139–40, 165–6
   "Official Manual for the Advice Doctor" (VMMAC) 123–5
   Proletarian Sexual Advice Centers 133–4
   public or private marriage advice, debate over 123
   responsibility, key message of Marriage Advice Centers 127–8
   sex-life behavior in families 124–5
   sexual knowledge 19, 118–140
   sexual misery *(Sexualnot)* and 130–31, 133, 135
   Sexual-Reform (League Against Forced Motherhood) 130, 131–2
   The Socialist Doctor 134
   Socialist Society for Sexual Advice and Research 133–6
   syphilis, questions about 125–6
   venereal disease (VD) and 119, 124–5, 126–7, 129
coeducation, mixed classrooms and 68–9, 97
compassion, emotion and 161–3
congenital abnormalities 124
"Constitution and Race Hygiene" (Tandler, J.) 31–2
contraceptive techniques, women and use of 98–101
Criminal Man (Lombroso, C.) 9
Csoklich, Fritz 169n4

culture
  context of, promulgation of marriage manuals and 92
  cultural modernism in Vienna 7
  sexual education and cultural improvement 74
  sexual knowledge, cultural historical perspective on 4–5
Czechoslovakia 2, 193n17

dangers of sexual knowledge 4, 153, 197–8
Danneberg, Robert 27
Darwin, Charles 10, 11, 147
  evolutionary theory 14
  social Darwinism 16–17
de Grazia, Victoria 20n7
Dean, Carolyn J. 25n67
Decker, Hannah S. 20n5, 49n3
Dickinson, Edward R. 13–14, 24n48, 25n65, 50n18, 53n105
divorce and abortion prohibitions in Austria 40–41
Dora see Bauer, Ida
Dostal, Thomas 192n2
Dreikurs, Rudolf 184
"Drinker Care Center" 122
Dürerbund ("Dürer League") 56–9, 66, 67, 86n5

economic warfare, welfare and hygiene approaches to 29
Eder, Franz X. 20n6
education at home, Skalla's work and 59–60
  see also sexual education
The Efficiency of Our Race and the Protection of the Weak (Ploetz, A.) 17
Eherechtreformvenein 105
Ehrlich, Paul 15
Eisenschiml, Wilhelm 52n62, 114n28
Ellis, Havelock 9, 91, 146–7
emergency health system in Austria 119
emotions and emotionality 198
  compassion, emotion and 161–3
  "emotional regimes," concept of 6, 156

emotionology, concept of 21n16
Er und Sie, emotion in 155–63
  guilt, emotion and 158–9
  hope, emotion and 159–60
  inclination, emotion and 156–8
  leavening of sexual knowledge with emotional testimonies 4, 68, 99, 112, 122, 172, 198
  see also Bettauer's Vienna Weeklies
entertainment and education, sexual knowledge as 131–2
"The Environmental Conditions of Youth Sexuality" (Kraus, S.) 72–3
Er und Sie ("He and She: Weekly Newspaper of Lifestyle Reform and the Erotic") 145–50, 152–63, 164–6, 168, 169, 170n11, 171n22, 172n48, 173n97
"Eros in Chains" (*Er und Sie* article) 159
"The Erotic Revolution" (*Er und Sie* article) 149
"Erotica from Around the World" (*Bettauer's Wochenschrift* column) 146, 156, 164
eugenics
  eugenic sexual knowledge, discourse of 120–21
  eugenically sound reproduction, concept of 197
  humanitarianism and 45–6
  population politics, eugenics and 42–6
  sexual knowledge and 16–18, 120–21
Evening Clinics for Venereal Disease 38, 127
"On the Evolution of the Erotic" (Schlesinger, T.) 105
Exner, Sigmund 10, 14
exogamy 43
"Experiences and Problems from Sex Advice Clinics for Workers and Employees in Vienna" (Reich, W.) 134–5

In Faith's Light: Christian Reflections on Sexual Life (Gatterer, M.) 76
Fallend, Karl 171n47, 194n54

families
  "histories of disease" in 124–5
  sex-life behavior in families 124–5
  sexual indiscretion, family life and 59–60
  sexual reform and the family 188
  and state, establishment of analogy between 43–4
Febvre, Jucien 21n14
Federn, Paul 193n9
Feistritzer, Hildegard 89n76
Felski, Rita 9, 23n31
Felt, Ulrike 114n10
feminism and sexual knowledge 3, 14, 16
Ferch, Betty 163, 179, 196
Ferch, Johann 111–12, 115n36, 163, 179, 196
fertility, female control of 99
Fetscher, R. 115n47
Fettinger, Franz 50n28
Fin-de-Siècle Vienna: Politics and Culture (Schorske, C.) 6–7
Finger, Ernest 10
Flaschitz, Willi 115n49
Fleischel, Ernst 10
Flich, Renata 88n53, 88n55
Forcucci, Lauren E. 20n7
Forel, August 101–2, 115n48
Förster, Friedrich Wilhelm 55
Foucault, Michel 21n12
At the Fountain of Life (*Dürerbund* publication) 56–9, 63, 66
Frauenfrage ("Women's Question"), expansion of 93
Freud, Sigmund 1–2, 2–3, 11–12, 18, 20n1, 23n39, 55, 62, 76, 93, 99, 115n38, 181
Freundlich, Emmy 41
Frevert, Ute 114n9
Friedjung, Josef K. 66–7, 68, 72, 87n36, 88n44, 89n69, 179, 188, 193n18, 195n60
  opening speech at WLSR in Vienna 180–81
Furst, Sidonie 190, 195n71

Galton, Francis 16, 30
Gasman, Daniel 24n46
Gatterer, Michael 76, 89n84
Gedye, G.E.R. 174n102
Gegenbauer, Victor 51n45, 51n57, 52n83
Gehmacher, Johanna 115n45
gender-neutrality in coeducational learning 69–70
General Hospital in Vienna, Department of Venereal Disease at 10
generative self-determination, rights to 189–90
genetic suitability for marriage 125
Germany
  Nuremberg Laws 17
  sex reform movement in 23–4n45
  Weimar Germany 7, 47
Gilman, Sander 23n36
Ginzburg, Carlo 21n15
Glaessner, Rudolf 96, 97, 99, 102, 111, 112, 114n17, 115n50
Glatterer, Michael 107–8, 116n74
Glöckel, Otto 27, 64–5, 150, 151, 169
Goldscheid, Rudolf 13–14, 29, 43, 90n117, 93, 113n7, 177, 181, 188–9, 193n11, 195n61
Goldstein, Jan 21n12, 21n13
Golias, Eduard 65, 69–70, 73, 88n40, 89n58
gonorrhea 10, 38, 98, 104, 125–6, 127
Gottlieb, Karl 51n58
government of Vienna 4–5
Grogan, Susan 113n2
Gross, Otto 23n42
Grossmann, Atina 23–4n45, 176, 193n7
Gruber, H. and Graves, P. 114n9
Gruber, Helmut 8, 22–3n29, 22n28, 49n1, 83, 90n116
guilt, emotion and 158–9
Gulick, Charles 50–51n40, 87n34, 88n37

Hacker, Hanna 25n67
Hacohen, Malachi 23n43, 24n47, 88n39, 148, 170n18

Haeberle, Erwin J. 113n1
Haeckel, Ernst 13, 16, 17, 86n2
Hainisch, Ernst 22n29
Hainisch, Michael 166
Haire, Norman 193n15, 195n68
Hall, Murray C. 144–5, 169–70n5, 169n1, 170n6, 173n84, 173n96
Hamburger, Franz 39
Harmat, Ulrike 52n76, 113n4
Harrowitz, N.A. and Hayams, B. 24n52
Hartmann, Elise 115n49
Hauser, Renate 23n32
Hayams, B. and Harrowitz, N.A. 24n52
health empire, Tandler's construction of 33
"healthy sex" state concern for 27–8
Hecke, Wilhelm 39, 52n67, 52n71
heterosexual knowledge 18
Hirschfeld, Magnus 9, 55, 91, 181–2, 188, 193n21, 194n23, 195n76
  closing remarks at WLSR in Vienna 191–2
"histories of disease" in families 124–5
historiography of sexual knowledge in Vienna 6–9
Hitler, Adolf 9, 169
Hoffmann, Erich 15
Hoffmann, Jakob 61, 62, 63, 87n25
homoerotic practices of schoolboys 61–2
homoeroticism thwarted 162
homosexuality 9, 10, 11, 12, 17–18, 87n24, 91, 95, 104, 127, 136, 154, 161–2, 192, 197
Horn, David G. 20n7
How to Teach Your Child ("From a Friend of the Youth," Salzburg diocese) 77–8
How Woman Experiences Man (Lazarsfeld, S.) 96
Hubenstorf, Michael 50–51n40
The Human Birth (educational film) 103
humane realism, argument for 129–30
Hunt, Lynn 21n12
Huss, Marie-Monique 20n7
hygiene, Skalla's message on 60–61

Hygiene of Married Life: The Guide to love and Marital Bliss (Schlegel, J.C.) 98, 103–4

Ideal Marriage (Van der Velde, T.) 96–7
illegitimate children, municipal interest in 39–40
illicit sex, Viennese reputation for 27–8
Impotence in Men (Steckel, W.) 154
In the Light of Belief: Christian Thoughts on Sexual Life (Glatterer, M.) 107–8
incest 43, 46, 63, 159
inclination, emotion and 156–8
innovations
  in contraception 106
  in sex education 7, 64–5, 69, 170, 198
  in welfare arrangements 27–8, 35–42, 179
instability and political violence in Austria 8–9, 168–9, 169n2
International Conference for Birth Control (1930) 132–3
international sex reform movement 33, 54, 128, 175–6
Ivory, Yvonne 87n24

Jagschitz, Gerhard 192n3
Jaksch, Rudolf von 15
Jalik, A. and Toulmin, S. 21n18
Jesus Christ 78
Journal for Austrian Preparatory Schools 59
The Joyless Street (Bettauer, H.) 146
Jusek, Karin J. 14, 24n53, 24n55, 50n18
justice, WLSR call to 182–3

Kammerer, Paul 11, 23n35
Kanitz, Otto Felix 66, 67, 69, 73, 88n41, 88n47, 89n60, 89n74, 187–8, 194n56
Kautsky Jr., Karl 41, 52n79, 90n117, 104
Kelly, Alfred H. 13, 24n46, 86n2
Keun, Irmgard 113–14n8
Key, Ellen 182
Kinderfreunde movement (parent association) and 64–6, 67, 68–9

Kitaj, Jakob 94–5, 104, 112, 114n12
Klar, Josef 51n49, 51n55
Konrad, Helmut 22n28, 22n29
Körner, Theodor 27
Krafft-Ebing, Richard von 7, 10, 14, 55, 91, 93, 157, 181
Kraus, H. 100
Kraus, Karl 7, 20n6, 94, 145
Kraus, Siegfried 72–3, 89n70, 181, 184–5

Lad and Lassie in God's Hands: A Ministerial and Pedagogical Contribution to the Sex Problem (Schmitz, P.) 81, 82, 83
Lamarck, Jean-Baptiste 10–11
Lang, Edward 10
Laquer, Thomas 21n12
Lazarsfeld, Sofie 96, 97, 98, 100, 102, 111, 112, 114n16, 114n20, 179
Le Rider, Jacques 21n18, 24n52
League Against Forced Motherhood 128–33, 141n32
  birth control clinics 128, 137
Lehner, Karin 22–3n29, 49n5, 53n100, 113n6
Lehnert, Detlef 22n25
Lepicard, Etienne 116n84
Lesky, Erna 23n33
Leunbach, J.H. 193n14
"Life's Problems" (*Er und Sie* column) 146, 155–6, 158, 159–60, 162, 163, 164
Lifestyle Reform and the Erotic, Weekly Newspaper of *see Er und Sie*
Lombroso, Cesare 9
"Lonely Woman" (*Er und Sie* column) 160
Lowenberg, Peter 49n3
Lueger, Karl 7
Luft, David S. 24n51

McGrath, William J. 11, 23n37
McGuire, Kirstin 25n65
Mach, Ernst 10
McLaren, Angus 115n41
Maderthaner, Wolfgang 7, 22n20, 22n29

Magazine for Applied Anatomy and Constitutional Research 31–2
Magazine for Human Inheritance and Constitutional Research 32
"Mailbox" (*Er und Sie* column) 169
The Man - A Book for Women (Tauber, E. and R.) 97, 102–3
Mantegazza, Paolo 1
Marcuse, Max 87n20
marital continence 99–100
marriage advice
  discourse surrounding sexual knowledge and 93
  and *Frauenfrage* ("Women's Question") 93–4
"Marriage and Population Politics" (Tandler, J.) 42, 44–6, 47, 48
marriage and procreation, dangers of 137
Married Love (Stopes, M.) 100
masturbation 12, 13, 18, 95, 102, 107, 134, 135–6, 154, 181, 187
Masturbation and Homosexuality (Steckel, W.) 154
Matte, Nicholas 193n13
Matysik, Tracie 25n67
Mayreder, Rosa 24n49
Meisel-Hess, Grete 16, 24n49, 25n63
Melander, Ellinor 16, 25n64
Melody, M.E. and Peterson, L.M. 114n19
"Memoirs of a Midwife" (*Er und Sie* column) 156, 158–9
Mendel, Gregor J. 181
Menschenökonomie ("economy of humanity") in Vienna 13–14, 50–51n40, 84–5, 90n117, 113n7, 120, 129, 180–81, 188, 191
mentally insane, care for 44–5
"The Merry Women of Vienna" (*Er und Sie* article) 146, 155
Mesner, Maria 115n34
methodology for study 4–6
Meynert, Thomas 10
Milkula, Regina 88n54

Mocek, Reinhard 48, 53n103
Monism 13–14, 16, 55, 86n2
morality
    biological and moral, separation of 59–61
    moral *Aufklärung*, sexual education and 61
    moral well-being of youth, Vienna Weeklies as danger to 148
    socialistic world view of sexuality and 73
    WLSR perspective on 182
Morel, Bénédict Augustin 9
mortality rates 30
Mosse, George 20n8
motherhood
    duty towards sexual education 77
    Golias on 70–71
municipal health and hygiene 18, 26–48
    birth control, municipal policies for 36–7
    Catholicism, struggle with politics of 35, 40, 42, 46
    childcare, municipal policies for 35–6
    economic warfare, welfare and hygiene approaches to 29
    eugenics, humanitarianism and 45–6
    family and state, establishment of analogy between 43–4
    health empire, Tandler's construction of 33
    "healthy sex" state concern for 27–8
    illegitimate children, municipal interest in 39–40
    "Marriage and Population Politics" (Tandler, J.) 42, 44–6, 47, 48
    mentally insane, care for 44–5
    mortality rates 30
    personal freedom, subordination of 30–31
    population politics, eugenics and 42–6
    productive population politics 44
    race hygiene 31
    "The Reconstruction of People's Health" (Böhm, A.) 34
    reproduction, municipal policies for 35–6, 36–7, 44
    research and analysis, transformation of human constitution through 31
    responsibility for children, state organization and 43
    sexual hygiene directives 42
    sexual knowledge 18, 26–48
    sexually transmitted diseases, intensity of war against 38–9
    social medicine
    Tandler as model for 34–5
    Tandler's early career in 28–35
    social powers invested in health officials 33–4
    social repair, requirements of 30–31
    societal transformation, goal of 33
    venereal disease (VD) 26–7, 30–31, 34, 35, 37–8, 46
    "War and Population" (Tandler, J.) 29, 30, 31, 38
    welfare innovation 35–42
    welfare ministry, aims of 32
    welfare system in Vienna
    progressive nature of 27
    scope of 40
    World War I, effects of 29–30
Municipal Marriage Advice Center 26, 27, 40–41, 104, 116n61, 119, 121, 128–9, 133, 134–5, 137, 138, 139–40, 165–6
Museum of Sociological and Economic Sciences in Vienna 19, 176, 193n5
Musil, Robert 61–2, 87n27
Musner, Lutz 7, 22n20

Naiman, Eric 20–21n8
National Socialist Party of Austria 168, 169, 176, 192n3, 193n10
natural nature of sexual urges 83–4
Nazi Germany 17
    Anschluß on Austria 6, 8, 120, 169

Nervenarzt (anonymous columnist) in Vienna Weeklies 153–4, 171n42, 172n74
Neue Freie Presse 146, 176–7
Das Neue Wien 50n31, 51n42, 51n51, 52n60
Neurath, Otto 193n5, 195n73
The New Woman (SDAP pamphlet, 2924) 105, 116n66
Nietzsche, Friedrich 62
Normal and Pathological Sexual Life of the Male and Female (Kitaj, J.) 94–6, 104
Nowotny, Paula 173n83

"office hours," system of 164–5
official advice, personal delivery of 62–3
"Official Manual for the Advice Doctor" (VMMAC) 123–5
official morality, new sexual ethic and 181–2
Ogino, K. 100
Olden, Rudolf 147, 154, 164, 169
"One Beset by Release" (*Er und Sie* article) 161
Oosterhuis, Harry 21n18, 23n32, 113n1
Orel, Anton 152–3
"Orgasm, Theory of" (Reich, W.) 12
orgiastic satisfaction, Reich's theory of 135–6
Oxaal, Ivar 7, 22n22

Pabst, P.W. 146
Pallester, Paul 52n77, 190, 195n72
Pan-German Party 7
Paradeiser, Hans 25n61
Pauley, Bruce F. 22n23
Pearson, Karl 30
Pelinka, Anton 7, 22n25
Peller, Sigismund 189–90, 195n66
"People Seeking One Another" (*Er und Sie* article) 155, 160
performing arts, sexual knowledge and 94
personal freedom, subordination of 30–31

Pfoser, Alfred 114n11
physical exertion and sublimation of sexual energy, Catholic emphasis on 75
Physiology of Love (Mantegazza, P.) 1
Pick, Daniel 23n30
Pius XI 42, 51n44, 75, 109–10, 116n86, 116n87, 117n88
Ploetz, Alfred 16–17, 49n11
plurality
  of Catholic opinion 75
  of sexual knowledge 21n12
politics
  cultural and political revolution, sexual knowledge and 3–4, 175–6, 178–9
  Lager System in Austria 7–8
  population politics, eugenics and 42–6
  productive population politics 44
  see also municipal health and hygiene
Pollack, Michael 7, 22n22
Pollak, Ludwig 34–5, 50n23
Pollard, Miranda 20–21n8
Popp, Adelheid 41, 189–90, 195n65
population patterns, tables of 190–91
population politics, eugenics and 42–6
pornography 157–8, 163–4, 166, 167, 170n10, 172n54, 172n56
  Bettauer and the *Prozeß* (trial) of 145–55
possibility, concept of "horizon" of 6
pre-War *Aufklärung* in Vienna 56–63
pregnancy, birth control and 98–9
"The Pressure to Bear Children" (*Er und Sie* article) 162
prevention of VD, local committees and aim of 183
primary information sources in Vienna, destruction of 21n11
"On the Problem of Motherhood" (Schlesinger, T.) 105–6
problem of sexual knowledge 3–4
process of sexual knowledge, historical perspective on 6–9, 19–20, 27, 196–7

productive population politics 44
Proft, Gabrielle 41
progressive education, *Dürerbund* and 56–9, 66, 67, 86n5
Proletarian Sexual Advice Centers 133–4
pronatalism 4, 20n7
prostitution in Vienna 14–15, 16, 20n6, 31, 58, 66, 72, 84, 94–5, 98, 106, 156, 181, 183, 185, 196–7
psychoanalysis 11–12, 13, 108, 145, 186
Psychoanalytic Dispensary in Vienna 12–13
Psychopathia sexualis (Krafft-Ebing, R. von) 10
public interest in WLSR 176–7
public or private marriage advice, debate over 123
published texts, working with 6
At the Pure Source of Life: A Guide Through Children's Sexual Education for the Christian Mother (Schmitz, P.) 76–7, 78, 83
purity, Catholic maxim of 15–16, 75–83

"The Question of Sexual Education in Socialist Teaching" (Schrott, A.) 68–9

Rabinbach, Ansor 22n24, 50n20
"racial hygiene" *(Rassenhygiene)* 17, 31
radical redirection of sexual knowledge 18–19
rationality and science, social and sexual justice through 183–4
Ratzenböch, Gertraud 113–14n8
"The Reconstruction of People's Health" (Böhm, A.) 34
Red Vienna 18, 26–48, 55, 63, 65, 74, 83, 93, 120
Red Vienna: Experiment in Working-Class Culture (Gruber, H.) 83
Reddy, William M. 21n16, 154, 172n48
reform
    reform literature 69–70
    voices (1919–1934) of 63–74

see also clinical sexual advice; municipal health and hygiene; sexual education; sexual knowledge
Reich, Wilhelm 12–13, 23n44, 96, 111, 115n52, 171n47, 179, 185, 188, 194n47, 196
    categories of sexual knowledge 136–7
    pressing issue of sexual reform for 186–7
Reise, Hertha 193n12, 193n14, 194n30
Renner, Karl 27
reproduction
    municipal policies for 35–6, 36–7, 44
    rationalization of 197
responsibility
    charges against Vienna Weeklies of lack of 148–9
    for children, state organization and 43
    emotional component in sexual knowledge 197
    key message of Marriage Advice Centers 127–8
    societal change, sexual morality and 189
Reverentia Puero! Catholic Reflections on the problem of Sexual Pedagogy (Bertram, A.) 76, 80, 83
The Riddle of the Universe (Haeckel, E.) 13
Ridler, Hilda 51n52
Rilke, Rainer Maria 62, 87n27
Ripe for Love! (Glaessner, R.) 96, 97, 111
Roberts, Mary L. 20n7
Rodlauer, Hannelore 24n52
Rosenfeld, Siegfried 52n65, 53n84
Rothstock, Otto 167–8

Sablik, Karl 49n2, 49n8, 49n11
salversan 15, 24n57
Sauerteig, Lutz D.H. 23–4n45, 86n3
Schaudinn, Fritz 15
Schlegel, Josef Carl 98, 103–4, 114n31
Schlesinger, Therese 41, 74, 89n76, 101, 105–6, 115n44, 116n64
Schmitt, Albert 82, 85, 90n111

Schmitz, Father Peter 76–7, 78, 79–80, 81, 82–3, 85, 86, 89n85, 90n92, 90n96
Schnitzler, Arthur 94
Schober, Johann 150
school lectures to parents 59
school reforms in Vienna 65
Schorske, Carl 6–7, 21n17, 49n4
Schrott, Andreas 68–9, 83–4, 88n56, 89n61
science and sex 9–13
Seipel, Ignaz 150–51, 168
    exchange with Seitz over Bettauer's Vienna Weeklies 151–2
Seitz, Karl 27, 149–50, 150–52, 168, 169
    exchange with Seipel over Bettauer's Vienna Weeklies 151–2
Sengoopta, Chandak 21n18
sex
    as science 9–13
    sex-life behavior in families 124–5
    sex-life within marriage, joy of 81
    as social reform movement 13–18
    venal sex 14–15, 27–8
Sex and Character (Weininger, O.) 14
Sex-Life Problems (Glaessner, R.) 102, 111
sexology 3, 9, 10–11, 12, 13, 23n39, 43, 55, 87n24, 91, 144, 192
    medical sexology and sexual knowledge 93–4
    sexological literature, decline of 196–7, 198
sexual abstinence 79–80, 85, 99
Sexual Aufklärung in Education: A Guide for Parents, Teachers and Doctors (Friedjung, J.) 66
sexual discourse, tools of 6
sexual education 18–19, 54–86
    adolescence, confusions of 58–9
    Aufklärung ("enlightenment") and 54, 55, 56, 58, 60–89
    Becoming a Complete Man! Aufklärung and Education for the Growing Male Youngster (Hoffmann, J.) 61, 81
    Catholic literature on 78–9
    Catholic responses to reform agenda 75–83
    for children, SDAP workshops on 74
    coeducation and mixed classrooms 68–9, 97
    cultural improvement and 74
    At the Doors of Life: On Sexual Aufklärung and Morality (Golias, E.) 65
    education at home, Skalla's work and 59–60
    "The Environmental Conditions of Youth Sexuality" (Kraus, S.) 72–3
    In Faith's Light: Christian Reflections on Sexual Life (Gatterer, M.) 76
    At the Fountain of Life (Dürerbund publication) 56–9, 63, 66
    gender-neutrality in coeducational learning 69–70
    homoerotic practices of schoolboys 61–2
    How to Teach Your Child ("From a Friend of the Youth," Salzburg diocese) 77–8
    humanity of children and 187–8
    hygiene, Skalla's message on 60–61
    international sex reform movement, central tenet of 54
    Kinderfreunde movement (parent association) and 64–6, 67, 68–9
    Lad and Lassie in God's Hands: A Ministerial and Pedagogical Contribution to the Sex Problem (Schmitz, P.) 81, 82, 83
    moral *Aufklärung* 61
    morality, socialistic world view and 73
    motherhood
        duty towards sexual education 77
        Golias on 70–71
    municipal debate, subject for 55
    official advice, personal delivery of 62–3

physical exertion and sublimation,
Catholic emphasis on 75
pre-war *Aufklärung* 56–63
progressive education, *Dürerbund* and
56–9, 66, 67, 86n5
*At the Pure Source of Life: A Guide
Through Children's Sexual
Education for the Christian Mother*
(Schmitz, P.) 76–7, 78, 83
"The Question of Sexual Education in
Socialist Teaching" (Schrott, A.)
68–9
reform literature 69–70
reforming voices (1919-1934) 63–74
*Reverentia Puero! Catholic Reflections
on the problem of Sexual Pedagogy*
(Bertram, A.) 76, 80, 83
right of all young people to 184–5
school lectures to parents 59
sex-life within marriage, joy of 81
sexual abstinence 79–80, 85, 99
*Sexual Aufklärung in Education: A
Guide for Parents, Teachers and
Doctors* (Friedjung, J.) 66
sexual hygiene, women's ignorance of 71
sexual knowledge and 18–19, 54–86, 188
appropriateness for children 55
*Sexual Pedagogy: Foundations and
Fundamentals* (Allers, R.) 76, 79,
108–9
sexual realities, children and exposure
to 71–2
sexual trends in modern life 71–2
sexuality, separation from everyday life
80–81
shaming and scare tactics 62
site of, debates concerning 65–6, 75–6
spiritual perspective on 79–80
spread of venereal disease (VD) and 77
sexual enlightenment *(Aufklärung)* 18, 36, 54
sexual hygiene
directives from municipal authorities
on 42

women's ignorance of 71
sexual indiscretion, family life and 59–60
sexual information
problem of venereal disease (VD) and
91, 94, 95, 96, 97–8, 106
promulgation of 19, 91–113, 191–2
sexual irregularities 186–7
sexual knowledge
abortion, legal status of 92–3
anatomical knowledge, sex reform and
96–7
anti-Semitism and ideas of 12–13, 14
appropriateness for children 55
Aufklärung ("enlightenment") and 91,
92, 94–5, 96, 99, 102, 103, 106,
111, 112
birth control 98–100
clinical sexual advice 19, 118–140
contraceptive techniques, women and
use of 98–101
creative transition between sexual
knowledge as science and as social
reform, rationale for 196–7
cultural context, promulgation of
marriage manuals and 92
cultural historical perspective on 4–5
dangers of, perceptions of 153, 197–8
dissemination (and creation) of 8, 9
emotional testimonies, leavening with
4, 68, 99, 112, 122, 172, 198
as entertainment and education 131–2
eugenics and 16–18, 120–21
feminism and 3, 14, 16
fertility, female control of 99
heterosexual knowledge 18
historiography 6–9
How Woman Experiences Man
(Lazarsfeld, S.) 96
*Hygiene of Married Life: The Guide to
love and Marital Bliss* (Schlegel,
J.C.) 98, 103–4
Ideal Marriage (Van der Velde, T.) 96–7
innovations in sex education 198

League Against Forced Motherhood 128–33
The Man - A Book for Women (Tauber, E. and R.) 97, 102–3
marital continence 99–100
marriage advice and
discourse surrounding 93
Frauenfrage ("Women's Question") 93–4
medical sexology and 93–4
methodology for study 4–6
moral and biological, separation of 59–61
morality, WLSR perspective on 182
municipal health and hygiene 18, 26–48
Municipal Marriage Advice Center 121–8
natural nature of sexual urges 83–4
Normal and Pathological Sexual Life of the Male and Female (Kitaj, J.) 94–6
performing arts and 94
plurality of 21n12
political and cultural revolution and 3–4, 175–6, 178–9
political contestation of 175–6
pregnancy, birth control and 98–9
problem of 3–4
process of, historical perspective on 6–9, 19–20, 27, 196–7
published texts, working with 6
purity, Catholic maxim of 15–16, 75–83
radical redirection of 18–19
Reich's categories of 136–7
responsibility, emotional component in 197
Ripe for Love! (Glaessner, R.) 96, 97, 111
science and sex 9–13
sex
 as science 9–13
 as social reform movement 13–18

sexological literature, transition away from 198
sexual education and 18–19, 54–86, 188
sexual information, promulgation of 19, 91–113, 191–2
sexual positions, creativity and 103
sobriety of sexual partners 100–101
social pretense of women's ignorance on sexual matters 3
social reform and interpretation of 13–18, 63–74, 196–7
social structures, sexual misery and 188
Socialist Society for Sexual Advice and Research 133–6
tensions surrounding 177–8
therapeutic benefits of 2–3
venal sex 14–15, 27–8
venereal disease, education of women in recognition of 97–8
in Vienna
 approach to 8–9
 boom in 91–2
 interdisciplinary studies in 10–11
 women's sexual knowledge 94–104
 see also Bettauer's Vienna Weeklies; World League of Sexual Reform (WLSR) in Vienna
The Sexual Life of Our Time (Bloch, I.) 55
sexual "misery" or "emergency" *(Sexualnot)* 19, 63–4, 72, 95, 104, 154, 161, 185, 186, 187, 190, 197
 clinical sexual advice and 130–31, 133, 135
sexual morality and venereal disease (VD) 85
Sexual Pedagogy: Foundations and Fundamentals (Allers, R.) 76, 79, 108–9
sexual positions, creativity and 103
sexual realities, children and exposure to 71–2
Sexual-Reform (League Against Forced Motherhood) 130, 131–2

sexual reformers in Vienna 8, 150, 175, 179, 191
  see also clinical sexual advice; municipal health and hygiene
sexual trends in modern life 71–2
sexuality
  concept of 179
  sensations and meanings attributed to 184
  separation from everyday life 80–81
Sexuality, Three Essays on the Theory of (Freud, S.) 12
sexually transmitted diseases, intensity of war against 38–9
  see also venereal disease (VD)
shaming and scare tactics in sexual education 62
Shorter, Edward 24n57
Singer, Peter 25n67
sites of sexual education, debates concerning 65–6, 75–6
Skalla, Lothar 59–60, 61, 62, 87n16
Smola, Rudolf 67–8
sobriety of sexual partners 100–101
Social Democracy 19, 26–7
  Christian Social and Social Democratic approaches to Bettauer's Vienna Weeklies, chasm between 153
  see also Social Democratic Workers' Party (SDAP)
Social Democratic Workers' Party (SDAP) 3, 5, 7–8, 27, 28, 32, 34–7, 40–42, 43, 46–7, 48, 49n3, 92–3, 107, 116n65, 148, 151, 152, 162–3, 166, 175, 196
  Advice Centers run by 36–7
  "Guidelines for the Sexual *Aufklärung* of Youth" 106
  Kulturkampf with CSP 2
  political culture, *Lager System* and 7–8
  Schutzbund 168–9
  sexual education and 63–4, 71–2, 73, 74, 83–4
  socio-cultural reform, focus on 7–8

women, sex and Social Democracy 104–6
Worker Temperance Association (*Arbeiter-Abstinenten Bund*) 101
social medicine
  Tandler as model for 34–5
  Tandler's early career in 28–35
  see also municipal health and hygiene
social powers of health officials 33–4
social pretense of women's ignorance on sexual matters 3
social reform and interpretation of sexual knowledge 13–18, 63–74, 196–7
social repair, requirements of 30–31
social structures, sexual misery and 188
The Socialist Doctor 134
socialist sexual education, challenge of 75
Socialist Society for Sexual Advice and Research 13, 21n11, 96, 111, 115n52, 133–6
The Socialistic Education (Kinderfreunde) 68–9, 69–70, 73
Society for Birth Control (*Bund für Geburtenregelung*) 99, 115n34
soldiers as carriers of VD 129, 197
Somerville, Siobhan B. 113n1
The Source (Socialist magazine) 66
Soviet Russia (USSR) 179, 186, 196
Spencer, Herbert 16–17
Spengler, Oswald 30
spiritual perspective on sexual education 79–80
Springer, Sidonie 115n46
state concern for "healthy" sex 27–8
Stearns, P.N. and Stearns, C.Z. 21n16, 172n48
Steckel, Wilhelm 154
Stein, Paul 41, 74, 89n76, 100, 115n43, 116n70
Steinach, Eugen 181
Steiner, Herbert 190, 193n6, 193n16, 194n43, 195n66, 195n70
Steininger, Rolf 22n24

Stekel, Wilhelm 99–100, 115n39
Stöcker, Helene 16, 163
Stopes, Marie 100, 115n41
Stourzh-Anderle, Helene 195n59
The Struggle (SDAP monthly journal) 34–5
Sully, Melanie A. 7–8, 22n27
syphilis 14–15
  questions about 125–6
Systematic Anatomy (Tandler, J.) 28

Tandler, Julius 18, 26–8, 90n117, 147–9, 151, 152, 153, 169, 179, 181, 185, 188, 191, 194n37, 196
  early career, social medicine and 28–35
  shaping of sexual behavior 183–4
  welfare innovations, vision of 35–42
Tauber, E. and R. 97, 102–3, 114n24
tensions
  within SDAP regarding pornography and Bettauer's Vienna Weeklies 150–51
  sexual knowledge, tensions surrounding 177–8
Textbook of Biology (Schmeil, O.) 57
Theory of Degeneration (Morel, B.A.) 9
therapeutic benefits of sexual knowledge 2–3
Three Letters to a Young Lad (Andreas-Salomé, L.) 62–3
Timm, Edward 21n18, 49n4
Timmering, H.E. 87n20
Toews, John E. 21n12
The Topographical Anatomy of Emergency Operations (Tandler, J.) 28
"The Turning Point" (*Er und Sie* article) 161

Ullman, Karl 24n56
University Medical School in Vienna 10–11, 26
"Unusual Love Accident" (*Er und Sie* article) 161
Die Unzufriedene („The Unsatisfied") 99, 104, 115n49, 170n14, 173n63
Usborne, Cornelie 23–4n45, 47, 53n104

Van der Velde, Theodore 96–7, 114n19, 115n42
venal sex 14–15, 27–8
venereal disease (VD) 2, 4, 10, 14, 20n6, 55, 68, 148, 163, 185
  children, urban environment and exposure to 72
  clinical sexual advice and 119, 124–5, 126–7, 129
  education of women in recognition of 97–8
  Evening Clinics for Venereal Disease 38, 127
  General Hospital in Vienna, Department of Venereal Disease at 10
  municipal health and hygiene 26–7, 30–31, 34, 35, 37–8, 46
  prevention of, local committees and aim of 183
  sexual education and spread of 77
  sexual indiscretion, family life and 59–60
  sexual information and problem of 91, 94, 95, 96, 97–8, 106
  sexual morality and 85
  soldiers as carriers of 129, 197
Vicinus, Martha 113n2
Vienna
  Atlantis narrative in interwar history of 169, 174n102
  birth control, access to 197
  creative transition between sexual knowledge as science and as social reform, rationale for 196–7
  cultural modernism in 7
  eugenically sound reproduction 197
  Evening Clinics for Venereal Disease 38
  General Hospital, Department of Venereal Disease at 10
  government of 4–5
  Menschenökonomie ("economy of humanity") in 13–14, 50–51n40,

84–5, 90n117, 113n7, 120, 129, 180–81, 188, 191
Municipal Marriage Advice Center 26, 27, 40–41, 104, 116n61, 119, 121, 128–9, 133, 134–5, 137, 138, 139–40, 165–6
Museum of Sociological and Economic Sciences 19, 176, 193n5
pre-War *Aufklärung* 56–63
primary information sources in, destruction of 21n11
prostitution in 14–15, 16, 20n6, 31, 58, 66, 72, 84, 94–5, 98, 106, 156, 181, 183, 185, 196–7
Psychoanalytic Dispensary 12–13
purpose of sexual knowledge, subtle shift in 197
Red Vienna 18, 26–48, 55, 63, 65, 74, 83, 93, 120
reproduction, rationalization of 197
reputation for illicit sex 27–8
school reforms in 65
sexual danger, discourse in 197–8
sexual knowledge in
  approach to 8–9
  boom in 91–2
  interdisciplinary studies in 10–11
sexual reformers in 8
University Medical School 10–11
World League for Sexual Reform (WLSR) in 19, 175–92
World War I, conditions during and after in 26–7, 55
Youth Aid Office in 37
Viennese Medical Journal (Wiener medizinische Wochenschrift) 15, 24n58, 42, 93–4
Virgin Mary 57
Der Volkssturm 152, 171n34

Walkowitz, Judith R. 25n60
"War and Population" (Tandler, J.) 29, 30, 31, 38

Wassermann, August Paul von 15
We Young Men: The Sexual problem of Educated Young Men Before Marriage (Wenger, H.) 60
Weber, Fritz 22n24
Weeks, Jeffery 21n12
Wegner, Hans 87n20
Weidenholzer, Josef 7, 22n26
Weininger, Otto 7, 13, 14, 20n6, 24n50, 93
welfare system in Vienna
  innovation within 35–42, 179
  ministry of, aims of 32
  progressive nature of 27
  scope of 40
Wenger, Hans 60–61, 62
"Where Can I Find Help?" *(Bettauer's Almanac)* 165
Wiener Stimmen 152
Wise Parenthood (Stopes, M.) 100
Wittgenstein, Ludwig 7
The Woman Question and the Economics of Humanity (Goldscheid, R.) 29
"women's issues" in Bettauer's Vienna Weeklies 166
women's sexual knowledge 94–104
World League for Sexual Reform (WLSR)
  aims of World League (Copenhagen, 1928) 178, 180, 182–3, 193n12
  birth control information, call for 190
  change, trajectories of 178–9
  congresses and conferences 179–80, 193n17
  debating points for 176, 178
  family, sexual reform and 188
  Friedjung's opening speech in Vienna 180–81
  generative self-determination, rights to 189–90
  Hirschfeld's closing remarks in Vienna 191–2
  justice, call to 182–3
  liberation and sexual reform 187

official morality, new sexual ethic and 181–2
population patterns, tables of 190–91
public interest in 176–7
rationality and science, social and sexual justice through 183–4
reflection, avenues for 177–8
Reich and pressing issue of sexual reform 186–7
responsibility, societal change, sexual morality and 189
sexual education
    humanity of children and 187–8
    right of all young people to 184–5
sexual irregularities 186–7
sexual knowledge
    political contestation of 175–6
    tensions surrounding 177
sexuality
    concept of 179
    sensations and meanings attributed to 184
Tandler and shaping of sexual behavior 183–4
in Vienna 19, 175–92
World of the Erotic (Ferch, J.) 111–12
World War I
    conditions during and after in Vienna 26–7, 55
    effects on municipal health and hygiene 29–30

Young Törless (Musil, R.) 61–2, 87n27
Youth Aid Office in Vienna 37

Die Zeit 146
Ziche, Paul 24n46
Zuckerkandl, Emil 28
Zweig, Stephan 24n54

www.ingramcontent.com/pod-product-compliance
Lightning Source LLC
Chambersburg PA
CBHW072152100526
44589CB00015B/2188